THE **RELATIVITY** OF **DEVIANCE**

EDITION
4

SAGE | 50 YEARS

THE RELATIVITY OF DEVIANCE

EDITION
4

John Curra
Eastern Kentucky University

Los Angeles | London | New Delhi
Singapore | Washington DC

Los Angeles | London | New Delhi
Singapore | Washington DC

FOR INFORMATION:

SAGE Publications, Inc.
2455 Teller Road
Thousand Oaks, California 91320
E-mail: order@sagepub.com

SAGE Publications Ltd.
1 Oliver's Yard
55 City Road
London, EC1Y 1SP
United Kingdom

SAGE Publications India Pvt. Ltd.
B 1/I 1 Mohan Cooperative Industrial Area
Mathura Road, New Delhi 110 044
India

SAGE Publications Asia-Pacific Pte. Ltd.
3 Church Street
#10-04 Samsung Hub
Singapore 049483

Printed in the United States of America

Library of Congress Cataloging-in-Publication Data

Names: Curra, John.

Title: The relativity of deviance / John Curra.

Description: Fourth Edition. | Thousand Oaks : SAGE Publications, Inc., 2016.
| Revised edition of the author's The relativity of deviance, 2014. |
Includes bibliographical references and index.

Identifiers: LCCN 2015038736 | ISBN 9781483377346 (pbk. : alk. paper)

Subjects: LCSH: Deviant behavior.

Classification: LCC HM811 .C87 2016 | DDC 302.5/42—dc23 LC record available at http://lccn.loc .gov/2015038736

This book is printed on acid-free paper.

Acquisitions Editor: Jeff Lasser
Editorial Assistant: Alexandra Croell
Production Editor: Jane Haenel
Copy Editor: Teresa Herlinger
Proofreader: Jeff Bryant
Typesetter: Hurix Systems (P) Ltd.
Indexer: Terri Morrissey
Cover Designer: Scott Van Atta
Marketing Manager: Johanna Swenson

Certified Sourcing
www.sfiprogram.org
SFI-00453

16 17 18 19 20 10 9 8 7 6 5 4 3 2 1

Brief Contents

Detailed Contents

Preface

Human attitudes, behaviors, and conditions—the ABCs of deviance—do not exist in a social vacuum; they are always of great interest and concern to others. Depending on time, place, situation, the particular temperament of the individuals involved, and a host of other factors, some attitudes, behaviors, and conditions are praised; some are condemned; and others are ignored, at least for a time. Readers of this book will see that what qualifies as deviance varies from place to place, time to time, and situation to situation. They will see that deviance cannot be understood apart from its social setting, and they will be introduced to many examples that show this to be true. What exists could almost always be otherwise, and a change in social settings and interpersonal relationships almost always produces a change in the nature of deviance. This book will be appealing to anyone who is fascinated by the great diversity in human experience and the even greater diversity in social representations or constructions of it. Readers will come to realize that no intrinsic or inherent qualities exist to separate deviance from nondeviance and that deviance is far from absolute and uniform. This book will encourage readers to evaluate critically their own understandings of deviance.

In this fourth edition, I have included new examples and concepts to demonstrate the relativity of deviance, while keeping what I hope is the best from previous editions. In the following pages, readers will meet the blue people of Kentucky, a woman who believes that she is a vampire, the thugs of India, tattooists, self-injurers, autoerotic asphyxiates, berdaches, terrorists, serial killers, and even a man who ate an entire airplane. Some of the examples are funny, some are sad, and some are shocking. These examples, however, are more than journalistic accounts of quirky events. They show that deviance is a social construction—an accomplishment—of individuals in particular situations at particular times. The only valuable way to understand deviance is to look at variables such as power, conflict, norms, labeling, culture, vocabularies of motive, retrospective interpretation, stigma, accounts, ideologies, techniques of neutralization, and social reactions, so these concepts (and many more) are discussed in the following pages.

Chapter 1 explains how deviance can be understood as a socially constructed event by discussing egocentricity, ethnocentricity, culture, norms, sanctions, and ideologies. This chapter will show that we live in a world of multiple realities and that deviance must be understood as a situational, interactive, and meaningful accomplishment of humans acting together. It explores the nature of relativity and how relativity helps to illuminate the relationship between human diversity and social deviance. It also discusses theories of deviance that help us to understand its relative nature.

Each of the book's remaining chapters discusses a different facet of the relativity of deviance. Chapter 2 (dealing with identities, responsibility, and stigma) shows that people can be labeled deviant for things over which they have little control. It also discusses physical appearance, bodily adornment (e.g., tattooing), self-injurers, and eccentrics (and their eccentricities). Chapter 3 deals with the role played by both power and organizational networks in the social construction of deviance. It illustrates that individuals in organizations regularly use their social positions to hurt others, posing a threat to our collective and individual well-being. It also shows that some people's deviance is considered perfectly all right, whereas other people's deviance is criminalized and punished to the fullest extent of the law. Chapter 4 shows how human diversity, social conflicts, power, organizational interests and resources, social control, and naming and diagnosing all work together to construct that social deviance known as mental disorder. It demonstrates that deviance is a contested social terrain and that different groups will do all they can to define deviance in a way that best serves their own economic and political interests. This is particularly clear in the medicalization of deviance in which so much human diversity and pathos have been redefined as treatable disease. Chapter 5 examines predatory violence. It shows that even serious acts, which produce great harm, are not deviant at all times and in all places. It contains information on serial murder, interpersonal violence, infanticide, capital punishment, and other kinds of killing and assault that are a part of most human societies. Chapter 6 deals with sexual violence. It shows that serious violence, erupting from sex and gender antagonisms and disagreements, may still be widely viewed as both normal and normative. Chapter 7, on suicide, presents readers with information about the framing of social events. They will see that suicide is a socially constructed category with diverse meanings that are determined by time and place. Chapter 8 deals with sex, gender, and sexuality. It shows that sexual diversity—rooted in biology, psychology, culture, and society—is transformed into sexual deviance whenever humans and what they do, think, or feel in regard to things sexual are pigeonholed and then devalued. Few universals exist, and sexuality is a complex and ever-changing human experience. Chapter 9 discusses drugs and deviance. Readers will see that some groups initiate moral crusades to brand other people's drug use as sick and wholly unacceptable. The book contains what I hope are interesting and thought-provoking examples of social deviance that show readers the great array in both human experience and narratives about it.

I have included information about the worldwide economic crisis, the relationship between deviance and social inequality, the killing of Osama bin Laden, the Penn State sexual abuse scandal, police violence, and changing definitions of drug use (e.g., marijuana use). I have also expanded the theoretical section in Chapter 1. The discussions of terrorism, sexual deviance, and drugs and deviance have also been expanded, as well as the exploration of predatory violence. New information is included on sexual minorities (e.g., lesbians, gays, transgendered people, exotic dancers, prostitutes) and on far-side sexual deviances. New information about deviant subcultures is included. New research from academic journals and books has also been added, which is why this fourth edition is longer than the previous three. I think all these changes strengthen the book, and I hope readers will agree.

The writing in this book is gender-neutral. When direct quotes from others are included, however, that was not always possible, especially when the authors lived and wrote at an earlier time in history. These authors were inclined to use masculine pronouns to represent all humans, male and female. Although this is unacceptable now, in order to keep the meaning and flow of the original citation, when a direct quotation is included, the original language has been unaltered.

1

The Dynamic Nature of Deviance

Kids, Crocodiles, and Social Control

On January 2, 2004, Steve Irwin, crocodile hunter, snake wrangler, television personality, and naturalist, brought his 1-month-old son with him into a crocodile pen at Australia Zoo in Brisbane. He held his son in his left arm and a dead chicken in his right hand. While his wife, visitors to the zoo, and a camera crew looked on, Irwin extended the chicken to a 13-foot crocodile. The reptile lunged forward, snapping its massive jaws shut on the chicken and swallowing it. At the same time, Irwin jumped safely away from the animal with his son held tightly in his arm. While the Irwins looked at the stunt as inconsequential, nothing more than a crocodile-feeding debut by the youngest member of a reptile-loving family, some other people were mightily upset by what happened. A film of the incident was shown several times on U.S. television, Steve Irwin was quizzed by various U.S. newscasters, and family services officials in Australia reprimanded the Irwins. Legal charges could have been filed against them for child abuse.

Steve Irwin was astonished that anyone could think he would put his infant son in harm's way. The child was in no danger, Irwin insisted, and getting up close and personal with dangerous reptiles is what it means to be a member of the Irwin family. Steve Irwin's 30 years of experience, tracking and capturing highly dangerous creatures, gave him the confidence that his son would be perfectly safe. His surprise gave way to defiance and eventually to a modicum of public remorse, an apology, and a pledge that nothing like it would ever happen again. (Steve Irwin was killed by a stingray in September 2006 when the sea creature pierced the man's heart with a poisonous barb.)

This incident involving kids, crocodiles, and social control illustrates central elements in the human social construction of deviance, especially showing that fundamental disagreements do exist over proper ways of acting, thinking, feeling, and being. Whose definition of the "crocodile stunt" is the "right" one? Were the Irwins bad parents, or were they carefully (and safely) exposing their child to a new and valuable experience? How different is this from what other parents do when they take their child for a ride in an airplane, for a trip by car, for a swim in an ocean, or for a horseback ride, any of which could end disastrously? Some parents would be inclined to do with their child exactly what Irwin did with his, just as some parents would *not* do it with their child under any circumstances. Likewise, some individuals, while they would not actually *do* what Irwin did, would still think (and feel) that what he did was perfectly okay; other individuals would think (and feel) just as strongly that it most certainly was *not* okay. The elements we find in this social event—expectations, human interactions (and the associated thoughts and emotions), social evaluations and judgments—are the social "stuff" from which *any* social deviance originates. This incident involving kids and crocs has much to teach us about *all* social deviance.

Relationships and Rule Breaking

The study of social deviance must involve an understanding of the *origination* of human attitudes, behaviors, and conditions—the ABCs of deviance (Adler & Adler, 2009)—it is true, but it must also involve an understanding of socially constructed *viewpoints* on human attitudes, behaviors, and conditions.

> Deviance is not a self-evident category. It does not just float down from the skies applying itself to people who quite obviously are deviant. Deviance is a historical term and its application and/or adoption can create a status which dwarfs all others in its consequences for the individual's existence. Even the most deviant of all deviants does not just "happen"; someone has to pass judgement, to portray, to stigmatize, to insult, to heap abuse, to exclude or to reject. (C. Sumner, 1994, p. 223)

Social reactions and cultural meanings strongly affect the type of deviance that exists in society, and patterns of deviance constantly evolve and change over time. What's more, human attitudes, behaviors, and conditions don't always line up in uniform ways with characterizations of them. At one time or place, for certain kinds of people (i.e., those of a certain age or sex), drinking alcohol is perfectly proper, while at another time or place, it is forbidden. At one time or place, smoking cigarettes is a sign of maturity and sophistication, while at some other, it is a sign of immaturity and irresponsibility. The *deviancy* of some attitude, behavior, or condition cannot be determined simply by examining it closely.

Very few, if any, human experiences exist in a social vacuum, and very few, if any, can be understood separately from social context.

> Plainly, people throughout the ages have worried over—told tales about, made laws for, designed rituals around—situations that disturb the peace or threaten the communal fabric. Equally plainly, the coming to group attention of a specific threat has largely depended upon how that threat is publicly named, shaped, cast, categorized, and put in context. (Schwartz, 1997, p. 289)

Human beings are simply too inventive in assigning positive and negative labels to the many things that they do for us to ignore in our explanations of social deviance how groups judge and evaluate what other groups and the people in them are doing, thinking, feeling, and being (O'Brien, 2006; Spector & Kitsuse, 1977). Because we seek to understand deviance as a social relationship, we cannot stop with an *explanation* of human diversity. We must also examine the diversity of claims, labels, narratives, constructions, or characterizations of it.

During the New Orleans Mardi Gras, certain forms of *creative deviance* that might normally be forbidden become customary (Douglas, Rasmussen, & Flanagan, 1977, p. 238). One of these is "parade stripping," in which women expose their naked breasts to people on parade floats so that they will be thrown glass beads and trinkets. People who are not so accepting of the practice refer to these women as "beadwhores," and they tend to view parade stripping as unbridled exhibitionism. Those individuals who are caught up in the playful atmosphere of Mardi Gras, however, view things differently (Forsyth, 1992, p. 395). Parade stripping represents a ritualized exchange of things of value. The float rider gets to see naked breasts, and the woman receives beads, trinkets, and confirmation that her breasts are grand enough to warrant a bestowing of gifts (Shrum & Kilburn, 1996, p. 444). In 1935, police officers in Atlantic City, New Jersey, arrested 42 *men* on the beach because they wore swimsuits without tops. Imagine what these officers would have done at Mardi Gras (or on a nude beach)!

Societies, Cultures, Groups, and Subcultures

Each society contains a culture, along with a multitude of groups, each of which has its own subculture (J. P. Williams, 2011). The word *culture* was first used in 1877 by the anthropologist Edward Tylor to describe the totality of humans' behavioral, material, intellectual, and spiritual products. It now refers to designs for living or shared understandings that members of a society use as they act together. A *subculture* is a culture within a culture, identifiable by its distinctive constellation of information (Kluckhohn, 1949). Poker players are a subculture, as are attorneys, guitar players, and stamp collectors. In these small groups and countless others, knowledge is created, enacted, and institutionalized (Fine, 2012). A focus on culture and subculture is one of the best ways to explain why people are the same in some ways but different in others (Blackman, 2014; Demerath, 2014).

Subcultures can be, and usually are, in conflict with one another. When you follow the rules and expectations of one subculture, it almost always means that you are violating the rules and expectations of a lot of other subcultures (Sellin, 1938). For example, youth culture contradicts other parts of U.S. culture in many ways, as it gives young people an outlet for some of the insecurities and anxieties that characterize adolescence (Danesi, 2010). When adolescents follow the rules of youth subculture—a reasonable thing for them to do—it can bring them into conflict with other subcultures that encourage different behaviors from their members (Haenfler, 2013). A strong motivation exists for individuals who are similar to bond together (Jung, King, & Soule, 2014). Birds of a feather flock together, and so do humans. This promotes group solidarity and collective identification (Enriquez, 2014; Irwin & Simpson, 2013; Whittier, 2014).

A number of communities exist that provide alternate identities to their members, giving them a sense of pride and significance even while they may be considered deviant from the standpoint of other communities (Cross & Hernández, 2011). A study of "catchout camp" (Wasserman & Clair, 2010), a locale in Birmingham, Alabama, populated by the homeless, shows how marginal people may display a creative resistance to what they see as a social system that is really not for them. The residents of this camp realized that their way of life was going to be criticized or condemned by many different groups of people—police, social workers, religious zealots, shopkeepers, politicians, ordinary citizens—under the cloak of care and concern. They concluded, therefore, that they lived in a hostile social environment. Residents did what they could to resist the imposition of labels attached to them and their lifestyle by others. Catchout camp inhabitants made their own world as best they could, one characterized by resilience, pride, independence, humor, and lively conversation (often about sports or sex). Variations can and usually do exist *within* any one group in its members' allegiances to its values, norms, and meaning systems (Hunt, 2010, p. 526).

Humans formulate cultural rules about "proper" and "improper" ways of thinking, acting, feeling, and being. These rules are called *norms*. The directive to "chew your food with your lips closed" is the statement of a norm, as is the sign found in many restaurants informing customers, "No shoes, no shirt, no service." These standards help to determine what is important, what fits where, and what is deviant (Busch, 2011, p. 10). Norms are usually coupled with *sanctions*. A *positive sanction* (e.g., a promotion at work or an award at college) conveys approval and encourages norm-following activities; a *negative sanction* (e.g., a ticket for speeding) conveys disapproval and is designed to discourage norm-breaking activities. Norms are an important part of culture and subculture, helping us to better understand regularities in human behavior (Becker, 1982). Modern societies work to eliminate as many uncertainties as possible. They try to accomplish this by formulating and applying extensive systems of rules and regulations to practically everything they can (Bauman, 1991, 2006, 2011).

Ferrell's (1993) study in Denver of graffiti and graffiti writers (i.e., the individuals who paint on public structures, such as walls, viaducts, buildings, trains, or fences) shows how subcultural dynamics, group processes, and social control coalesce to make social deviance. Graffiti writing requires an individual who paints well enough to be able to do it in the dark and with enough speed and daring to evade detection. This demands both technology (e.g., spray paint) and sufficient knowledge and skill to be able to paint a design. Graffiti writing, however, is almost always a group event with members of the graffiti underground learning from one another as they see each other's artistic products. Groups or crews develop, and their members work together on a graffiti project.

At one time, Denver police took a generally tolerant and disinterested approach to graffiti. However, by the end of the 1980s and into the next decade, this all changed. Local politicians and business leaders worked together to generate a sense of urgency and moral outrage about the dangers that graffiti posed to society and social order. These anti-graffiti crusaders portrayed it as a growing menace that could only be stopped by extreme measures. Instead of defining it as a form of adolescent fun, an outcome of boredom, or an alternate art form, crusaders against graffiti branded it as a form of violence, crime, ruthlessness, irresponsibility, and vandalism of the worst kind. Graffiti writers were portrayed as immoral, uncaring, disrespectful, untrustworthy, and selfish. Both graffiti and graffiti writers were depicted as the source of ecological destruction and anarchy with the potential to destroy the entire city of Denver. Negative images and catch phrases were used as often as possible to condemn both the writers and the graffiti: "graffitidiots," "graffiti creeps," "gauche graffiti goons," "graffiti vandals," and "spray-can cretins" (Ferrell, 1993, p. 137). The campaign against graffiti, though instigated principally in the interests of local politicians and business elites, was never widely understood by the general public to be the biased moral enterprise it was. They understood it more generally as acts of vandalism, crime, and deviance rather than as another way for business leaders and politicians to further their own interests, according to Ferrell.

The graffiti writer as vandal was a recurring theme in Ferrell's (1993) study. Just to be clear, it is not Ferrell who is treating these writers as vandals. Far from it. This was the objective of the moral enterprise initiated against them, which placed graffiti writers in the same category as people who paint obscenities on bridges, who wantonly break windows, and who damage cemeteries. Instead of using the more neutral verb "to paint" to describe graffiti writing, opponents and critics opted for the more inflammatory words "attack," "rob," or "destroy." The word "suicide" was even used to make it appear that graffiti writers were self-destructive because they were destroying the neighborhoods within which they lived and so, ultimately, themselves (p. 139). As if the branding of graffiti as a type of assault, robbery, suicide, or murder of the urban environment was not enough, the anti-graffiti campaigners had another inflammatory word at their disposal: They equated graffiti writing with rape ("We feel like we've been raped" [p. 142]). As Ferrell puts it, "It is difficult to say whether such tactics are more offensive to rape victims or graffiti writers; it is not difficult to see that such tactics are designed to locate graffiti in the worst possible context" (p. 142). The core objective of the anti-graffiti crusaders was to generate enough fear and outrage in the general public that any political response, no matter how excessive, seemed justified.

The relationship between graffiti writers and the forces amassed against them shows not only the relativity of deviance, but also its political nature. Graffiti writing in Denver was a form of primitive rebellion and resistance against cultural domination and the monotony, insecurity, and incivility of public life. It was issued as a challenge to the hegemony of corporate ads and governmental intrusion into public space.

> Graffiti provides a sort of public art outside political or corporate control, and by its presence reclaims public space from city planners, corporate developers, and their aesthetic of authority. In the railyards and the alleys, under viaducts and on back walls, graffiti signifies public life and community creativity amidst the prefabricated imagery of the city. With its sweeping scale and sudden

visibility, it comes closer to engaging the public in the process of art than do the pieces tastefully arranged around courthouse lawns and bank lobbies. (Ferrell, 1993, pp. 185–186)

The deviancy of what these graffiti writers produced is principally a result of the challenges it offered to governmental and economic elites, who wanted to have exclusive rights to determine how public space is used and who is allowed to use it. The real deviance of graffiti writers, according to Ferrell (1993), had little to do with their artistic creations. It mostly had to do with the fact that they refused to do what they were told to do, thereby resisting constituted authority.

Another example of how rules and relationships work together to make social deviance is the saga of Edward Snowden. At one time, he was a computer technician with the National Security Agency (NSA) of the U.S. government, and prior to that he was a system administrator with the Central Intelligence Agency (CIA). In 2013, thinking that he had to go beyond the law to do what was right for the country, Snowden divulged details about the U.S. government's extensive surveillance program in which government employees had collected information on American citizens' phone calls, emails, and texts (Harding, 2014). Snowden leaked thousands of classified documents that he had illegally obtained to a number of media outlets. These documents showed that the U.S. surveillance activities were extensive, involving other countries (e.g., Canada, New Zealand, the United Kingdom), as well as telecommunications companies (e.g., AT&T and Verizon).

The reactions to Snowden's whistle-blowing, and to Snowden himself, were mixed. Some people branded him a traitor. No doubt exists that what Snowden did was illegal. He divulged information about a program that few were even aware of, and he fled the country to avoid arrest and prosecution for his crimes. Other people, while acknowledging the illegality of his actions, believed that the ends justified the means and that Snowden therefore should be celebrated, not condemned, for acts of patriotism and courage. The constitutional abuses illuminated by the leaks, these supporters asserted, were far more serious than anything that Snowden did. They concluded that what he did may have been illegal, but it was not criminal. Former Vice President Al Gore insists that Snowden is closer to being a whistle-blower than a traitor (MacAskill, 2014). On June 14, 2013, the U.S. Department of Justice charged Snowden with violating the Espionage Act and theft of government property, which carry a sentence of up to 30 years in prison if he were ever to be arrested, tried, and convicted. (As of this writing, he lives in a secret location in Russia.) Is Snowden, like the graffiti writers, a criminal because he resisted constituted authority, or is something else operating?

Being Centered

As newborns, we humans are *egocentric,* meaning we are wrapped up in our own viewpoint (Piaget, 1948). We look out on the world and respond to the people in it, it is true, but early in life we have no external or outside position from which to view *ourselves* or to evaluate what we are and do. As we become more aware of others and participate in meaningful relationships with them, we start looking at our society and ourselves in new ways. We eventually come to think, feel, and act in *anticipation* of the impact we can have on others. It becomes less likely that we will intentionally hurt someone else, but it does not automatically guarantee that we won't. People—some more than others—will maintain some of their egocentricity throughout their lives (Kumbasar, Romney, & Batchelder, 1994, p. 499). They will continue to do what is good for them *as individuals,* even if it is contrary to the wishes and interests of others or even if contrary to cultural rules.

Another kind of centeredness is *ethnocentrism,* which exists when members of some society or group come to believe that their culture or subculture—the system of values, norms, and customs—is better than everyone else's. If Americans were to decide that they were better than, say, Italians, because Americans play baseball better, this could easily be a reflection of ethnocentrism. A custom in one culture (i.e., baseball) is being used to evaluate and then belittle members of some other culture who have little or no knowledge of the sport. Using the values, norms, or customs of one culture to evaluate people of some other culture will usually produce a great deal of distortion and misunderstanding. Ethnocentrism makes it more likely that some people will define as inferior other people who are merely *different* from them or who do things differently. Difference is easily transformed into deviance, and deviance is easily transformed into abnormality or degeneracy.

Too much ethnocentrism or egocentrism makes it less likely that people will be able to—or willing to—look at the world through others' eyes. *Empathy* (or *role taking*) is encouraged by interactive processes as we each mentally project ourselves into the positions of others and incorporate others' viewpoints into our selves (Mead, 1934). Some research exists, both thought provoking and controversial, that humans have *mirror neurons* in their brains, which seem to play a role in the ability to empathize successfully with others (Iacoboni, 2009). We must be cautious not to make too much of this research. Empathy is not identical to sympathy. Just because we can identify with others, and maybe even understand their viewpoints, it does not mean we necessarily can feel their pain or that we care at all about what happens to them (Cronk & Leech, 2013).

The opposite of ethnocentrism is *cultural relativity,* which is anchored on the idea that human experiences and conditions must always be viewed and understood in the particular social and cultural contexts within which they originate and develop. Cultural relativists usually use the concept of culture only to describe and explain relationships and regularities in human experience. They refuse to use culture to judge people or to compare people in different lands to one another. Franz Boas, for example, would not rank cultures from good to bad no matter how primitive some cultures might have appeared to outsiders (cited in Mintz, 1982, p. 501). He insisted that no universal standard or rule exists that can be used to decide exactly which attitudes, behaviors, or conditions are best. Boas's students, especially Ruth Benedict, Margaret Mead, and Melville Herskovits, carried on his legacy, believing that cultures had to be understood as both separate *and* equal to one another.

Although Boas and his students did reaffirm the importance and value of cultural relativity, their exaggerated devotion to it blinded them to its fundamental error: Just because all cultures are proclaimed to be equivalent doesn't mean that they actually are.

> Many would surely be troubled by the idea that the political systems of Iraq, Hitler's Germany, or the Khmer Rouge in Cambodia were, or are, as good as those in, say, Norway, Japan, or Switzerland. And they would probably react with disbelief to the assertion that there is no scientific basis for evaluating another society's practice of genocide, judicial torture or human sacrifice, for example, except as the people in that society themselves evaluate these practices. (Edgerton, 1992, p. 2)

As systems of power, knowledge, morality, and surveillance change, so do patterns of deviance (Ben-Yehuda, 2006; Foucault, 2003, pp. 55–75; Mills, 1943; Staples, 2000, pp. 15–39). This does not mean, however, that all human customs are equivalent to one another and identical in all ways (as Edgerton notes in the above quote). Norms forbidding slavery are different from norms that forbid nose picking or shoplifting. Some deviance is harmful and dangerous—or "hard"—while other deviance is "soft," meaning it is unique and original and poses little threat to a society or the people in it (Raybeck, 1991, p. 54).

Sociological Relativity

Peter Berger, in his *Invitation to Sociology* (1963), showed the value of a *relativizing motif*. This demands that we keep foremost in our explanations of human experience the fact that identities, ideas, and customs are specific to a particular time and place.

> The sociological frame of reference, with its built-in procedure of looking for levels of reality other than those given in the official interpretations of society, carries with it a logical imperative to unmask the pretensions and the propaganda by which men cloak their actions with each other. (p. 38)

To fully explain—and therefore to fully understand—we must develop and then nourish whatever capacity we have to alternate from one perspective to another and to take account of meaning systems that stand in opposition to one another. This leads neither automatically nor inevitably to a greater tolerance of group or cultural differences. What it does lead to, however, is the willingness to scrutinize and then call into question what most other people take for granted (Bauman & May, 2001; Portes, 2000).

Practically anything that can be done with the human body has been done, either as a source of individual pleasure or as a matter of group custom, by somebody (or somebodies), somewhere, sometime. This means an incredible diversity exists in human attitudes, behaviors, and conditions. An even greater diversity exists in the *judgments* and *evaluations* humans make of attitudes, behaviors, and conditions that they find (Cohen, 1974). Definitions of deviance change over time and as we move from one group to another at one point in time (Adler & Adler, 2006, p. 132). In other words, deviance is defined up and down all the time (Krauthammer, 1993; Moynihan, 1993). Things that were mightily upsetting to one generation are trivial to the next (i.e., defining deviancy down) and vice versa (i.e., defining deviancy up). Serious deviances in one group are routine and regular happenings in some other group. Goffman (1963) asserted that "normal" and "stigmatized" are not inherent qualities of individuals but *perspectives* on individuals (p. 138). If anything intrinsically real or objective may be found in the human condition, it is the intrinsically situational nature of both rules and reactions, producing a dynamic, negotiated social order (Becker, 1973, p. 196).

Deviance is not a quality of the act a person commits, Becker (1963, p. 9) instructs. It is a function of the application of rules and sanctions to a suspect individual. Those traits individuals possess that are objects of reverence to their friends are—or can be—objects of disgust to their enemies. The traits have not changed, but the meanings of them have. Such assessments depend as much or more on *who* is doing the evaluating than they do on *what* is being evaluated. "No trait is normal or pathological in itself but only acquires the quality of normality (or deviance) with regard to the environment in which it arises" (Horwitz, 2008, p. 366). How things look and get defined depends a lot on where you're standing. If any human universal has relevance for our understanding of social deviance, then it must surely be the human inclination to construct social differences and then to persecute anyone who seems to be out of step with everybody else (Moore, 1987).

Sociological relativity demands that social scientists who want to understand groups of people, even ones that are very different from their own, must suspend their moral judgments and look at the world through the eyes of the people they wish to understand. This requires the "practice of putting yourself in your adversary's shoes, not in order to wear them as your own but in order to have some understanding (far short of approval) of why someone else might wear them" (Fish, 2001, p. A23). Relativists may be less inclined to be ethnocentric or egocentric because by looking through the eyes of people in a multitude of situations, it may increase their tolerance for practices different from their own. Goffman (1961) shows how this can work in the following:

> [T]he awesomeness, distastefulness, and barbarity of a foreign culture can decrease to the degree that the student becomes familiar with the point of view to life that is taken by his subjects. (p. 130)

Goffman's assertion is true, but it's not the whole truth. Although some things that initially seemed foreign or strange may become less so with greater familiarity, it is also possible for things that once seemed ordinary to look strange as an observer's familiarity with them increases.

A powerful tension exists between wanting to understand people and wanting to help them (Riesman, 1963), a tension that is at the core of a paradox that afflicts *any* relativistic approach. Sociologists and anthropologists must use tenets of relativism to understand and explain human experience, but by using the tenets of relativism, they put themselves in a contradictory moral position. The *decrease* in ethnocentrism and the *increase* in tolerance that can come from a relativistic approach must be tempered by the knowledge that some of the things that an individual may find in the groups he or she is studying may be too maladaptive or damaging for them to be overlooked. Relativity is difficult to defend if it demands acceptance of things such as murder, slavery, mutilation, or assassinations, all under the banner of a doctrinaire acceptance of cultural equivalency and celebration of diversity. If relativity becomes too relativistic, it invites criticism and rejection from non-relativists for its moral indifference (Gibbs, 1966).

Contrary to the cultural relativity of Boas and his students, all outcomes are not equivalent. A well-played basketball game is different from a poorly played one; a well-run company is not identical to one that is inefficient; stealing other people's money is not the same as earning it; a badly written novel is not the same as a well-written one; getting a ship safely to port is not the same as smashing it into an iceberg; dishonesty is different from honesty; an interesting lecture is different from a dull one; and a silk purse is not the same as a sow's ear. Meanings are not necessarily randomly or capriciously attached to human attitudes, behaviors, and conditions (Lemert, 1972). A sociological relativist is unlikely to believe that anything goes and is acceptable just because a majority of people says it does and is. However, he or she is likely to believe that a wide range of things *could* go. It is the belief in human potentialities, coupled with a determination to explain correctly, that characterizes sociological relativity. What if Steve Irwin had for some reason (e.g., confusion, insanity, or wickedness) held the chicken in his left arm and actually fed his *son* to the crocodile? Can anyone seriously believe that relativists would view this as no different from what actually happened?

The Social Construction of Reality

Making Sense of Common Sense

Some human activities can exist independently from a socially constructed system of rules. Eating, drinking, sleeping, and waste elimination are *regulated* in all places and at all times by rules and shared expectations, but these activities would occur even without rules. For example, humans cough due to an involuntary muscular spasm in the throat that clears air passages. We get things stuck in our throats and we cough. The expulsion of air from the body that makes a cough, however, is regulated by cultural rules. Years ago (in the United States), the "correct" or "proper" way to cough was to expel air into an open hand that covered the mouth. The H1N1 (swine flu) virus, which first appeared in 2009, was an impetus to change how we cough (or, more correctly, how we *regulate* how we cough). Now, it is the elbow that is the "correct" or "proper" target of the expelled air. However, some kinds of human activity are *constituted* by rules, not merely regulated by them. If the rules were nonexistent, the activity in question would be as well. For example, if you refuse to follow the rules of chess, then you are not playing the game (Searle, 1995).

Although all cultural rules—both regulative and constitutive—have a provisional quality (Troyer, 1992), their conventional nature is sometimes easy to miss. The social world (or parts of it) can reach the point where it "thickens" and "hardens" so much that its members think and feel it is natural and inevitable, no longer amenable to change (Berger & Luckmann, 1966; Kraaykamp & van Eijck, 2010). Some cultural ideas endure so long that they attain the enviable status of "common sense," something that seems to be true beyond dispute. If these ideas weren't true, conventional wisdom instructs, why do so many of us believe them?

Common sense is actually a constellation of inconsistent, incoherent ideas, each of which seems right at a given time but that carries no guarantee of being right at any other time. Common sense makes us think we know and understand more than we do (Watts, 2011, 2014).

> Bad things happen not because we forget to use our common sense, but rather because the incredible effectiveness of common sense in solving the problems of everyday life prompts us to put more faith in it than it can bear. (Watts, 2011, p. 23)

Berger (1963) concludes that the commonsense view is nothing more than the grown-up view taken for granted. We must not confuse commonsense notions with empirically correct descriptions and understandings.

Benjamin Franklin wrote that honesty is the best policy, and individuals of all ages are encouraged to "always tell the truth." Even a bit of fortune cookie philosophy for the wayward reaffirms honesty's importance: "Never forget that a half truth is a whole lie." However, the cultural encouragement of honesty may be mostly rhetoric. Ruane and Cerulo (2015) emphasize the following: "Clearly, we would be lying to say that our culture firmly endorses honesty as the best policy" (p. 197). As we learn that lying is wrong (and give lip service to honesty's importance), we also probably learn how to lie, when to lie, how to excuse and justify the lies we've told, and who deserves to hear the truth and who does not.

Social context has a substantial impact on the whole process of lying: whether lies are told and even what qualifies as a lie in the first place. While honesty is one way to achieve life's goals, dishonesty may be an easier, more effective, or less stressful way to achieve them. Whenever greater emphasis is placed on achieving goals than on how they are achieved—"winning isn't everything; it's the only thing"—deviances of all types become more likely (Merton, 1938). The Josephson Institute (2012) surveyed 23,000 high school students in 2012 and reported that 76% of the sample had lied to a parent about something significant, while 55% had lied to a teacher. Some lies and lying are normal or at least expected, while others are both deviant and criminal (Ruane, Cerulo, & Gerson, 1994). Ruane and Cerulo (2015) conclude that the normal lie is a crucial mechanism for maintaining the flow of social interaction. It practically goes without saying that what qualifies as normal is open to interpretation.

Creating Deviance

The existence of social deviance in human societies cannot be separated from the human ability to create and internalize symbols. A *symbol* is a physical gesture or sound (i.e., a word) that represents something else because of group agreement. Humans do not live only in a physical world of smells, sights, sounds, tastes, and touches. We live in a world of "hot and humid"; "felonies and misdemeanors"; "pepperoni pizzas"; "governments by the people and for the people"; and many other things, material and nonmaterial, that are identified and represented in a culture or subculture. Symbols make it possible for individuals to become active and interactive members of a society or group.

A parent may ask the younger child, "Why can't you be more like your older brother?" The parent has an understanding made possible by his or her ability to organize experiences symbolically and to recognize that the younger child acts differently from the older child and from how the younger child *could* and *should* act. Humans are able to recognize the difference between what is, what was, and what should be. The human communication process is a powerful force, having the capacity to encourage both prosocial behaviors (e.g., healthy eating habits) and antisocial behaviors (e.g., crime or delinquency) (Gladwell, 2000; Rosenberg, 2011). Groups will symbolize risks—identifying them and then offering their claims about how to eliminate them—in ways that further their own interests (Mohun, 2013).

Deviants can be symbolized in ways that prevent their deviances from posing any serious threats to the dominant construction of reality and the shared understandings on which it is based. If anything, the existence of deviance is used by supporters of the status quo to encourage an allegiance to conformity and conventionality (Reiman & Leighton, 2010). Deviance is branded as sick, evil, or abnormal, rather than as a cultural alternative or functional group difference. The definition of alternate realities as inauthentic, pathological, or just plain nuts reinforces the dominant view of reality and makes the status quo appear more immutable, concrete, and commonsensical than it actually is. The construction of deviant labels and their assignment to particular individuals serves to mask social conflicts, making labelers more confident that their way is the only *right* way (Parsons, 1951).

Westboro Baptist Church (WBC) was formed in Topeka, Kansas, in 1955, by Fred Phelps (who died in March 2014). He had a strict and fundamental view of God and Christianity, and he attracted people to his congregation who held beliefs as rigid and fundamental as his own. Members of WBC are fervently convinced that God is hell bent on punishing anyone who commits sexual trespasses. They believe that God's distaste for sexual deviances knows no bounds and so transgressors should be punished, both in this life and in the hereafter for all eternity (Baker, Bader, & Hirsch, 2015). Church members view homosexuality as the baddest of the bad, being both unnatural and immoral.

Had members of the congregation been content merely to condemn homosexuality and homosexuals, they could have been dismissed as bigots, bullies, or zealots. Their condemnation of homosexuality does not make them much different from other fundamentally conservative religious groups, but their political activities do. Phelps and his followers were continually "upping the bar" in their public protests to garner more and more attention for their denunciation and condemnation of homosexuality and homosexuals. They showed their contempt by protesting at funerals of AIDS victims; at lesbian, gay, bisexual, and transgender (LGBT) pride events; and at funerals of prominent supporters of LGBT rights. They even protested at the funeral of Matthew Shepard (in 1998), a victim of a homophobic hate crime. However, what put them on the radar screen of so many people who wanted to end their campaign of hate and damnation was that members of the church protested at funerals of U.S. soldiers killed in Afghanistan and Iraq. The parishioners' rationale was that the U.S. military itself was a sinful abomination and affront to God, deserving nothing other than damnation because it was allowing openly gay men and women to serve (Baker et al., 2015).

The protest activities of the church grew increasingly—or were defined that way—irritating and objectionable to more and more people. Their protests at soldiers' funerals, which regularly involved burnings of U.S. flags, were more than an affront to the memory of the deceased soldier and his or her mortal remains. They were a desecration of both the American identity and the entire U.S. social fabric (Baker et al., 2015, pp. 46–47). WBC and its members were increasingly defined as the problem, not what they were protesting, and fewer and fewer people had any sympathy for the protestors and their activities.

Though the actions and claims of WBC may have been offensive, if not thoroughly contemptible, one problem remained: They were entirely legal. Members of WBC know the law—Phelps had been a prominent civil rights attorney until he was disbarred for being too outspoken and vindictive—and they are meticulous in refusing to do anything even slightly against it. Their protest activities are legally protected as forms of free speech and free action. WBC always followed local ordinances in regard to when and where they could protest, and they always acted in a peaceful manner. However, as they became increasingly mean-spirited—or were defined that way—they reached a point where they could no longer be overlooked and ignored. They generated enough adverse publicity and hostility that politicians at several levels of government moved to regulate and restrict them and what they were doing (Baker et al., pp. 56–57).

In 2006, the Respect for America's Fallen Heroes Act (H.R. 5037) was introduced and was overwhelmingly supported by both the House and the Senate. It was signed into law by then-President George W. Bush on Memorial Day. It gave each state the power to restrict demonstrations at any military funeral. Within 2 years, most states had passed laws that defined funeral protests as forms of disorderly conduct, making it possible for protesters to be contained and their protests to be neutralized. However, laws, even harsh ones, can do nothing more than *restrict* Westboro's protest activities. They cannot completely eliminate them.

Theoretical Views: The Old and the Not-So-Old

Bad Actors and Bad Acts

One of the earliest conceptions of deviance and deviant was founded on a belief that deviants could be separated from nondeviants on the basis of inherent or intrinsic characteristics of the individual rule breaker (Devroye, 2010; Rafter, 1997). Usually, some biological or psychological factor, such as body chemistry, intelligence, or brain dysfunction, was identified and then blamed for the trespass (Bernard, Snipes, & Gerould, 2010; Lilly, Cullen, & Ball, 2015; F. P. Williams & McShane, 2014). Because the deviance was almost always viewed as unacceptable, correctible, and unnecessary, the temptation to see defect, abnormality, or degeneracy in the biology or psychology of deviants was too great to resist. Simply put, deviants were viewed as both distinct (identifiable and all alike) and inferior, so deviance was anything that abnormal people did (or were). This claim, however, of uniform and universal inferiority was based on both bad logic and bad science (Merton & Ashley-Montagu, 1940).

The belief developed that with certain kinds of deviance (e.g., crime), the deviant had inherited physical traits or markers of his or her degeneracy that could be recognized by dispassionate observers (e.g., asymmetry of the face, too-large jaws or cheekbones, too-large or too-small ears, abnormal teeth, too-long arms, extra fingers or toes). This kind of marginal thinking that deviance was inherited was not restricted to marginal thinkers. Former U.S. Supreme Court Judge Oliver Wendell Holmes Jr., in a 1927 case

(*Buck v. Bell*), upheld the forced sterilization of an adolescent female. She had been deemed by the state of Virginia to be both retarded and a deficient mother. Holmes reasoned that

> it is better for all the world if, instead of waiting to execute degenerate offspring for crime, or to let them starve for their imbecility, society can prevent those who are manifestly unfit from continuing their kind. . . . Three generations of imbeciles are enough. (Schnakenberg, 2009, pp. 46–47)

Some theorists focused on deviant acts instead of deviant individuals, classifying these acts as inherently or intrinsically deviant. For example, Parsons (1951) insisted that deviance produces a disturbance in the equilibrium of interactive systems, and Schwendinger and Schwendinger (1975) asserted that deviance is behavior that is harmful. As sociologists and anthropologists demonstrated the great array that exists in human customs and conditions, the meaning of deviance changed. Attention was less on deviants and what they did and more on the relativity of reactions and relationships (Best, 2004).

Relativity is found in the works of both Karl Marx and Émile Durkheim. Marx (1846/1978) was inclined to believe that the economic forms within which humans produce, consume, and exchange are transitory and historical. No final conclusion, theory, or premise exists that applies universally to all times, places, and circumstances. However, the first thorough-going application of relativity to an understanding of deviance is found in Durkheim's *The Rules of Sociological Method* (1895/1938), where he contrasts the "normal" with the "pathological." Durkheim asks us to imagine a society of saints where each individual is exemplary, so crimes such as murder, rape, or assault will not exist (pp. 68–69). This does not mean, however, that crime will be unknown. Offenses that might seem trivial and ordinary to us would appear quite scandalous in this saintly society. Durkheim was indicating that it is the *attitude* about, and *reaction* to, some social arrangement that is responsible for its categorization as criminal.

Relativity also appears in his *The Division of Labor in Society* (1893/1933), where Durkheim asserts that many acts are regarded as criminal even though they are not intrinsically harmful, such as touching a forbidden object, allowing a sacred fire to die out, or failing to make a required sacrifice (p. 72). Although we might now refuse to classify normative violations like these as crimes, Durkheim's point stands. Crime is whatever people say it is, and it is social reaction that establishes what is harmful, not the other way around. Deviance as an analytical and empirical category may be nearly universal, but the particular form that deviance takes is not (Ben-Yehuda, 1990, 2006).

The Chicago School

In the United States, a group of sociologists in the Department of Sociology at the University of Chicago were the first to use a relativistic approach to deviance. Known as the Chicago School, they were to exert a tremendous amount of influence on practically all subsequent approaches to deviance and crime that had any sociological leanings (Lanier, Henry, & Anastasia, 2015). Bernard et al. (2010) declare that the Chicago School is a gold mine that continues to enrich the study of crime even today. For representatives of the Chicago School, neither absolutes nor universal rules of human behavior existed (F. P. Williams & McShane, 2014).

The Chicago School emphasized the powerful role played by context and social setting in the creation of deviance and crime by showing that coexisting and yet incompatible subcultures could encourage different ways of acting, thinking, and feeling. The Chicago School also showed that different groups could evaluate the same conduct or social arrangement in different ways. As these Chicago sociologists moved from one area to another in the urban milieu, they found different group customs and subcultural meanings. They concluded that deviance and crime were highest in zones or natural areas with the highest levels of deregulation and social disorganization. Research does indicate that rapid social and political change, as well as changes in the distribution of scarce resources, can produce confusion and deregulation, which can lead to deviance and crime (Zhao & Cao, 2010).

The Chicago School, embodied particularly in the works of Edwin Hardin Sutherland (1947), clarified how differential association makes it possible for some individuals to learn things that other individuals do not. By focusing on symbolic interaction and learned behavior, Sutherland developed a social and interactive understanding of the development of crime, while he offered a contextual understanding of shared rules and subcultural values. This transformed the meaning of social disorganization into something closer to what actually exists in the real world: differential social organization. Moreover, this helped to erode even further the idea that deviants were degenerate and that deviance was inherently abnormal.

The principal factor in understanding why some people break the law, Sutherland (1947) insisted, is to be found in the meanings or definitions they give to events in the social world. Most juvenile delinquency, for example, is learned from others with whom the juvenile has meaningful and rewarding contacts. It is rarely an outcome of fractured interpersonal relationships or a response to isolation and despair (Smångs, 2010). Having delinquent companions is one of the best and most consistent predictors of a teenager's own delinquent activity (Chapple, Vaske, & Worthen, 2014; Menard &

Johnson, 2015; Warr, 1993, 2002). Delinquent acts may be an expression of *subterranean values*, such as autonomy, daring, street smartness, avenging masculinity, and conspicuous consumption (Matza & Sykes, 1961).

Sutherland (1947) believed that face-to-face interaction was the only way that definitions favorable to violating the law could be learned. However, in this day and age, where the information superhighway is so wide and long, television, movies, and cell phones play a prominent role in our lives. Many of us are now part of *portable communities* (Chayko, 2008, p. 8), networks of interactants who are connected through online and mobile technologies, regardless of whether we meet face-to-face frequently, infrequently, or never (Ling, 2012). The chance that an individual will engage in deviant behavior is an outcome of learning favorable definitions about such behavior, the reinforcement one receives for it, and the chances that exist to observe and copy the deviance of others (Alleyne & Wood, 2014). Deviance is more likely when an individual's friends engage in deviance (Tedor, 2015).

With the passage of time, Sutherland's view of learning was fleshed out by adding newly developed (and still developing) ideas from psychology and social psychology about how humans learn (Tibbetts & Hemmens, 2010). One of the more important reformulations of Sutherland's differential association theory has been done by Burgess and Akers (1966), which itself was expanded by Akers (1985). These theorists contributed additional (and valuable) information about how humans acquire deviant behaviors through imitation and vicarious learning (F. P. Williams & McShane, 2014).

Norms and Naughtiness

By the middle of the twentieth century, more and more sociologists had reached the conclusion that deviance was never going to be suitably understood by looking at intrinsic or essential qualities of deviants that distinguished them from nondeviants. Attitudes, behaviors, and conditions are simply too relative and dynamic to be pigeonholed into two mutually exclusive categories of normality and abnormality. The concept of *norm* was adopted as a better way—or so it seemed—to explain and understand the nature of social deviance than any account based on the notion of degeneracy or abnormality.

William Graham Sumner's (1906) discussion of *folkways*, a type of norm, had indicated that they are inherited from the past and that they direct human behavior almost automatically. When rules are followed, they facilitate the adjustment of individuals to life conditions and to the particular demands of time and place. It was an easy leap to the view that deviance is a normative departure and that norms could make anything right or wrong, depending on the case (Gibbs, 1966; W. G. Sumner, 1906). Becker (1963) retained the idea of norm but changed the thinking about responsibility. It was no longer the rule breaker who was at fault. Becker reasoned that it is the group *itself* that creates deviance by making rules whose violation qualifies as deviance, identifying rule breakers, and treating them as outsiders.

We must see deviance as an outcome of a process of interaction between people, some of whom in their own interests make and enforce rules that catch others who are doing (or being) something that gets them labeled as deviants and treated accordingly.

> A successful, and enforceable, social construction of a particular label of deviance depends on the ability of one, or more, groups to use (or generate) enough power so as to enforce *their* definition and version of morality on others. . . . Deviance . . . always results from negotiations about morality *and* the configuration of power relationships. (Ben-Yehuda, 1990, pp. 6–7)

Some of these moral crusades are very successful, having enduring effects, while others are short-lived, dying quickly and with little fanfare.

No longer were norms necessarily viewed as reflective of a society-wide consensus or a universal morality. C. Wright Mills (1943), one of the most influential sociologists in the history of the discipline (Oakes, 2011), showed that the prevailing norms always reflect some specific group's biased view of what is proper or improper; norms reflect the power, interests, and outlooks of the groups that create them. Under Mills's gaze, not only did norms produce efficiency and predictability in human behavior but they also served as smokescreens to hide the wellspring of power and class interests. Norms are "propaganda for conformity," embodying and demanding adherence to standards that are biased, reflecting a confluence of class, status, and power (p. 179).

The Labeling or Social Reactions Perspective

Once theoretical explanations of deviance were sensitive to the role played by the "other" in the construction of deviance, a whole new world of possibilities was opened. It could be maintained with credibility and confidence that social control *itself* has the ironic effect of actually creating deviance and channeling the direction that it takes (Lemert, 1972). Tannenbaum (1938) insisted that social labels (and other social reactions) actually create deviance: "The process of making the criminal, therefore, is a process of tagging, defining, identifying, segregating, describing, emphasizing, making conscious and self-conscious; it becomes a way of stimulating, suggesting, emphasizing, and evoking the very traits that are complained of" (pp. 19–20). A new wrinkle had been added: The understanding of social deviance required an analysis of the processes by which persons are defined and treated *as deviant* by others. The definition of deviance changed to reflect this new understanding: "Deviance is not a property *inherent in* certain forms of behavior; it is a property *conferred upon* these forms by the audiences which directly or indirectly witness them" (Erikson, 1962, p. 308).

How can social control create deviance? One way is by naming, labeling, or categorizing some attitudes, behaviors, or conditions as types of deviance, separating them from other attitudes, behaviors, or conditions that are considered to be proper or even desirable.

> Deviance may be conceived as a process by which the members of a group, community, or society (1) interpret behavior as deviant, (2) define persons who so behave as a certain kind of deviant, and (3) accord them the treatment considered appropriate to such deviants. (Kitsuse, 1962, p. 248)

A second possibility is that the *reactions* of other people to an individual's initial or primary deviance—what these others say, do, or believe—can powerfully impact the nature and form of all subsequent deviant behavior of the labeled individual.

> [W]e start with the idea that persons and groups are differentiated in various ways, some of which result in social penalties, rejection and segregation. These penalties and segregative reactions of society or the community are dynamic factors which increase, decrease, and condition the form which the initial differentiation or deviation takes. (Lemert, 1951, p. 22)

According to Lemert's (1951, 1972) *secondary deviance proposition,* an individual's deviant behavior evolves to the point where it is constructed principally as a means of defense, attack, or adaptation to the problems created by the real or anticipated disapproving, degradational, or isolating reactions of others.

About the same time that Lemert was exploring the role of secondary processes in human deviance, Merton was exploring how collective events (i.e., human actions, decisions, or beliefs) can have unanticipated consequences. One possibility, which Merton (1948) called the "self-fulfilling prophecy" (p. 195), is that a *false* or *incorrect* definition of a situation changes subsequent events sufficiently that it actually becomes true.

Students, for example, convinced that they are destined to fail an exam, become so nervous and anxious that they worry more than they study, and they do fail. Merton (1968) also acknowledged—though he spent no time developing the idea—that beliefs (and reactions based on them) can be self-destroying, an idea he credited to John Venn, a nineteenth-century logician. Merton (1948) called this a "suicidal prophecy" (p. 196). The suicidal prophecy prevents or "kills off" the fulfillment of an outcome that would otherwise have developed. The hare in the famous fable about its race against the tortoise demonstrates a suicidal prophecy. The rabbit was so certain that it would beat the slow-moving reptile that it behaved imprudently, and it did not win the race. Another example is found in the situation where a teacher tells a student that he or she will never amount to anything, which results in the pupil working hard to prove the teacher wrong.

These two prophecies have not been treated equally in subsequent analyses of deviance. Becker (1963), for example, only felt obliged to use a self-fulfilling prophecy in his analysis of deviant careers (failing to credit Merton when he did). This gave the false or at least distorted impression that the only situations of importance to an analysis of deviance are when social mechanisms work together to shape individuals into the images that people have of them. Although it is true that sometimes an individual's deviance is amplified by the reactions of others, this is not the only possibility.

The Normality of Deviance

Deviance came to be viewed as an inevitable and rather ordinary feature of life in a pluralistic society, and deviants came to be viewed as more sinned against than sinning. In fact, siding with deviants became as defensible as siding with representatives of conventional society, such as police, judges, or psychiatrists. The deviant's right to be different and to be free from stigma and harassment was actively defended. Deviance was defined increasingly in political terms. Power—the power to label and the power to legitimate one's own view of proper and improper—emerged as a central explanatory variable in understanding deviance (Young, 2011). Deviance was conceptualized more than ever before as a name, label, category, definition, vocabulary, discourse, typification, or narrative that was applied to individuals and what they think, do, and are (Dellwing, 2011). One conclusion from the relativistic approaches, especially conflict-oriented ones, was that state intervention created crime more often than it eliminated it (Lilly et al., 2015).

The emergence of a radical view of deviance meant that some theorists took the side of deviants with a vengeance. Not only did these theorists defend the right of deviants to be different, but they also condemned representatives of conventional society and branded them as the dangerous, odd, or misguided ones. Life in an unequal, competitive, insecure, acquisitive society, they believed, was brutalizing for some people, and brutal conditions generate brutal behaviors. Radicals viewed deviance as one of the choices that people consciously make in order to manage some of the difficulties posed for them by life in a contradictory society (Taylor, Walton, & Young, 1973). These theorists focused more on the process of law making than on law breaking. The principal reason is that they were inclined to view official definitions of crime as one of the tools that privileged and powerful groups use to maintain their own positions while restricting the social mobility and power of the less privileged (Miller, Schreck, Tewksbury, & Barnes, 2015; Tibbetts, 2012).

Radicals insist that the control of deviants and the suppression of deviance are principal ways that threats to the economic and political systems are counteracted so that the status quo is preserved for the benefit of the privileged and powerful (Quinney, 1970, 1974; Reiman & Leighton, 2010). Quinney (1973) went so far as to claim that the really bad people in a society are those who make laws to protect their own interests and to legitimate the suppression of threatening or disliked groups. Radical deviance theorists, as well as other theorists who consider power and social conflict to be central variables in any understanding of social deviance, now are inclined to use the term "postmodern" to identify their work (Cote, 2002; F. P. Williams & McShane, 2014). (Arrigo and Bernard [1997], however, concluded that postmodern criminology is an independent orientation despite having some areas of agreement with conflict criminology and radical criminology.) An important contribution to the postmodern approach is known as *cultural criminology*, whose representatives work to understand how culture and crime interpenetrate one another in a world that is unequal, exclusionary, ambiguous, and constantly changing (Ferrell, Hayward, & Young, 2015).

Postmodernists (Arrigo & Bernard, 1997; Ferrell, 1999; Henry & Milovanovic, 1991, 1996; Katz, 1988; Milovanovic, 1997) conceptualize deviance as a joint construction of social actors, and a core theme is postmodernists' refusal to reduce social deviance down to the concrete and discrete action of any one individual (Henry & Milovanovic, 1991). Postmodernists assert that the meanings, definitions, discourses, and narratives used to describe and understand both deviance and its control are always problematic and contentious, just like the social world itself (Henry & Milovanovic, 1996; Lyman & Scott, 1989). Postmodern theorists, especially when they study crime, look at the linguistic constructions (i.e., words, statements, or narratives) made about it by influential representatives of official institutions (Lilly et al., 2015).

Postmodernists focus on how humans jointly produce social deviance (crime in particular) through modes of discourse that they conveniently forget they have jointly produced. Structures of control, as well as that which is being controlled (i.e., deviance), are shaped by human collective actions, interactions, and the discourses that are such essential parts of the reproduction of what is being described. Postmodernists give great importance to the means of linguistic production because of their view that human knowledge—human thoughts and emotions particularly—is inseparable from language and shared systems of discourse. We must always know who the individuals are that are deciding that something is deviant, why they are making their claims about it, and their level of success in convincing others that what they claim is true (Best, 1990; Spector & Kitsuse, 1977). We must also have a clear understanding of how these discourses or narratives change those individuals who make them, as well as how they change the individuals about whom they are made (Meyer & Rohlinger, 2012).

Language itself is far from neutral, privileging some points of view while invalidating others (Bernard et al., 2010; Coyle, 2013; Foucault, 2003). Agents of social control try to make what they do to control others appear to be the only reasonable way for them to proceed, a way for them to be able to help the people being controlled to lead better, more productive lives. This is a fiction, according to postmodernists, who believe that the principal objective of control agents is to regulate and manage any troublesome population wherever and whenever it is found. This is an enterprise in which a constellation of interlocking agencies from different institutions work together to maintain the status quo (Foucault, 1977; Henry & Milovanovic, 1991).

It may be the *functionality* of both deviance and the deviant that is a central reason for their existence. Conventional groups do many things, both intentionally and unintentionally, to ensure that deviance exists because, despite surface appearances or public proclamations, deviance actually contributes in many ways to preservation of the status quo. The war on crime, for example, justifies the existence of police, courts, and prisons (Reiman & Leighton, 2010). It is the same for other kinds of deviance. Groups and organizations that have the mandate to eliminate deviance usually benefit too much from its existence to do the job well enough to make much of a difference. Deviants can be used as scapegoats to explain away continuing or worsening social problems (Gamson, 1995). Both under-conformity (being too "bad") to norms and over-conformity (being too "good") can evoke negative reactions from powerful individuals when these reactors conclude that their interests are being threatened (Heckert & Heckert, 2002) (though being too bad is more likely to be defined as a problem than is being too good).

Relativity and Social Deviance

Pathology, Harm, and Human Rights

To describe some culture, society, social arrangement, group, or individual as degenerate, pathological, or abnormal may be convenient, but none of these terms adds very much to our understanding of social deviance. "If persons are miserable, they may be so designated, and the quality of that misery described. Nothing but confusion is added by rendering that misery a pathology" (Matza, 1969, p. 43). We do not need to categorize something as degenerate, pathological, or abnormal in order to recognize that it is something that humans would be better off without. A society's structures and existing institutions can be the reason for much of the suffering of its citizens (Wright, 2012). Nothing is to be gained of lasting value from portraying social contradictions as individual pathologies.

Preservation of basic human rights emerged as a global concern, mainly in response to the Holocaust and World War II. These rights were formalized in the Universal Declaration of Human Rights (UDHR) of the United Nations (1948). This document is premised on the idea that all human beings should have the same fundamental rights no matter where they live (Turner, 1997; Zechenter, 1997). The UDHR was ratified by each member country of the United Nations in 1948, and it continues to be an important standard against which human decency is measured (Nagengast & Turner, 1997).

Provisions of the UDHR prohibit murder, torture, and slavery, while they guarantee freedom of conscience, speech, and dissent. Specific sections provide guarantees to employment and fair working conditions; to health, food, and social security; to education; and to participation in the cultural life of the community (United Nations, 1948). The history of a global concern with human rights has been uneven, precarious, and difficult. A "Responsibility to Protect" doctrine has been evolving in spurts and fits (Moyn, 2010). This doctrine is founded on the idea that human rights are universal, so every state or government should do what it can to protect them. If a political entity drags its feet or fails to protect its citizens altogether, other political entities (e.g., the United Nations) should step in to do the job.

Indigenous populations have been thrown off of their lands, legally and illegally; women have been denied equal access to food, health care, and other medical necessities; individuals (especially women and children) have been forced to perform slave labor; people across the planet have been deprived of both property and liberty without due process; and people have been tortured and killed merely because they were defined as political threats by powerful elites (Hagan & Rymond-Richmond, 2009; Levy & Sznaider, 2010; Totten, 2013). Some nations further their economic, political, and cultural interests in ways that are destructive to the sanctity and well-being of people worldwide (Ritzer, 2008; Turner, 1997). In addition, the actions of some groups within a given society threaten fundamental human rights of other groups in that same society (Gross, 2010; Lovell, 2012).

We must be able to identify how and when human rights are being violated, by whom, for what reasons, and with what consequences. Attention to the existence of harm is a valuable contribution to our understanding of deviance (Costello, 2006, 2009). It would be a mistake, however, to conclude that a harm-based conception of deviance invalidates sociological relativity. A government, because of its monopolization of power, can blame individuals for harms that are really no different from the harms imposed by the government itself (Kennedy, 1976). It can also blame individuals for harms that are really not their fault. Decisions about what qualifies as harm and who is responsible for it are subject to a great deal of relativity (Ghatak, 2011; Presser, 2013; Savelsberg & King, 2011). It is no easy task to develop a concept of universal human rights in the face of such profound and enduring conflicts and disagreements all across the world in regard to moral and ethical norms (Agier, 2011; Brunsma, Smith, & Gran, 2013; Findlay & Henham, 2010; Glenn, 2011; Zechenter, 1997).

Being a relativist does not inevitably dull one's moral sensibilities, and relativists can be as passionately committed as anyone else to ending human suffering. As Berger (1963) notes, a use of relativity to better understand human experience frees no one from finding his or her own way morally. For example, even though we might be able to understand that one nation's terrorist is another nation's freedom fighter or martyr, it certainly does not mean that we must cast an approving eye toward the attacks on the U.S. World Trade Center on September 11, 2001. Likewise, even though we can understand that laws against theft are culturally specific and historically based, reflecting some groups' interests and power more than others', it does not mean that we have to grin and bear it when our homes are burglarized and our possessions taken. We can still commit to the intellectual position of sociological relativity and yet be passionately committed to one course of action instead of another. For instance, it is "possible to be fully aware of the relativity and the precariousness of the way by which men organize their sexuality, and yet commit oneself absolutely to one's own marriage" (p. 159). We do the "right" thing because we can, justifying it on the basis of neither nature nor necessity.

Relativity does not require moral indifference, and it does not mean that we can never be upset or horrified by what we see or experience in a group or society (Goode & Ben-Yehuda, 1994). Relativity just reminds us that our personal beliefs or our cultural understandings are not necessarily found everywhere. If we condemn some practice, we must be certain that we are doing it for reasons other than our own particular ethnocentric or egocentric biases. Our biases cannot be avoided completely, it is true, but relativity allows us the best chance to recognize them for the partialities that they are.

The Serious Implications of Taking Relativity Seriously

According to Matza (1969), the sociology of deviance encourages an appreciation of human diversity and a rejection of the simplistic notion that deviants are inherently pathological.

> The growth of a sociological view of deviant phenomena involved, as major phases, the replacement of a correctional stance by an *appreciation* of the deviant subject, the tacit purging of a conception of pathology by new stress on human *diversity*, and the erosion of a simple distinction between deviant and conventional phenomena, resulting from more intimate familiarity with the world as it is, which yielded a more sophisticated view stressing *complexity*. (p. 10)

Social scientists, just like the humans they study, must be able to deal with— and construct theories that make sense of—the ambiguity, uncertainty, and complexity of social life (Crewe, 2013). Sociology itself, Goode (2003) asserts, is "wedded" to the concept of deviance (pp. 519–520). If the marriage works, it is due in no small part to the relativity that is at the core of both.

Humans have a remarkable capacity to make practically anything proper or improper, as the case may be. The world is constantly in flux, and people have done, are doing, and will continue to do a multitude of things that will lead to the delight, indifference, or dismay of others (Gibbs, 1994). A colleague of mine once observed that the ties that bind—traditions and customs, ways of doing things, standard notions of proper and improper—also qualify as the ties that *blind* (Winther, 1994, personal communication). Human beings assign meaning to practically everything that can be seen, felt, smelled, tasted, or heard. Once this is done, it tends to blind them to other possibilities and to alternate ways of thinking, feeling, acting, or being. One individual's object of outrage or disgust might be, and probably is, another individual's object of reverence, worship, or desire; one individual's revulsion might be another individual's attraction; and the object or objects of hatred for members of one human society just might be, and probably are, the objects of adoration for members of another society.

Culture shock is the feeling of disorientation or uneasiness that one might experience when traveling to a different place and being forced to accommodate to new ways of thinking, feeling, or acting. Sometimes the culture shock is mild. If you went from a hot climate, such as one finds in Southern California or Florida, to a much colder climate, such as one finds in Illinois or New York, you might experience things in the winter to which you were unaccustomed. People would seem to be dressing in unusual ways and doing unusual things, such as buying snow blowers and snow shovels, but it would be easy to adjust to these changes. They would be only temporarily disorienting. What if you were told, however, that the stew you had just eaten was made with dog meat, horse meat, sheep eyes, or the flesh of recently killed rattlesnakes? How would you feel if you were told that the crunchy snack you had just eaten was not a party mix but baked locusts and termites? In these cases, culture shock may be acute and quite unsettling. Sometimes it is an experience an individual will never forget.

Berger (1963) observed that sociological discovery is culture shock without geographical displacement. Just as travelers to another land may experience a sense of uneasiness, disorientation, or surprise when faced with people whose customs are different from their own, so can we be shocked by seeing familiar happenings in our own society in a new and disturbing way. This culture shock may propel us in the direction of greater ethnocentrism. No way, we tell ourselves, would we ever do *that;* we would have to be sick, crazy, or out of our heads. Yet we must make every effort to understand the context of action. We must understand that if we had been raised in a culture where people eat dogs, horses, sheep eyes, rattlesnakes, locusts, or termites, we would, in all likelihood, be eating and enjoying them, too.

Viewing deviance as something that can produce culture shock but that is not intrinsically bad or inherently sick is valuable. Just as we might study any form of behavior in a foreign land, we can study deviance "at home"—even in our own homes—as part of changing social relationships and alternating cultural or subcultural meaning systems. Because our goal is to understand social context and how and why behavior is defined and evaluated the way it is, we will not spend much time trying to decide if deviance is abnormal or sick, in need of cure or correction. Just as it would be too ethnocentric to conclude that eating dog meat instead of cow meat is abnormal or sick, it is too ethnocentric to conclude that people who inhale certain kinds of substances (e.g., marijuana) are more abnormal or sicker than people who inhale other kinds of substances (e.g., tobacco). Deviance in practically all its forms is a normal feature of human societies, and we must fight the temptation to equate deviance with disease or abnormality. Some deviance is unsettling or shocking to people who are unfamiliar with it, but this does not mean that deviance is essentially or necessarily abnormal or sick everywhere and at all times.

Whose Side Are We On?

The concept of sentimentality (Becker, 1963, 1964, 1967) offers a powerful reminder that sides exist in deciding who or what is deviant, and it matters greatly whose side is taken. Becker (1964) defined *sentimentality* as a disposition on the part of a researcher to leave certain variables in a research problem unexamined or to refuse to consider alternate views of some social happening or distasteful possibilities. Becker borrowed the term from Freidson's (1961) study of physicians and their patients. Freidson was willing to give credibility and authority to patients' views of their physicians even when those views were at odds with what physicians thought of themselves. Sides exist even in the seemingly straightforward relationship between physician and patient, and it is possible that a patient's view is more credible and correct than is the physician's.

Sometimes, a researcher's bias is to side with representatives of the official world (e.g., police, judges, or psychiatrists), in which case he or she is adopting *conventional sentimentality*; at other times, a researcher's bias is to side with representatives of deviant worlds (e.g., criminals or the mentally ill), in which case he or she is adopting *unconventional sentimentality* (Becker, 1964, p. 5). Researchers are sentimental when they overidentify with either conventional or unconventional human beings only because they do not want to face the possibility that some cherished sympathy of theirs could be shown to be untrue (Becker, 1967). Alternation between these two different sides will increase the chances of developing an actor-relevant, empirically correct understanding of both rule breakers *and* rule makers.

Social scientists are required by the demands of their disciplines to understand as fully as possible the social systems they are studying. This means that they will almost always have to uncover and critically evaluate the myths, ideologies, and verbal smoke screens that humans use to hide, distort, or legitimate whatever they are doing (Berger, 1963). Carried to extremes, romanticizing or glorifying diversity will have the unfortunate outcome of making it more difficult to see and deal with the extreme suffering that deviance can cause in the lives of people who are adversely affected by it (Matza, 1969). We must not be relativistic in the extreme, because it would hamper our ability to understand social deviance (Goode, 2015; Rafter, 1992).

The social construction of values and norms is often accidental and arbitrary, it is true, but it is also (or can be) rational and reasonable (Bloom, 1987). By restricting ourselves to one particular group and time, the acts, attributes, ideas, and identities can be ranked in some rough fashion from good to bad, appropriate to inappropriate, or injurious to benign. To act as if it is unimportant exactly *what* attitudes, behaviors, and conditions individuals profess, display, or have would be a mistake. Feeding a dead chicken to a crocodile is identifiably different from, and morally superior to, feeding your infant son to the reptile. The issue gets murky, however, when you try to compare customs from different cultures and subcultures or time periods to one another along some universal dimension of goodness and badness. What one group calls a "freedom fighter" or "martyr," another group calls a "terrorist," and it does little good to try to figure out who is right, independent from a consideration of who exactly is making the determination and why.

The concept of relativity, which was developed partly to encourage an awareness of, and respect for, human variability and diversity, has returned to haunt us. Relativity has been used to justify the differential treatment of indigenous groups, women, and minorities, as well as to excuse human rights abuses (Moyn, 2010; Nagengast, 1997). Countries that violate the human rights of their populations most often are the ones that justify their actions in the international arena by appealing to sovereignty and cultural relativity (Nagengast & Turner, 1997). Their rulers defend practices such as corporal or capital punishment, the abuse of women (including genital mutilation), sexism and racism, and violence by claiming that their critics are ethnocentric or indifferent to the integrity of local customs.

Self-interest can be masked as the common good, and socially constructed roles can serve as alibis for acts of personal cruelty or cowardice (Berger, 1963). It is quite proper—and not at all inconsistent with sociological relativity—to be critical of sovereign nations whenever they have institutionalized practices that interfere with human rights for reasons unrelated to community survival or the safety and security of their citizens. Customs that are a product of ideological thinking (e.g., male dominance) or stark economic inequalities are the ones that are most in need of a relativist analysis.

Conclusions

Understandings of deviance have evolved over time. Early views were based on a belief that intrinsic characteristics separated both deviants and deviance from their opposites. They assumed that deviance is what abnormal people do. Attention ultimately shifted to norms and then to labels and social reactions. Social deviance came to be viewed as a regular feature of life in a pluralistic society that could be caused by social control itself. Deviance emerges from social differentiation, social conflict, and social disagreement; the meanings of deviance are always problematic and contentious.

A great deal of diversity can be found as we move from society to society or group to group. Relativity is a way of examining standards and customs by understanding their context. Deviance, like beauty, is in the eye of the beholder. It exists because some groups decide that other groups ought not to be doing and being what they are, in fact, doing and being. Deviance results from dynamic relationships among many people; it is not an unchanging or immutable condition with intrinsic or inherent qualities. We must remember that all things are transitory and impermanent, including human understandings about proper and improper ways of acting, thinking, feeling, and being.

The author Victor Hugo claimed that nothing is as powerful as an idea whose time has come. This is certainly true for sociological relativity. Sometimes, examples of deviance will be found—glaring examples of inhumanity and incivility—that will shock our sensibilities so much that we will be inclined toward intolerance and a quest for harsher and swifter penalties for deviants. Some individuals or groups will do things that are so harmful or outlandish that they push practically everyone else into a strong defense of the status quo and conventional morality. However, it is relativity that offers social scientists—especially sociologists—the best hope for understanding the social construction of both reality and social deviance.

Sociological relativity is just too powerful an idea and too much a part of what makes the sociological imagination important and valuable for it to be dumped in the intellectual waste bin. A relativistic approach to social deviance will enrich us in countless ways. Sociological relativity's vision of society (socially constructed), vision of human nature (broad and flexible), scientific methodology (actor-relevant and empathic), and moral stance (unsentimental) all offer great power and potential to anyone who wants to understand and explain social deviance.

References

Adler, P., & Adler, P. (2006). The deviance society. *Deviant Behavior, 27,* 129–148.

Adler, P., & Adler, P. (2009). Defining deviance. In P. Adler & P. Adler (Eds.), *Constructions of deviance: Social power, context, and interaction* (6th ed., pp. 11–15). Belmont, CA: Thomson/Wadsworth.

Agier, M. (2011). *Managing the undesirables: Refugee camps and humanitarian government.* Cambridge, UK: Polity Press.

Akers, R. L. (1985). *Deviant behavior: A social learning approach* (3rd ed.). Belmont, CA: Wadsworth.

Alleyne, E., & Wood, J. L. (2014). Gang involvement: Social and environmental factors. *Crime & Delinquency, 60,* 547–568.

Arrigo, B. A., & Bernard, T. J. (1997). Postmodern criminology in relation to radical and conflict criminology. *Critical Criminology, 8,* 39–60.

Baker, J. O., Bader, C. D., & Hirsch, K. (2015). Desecration, moral boundaries, and the movement of law: The case of Westboro Baptist Church. *Deviant Behavior, 36,* 42–67.

Bauman, Z. (1991) *Modernity and ambivalence.* Cambridge, UK: Polity Press.

Bauman, Z. (2006) *Liquid fear.* Cambridge, UK: Polity Press.

Bauman, Z. (2011). *Culture in a liquid modern world* (L. Bauman, Trans.). Cambridge, UK: Polity Press.

Bauman, Z., & May, T. (2001) *Thinking sociologically* (2nd ed.). Oxford, UK: Blackwell.

Becker, H. (1963). *Outsiders: Studies in the sociology of deviance.* New York: Free Press.

Becker, H. (1964). Introduction. In H. Becker (Ed.), *The other side: Perspectives on deviance* (pp. 1–6). New York: Free Press.

Becker, H. (1967). Whose side are we on? *Social Problems, 14,* 239–247.

Becker, H. (1973). Labeling theory reconsidered. In H. Becker (Ed.), *Outsiders: Studies in the sociology of deviance* (pp. 177–212). New York: Free Press.

Becker, H. (1982). Culture: A sociological view. *Yale Review, 71,* 513–527.

Ben-Yehuda, N. (1990). *The politics and morality of deviance: Moral panics, drug abuse, deviant science, and reversed stigmatization.* Albany: State University of New York Press.

Ben-Yehuda, N. (2006). Contextualizing deviance within social change and stability, morality, and power. *Sociological Spectrum, 26,* 559–580.

Berger, P. (1963). *Invitation to sociology: A humanistic perspective.* Garden City, NY: Anchor.

Berger, P., & Luckmann, T. (1966). *The social construction of reality.* Garden City, NY: Anchor.

Bernard, T. J., Snipes, J. B., & Gerould, A. L. (2010). *Vold's theoretical criminology* (6th ed.). New York: Oxford University Press.

Best, J. (1990). *Threatened children: Rhetoric and concern about child victims.* Chicago: University of Chicago Press.

Best, J. (2004). *Deviance: Career of a concept.* Belmont, CA: Thomson/Wadsworth.

Blackman, S. (2014). Subculture theory: An historical and contemporary assessment of the concept for understanding deviance. *Deviant Behavior, 35,* 496–512.

Bloom, A. (1987). *The closing of the American mind.* New York: Simon & Schuster.

Brunsma, D., Smith, K., & Gran, B. (Eds.). (2013). *Handbook of sociology and human rights.* Boulder, CO: Paradigm.

Buck v. Bell, 274 U.S. 200 (1927).

Burgess, R. L., & Akers, R. L. (1966). A differential association-reinforcement theory of criminal behavior. *Social Problems, 14,* 128–147.

Busch, L. (2011). *Standards: Recipes for reality.* Cambridge: MIT Press.

Chapple, C., Vaske, J., & Worthen, M. G. F. (2014). Gender differences in associations with deviant peer groups: Examining individual, interactional, and compositional factors. *Deviant Behavior, 35,* 394–411.

Chayko, M. (2008). *Portable communities: The social dynamics of online and mobile connectedness.* New York: State University of New York Press.

Cohen, A. (1974). *The elasticity of evil: Changes in the social definition of deviance.* Oxford, UK: Blackwell.

Costello, B. (2006). Cultural relativism and the study of deviance. *Sociological Spectrum, 26,* 581–594.

Costello, B. (2009). Against relativism: A harm-based conception of deviance. In P. Adler & P. Adler (Eds.), *Constructions of deviance: Social power, context, and interaction* (6th ed., pp. 46–52). Belmont, CA: Thomson/Wadsworth.

Cote, S. (Ed.). (2002). *Criminological theories: Bridging the past to the future.* Thousand Oaks, CA: Sage.

Coyle, M. J. (2013). *Talking criminal justice: Language and the just society.* New York: Routledge.

Crewe, D. (2013). *Becoming criminal: The socio-cultural origins of law, transgression, and deviance.* Hampshire, UK: Palgrave Macmillan.

Cronk, L., & Leech, B. L. (2013). *Meeting at Grand Central: Understanding the social and evolutionary roots of cooperation.* Princeton, NJ: Princeton University Press.

Cross, J. C., & Hernández, A. H. (2011). Place, identity, and deviance: A community-based approach to understanding the relationship between deviance and place. *Deviant Behavior, 32,* 503–537.

Danesi, M. (2010). *Geeks, goths, and gangstas: Youth culture and the evolution of modern society.* Toronto, Ont., Canada: Canadian Scholars' Press.

Dellwing, M. (2011). Truth in labeling: Are descriptions all we have? *Deviant Behavior, 32,* 653–675.

Demerath, L. (2014). *Explaining culture: The social pursuit of subjective order.* Lanham, MD: Lexington Books.

Devroye, J. (2010). The rise and fall of the American Institute of Criminal Law and Criminology. *Journal of Criminal Law & Criminology, 100,* 7–32.

Douglas, J., Rasmussen, P., & Flanagan, C. (1977). *The nude beach.* Beverly Hills, CA: Sage.

Durkheim, É. (1933). *The division of labor in society* (G. Simpson, Trans.). New York: Free Press. (Original work published 1893)

Durkheim, É. (1938). *The rules of sociological method* (8th ed.; George Catlin, Ed.; S. Solovay & John Mueller, Trans.). New York: Free Press. (Original work published 1895)

Edgerton, R. (1992). *Sick societies: Challenging the myth of primitive harmony.* New York: Free Press.

Enriquez, L. E. (2014). "Undocumented and citizen students unite": Building a cross-status coalition through shared ideology. *Social Problems, 61,* 155–174.

Erikson, K. (1962). Notes on the sociology of deviance. *Social Problems, 9,* 307–314.

Ferrell, J. (1993). *Crimes of style: Urban graffiti and the politics of criminality.* Boston: Northeastern University Press.

Ferrell, J. (1999). Cultural criminology. *Annual Review of Sociology, 25,* 395–418.

Ferrell, J., Hayward, K., & Young, J. (2015). *Cultural criminology: An invitation* (2nd ed.). Thousand Oaks, CA: Sage

Findlay, M., & Henham, R. (2010). *Beyond punishment: Achieving international criminal justice.* Basingstoke, UK: Palgrave Macmillan.

Fine, G. A. (2012). *Tiny publics: A theory of group action and culture.* New York: Russell Sage Foundation.

Fish, S. (2001, October 15). Condemnation without absolutes. *New York Times,* p. A23.

Forsyth, C. (1992). Parade strippers: A note on being naked in public. *Deviant Behavior, 13,* 391–403.

Foucault, M. (1977). *Discipline and punish: The birth of the prison* (A. Sheridan, Trans.). New York: Pantheon.

Foucault, M. (2003). *Abnormal: Lectures at the Collège de France* (V. Marchetti & A. Salomoni, Eds.; G. Burchell, Trans.). New York: Picador.

Freidson, E. (1961). *Patients' view of medical practice.* New York: Russell Sage Foundation.

Gamson, W. (1995). Hiroshima, the Holocaust, and the politics of exclusion (1994 presidential address). *American Sociological Review, 60,* 1–20.

Ghatak, S. (2011). *Threat perceptions: The policing of dangers from eugenics to the war on terrorism.* Lanham, MD: Lexington Books.

Gibbs, J. (1966). Conceptions of deviant behavior: The old and the new. *Pacific Sociological Review, 9,* 9–14.

Gibbs, J. (1994). *A theory about control.* Boulder, CO: Westview Press.

Gladwell, M. (2000). *The tipping point: How little things can make a big difference.* Boston: Little, Brown.

Glenn, E. N. (2011). Constructing citizenship: Exclusion, subordination, and resistance (2010 presidential address). *American Sociological Review, 76,* 1–24.

Goffman, E. (1961). *Asylums.* Garden City, NY: Doubleday.

Goffman, E. (1963). *Stigma: Notes on the management of spoiled identity.* Englewood Cliffs, NJ: Prentice Hall.

Goode, E. (2003). The MacGuffin that refuses to die: An investigation into the condition of the sociology of deviance. *Deviant Behavior, 24,* 507–533.

Goode, E. (2015). *Deviant behavior* (10th ed.). Upper Saddle River, NJ: Pearson.

Goode, E., & Ben-Yehuda, N. (1994). *Moral panics: The social construction of deviance.* Oxford, UK: Blackwell.

Gross, J. A. (2010). *A shameful business: The case for human rights in the American workplace.* Ithaca, NY: Cornell University Press.

Haenfler, R. (2013). *Goths, gamers, grrrls: Deviance and youth subcultures* (2nd ed.). New York: Oxford University Press.

Hagan, J., & Rymond-Richmond, W. (2009). *Darfur and the crime of genocide.* New York: Cambridge University Press.

Harding, L. (2014). *The Snowden files: The inside story of the world's most wanted man.* New York: Vintage.

Heckert, A., & Heckert, D. M. (2002). A new typology of deviance: Integrating normative and reactivist definitions of deviance. *Deviant Behavior, 23,* 449–479.

Henry, S., & Milovanovic, D. (1991). Constitutive criminology: The maturation of critical theory. *Criminology, 29,* 293–315.

Henry, S., & Milovanovic, D. (1996). *Constitutive criminology: Beyond postmodernism.* London: Sage.

Horwitz, A. (2008). Keyword: Normality. In J. Goodwin & J. Jasper (Eds.), *The contexts reader* (pp. 363–367). New York: Norton.

Hunt, P. M. (2010). Are you kynd? Conformity and deviance within the jamband subculture. *Deviant Behavior, 31,* 521–551.

Iacoboni, M. (2009). *Mirroring people: The science of empathy and how we connect with others.* New York: Picador/Farrar, Straus & Giroux.

Irwin, K., & Simpson, B. (2013). Do descriptive norms solve social dilemmas? Conformity and contributions in collective action groups. *Social Forces, 91,* 1057–1084.

Josephson Institute. (2012). *The ethics of American youth: 2012.* Retrieved January 30, 2015, from http://charactercounts.org/programs/reportcard/2012/installment_report-card_honesty-integrity

Jung, W., King, B. G., & Soule, S. A. (2014). Issue bricolage: Explaining the configuration of the social movement sector, 1960–1995. *American Journal of Sociology, 120,* 187–225.

Katz, J. (1988). *Seductions of crime: Moral and sensual attractions in doing evil.* New York: Basic Books.

Kennedy, M. (1976). Beyond incrimination: Some neglected facets of the theory of punishment. In W. Chambliss & M. Mankoff (Eds.), *Whose law? What order?* (pp. 34–65). New York: Wiley.

Kitsuse, J. (1962). Societal reaction to deviant behavior: Problems of theory and method. *Social Problems, 9,* 247–257.

Kluckhohn, C. (1949). *Mirror for man: The relation of anthropology to modern life.* New York: McGraw-Hill.

Kraaykamp, G., & van Eijck, K. (2010). The intergenerational reproduction of cultural capital: A threefold perspective. *Social Forces, 89,* 209–232.

Krauthammer, C. (1993, November 22). Defining deviancy up. *New Republic,* 20–25.

Kumbasar, E., Romney, A. K., & Batchelder, W. H. (1994). Systematic biases in social perception. *American Journal of Sociology, 100,* 477–505.

Lanier, M. M., Henry, S., & Anastasia, D. J. M. (2015). *Essential criminology: Contexts and consequences* (4th ed.). Boulder, CO: Westview Press.

Lemert, E. (1951). *Social pathology.* New York: McGraw-Hill.

Lemert, E. (1972). *Human deviance, social problems, and social control* (2nd ed.). Englewood Cliffs, NJ: Prentice Hall.

Levy, D., & Sznaider, N. (2010). *Human rights and memory: Essays on human rights.* University Park: Pennsylvania State University Press.

Lilly, J. R., Cullen, F. T., & Ball, R. A. (2015). *Criminological theory: Contexts and consequences* (6th ed.). Thousand Oaks, CA: Sage.

Ling, R. (2012). *Taken for grantedness: The embedding of mobile communication into society.* Cambridge: MIT Press.

Lovell, G. I. (2012). *This is not civil rights: Discovering rights talk in 1939 America.* Chicago: University of Chicago Press.

Lyman, S., & Scott, M. (1989). *A sociology of the absurd* (2nd ed.). Dix Hills, NY: General Hall.

MacAskill, E. (June 10, 2014). Edward Snowden's NSA leaks "An important service," says Al Gore. *The Guardian.* Retrieved May 10, 2015, from www.theguardian .com/world/2014/jun/10/edward-snowden-nsa-leaks-important-service-al-gore

Marx, K. (1978). Society and economy in history. In R. Tucker (Ed.), *The Marx–Engels reader* (2nd ed., pp. 136–142). New York: Norton. (Original work published 1846)

Matza, D. (1969). *Becoming deviant.* Englewood Cliffs, NJ: Prentice Hall.

Matza, D., & Sykes, G. M. (1961). Juvenile delinquency and subterranean values. *American Sociological Review, 26,* 712–719.

Mead, G. H. (1934). *Mind, self, and society: From the standpoint of a social behaviorist.* Chicago: University of Chicago Press.

Menard, S., & Johnson, M. C. (2015). An intergenerational test of integrated theory. *Deviant Behavior, 36,* 87–100.

Merton, R. K. (1938). Social structure and anomie. *American Sociological Review, 3,* 672–682.

Merton, R. K. (1948). The self-fulfilling prophecy. *Antioch Review, 8,* 193–210.

Merton, R. K. (1968). Introduction. In R. K. Merton, *Social theory and social structure* (enlarged ed., pp. 175–184). New York: Free Press.

Merton, R. K., & Ashley-Montagu, M. F. (1940). Crime and the anthropologist. *American Anthropologist, 42,* 384–408.

Meyer, D. S., & Rohlinger, D. A. (2012). Big books and social movements: A myth of ideas and social change. *Social Problems, 59,* 136–153.

Miller, J. M., Schreck, C. J., Tewksbury, R., & Barnes, J. C. (2015). *Criminological theory: A brief introduction* (4th ed.). Boston: Pearson.

Mills, C. W. (1943). The professional ideology of social pathologists. *American Journal of Sociology, 49,* 165–180.

Milovanovic, D. (1997). *Postmodern criminology.* New York: Garland.

Mintz, S. (1982). Culture: An anthropological view. *Yale Review, 71,* 499–512.

Mohun, A. P. (2013). *Risk: Negotiating safety in American society.* Baltimore, MD: Johns Hopkins University Press.

Moore, R. I. (1987). *The formation of a persecuting society: Power and deviance in Western Europe, 950–1250.* New York: Basil Blackwell.

Moyn, S. (2010). *The last utopia: Human rights in history.* Cambridge, MA: Belknap Press of Harvard University Press.

Moynihan, D. P. (1993). Defining deviancy down. *American Scholar, 64,* 25–33.

Nagengast, C. (1997). Women, minorities, and indigenous peoples: Universalism and cultural relativity. *Journal of Anthropological Research, 53,* 349–369.

Nagengast, C., & Turner, T. (1997). Introduction: Universal human rights versus cultural relativity. *Journal of Anthropological Research, 53,* 269–272.

Oakes, G. (2011). Mr. Big. *Contemporary Sociology, 40,* 549–552.

O'Brien, J. (2006). Shared meaning as the basis of humanness. In J. O'Brien (Ed.), *The production of reality* (4th ed., pp. 64–82). Thousand Oaks, CA: Pine Forge/Sage.

Parsons, T. (1951). *The social system.* New York: Free Press.

Piaget, J. (1948). *The moral judgment of the child.* New York: Free Press.

Portes, A. (2000). The hidden abode: Sociology as an analysis of the unexpected (1999 presidential address). *American Sociological Review, 65,* 1–18.

Presser, L. (2013). *Why we harm.* New Brunswick, NJ: Rutgers University Press.

Quinney, R. (1970). *The social reality of crime.* Boston: Little, Brown.

Quinney, R. (1973). There are a lot of folks grateful to the Lone Ranger: With some notes on the rise and fall of American criminology. *Insurgent Sociologist, 4,* 56–64.

Quinney, R. (1974). *Critique of the legal order: Crime control in capitalist society.* Boston: Little, Brown.

Rafter, N. (1992). Some consequences of strict constructionism. *Social Problems, 39,* 38–39.

Rafter, N. (1997). *Creating born criminals.* Chicago: University of Illinois Press.

Raybeck, D. (1991). Hard versus soft deviance: Anthropology and labeling theory. In M. Freilich, D. Raybeck, & J. Savishinsky (Eds.), *Deviance: Anthropological perspectives* (pp. 51–73). New York: Bergin & Garvey.

Reiman, J., & Leighton, P. (2010). *The rich get richer and the poor get prison: Ideology, class, and criminal justice* (9th ed.). Boston: Pearson/Allyn & Bacon.

Riesman, D. (1963). Foreword. In E. S. Bowen, *Return to laughter* (pp. ix–xviii). Garden City, NY: Anchor/Doubleday.

Ritzer, G. (2008). *The McDonaldization of society* (5th ed.). Thousand Oaks, CA: Pine Forge/Sage.

Rosenberg, T. (2011). *Join the club: How peer pressure can transform the world.* New York: Norton.

Ruane, J. M., & Cerulo, K. A. (2015). *Second thoughts: Sociology challenges conventional wisdom* (6th ed.). Thousand Oaks, CA: Sage.

Ruane, J. M., Cerulo, K. A., & Gerson, J. M. (1994). Normal lying in an occupational setting. *Sociological Focus, 27,* 91–109.

Savelsberg, J. J., & King, R. D. (2011). *American memories: Atrocities and the law.* New York: Russell Sage Foundation.

Schnakenberg, R. (2009). *Secret lives of the Supreme Court: What your teachers never told you about America's legendary justices.* Philadelphia: Quirk Books.

Schwartz, H. (1997). On the origin of the phrase "social problems." *Social Problems, 44,* 276–296.

Schwendinger, H., & Schwendinger, J. (1975). Defenders of order or guardians of human rights? In I. Taylor, P. Walton, & J. Young (Eds.), *Critical criminology* (pp. 113–146). London: Routledge/Kegan Paul.

Searle, J. (1995). *The construction of social reality.* New York: Free Press.

Sellin, T. (1938). *Culture conflict and crime* (Bulletin 41). New York: Social Science Research Council.

Shrum, W., & Kilburn, J. (1996). Ritual disrobement at Mardi Gras: Ceremonial exchange and moral order. *Social Forces, 72,* 423–458.

Smångs, M. (2010). Delinquency, social skills and the structure of peer relations: Assessing criminological theories by social network theory. *Social Forces, 89,* 609–632.

Spector, M., & Kitsuse, J. (1977). *Constructing social problems.* Menlo Park, CA: Cummings.

Staples, W. (2000). *Everyday surveillance: Vigilance and visibility in postmodern life.* Lanham, MD: Rowman & Littlefield.

Sumner, C. (1994). *The sociology of deviance: An obituary.* New York: Continuum.

Sumner, W. G. (1906). *Folkways: A study of the sociological importance of usages, manners, customs, mores, and morals.* Boston: Ginn.

Sutherland, E. H. (1947). *Principles of criminology* (4th ed.). Philadelphia: J. B. Lippincott.

Tannenbaum, F. (1938). *Crime and the community.* Boston: Ginn.

Taylor, I., Walton, P., & Young, J. (1973). *The new criminology: For a social theory of deviance.* New York: Harper & Row.

Tedor, M. F. (2015). The moderating effect of type of deviance on the relationships among gender, morality, deviant peers, and deviance. *Deviant Behavior, 36,* 221–244.

Tibbetts, S. G. (2012). *Criminological theory: The essentials.* Thousand Oaks, CA: Sage.

Tibbetts, S. G., & Hemmens, C. (2010). *Criminological theory: A text/reader.* Thousand Oaks, CA: Sage.

Totten, S. (Ed.). (2013). *Impediments to the prevention and intervention of genocide.* New Brunswick, NJ: Transaction.

Troyer, R. (1992). Some consequences of contextual constructionism. *Social Problems, 39,* 35–37.

Turner, T. (1997). Human rights, human difference: Anthropology's contribution to an emancipatory cultural politics. *Journal of Anthropological Research, 53,* 273–291.

United Nations. (1948). *The universal declaration of human rights.* Adopted and proclaimed by General Assembly Resolution 217 A (III) of 10 December 1948. Retrieved January 18, 2013, from http://www.un.org/en/documents/udhr/index .shtml

Warr, M. (1993). Age, peers, and delinquency. *Criminology, 31,* 17–40.

Warr, M. (2002). *Companions in crime: The social aspects of criminal conduct.* New York: Cambridge University Press.

Wasserman, J. A., & Clair, J. M. (2010). *At home on the street: People, poverty and a hidden culture of homelessness.* Boulder, CO: Lynne Rienner.

Watts, D. J. (2011). *Everything is obvious, once you know the answer: How common sense fails us.* New York: Crown Business.

Watts, D. J. (2014). Common sense and sociological explanations. *American Journal of Sociology, 120,* 313–351.

Whittier, N. (2014). Rethinking coalitions: Anti-pornography feminists, conservatives, and relationships between collaborative adversarial movements. *Social Problems, 61,* 175–193.

Williams, F. P., III, & McShane, M. (2014). *Criminological theory* (6th ed.). Upper Saddle River, NJ: Pearson.

Williams, J. P. (2011). *Subcultural theory: Traditions and concepts.* Malden, MA: Polity Press.

Wright, E. O. (2012). Transforming capitalism through real utopias (2012 presidential address). *American Sociological Review, 78,* 1–25.

Young, J. (2011). Moral panics and the transgressive other. *Crime, Media, Culture, 7,* 245–258.

Zechenter, E. (1997). In the name of culture: Cultural relativism and the abuse of the individual. *Journal of Anthropological Research, 53,* 319–347.

Zhao, R., & Cao, L. (2010). Social change and anomie: A cross-national study. *Social Forces, 88,* 1209–1230.

2

Being Deviant

The Original Blue Man (and Woman) Group

Over six generations ago, Martin Fugate and his bride settled on the banks of eastern Kentucky's Troublesome Creek. They had children, who had children, who had children. Most of them were healthy and lived well into old age. When Martin Fugate's great-great-great-great-grandson was born, he was as healthy as a newborn could be. He did, however, have one curious trait: dark blue skin, the color of a ripe plum or dark denim blue jeans. The attending physicians were concerned. Did the child have a blood disorder? The child's grandmother told them not to worry. Many of the Fugates had blue skin (Trost, 1982).

A young hematologist from the University of Kentucky was curious about the unusual skin color. With the help of a nurse and a blue couple, the physician eventually uncovered the reason for the blue tint. It was caused by a hereditary condition that allowed too much methemoglobin (a form of hemoglobin that is blue) to accumulate in the blood. The blue people, it seemed, lacked an enzyme that is necessary for the regulation of methemoglobin. Due either to a quirk of fate or an affair of the heart, Martin Fugate had married a woman who carried the same recessive gene for blueness that he did. Because members of the Fugate line were content to remain where they were born, people with the recessive gene that caused the blueness often married and had children with others who had the same hereditary trait. As a result, the number of blue people around eastern Kentucky's Troublesome Creek increased.

The physician and the nurse had more than an academic interest in the blue skin color. As befitted their medical training, they were really hoping to find a "cure" for it. Once they knew the reason for the skin color, it was easy enough for them to find an "antidote." Methylene blue is a chemical that changes the color of methemoglobin. When it was injected into the blue people, it had the desired effect: Their skin turned pink. However, because the effects of methylene blue are short-lived, the *former* blue people of Kentucky would have to take a pill every day for the transformation to last. (Physicians no longer see this blood condition very much because mountain people are more inclined than they once were to leave the mountains, so the gene pool is more diverse.) What could show the relative nature of deviance better than the fact that people can be stigmatized for characteristics over which they have little or no control? If being blue among a bunch of other blue people can be labeled as deviant and in need of correction, then anything can be.

Being and Doing

An individual's identity contains two separable parts (Goffman, 1971). One part is *social identity,* which consists of general social statuses, such as gender, race, class, and nativity. The other part is *personal identity,* which is more idiosyncratic and requires familiarity with an individual for it to be known. It includes an individual's name and appearance, as well as distinctive attributes, traits, or marks. These two identities, of course, complement one another, and social identity is always "fleshed out" by personal identity. Although being a "mother" is part of social identity, each mother has unique characteristics that make up her personal identity (e.g., *this* mom likes to mow the lawn and jog 5 miles a day). Some relationships are *pegged* or *anchored,* and interactants know one another personally and know that they are known in both their social and personal identities. Other relationships, however, are *anonymous,* and interactants know one another only in terms of social identity (p. 189). We each have access to many identities, both social and personal, that we can present to others (Shanahan, Bauldry, Roberts, Macmillan, & Russo, 2014).

An individual may do all he or she can to keep a deeply discrediting act or attribute hidden entirely or restricted to personal identity alone so that only a few others will be aware of it (Ridolfo & Ward, 2013). It may be a central part of one's life to keep discrediting parts of personal identity from contaminating social identity (and vice versa) (Schroeder & Mowen, 2014). Social and personal identities are in many ways a negotiated reality, being flexible, contingent, and relative to time and place (Burke & Stets, 2009; MacKinnon & Heise, 2010; Richardson, 2010; Thompson & Thompson, 2014). Some of what we are we embrace willingly and fully, while other parts we take on reluctantly, as something imposed on us against our wills. The human body is both a possession and a prison (Kosut & Moore, 2010; Lizardo & Collett, 2013).

Garot (2010) studied gang memberships of students in an alternative school (called Choices Alternative Academy) in an area characterized by some of the highest levels of crime and poverty in the western United States. These students had histories of violence, drug use, truancy, dropping out of school, and teen pregnancy. Garot's subjects, who were mostly African Americans or Latinos, were rough and tough, the baddest of the bad. They knew how to take care of themselves, regularly using violence to do so (p. 15). Garot found, however, that gangs were not filled with ruthless killers, bent on carrying out whatever missions their leaders demanded of them. Gang members were individuals—more normal than not—who were trying to construct identities in social environments that they found irrelevant and alienating. Whatever gang members are, they are more than just members of gangs. They do what they can to make lives for themselves that matter out of inferior materials in alienating and dangerous environments (Venkatesh, 2008).

The experiences of people who are treated as deviant for what they *are*— their shame, guilt, rejection by others—may not be appreciably different from the experiences of people who are treated as deviant for what they *do*. Both human behaviors and human beings must be part of our understanding of deviance, because deviance is sometimes a matter of being rather than doing (Sagarin, 1975).

> The belief that one is a certain thing, particularly when the concept of isness carries with it a sense of destiny . . . creates a feeling of immutability in that role. The language reinforces both the identity and the immutability, and the role occupant at that point finds it impossible to believe that he can be or is other than what he has defined himself as being. (Sagarin, 1975, p. 152)

Role engulfment can occur in which an individual feels trapped in some particular role and powerless to leave it (Schur, 1971). Others may think this person is *only* what he or she is believed to be (Hills, 1980). We sometimes do feel imprisoned by our bodies rather than liberated, and we are imbued with all kinds of meanings and understandings, coming from both the self and others (Etorre, 2010; Fiske, 2012; Moore & Kosut, 2010).

Deviance and Responsibility

Attaching Blame

The *fundamental attribution error* (FAE) is the mistake of attaching responsibility for some happening to an individual (or individuals) rather than to the social situation within which it occurs; it is the error of giving too much responsibility to individual disposition and not enough to environmental or contextual factors (Nisbett & Ross, 1991; O'Brien, 2006). In one experiment, observers were asked to view two teams of equally talented basketball players. One team was playing in a gymnasium that had plenty of light, and the second team was playing in a poorly lit gym (and doing far worse at making shots). The observers were asked to rate the players, and they decided that the players in the brighter gym were better (Gladwell, 2000). They confused context with character, deciding that it was players' *character traits* that explained what happened rather than an obvious and important difference in environmental conditions.

Although we should never miss the role played by individual factors in what humans are, we must also be fully aware of the power of context. We will find, more often than not, that what we do and are, as well as how what we do and are is evaluated, reflects context more than anything else. We may be more fun at parties—and viewed that way by others—precisely because parties *are* fun. If we found ourselves in a bar fight, however, all this would change. We wouldn't be fun people at all (nor would we be viewed that way by others).

The attribution of responsibility is strongly influenced by whether deviance is considered to be ascribed or achieved. *Ascribed deviance* exists if a rule breaker is defined as having a physical or visible impairment, and the individual can acquire that status regardless of his or her behavior or wishes. By contrast, *achieved deviance* involves some intentional or deliberate activity on the part of a rule breaker. Ascribed deviance would cover the situation of individuals who are rejected for physical disabilities, and achieved deviance would cover embezzlers or bank robbers. Unlike the ascribed, the achieved have had to acquire rule-breaking status, at least to some extent, on the strength of what they do (Mankoff, 1976, pp. 241–242).

If deviance is ascribed, it is more likely to be viewed as a misfortune—devalued perhaps, but not in the same category as achieved deviance. With achieved deviance, because something has indeed been done, negative reactions are more likely to be warranted and are easier to justify. It practically goes without saying that *behavior* that breaks rules or violates expectations will regularly be viewed as achieved, and *conditions* or *attributes* that break rules or violate expectations are more likely to be viewed as ascribed. It is also possible for individuals to fall somewhere in between, displaying something that is perceived to be voluntary, but still what one *is* rather than what one *does* (Sagarin, 1975). An individual who is hard of hearing but who refuses to get a hearing aid falls in this category. Because the individual could hear better by purchasing a hearing aid but chooses not to get one, he or she is perceived to be "deaf by choice." The deviance exists not because the individual is hard of hearing, but because he or she is defined by others as being able to do something to hear better but choosing not to. It is generally true, however, that "isness" is less blameworthy than "didness."

Some individuals get labeled as deviant and negatively sanctioned because they are viewed by others as a bothersome annoyance. In Irwin's (1985) words, they are *rabble*. If rabble keep to themselves and cause nobody any trouble, they are given little attention. However, if they take their annoying traits or conduct to places where they do not belong—or are defined as not belonging by influential or powerful individuals—police will usually be called to return them to places where rabble are more likely to be tolerated or to cart them off to jail (Fitzpatrick & Myrstol, 2011; Huey, 2012; Way & Patten, 2013). It is not their danger but their offensiveness to standards of decency and propriety that mobilizes the forces of social control against them. Dominant groups are most likely to act to control minority groups (i.e., race/ethnicity) when they are viewed as a threat (Chiricos, Stupi, Stults, & Gertz, 2014; Olzak & Shanahan, 2014).

When it comes to issues of deviance and responsibility, cause and blame are sometimes confused, but they are not the same (Felson, 1991). *Cause* is objective and verifiable, referring to observed patterns of association and ordering. If drinking ethyl alcohol causes poor driving ability, it is because the drinking precedes erratic driving and is responsible for it. *Blame* (or the assessment of responsibility) is a value-laden term, more of a moralistic judgment than a scientific determination based on logic and observation. If an individual had been in the World Trade Center on September 11, 2001, and was killed in the terrorist attack on that day, one *cause* of his or her death would have been that the individual decided to enter the building. However, the individual should not be *blamed* for what happened. Goode (2011) clarifies matters when he notes that, "[i]f I take a plane to Los Angeles and the plane crashes and I die, my taking the plane is one *cause* of my death—but I should not be *blamed* for my death" (p. 130).

No perfect correlation exists between cause and blame, and blaming someone for some trespass is different from identifying its cause. Though we may agree, from our observation of changes in variables, about what causes what, attaching blame is a more contentious issue. Different groups can have very different understandings about who is at fault and how much responsibility the individual should bear for the trespass (even while group members might agree on its cause).

Discreditable and Discredited Deviants

According to Schur (1971), deviance is a *personally discreditable* departure from a group's or society's normative expectations. *Discreditable* attitudes, behaviors, or conditions could lead to social censure and stigma if they ever reach the light of day, so they may be expressed or performed in private and in secretive ways (Goffman, 1963). An example of discreditable behavior is ritualized self-injury. In the sample of 25 self-injurers studied by Adler and Adler (2009), the majority (80%) engaged in their acts of self-mutilation while they were alone, and they most frequently cut themselves, although they also burned, branded, and shocked themselves. Because the injurers could control where, when, and how the pain occurred, it replaced—at least temporarily—all the other pain in their lives, actually giving them a measure of comfort and relief. Their pain was a "warrior mark," less an unfortunate consequence of the experience than one of its central objectives (Atkinson & Young, 2008). Their ability to endure pain was, at least to the injurers, an indicator of strong character, courage, and integrity. The immersion of self-injurers in their own private world of injury and secrecy leads to greater and greater isolation from others and, if discovered, strong pressures for them to stop the injury, which leads ultimately to greater loneliness, which is the principal reason that they began to injure themselves in the first place (Adler & Adler, 2009).

Passing as something other than a deviant requires impression management and strategic interaction to control what others learn about the deviant (Furst & Evans, 2015; Goffman, 1959, 1969). It involves information control and the manipulation of others in the interest of presenting and sustaining a fabricated self (Brune & Wilson, 2013, Lasky, Jacques, & Fisher, 2015; Shippee, 2011). A qualitative study of 73 participants in the bondage/discipline/sadism/masochism subculture (BDSM), by Stiles and Clark (2011), reports that these sexual deviants were inclined to conceal their deviance from others whenever they could. They hid information about their sexual interests and practices, as well as about their deviant identity, when interacting with people whom they deemed likely to be both offended and judgmental. The largest portion of the sample (38%) told nobody outside of the subculture, following a strict need-to-know decision rule ("absolute concealment"). The rest told only close friends or family members. Only a small percentage (1%) was completely open about their sexual activities. Some of the sample (8%) had been forced out of the closet ("outed") against their wishes. The principal reasons members of this sample opted for concealment were self-protection and to protect others from information that these sexual deviants thought might be upsetting or unpleasant for them.

Individuals who have been caught and labeled for their trespasses find themselves in a different situation from the discreditable. They are *discredited deviants,* and their main problem is managing tension during social contacts with individuals who do not share their condition (Goffman, 1963). Goffman relates the case of a 16-year-old female who wrote to "Miss Lonelyhearts," asking for advice about a "problem." The teenager told the columnist that she would like to go out on dates like everyone else, but males won't take her out even though she is a good dancer, wears nice clothes, and has a nice figure. The reason males avoid her as a dating partner is because she was born without a nose, having a "big hole" in the middle of her face. Her main question for the columnist is whether she should take her own life. In situations as extreme as this one, the discrediting trait is very difficult, if not impossible, to manage successfully no matter how much an individual tries. Some people are quick to judge and quick to reject anyone who is perceived to be different from them, while others are much more accepting (Edgell & Tranby, 2010). Hostile reactions may keep an already marginalized population from trying to integrate into mainstream society (Brayne, 2014).

A study by Rassin (2011) of individuals with HIV in the largest AIDS clinic in Israel shows that the division between the discredited and the discreditable falls apart in the real world. Because the demands of passing are so intense for individuals who must do it on a continual basis, *both* tension control and information control are required. Part of the reason that these HIV sufferers decided to keep their condition a secret is that the initial reaction of family members who had been told of the diagnosis was prejudicial, discriminatory, and hurtful. Even those HIV sufferers who had received a favorable response had reasons to hide their disease from most others. They feared that their families might become the target of hostility or persecution. Most of them hid their disease because it made it possible for them to continue to lead a normal life for as long as possible.

Maggard and Boylstein's (2014) study of a small number of individuals ($n = 8$) who participated in the marijuana trade as users, sellers, and indoor growers in central Florida, over a period of about 15 years, shows some of the complexities involved in identity construction and maintenance. One core objective of the participants in this deviant subculture was to be able to successfully maintain secrecy about the nature and extent of their involvement in the marijuana trade. They wore a great many "masks" in their relationships with others (p. 600), but the deviant identity that they most wanted to keep hidden from outsiders was that of grower. This study showed how significant marijuana is to members of this subculture. It brought personal identity, while solidifying and reaffirming social bonds among members of the group.

Responsibility and Moral Careers

McHugh (1970) identified two decision rules that observers use to attach moral responsibility or blame to individuals for their untoward attitudes, behaviors, or conditions. The first decision rule, called *conventionality,* refers to whether observers believe that the attitude, behavior, or condition "could have been otherwise." If, in their opinion, it could have been, then it is a good candidate for consideration as something deviant instead of something accidental, coerced, or miraculous. It is the perceived inevitability of nonconventional events that makes the difference. Slipping on ice and falling, getting hurt in the process, is a different event from the standpoint of conventionality than is using your body in a game of football to block an opponent. The extent of the injuries may be identical, but slipping is an accident—nonconventional—while body blocking in an athletic contest is something that is conventional (i.e., the athlete elected to do it to help win the game). McHugh's second decision rule is *theoreticity.* It concerns whether the untoward attitude, behavior, or condition is viewed as having been intentional, unfolding according to some plan or purpose (making it "theoretic" instead of "practical" action). Individuals who deviate in a conventional and theoretic way are held responsible (i.e., blamed) for disrupting the social order. They are expected to show that they understand the wrongfulness of their trespass. They are also expected to repair the damage they've done to the flow of social interaction and the moral understandings on which it is based.

These two rules are neat and tidy—sort of—but the real world is far more complicated. The boys still won't ask the teenager with no nose out on dates, and she anguishes over her physical condition so much that she contemplates suicide. She can take some small comfort in knowing that had she intentionally removed her own nose (when she did not have to), her situation would have been even worse. She herself would have been held entirely responsible for her plight. We can see that even in the absence of the assessment that an individual is responsible for his or her condition, it is still possible for a great deal of stigma and unhappiness to result from being different from everyone else.

We must include in our understanding of deviance a category called *involuntary deviants*. These are individuals who are not held responsible for either their devalued traits or the social reactions based upon them (Montanino & Sagarin, 1977). They are still devalued and stigmatized, however, for conditions they are viewed as having had no responsibility in creating (Butera & Levine, 2009). In fact, people with disabilities are the target of both hate and violence because of their disabilities, and *disablism*—prejudice against people with disabilities—is a far-too-frequent fact of life for these involuntary deviants (Davis, 2014; Sherry, 2010; Wappett & Arndt, 2013). They may be defined as disabled people instead of being viewed as people with disabilities (Cahill & Eggleston, 2005; Campbell, 2009).

Disagreements exist over whether something is conventional or theoretic, and who or what is to blame is a contentious issue (as noted previously). A child is asked by a father to carry a plate of cookies, but the child then drops it. The mother may think that her husband is at fault for expecting capabilities beyond most children; the father, however, may think the child is to blame for not paying sufficient attention to the task at hand to do it correctly. An important factor in how a deviant is judged and reacted to is whether he or she is trying to evade the norms secretly, making him or her a *cynical deviant,* or openly defying them, making him or her an *enemy deviant* (Gusfield, 1967). Other things being equal, cynical deviants, because they are not openly challenging the status quo and the moral order on which it is based, are generally easier to deal with and accept than are enemy deviants. Both the cynical and enemy deviants are different from a deviant like the cookie-dropper, who is neither intentionally resistant to, nor stubbornly defiant of, the normative system.

The Social Construction of Spoiled Identities

Appearance and the Sociocultural Matrix

Symmetry, Learning, and Relativity

Physical appearance is one of the more obvious and immediate cues that people bring to their encounters with others, a fundamental element in personal identity that impacts social identity. It is used as a signifier of other, more difficult-to-measure personal factors, and it plays an important role in patterns of social interaction and in the differential treatment that people receive. Physical attractiveness is a valued trait that is valuable for an individual who is defined as having it (Vecitis, 2011). The determination that someone is beautiful or ugly (or any gradation in between) involves selective viewing, classification, and evaluation. Beauty, just like deviance, is in the eye of the beholder, and *attentional adhesion*—the difficulty of pulling one's attention or gaze away from a particular individual—is a documented fact (Maner, Gailliot, Rouby, & Miller, 2007). Appearance norms exist in all cultures, and violations of these norms can lead to the assessment that something deviant—or at least devalued—has occurred (Schur, 1983).

Studies have been done in which images of composite faces are constructed on a computer from individual pictures of faces. The greater the number of pictures of faces that went into the construction of the composite photo, the more average or symmetrical the composite became. So, if eight separate photos were used to make the composite, the composite was more symmetrical, typical, or average than if four separate photos had been used to make it. The central finding was that the composite image constructed from 32 separate pictures of faces was ranked as more attractive than a composite made from 16, 8, or 4 separate pictures of faces (Buss, 1994). The equating of facial symmetry with beauty and asymmetry with ugliness is interesting but flawed. People use things in addition to the face to determine attractiveness (figure, health cues, character, personality, age), and we can certainly think of times when a symmetrical face would *not* be judged particularly attractive (think Darth Vader in *Star Wars,* or other such villains).

Most of us suspect that the world's "most beautiful people" have gotten that way by being more than just average. Using symmetrical to mean "average" is not the same as using it to mean "ideal" or "flawless," and perhaps these words are closer to what is meant by beautiful. When American men and women are given the task of constructing an ideal or perfect human face, they seem to agree. The ideal or perfect female face is a very youthful one with full lips and a narrow mouth. The perfect male face (based on the responses of American female undergraduates) has large eyes, a large chin, a small nose, and prominent cheekbones. It is an open, pleasant face with rugged features (Small, 1995).

None of these traits seems extraordinary, but maybe it is unusual to find so many diverse indicators of female attractiveness on the same female or of male attractiveness on the same male. What is true about sexual selection—a fact of which Darwin was fully aware—is that if females show a specific preference in selecting mates, then males with the desirable trait will be at a reproductive advantage. They will leave a greater number of offspring, and the frequency of that trait will increase in a population (Jones & Ratterman, 2009).

Are uniform and universal cues for beauty and ugliness to be found? Some traits—festering sores, hacking coughs, incessant sneezes, unpleasant body odors—are probably widely defined as unattractive or ugly, and they could easily repel potential mates in practically any situation. Other traits—youthfulness, vitality, sincerity, integrity, kindness, poise, intelligence, pleasantness—are likely to be viewed as attractive, and they may be used to classify people as beautiful. However, that is a far cry from the claim that objective and universal beauty cues exist that have been programmed into our biology and psychology to ensure reproductive success (Buss, 1994; Ridley, 1993). Just because people say that they find some particular qualities attractive in a mate does not necessarily mean that their fantasies are echoes of some genetic predisposition established long ago (Small, 1995).

How beautiful or ugly a partner looks to us depends on our needs, our interests, the nature of our relationship to him or her, and—importantly—our relationship to other "hims" or "hers." We may have an ideal image of beauty in our minds, but it is usually broad and alterable. Though a partner's age and health are supposed to be important indicators of beauty or handsomeness in long-term relationships oriented toward reproduction, it may be just those relationships in which they are the least important. People do not usually divorce or separate on the grounds that their partner is too old or too sick. In fact, growing old together may enhance the quality of the relationship for both partners. It is almost certain that if we looked, we could find *both* beautiful and ugly things in every person on earth, and a trait that looks ugly at one time may look beautiful at another (and vice versa).

Learning must certainly play a big role in what and whom people find attractive, and culture must have an impact on what a group defines as beautiful or ugly that parallels or surpasses any influence of biology. Women and men want mates who are enjoyable to be around, who will make them feel special and needed, and who are accommodating and sensitive enough to be responsive to their wants and needs. In the absence of these, a partner's youth, health, fecundity, or high social status will matter very little. What initially draws us to a relationship (attentional adhesion) may be very different from what keeps it going for the long run. The evaluation of potential mates and actual partners is a flexible, ongoing enterprise.

Beauty Norms and Cultural Dynamics

All the different body forms, skin colors, nose shapes, ear designs, and facial configurations, along with all the deliberate modifications of the human form, make it hard to believe that any universal and uniform standard of beauty and ugliness could ever be found.

A cross-cultural survey of notions of beauty is sure to include such "oddities" as a preference for cross-eyes (Mayans), flattened heads (Kwakiutl), black gums and tongue (Maasai), black teeth (Yapese), joined eyebrows (Syrians), absence of eyebrows and eyelashes (Mongo), enormously protruding navels (Ila), pendulous breasts (Ganda), gigantic buttocks (Hottentot), fat calves (Tiv), crippled feet (Chinese), and so on. (Gregersen, 1983, p. 81)

Certainly, it is not hard to find examples that challenge the claim that standards for beauty are universal and programmed into us at birth.

The erotic potential of female genitalia is found throughout the world, but the Tswana-Kgatla (Africa) put their own spin on it:

> With the onset of puberty Kgatla girls start pulling their labia and sometimes will ask a girlfriend to help. If the labia do not get longer as quickly as desired, the girls resort to magic. They kill a bat and cut off its wings, which they then burn. The ashes are ground up and mixed with fat. Each girl makes little cuts around her labia and smears the bat-ash ointment into the cuts. (Gregersen, 1983, p. 92)

This little bit of magic is designed to get the labia to grow quickly to the size of bat wings.

Teeth are an important part of one's appearance, and having a "nice" smile is usually considered an asset. The existence of "best smile" contests suggests that judges know a great smile when they see one (or believe that they do). Yet, what qualifies as a "great smile" varies across the globe. Teeth have been permanently colored, knocked out, dug out, filed down, decorated, drilled, and chipped in order to heighten their attractiveness (Gregersen, 1983). U.S. models and actresses (and others, thanks to the influence of television advertising) spend considerable time and money on the whitening of their teeth. The Nilotes of East Africa would find these efforts at whitening incomprehensible. Beauty for them involves knocking out the lower front teeth (up to six), usually at the start of adolescence (p. 97).

Standards for the "proper" girth and weight for individuals to meet are variable things, too. In places where food and a full stomach are both luxuries, corpulence is coveted, and thinness is taken as a sign of poverty or sickness, not self-control and good form (Brownmiller, 1984).

> In Mexico, for example, people are significantly less concerned than U.S. citizens about their own weight and are more accepting of overweight people. In Niger, being overweight—ideally with rolls of fat, stretch marks, and a large behind—is considered an essential part of female beauty. Women who aren't sufficiently round are considered unfit for marriage. In Mauritania, girls as young as 5 and as old as 19 are sometimes forced by their parents to drink five gallons of fat-rich camel's milk each day so they become fat. Among the

Calabari people of southeastern Nigeria, soon-to-be brides are sent to farms where caretakers feed them huge amounts of food to fatten them up for the wedding day. (Newman, 2008, p. 161)

The existence of cross-cultural differences in appearance norms for body size ratifies the truth of novelist Erica Jong's (1990) Proverb Number One for Free Women: "You're not too fat; you're just in the wrong country" (p. 296). If she's right, it means that finding that one's body proportions are not only accepted, but even admired, has more to do with *where* an individual is than with the size of an individual's stomach. Corpulence was not always considered an indication of either physical disease (e.g., glandular malfunction) or weak character in the United States, and it still is not in many places in the world even today (Ruane & Cerulo, 2015; Saguy, 2013).

Body Blame

Most adult women in the Western world have at some time in their lives been displeased to a greater or lesser extent with the shape and weight of their bodies, and they have tried to alter them in one way or another by reducing their food intake (Grogan, 2009). Studies in the United States, Australia, and Great Britain, using figural rating scales (a series of silhouettes of a body, going from very thin to very fat), indicate that respondents were inclined to find as most attractive a body shape that was thinner than their own. Slenderness and confidence are positively linked for most women, and most of them can more easily identify something wrong with their bodies than right with them. Glass, Hass, and Reither (2010) report from their research done in Wisconsin that heavy females in their sample were less inclined than lighter females to pursue post-secondary schooling, even though they were just as academically capable. Part of the reason they avoided advanced education was low self-esteem, depression, and a fear of failing. Obese women do face significant and enduring discrimination and disadvantage in their jobs because of their body size (Mason, 2012). A study of 57 college women in a large, public university in the western United States shows that some of them are so dedicated to staying thin that they are willing to resort to heavy and potentially dangerous drug use to help do it (Vecitis, 2011). They overidentify with a specific and highly inflexible set of cultural understandings about physical attractiveness, and they do all they can to control information to hide from practically everyone just how desperately they try to stay thin.

Individuals who view obesity as deviant are the ones who are most likely to define it as a result of individual laziness and weak will, a failure by overweight people to exercise often enough or to exert sufficient personal control over their eating habits (Guthman, 2011). These negative evaluators view obesity as a blemish of character, as well as of body, instead of the operation of impersonal forces over which an individual has little or no control (Goode, 2002, 2015). They view it as something that could and should be changed. The obese body is more than a lump of flesh and bone; it is a moral area and a contested terrain that is viewed in different ways by different audiences or groups, some accepting of it and some not (Badger, 2010; English, 1993; Gruys, 2012; Kwan, 2009).

The U.S. media usually offers a biased and distorted view of eating problems and of what should be done to manage them (Boero, 2012). Obesity is usually portrayed as an individual problem with roots in fundamentally bad choices. Social factors (e.g., class, race, gender, ethnicity, opportunity, accessibility, affordability), despite their clear role in how, what, and how much we eat, are given scant attention (Roberts & Edwards, 2010). Obesity is more often found among the poor and ethnic minorities, and rates are highest in countries with small or poorly developed (i.e., stingy or miserly) welfare systems. A principal reason is that overeating and binge drinking of fattening beverages are reactions to the stress and depression that result from economic insecurity and uncertainty (Ford, Schroeder, & Dotson, 2014; Offer, Pechey, & Ulijaszek, 2012).

Blame and responsibility are attached differently to the too-thin and the too-fat. Overeaters or binge eaters are looked on as weak and lazy; anorexics and bulimics are looked on as victims of social or biological forces beyond their control. Thin bodies, though extreme, are still viewed as associated with responsibility and self-denial, albeit of a perverse form, while fat bodies are viewed as the epitome of gluttony and irresponsibility (Saguy, 2013; Saguy & Gruys, 2010). In the public realm, fat bodies are viewed as something that must be changed in order to make other bodily functions and individual accomplishments possible (Saguy, Gruys, & Gong, 2010). The fat body is the contaminated body, crying out in a multitude of ways to be saved from itself (Kent, 2010; Sender, 2012). Atkinson's (2011) study of how male athletes (marathon runners, wrestlers, swimmers, tennis players) stay thin reported that dangerous eating practices were justified by these men as both normal and desirable. They viewed their emaciation as a sign of self-reliance and emotional maturity, which meant that they experienced low levels of stigma and guilt over their risky behaviors.

Physical appearance cues influence how individuals are treated (McClintock, 2014). For males, being tall helps increase their earnings throughout their careers, and tall men are more desired as dating partners than are short men. Individuals with above-average appearances earn much more in their jobs during their lifetimes than do people with below-average looks (Hamermesh, 2013). Although both males and females may dislike getting old, more females than males report that they do not want to *look* old. A double standard exists that works to the advantage of older men, who can still be viewed as "distinguished," even well into old age, in a way that few women can achieve (Jaeger, 2011). Most women surveyed—heterosexual ones, at any rate—profess that an important factor that makes them think they look old is that they no longer receive approving looks from men (Slevin, 2010).

Attitudes toward cosmetic surgery are changing worldwide so that now the new shame may be to *not* have work done, especially where it is available and affordable (Stein, 2015). Cosmetic surgery is usually done to enhance an individual's erotic potential or sexiness (e.g., breast augmentation surgery or penile enlargement), to create a "normal" appearance (e.g., nose reconstruction), or to create or maintain a "youthful" appearance (e.g., face-lifts or hair transplants). Clearly, a great deal of overlap exists, and it is not easy to know if a given procedure was done to sexualize, to correct a perceived defect, or to rejuvenate an aging body. (Did she get the breast lift to appear more attractive, to look younger, or to undo what was done to her mammary glands because of childbirth and breast-feeding?) More and more males are feeling the same pressure that females have felt to surgically correct the parts of their bodies that they find displeasing. The number one surgical procedure in the United States for men is a nose job; breast augmentation is the top cosmetic surgery for females (Stein, 2015).

Though many competing views, both cultural and personal, coexist about the benefits and desirability of altering a body in the interest of vanity rather than health, cosmetic surgery is no longer viewed as something that is received only by the marginal and maladjusted (Pitts-Taylor, 2007). Prominent boosters and cheerleaders for reconstructive surgery help to advance its public acceptance when they extol its benefits (as when a transgender woman, such as Caitlyn Jenner, whose birth name was Bruce Jenner, reports that she has been empowered due to her facial feminization surgery that she claims makes her feel better about herself and more easily accepted as who she really is).

It is a long way from laboratory studies of symmetry and attentional adhesion to the real world of finding and uniting with a desired partner. A few things—a very few things—*might* be universally viewed as beautiful or ugly. However, what appears to be more important is the total package a person brings to a relationship—or the other's perception of that package. Having a beautiful face—or any other specific trait—is not that important, at least not for long, or at least not in long-term relationships. Many things—opportunity, accessibility, availability, personal objectives, individual motives, physical qualities, personality characteristics, social attributes (e.g., status)—are assessed by people as they form relationships. Humans find a wide range of things attractive, some of which reflect cultural meanings and others reflect more idiosyncratic preferences. No matter whom we are with or what we find attractive, most of us realize that if we'd come to a different fork in the road and taken a different path, our partners would have been different from who they now are.

Status and Stigma

Each individual is a cluster of different attributes and appearance cues (in both social and personal identities), and each person displays a large number of different behaviors during the course of his or her life. We must wonder, therefore, why certain designations or characterizations are used more often than others to describe us, and why some of them stick to us more readily in describing what we are and what we do. E. C. Hughes (1945) coined the term *master status* to describe a status that evolves into the dominant way an individual is interpreted and categorized by others. A person's sex is usually a master status, as are skin color and occupation. These are major identity pegs, and they play a role in most human relationships. The status of deviant, Becker (1963) informs us, is also a master status. It can predominate over many other statuses that an individual occupies and can become a controlling one in his or her relationships to others (Pager, 2007). A strong possibility exists that as a deviant identity becomes a master status, the level of social censure will increase and the individual will experience stigma (Goffman, 1963).

At one time, the word *stigma* meant a distinguishing mark or brand cut into an individual's flesh for the purpose of identifying him or her as a tainted or despised individual. Now, stigma means *any* attribute—a physical sign or character cue—that is accompanied by shame or disgrace. Too-tall Jones is identified by body, and Otis the town drunk is identified by character. Stigma can also have little directly to do with body or character: It can exist because a person is a member of a persecuted or despised group, what Goffman (1963) called *tribal stigma*. He reminds us that when speaking of stigma, what is really needed is a language of relationships rather than of attributes, because no attribute is automatically crediting or discrediting. Stigma always involves a relationship between an attribute and its perception and symbolization by others. "Normal" and "stigmatized" are not persons but *perspectives* on persons (p. 138).

A tattoo, for example, may be either a *stigma symbol* (i.e., discrediting) or a *prestige symbol* (i.e., status-enhancing), depending on who the tattooee is, what the tattoo represents, where the tattoo is placed, and the nature of the relationship between the tattooee and his or her evaluating others. Tattoos have been used to identify social outcasts and to make it more difficult for them to blend in with others. In Japan in the sixth century, criminals were tattooed on the arms and face, and in the 1800s, convicts in correctional facilities in Massachusetts had "Mass S. P." and the date of their release tattooed on their left arms (Sanders, 1996).

At some times and in some places, tattoos are viewed by some individuals as tarnished cultural products, an indication that the tattooed individual lacks enough maturity to be able to consider the consequences of his or her actions (J. Adams, 2012). Tattoos on teenagers are still stigmatizing, indicating to the general public that the bearer is unconventional in outlooks and interests. Adolescents with tattoos are reported to be more inclined toward deviance, less academically oriented than adolescents without tattoos, and less interested in attending college (Silver, Silver, Siennick, & Farkas, 2011).

Some individuals do not consider tattoos to be stigmatizing. In fact, they collect tattoos on their bodies, viewing these markings as a fundamental and attractive part of their personal and social identities. They use a tattoo to increase their feelings of self-worth and to transform their identities in the eyes of others (Goode & Vail, 2008; Sanders, 1996). In fact, for some people, tattoos are said to be like potato chips in that one is not nearly enough (Vail, 2008). Even genital piercings, once considered abnormal and degenerate, are a body adornment that is becoming more mainstream and conventional (Thomas, Crosby, & Milford, 2015).

How tattoos are viewed, especially by those individuals inclined to view them as disreputable, cannot be separated from the tattoo industry itself. Tattoo artists have not had the same level of success as practitioners in related industries (e.g., cosmetologists, barbers, beauticians, manicurists) in changing the public image that they are engaged in what E. C. Hughes (1951) called *dirty work*. This is work that is defined as unpleasant, with clients or customers who are defined as unsavory or immoral (J. Adams, 2012). In November 2012, Walter Smith, a self-described tattoo artist, was forbidden to share information about tattooing with students during "Career Day" at Clearwater Fundamental Middle School (Clearwater, FL). His daughter was a student at the school, and Smith had participated in years past. The reason for the ban cited by the school principal was parental complaints that Smith would be promoting an alternative lifestyle.

Stigma may be an outcome of having "bad" companions or associates (or those defined as bad), a stigma by association called *courtesy stigma* (Goffman, 1963). (A daughter who is embarrassed because her father is viewed as the town drunk is suffering from this kind of stigma.) A study of stigma by association, experienced by Hollywood artists and performers during the "Red Scare" of the 1950s, illustrates how this can work. After the Second World War (circa 1945–1960), some powerful and influential people in Hollywood became convinced—or acted is if they were—that the film industry had been infiltrated by communists and communist sympathizers. Of the approximately 30,000 artists (31,781, to be exact) who worked in Hollywood during those years, 300 were officially blacklisted and kept from performing. Practically anyone who had any connections with them, no matter how slight, also became the target of persecution. They, too, found that they had trouble finding work. One contact with a tainted individual was usually enough to have adverse consequences for a performer's career. Even contact with a blacklisted writer proved to be a liability (Pontikes, Negro, & Rao, 2010).

The "Red Scare" shows that some individuals are accused of doing things they haven't or of being things they aren't. They are, in other words, *falsely accused* (Becker, 1963, p. 20). Even in a court of law, some people are tried and convicted of crimes that they did not commit—known as a "bum rap"—even though a number of safeguards exist to make it unlikely that the innocent are wrongfully convicted (Barkan & Bryjak, 2014). False accusations are even more likely to occur outside a legal setting where few, if any, safeguards exist to ensure that individuals are not accused of doing things that they did not do (Becker, 1963; Menard & Pollock, 2014). A label, even if it is false, can still have major consequences for both the labelers and the falsely accused (Rocheleau & Chavez, 2015). False accusations of criminal conduct are more likely with individuals who have prior records, deviant friends, or poor educational performances, and with those who are male, nonwhite, and lower-class (Menard & Pollock, 2014). A false label may even become a self-fulfilling prophecy, creating deviance that would otherwise not occur.

The social construction of a spoiled identity usually includes *retrospective interpretation* (Kitsuse, 1962). In retrospective interpretation, an accused deviant's biography is scrutinized, and prior experiences with the accused are played over in memory, searching for anything that might help to account for the individual's current display of deviance. The rule breaker is recast in the eyes of others, and he or she is viewed in a new way (Schafer, Ferraro, & Mustillo, 2011; Schur, 1971). What was once viewed as normal in the identity of the individual comes to be viewed as a façade that was actually hiding a deeper, more sinister, more authentic constellation of traits and attributes (Garfinkel, 1956). Retrospective interpretation works to create order out of what seems to be disorder. It allows observers to understand better how a seemingly ordinary person could do or be something so unusual. This individual is found to not be as ordinary as originally thought; despite surface appearances, he or she actually had been a deviant all along.

If something is found in the accused deviant's personal history that can explain the deviance, even remotely, it becomes part of the reconstructed biographical record. We may discover, for example, that a mass murderer had an abusive childhood and liked guns, information that would never have come to light—or been given much significance—if the individual had not committed random acts of violence. The process of retrospective interpretation is selective, and factors that might refute, challenge, or complicate the biographical sketch may be ignored, dismissed, or downgraded. It is also possible for the biographical reconstruction to include fabrications or lies. For example, a deviant's parents might be viewed as having been abusive when they really were not. All deviants may undergo processes of retrospective interpretation, especially when the need is great to explain or understand what seems to be inexplicable.

Deviants themselves may engage in an *autobiographical* retrospective interpretation as they search through their own life experiences to come to some understanding of why they can't be like everybody else or even why others are so annoyed by them. A study of 10 street prostitutes, who were in rehabilitation for their heavy drug use while trying to disengage from sex work, shows how this works. They used their former drug addictions as a way to explain and therefore handle some of the stigma associated with prostitution. They retrospectively made sense of their own involvement in prostitution by tying their sex work and their drug abuse together, presenting them as remnants of a former life with its corresponding former self (McCray, Wesely, & Rasche, 2011). This retrospective interpretation allowed them to move from a deviant to a nondeviant identity more easily. They were, in the words of Gusfield (1967), *repentant deviants.*

Managing Stigma

Deviance Avowal

Individuals are objects of their own experience, holding opinions and making evaluations of their personal attributes and social identities. Just because other people may condemn an individual for some behavior or attribute does not mean that he or she must share their opinions (LeBel, 2012). Individuals may take pleasure and pride in what they are, precisely because other people *do* condemn it, or they may simply be indifferent to the reactions of others, marching to the beat of a different drummer (Steinmetz & Gerber, 2014). Stigma is based on negotiated understandings and situational factors, not universal and absolute decision rules (Haenfler, 2013).

People with devalued attributes can still maintain a positive self-image, not only by hiding or covering the troubling condition, but also by believing that their personal condition is actually a good and valued trait regardless of what others may think. They may view their condition as righteous, requiring neither apology nor regret. In some cases, stigmatized individuals find ways to exploit their conditions for positive gains (Herman & Miall, 2005). They will transform negative labels into positive ones through a process of reinterpretation so that a once-stigmatizing label no longer is ("I'm bald *and* beautiful"). Little evidence exists that people who are defined as deviant by others *inevitably* hold poor opinions of themselves (Darling, 2013).

A once-stigmatizing trait also may be redefined by others as something positive (or vice versa). Rudolph the Red-Nosed Reindeer, the famous character from the Christmas song, shows how this can happen. His nose, once a source of embarrassment and shame (a stigma symbol), which kept the animal from joining in any reindeer games, became a prestige symbol because it came to be evaluated so positively by Santa Claus, majordomo of the North Pole. Women with naturally curly hair may be displeased with what sits atop their heads until style standards change and straight hair is no longer all the rage. During the Victorian era in both England and the United States, respectable women of means all carried parasols when they were outside in order to avoid any tanning of their skin. The bearer of untanned skin was viewed as attractive, because her ivory exterior showed that she did not have to toil in the fields to earn her daily bread. The meaning of suntan changed, however, and tan skin is now likely to be viewed as more attractive than is untanned skin. An important reason for the reversal is that fewer of us labor in the fields, finding our work activity indoors rather than outdoors (Gregersen, 1983). This means that having a tan, especially a full-body tan, indicates that the bearer has both the time and resources to be able to attain one in recreational pursuits; it is no longer necessarily a by-product of a life of toil on the land.

Whether negative reactions from others lead to reduced feelings of self-worth depends a lot on the type of deviance, how committed the individual is to the deviance, how involved the individual is with conventional society, the nature of the relationship between the accusers and the accused, and whether the condition is shared with others. Certain kinds of deviance are actually status enhancing, and deviants readily avow their deviance (Turner, 1972). *Deviance avowal* exists when people want to occupy a deviant status and actively pursue it if they can. This reminds us that deviance can be functional, even righteous, for individuals. In fact, nondeviants may fake or exaggerate unrespectability (Ball, 1970). Even extreme acts of deviance (e.g., murder, robbery, or drug dealing) can be consciously chosen in order to give an individual a sense of purpose, belonging, and respect (Lindegaard & Jacques, 2014).

Kitsuse (1980) proposed the term *tertiary deviation* to cover all those situations in which deviants embrace a deviant status but reject the negative identity and stigma associated with it. This transforms a deviant identity into something that is both positive and desirable. He referred to individuals who do this successfully as the "new deviants":

> Fat people, little people, ugly people, old people, and a growing number of others—who have called into question the very concept of "deviant," not by denying what they are, but by affirming and claiming it as a valued identity deserving of the rights accorded any member of society. (p. 8)

One thing that tertiary deviants may do is to join with other devalued or deviant people to collectively fight against or resist the societal exclusion, segregation, prejudice, and discrimination to which they are subject. One positive result of such a banding together is the Convention on the Rights of Persons with Disabilities (CRPD), a United Nations treaty that was adopted in 2006. Its principal objective is to remove any barriers that may exist for individuals with disabilities in the areas of education, health care, and civic involvement (Sabatello & Schulze, 2014).

At one time, people with certain types of spoiled identity—they used to be called "freaks"—could find a place in the world of popular entertainment and amusement. Siamese twins, bearded ladies, tattooed men, giants, dwarfs, armless men, the obese, the extremely thin—you name them, they were there. Though some of them were exploited, most of them were performers and entertainers who were applauded for having turned a potential liability into a profitable and valuable identity peg. According to Bogdan (1988), these human exhibits had no objection to being put on display; in fact, most of them enjoyed the attention. They were comfortable with what they were, and though they were called freaks, they did not believe they were freakish. Their approach to life and their view of their disabilities was different from that of Joseph Carey Merrick (1862–1890), nicknamed "the Elephant Man," whose story was movingly depicted in a Broadway play and a film. He believed he needed to hide his physical deformities under a mask whenever he could.

By the beginning of the twentieth century, the display of human oddities for amusement had fallen into disrepute in the United States. Part of the reason was the growing fear that these individuals might reproduce and transmit their physical traits to future generations. The major factor, however, was that after physicians organized into the American Medical Association (in 1847), they worked to establish their claim that they had special expertise and knowledge in regard to understanding and treating *all* human deviation. Human oddities, like those displayed in the freak shows, came to be medicalized as abnormal but curable rather than as exotic exhibits for the amusement of paying customers (Bogdan, 1988). How disabilities and people who have them ought to be viewed and understood is a constantly changing social terrain with many competing images: people who are strange, exotic, eccentric, pitiful, pathetic, sick, odd, freakish, helpless, dangerous, normal, admired, or beloved (Bogdan, 2012). The population of "people with disabilities" is a heterogeneous one (Darling, 2013).

Some attributes of individuals, though potentially discrediting, are tolerated or even accepted because they are assessed in light of other attributes of these same individuals. A different cluster of attributes would have produced very different reactions from others. Consider the following letter to "Dear Abby" from a "Happy Wife":

Dear Abby:

When our daughter was a baby, I found her pacifier in our bed. I thought it had dropped out of her mouth while she was in our bed, but later I found the pacifier in the drawer of our nightstand table, and I couldn't for the life of me figure out how it got there.

Then one morning I woke up early and saw my husband sound asleep with the pacifier in his mouth! We had a good laugh over it, and that evening when I fixed the baby's bottle I jokingly asked him if he wanted a bottle too. He said yes, so I fixed him one.

He loved it, so I kept fixing him a bottle right along with the baby's. I took the baby off the bottle when she was fourteen months old, but my husband still has one every night, and he is thirty-seven. Please don't use our names as my husband is well known here. He works on the space program. Thank you. (Van Buren, 1981, p. 175)

How can the husband *not* be deviant? The wife is embarrassed to have their name printed, and both she and her husband seem to realize that most other fathers are not nursing on their babies' pacifiers or drinking from their babies' bottles. Yet how can he *be* deviant? Both the wife and husband laugh over the husband's acts, and the wife really seems to experience very little consternation over her spouse's fondness for infant paraphernalia. Other characteristics in his cluster of traits (employee on the space program, good provider, good sense of humor) seem to be sufficient for his wife to be accepting of his less commendable traits.

Deviance and Respectability

People differ on what they accept or reject in others and on what they consider respectable. In November 1996, a 13-year-old female student named Karla Chapman did what she had done many times before. She went to class at Runyon Elementary School in Pike County, Kentucky. This day, however, she was declared to be a distraction by Rosa Wolfe, the principal. Three times the principal had warned her, and three times Karla Chapman had defied the principal's authority. The problem? Karla Chapman wore *black* lipstick. At another time or place, with different people, this probably would have been no big deal. However, at this time and place, with these people, it developed into a very big deal indeed.

Karla found that her choice of lipstick color (which she insisted was her business, not the school's), coupled with her refusal to wipe the stuff off as ordered, got her suspended for 3 days. On the day that her suspension ended, Karla got ready for school, donned a different-colored lipstick, and arrived at the elementary school ready for classes to start. However, she was once again reprimanded and prohibited from entering the school, because her new choice of lipstick color—dark purple—was still unacceptable to school personnel. Because the principal would brook no opposition, Karla was put in a difficult situation. If she did not return to school, she would be considered a truant—which at Karla's age qualified her as a delinquent—but if she did return to school, she could not wear lipstick that was considered distracting by the principal (Mueller, 1996).

It is difficult for an outsider to this incident to understand what it is about black lipstick that makes it so distracting and what exactly made Karla Chapman such a problem to the principal. Certainly, nothing unique to black lipstick makes it more upsetting than any other color of lipstick. Even red lipstick could be distracting on a 13-year-old (depending, of course, on how it was applied). One wonders if the problem was not so much the black lips as the fact that a teenager would refuse to comply with orders by the principal to wipe the stuff off (and thereby challenge the authority of those who have the power to decide what qualifies as a respectable appearance).

If Karla Chapman had been *born* with black lips, it is the principal who would have found herself in a difficult situation in trying to expel her. Though Karla still would have been sporting a "distracting" color, the attribute would be viewed as something over which Chapman had little or no control. The power and authority of school administrators would not have been challenged directly by a young person's *deliberate* act of insubordination, and they could have afforded to be more gracious and understanding than they were in this particular instance. Clearly, stigma is one possible outcome of the negotiations between people about the propriety of conditions that some of them find disturbing and unnecessary.

Deviants can encounter two different types of potentially supporting or confirming others. Goffman (1963) refers to one group as *the own*—individuals who also have the deviant's devalued trait. Although these individuals are more likely than others to be accepting of people like themselves, this is not guaranteed. Bullies don't like other bullies very much, and hyperactive people are not automatically more accepting of people like themselves. The stigmatized may, in fact, stigmatize others. The other group is *the wise*. These are individuals who do not themselves possess the devalued trait but who are familiar enough with the plight of deviants to be both understanding and accepting of them. We seem to be attracted to people who are like us and repelled by (or at least not attracted to) people who are dissimilar to us (Skvoretz, 2013).

Bogdan and Taylor (1989) studied individuals who were in a caring and accepting relationship with persons who had severe and debilitating mental retardations and physical disabilities. These individuals with disabilities sometimes drooled, soiled themselves, and could not talk or walk well. How was it possible for caretakers to be accepting and loving toward individuals who were so visibly impaired? First, the individual with a disability was granted the capacity for thinking and feeling, for being more aware and responsive than he or she might appear. Second, the individual with a disability was viewed as someone who had a unique personality, specific likes and dislikes, and a personal history—all of which underscored the person's specialness or exceptionality. Third, the individual with a disability was defined as an active participant in social life. He or she was seen as fun, important, and someone with whom people without disabilities enjoyed interacting. Finally, a social place was reserved for the individual with a disability. He or she was defined as an important member of the family (or group), and he or she was included in its routines and rituals. The wise are able to avoid stigmatizing, stereotyping, and rejecting others, even those who have obvious and debilitating conditions, by seeing them as equals and as enjoyable instead of inferior and annoying. Though raising and caring for a child with a severe disability creates a great deal of stress for other members of the family and the entire family relationship (e.g., divorce rates are higher and financial strains are greater), the presence of a child who needs so much continuing care and support from others can also be a source of pleasure, purpose, and inspiration (Hogan, 2012).

Neutralization and Stigma Management

An individual may find it necessary to manage or lessen whatever stigma he or she is experiencing through the use of *techniques of neutralization* (Sykes & Matza, 1957). These techniques, regardless of their specific form, are verbalizations that make it possible for individuals to temporarily suspend forces of social control, making them inoperative or insignificant (though neutralization could persist indefinitely). This makes it possible for an individual to engage in deviance without experiencing serious damage to his or her self-concept and without feeling constrained by feelings of stigma or embarrassment. Sykes and Matza identified five techniques of neutralization:

1. *Denial of responsibility:* The deviant insists that whatever happens is not his or her fault.
2. *Denial of injury:* The deviant insists that what happened hurt nobody.
3. *Denial of victim:* The deviant insists the victim was actually the one responsible for the deviance that occurred.
4. *Condemnation of the condemners:* The deviant insists that those who are criticizing him or her have no legitimacy, and it is they who are the real deviants.
5. *Appeal to higher loyalties:* The deviant insists that what he or she did was actually for the good of the whole—the nation, the society, the community, the gang—to achieve some higher purpose.

Some deviants will deny responsibility, thereby neutralizing whatever tension they might otherwise experience; others will insist that nobody was hurt or that the victim deserved what he or she got; still others will condemn those who condemn them and portray those others as stupid, spiteful, or mean; and still others will manage tension by claiming that they march to the beat of a different drummer (i.e., appeal to higher loyalties).

Neutralization techniques can also serve as *rationalizations*. These come *after* some untoward act occurs, and they help a deviant handle whatever tension or stigma might come from the trespass ("They had it coming, so what's the harm?"). The use of what Hitlin (2008) calls *lawyer logic* fulfills a rationalizing function ("I did it, but they can't prove it."). What kind of deviance occurs has a lot to do with the kind of neutralization techniques and rationalizations an individual is able to muster. Most deviants are aware that their trespasses are condemned by others and so engage in neutralizations of one form or another (Goode, 2013). A study of "sexting" at a small liberal arts college in the northeastern United States (with a student body of 535) shows that participants in the exchange of sexually explicit words or photographs through cell phones or other electronic devices realize that sexting is deviant and that doing it could lead to unpleasant and unwanted consequences (Renfrow & Rollo, 2014). These sexters mustered all kinds of neutralizing and rationalizing strategies to minimize the risks of sexting, such as emphasizing its playfulness, exaggerating its normality ("everyone is doing it"), and stressing its benefits (e.g., as a way to strengthen a romantic relationship and to encourage more open communication).

When it comes to stigma, it may not be so much that the deviant *did* (or *was*) the wrong thing as that the deviant failed to *present* what he or she did in the most appropriate, socially acceptable way. Some people can get away with things that other people cannot, because they are skilled at managing impressions for the benefit of others. One thing that a deviant can do is to perform *atonement*. This means doing the "right" thing immediately after it was done "wrongly." I once saw a tape of a weather report in which the reporter incorrectly informed her viewing audience that "from the north came cold mares' asses," while pointing to a map of the United States. She paused momentarily and then said it again, the right way: "From the north came cold air masses." Her atonement helped lessen some of the discomfort that her initial misstatement could have caused, both for the audience and for her. Another thing that deviants can do is to use an *apology* (Goffman, 1971). An apology is functional, both for the recipients and for the individual offering it. It shows that the individual realizes the wrongfulness of the trespass, tacitly supporting the normative order and the values on which it is based, while indicating that the rule breaking will never happen again. When successful, an apology promises a new self in an old body, one that will be more diligent in honoring the social contract.

Accused deviants can account for their trespasses (Scott & Lyman, 1968). An *account* is a verbal statement that functions to relieve individuals of responsibility for what they have done. Two types of accounts exist, *excuses* and *justifications*:

> An excuse is an admission that the act in question was bad, wrong, or inept, coupled with a denial of full responsibility. A justification is an admission of full responsibility for the act in question, coupled with a denial that it was wrongful. (Lyman & Scott, 1989, p. 136)

If a defendant in a court of law were to claim that he or she was insane at the time of the crime, this would be an excuse. The defendant is claiming that he or she did not know the difference between right and wrong and so should not be held responsible for what happened. If, however, a defendant were to claim that he or she broke into a stranger's cabin to avoid an impending blizzard, this is a justification (called *necessity* in a U.S. court of law). The accused is not claiming that something external (or internal) negated personal *responsibility* for the breaking and entering; the intruder knew fully and exactly what he or she was doing. However, in this situation, the possibility of greater harm (death by freezing) is being used to *justify* the illegal entry (i.e., breaking and entering) of someone else's cabin. Humans, even when they are *outside* a courtroom, will use similar strategies to convince others (or try to) that they were not responsible for whatever happened or even that the deviance was actually necessary (i.e., justified) under the circumstances.

The existence of an exception to following rules that are still viewed as important and necessary is a regular part of human encounters. When excuses "work" (i.e., are accepted as reasonable claims), the individual who might have been held responsible for the deviance is let off the hook, because it is concluded that the reason for the trespass was some factor (external or internal) over which the rule breaker had no control. When justifications "work" (i.e., are accepted as reasonable claims), a rule breaker is forgiven for the trespass, because it is concluded that it was actually demanded by the situation, being therefore unavoidable and thus blameless (Yagil & Luria, 2014). We are prepared to exonerate some individuals for some rule breaking *if* they are able to account for these trespasses in acceptable ways. Individuals who refuse to offer accounts to others for their trespasses—or fail to apologize for them—face the prospect of not being reintegrated into the group (Young & Thompson, 2011).

One of the best things for a rule breaker is to be in a situation where nobody even knows that something untoward has happened, even those who have suffered some loss because of it. This is the case with *hidden* or *secret deviants.* They need not worry about dealing with injured parties who may demand restitution or even want the rule breaker punished for what was done to them. It is possible for some rule breakers to take advantage of others in one way or another, causing losses for them, but still keep them from realizing that they have been intentionally victimized. This may involve what Goffman (1952) called "cooling the mark out."

The various methods of *cooling the mark out* all boil down to a nudging of a victim, injured party, or offended individual in the direction of believing that what happened to him or her was nobody's fault. It was simply bad luck. Though Goffman's (1952) principal objective was to show how victims are encouraged by coolers to adapt to failure and live with their losses in cases of criminal fraud (i.e., confidence games), his analysis has wider applications. "Persons who participate in what is recognized as a confidence game are found in only a few social settings, but persons who have to be cooled out are found in many" (pp. 452–453). Whenever a rule breaker is skillful enough to be able to cool the mark out successfully, or when the mark cools out on his or her own, no other strategies are necessary (such as apologizing, atoning, or accounting). One example is when an individual who has been cheated during a game of cards, losing both money and self-respect, comes to believe that the outcome was simply a matter of bad luck and thus was nobody's fault.

Square Pegs and Round Holes: Eccentrics and Eccentricities

Danielle Willis is a vampire, or so she claims. She sleeps by day; works by night (she's a fiction writer); and drinks human blood, partly for nourishment and partly because it excites her. She paid her dentist to install a permanent set of porcelain fangs over her incisors. She does not change into a bat and then bite hapless victims on the neck, however. What she does is use a syringe to extract blood from a willing partner (whom she is confident has no blood-borne diseases) and then drink it, either right on the spot or at some later time. For Willis, the consumption of the bodily fluids of another is an expression of intimacy and trust. Hundreds of vampires like Willis live throughout the United States, and some of them believe (or at least hope) that drinking blood ensures their immortality ("Interview With a Vampirette," 1997). Are these people real bats, just batty, or something else?

Eccentrics are quirky or even odd people who have thrown off the bonds of conformity and who pursue whatever wild hair intrigues them. Some eccentrics are successful people, and their eccentricities are just part of what they are. Other eccentrics have gained fame and fortune because of their eccentricities, which shape their lives and their identities (Nash, 1982). Still other eccentrics are abysmal failures at practically everything they do, partly because they are obsessed with their eccentricities. If an individual has the forbearance, ability, or good luck to triumph in some field, his or her eccentricity is likely to be overlooked or even admired. However, if an eccentric fails to gain prominence in some valued field of human endeavor, then his or her oddness is more likely to be disturbing to others, and he or she is more likely to be condemned or ridiculed (Wallace, 1957).

The label of eccentric—like all labels—is relative, and the ground rules for what makes one eccentric change all the time. Alexander Wortley had a deep suspicion of zippers in men's trousers, so he removed them from any pair he purchased. The reason? He did not want a lightning conductor so close to such a sensitive body part (S. Adams & Riley, 1988). Wortley's anxiety over genital shocks is not at all unreasonable; it is how he went about protecting himself from electrocution that seems strange. The Reverend George H. Munday was a renowned Quaker preacher in nineteenth-century Philadelphia. Parishioners gathered by the hundreds to hear his sermons but mostly to observe his odd trait: He refused to wear a hat at a time when all male Quakers did (Sifakis, 1984). Joseph Palmer moved to the city of Fitchburg, Massachusetts, in 1830. Some of his new neighbors shunned him, and others threw rocks at him (and at his house). Businessmen refused to cater to him, and religious people prayed for his redemption. Women avoided and feared him, often crossing to the other side of the road when they saw him coming. What was Palmer's problem? He was one of the first individuals in the United States to grow a long beard. This was so upsetting to others that one day, four men armed with scissors and a razor attacked him, threw him to the ground, and tried to shave him forcibly. Through all his trials and tribulations, he steadfastly kept his beard. His gravestone in Evergreen Cemetery in Leominster, Massachusetts, tells the story. It reads, "Persecuted for wearing the beard" (Sifakis, 1984, pp. 69–70).

Some eccentrics are what they are because accidents of birth made their pursuit of novelty more likely. Michel Lotito (1950–2007), also known as Monsieur Mangetout ("Mister Eat Everything"), a Frenchman from Grenoble, had an amazing ability: He could eat practically anything. When he was 16, he was drinking mint tea with friends at a French cafe, and the rim of the glass accidentally broke off in his mouth. Instead of spitting the piece out and complaining about the defective glass, he chewed the piece up and swallowed it. Because he experienced no adverse effects, he soon realized that he had a special talent (Flaherty, 1992). He went on to become a professional entertainer whose performance consisted of eating his way through things, such as television sets, aluminum skis, supermarket carts, bicycles (he liked the chain the best), razor blades, coins, glasses, bottles, bullets, and phonograph records. He even ate an entire airplane—a Cessna two-seater—piece by piece. Lotito would cut objects into bite-size pieces, lubricate his digestive tract liberally with mineral oil, and drink lots of water as he ate the debris. Surprisingly enough, though he could eat stuff that would kill an ordinary person, he had difficulty digesting bananas and eggs (S. Adams & Riley, 1988). Lotito was awarded a brass plaque by the *Guinness Book of World Records* to commemorate his eating eccentricities. He was so honored that he ate it (Flaherty, 1992).

Gourmandizing, which is excessive eating, was popular in the United States in the early 1900s as a form of freak entertainment. Now it is a competitive sport, and contests are regularly held with winners receiving prizes worth thousands of dollars. An International Federation of Competitive

Eating even exists to promote the sport. In 2014, a competitive eater named Molly Schuyler, 5-foot-7 and 125 pounds, broke a Texas restaurant's record for eating steak. She ate almost 10 pounds of steak, along with side dishes of baked potato, salad, shrimp, and bread rolls, in just about 15 minutes. In February 2014, at a Philadelphia restaurant, the woman ate 363 chicken wings in 30 minutes.

Other eccentrics methodically plan ways to be different and systematically carry them out. One such person is Ashrita Furman (born Keith Furman), who as of this writing has the most records in the *Guinness Book of World Records* held by a single individual. He has traveled to about 30 different countries to try to break records. One of the ways he gets in the book is by inventing new things to do that will establish a record, such as the fastest mile by someone balancing a baseball bat or underwater pogo stick jumping. Sometimes, Furman does ordinary things in extraordinary ways or in unusual places. For example, in 1979, he set his first record by doing 27,000 jumping jacks, and in 1986, he did somersaults along the same 12-1/4 miles that was traveled by Paul Revere on his famous ride in Massachusetts in 1775.

Eccentrics occupy an indeterminate status. They are fascinating to others (and may even be a source of envy), while they are also upsetting to them. Eccentrics believe that they are right in what they do, and they are not usually unhappy with their unconventionality. They tend to do exactly as they please, and they are usually unconcerned with what is proper or what others want them to do.

> Eccentrics are people who take boundless joy in life, immoderate men and women who refuse to violate their ideals. Their minds are always buzzing furiously with ideas. . . . At the root of eccentricity is a healthy and determined irreverence. (Weeks & James, 1995, p. 254)

The eccentric's unbridled freedom and independence of thought and action (or is it irresponsibility or some slavish obedience to the goal of being weird?) may rub others the wrong way. What gives eccentrics the right to do whatever they want when the rest of us cannot?

Eccentrics may actually be more alarming than some other kinds of deviants. To be sure, their eccentricities rarely break the law, but this does not mean that eccentrics are simply amusing oafs, providing some spice to life. Whereas most deviants know the difference between right and wrong and do not flaunt or challenge the rules openly, the eccentric seems to be out of touch with the ordinary concerns of ordinary folk. Not only is the eccentric odd in the eyes of others, but he or she also goes to great lengths to be different and separate, defends his or her oddness as perfectly proper, is indifferent to the expectations and wishes of others, and appears unable or unwilling to understand why others would be upset by him or her. Whatever tensions that might exist between individual desires and the forces of social control have been resolved successfully by the eccentric in favor of his or her own interests (Suran, 1978). Eccentrics' trespasses may be minor and relatively benign, but they do them with such gusto, irreverence, self-centeredness, assurance, and guiltlessness that their trespasses can take on an ominous and foreboding quality.

Conclusions

This chapter has shown that attributes (the principal element in "conditions" in the ABCs of deviance) are themselves a source of categorization and judgment. People are stigmatized for things over which they have little or no control. "Normal" and "stigmatized" are *perspectives* on persons, so we always will need a language of relationships to be able to discuss and understand any discrediting or discreditable attributes. An error occurs, called the fundamental attribution error, when observers attribute the cause for some happening to individual character instead of to the social context in which it occurs. Cause and blame are not identical, but decisions about blame and responsibility always have direct implications for who and what is deviant.

When the label of deviance is attached to some attitude, behavior, or condition, it usually involves some fundamental decisions about conventionality (Could it have been otherwise?) and theoreticity (Did the individual know what he or she was doing?). These decision rules help assess responsibility for some event, which leads quite easily into decisions about who or what is deviant. Such interpersonal processes are responsible for the social construction of spoiled identities and the stigma that comes from it. Deviance can easily evolve into a master status and be accompanied by a great deal of shame and embarrassment. Reputations can be tarnished or even irreparably damaged. Retrospective interpretation is a dynamic process in which a person's social identity is reconstituted in the eyes of others. It is possible for accused deviants to impact what happens to them by using neutralizations, rationalizations, atonements, apologies, accounts, or cooling-out strategies. When any of these is successful, it is possible to have a great deal of deliberate rule breaking without anyone being held responsible for it.

References

Adams, J. (2012). Cleaning up the dirty work: Professionalization and the management of stigma in the cosmetic surgery and tattoo industries. *Deviant Behavior, 33*, 149–167.

Adams, S., & Riley, L. (1988). *Facts and fallacies*. New York: Reader's Digest Association.

Adler, P., & Adler, P. (2009). Self-injurers. In P. Adler & P. Adler (Eds.), *Constructions of deviance: Social power, context, and interaction* (6th ed., pp. 379–386). Belmont, CA: Thomson/Wadsworth.

Atkinson, M. (2011). Male athletes and the cult(ure) of thinness in sport. *Deviant Behavior, 32*, 224–256.

Atkinson, M., & Young, K. (2008). Flesh journeys: The radical body modification of neoprimitives. In E. Goode & D. A. Vail (Eds.), *Extreme deviance* (pp. 15–26). Thousand Oaks, CA: Pine Forge/Sage.

Badger, S. (2010). "Where the excess grows": Demarcating "normal" and "pathologically" obese bodies. In E. Etorre (Ed.), *Culture, bodies and the sociology of health* (pp. 137–154). Burlington, VT: Ashgate.

Ball, D. (1970). The problematics of respectability. In J. Douglas (Ed.), *Deviance and respectability: The social construction of moral meanings* (pp. 326–371). New York: Basic Books.

Barkan, S. E., & Bryjak, G. J. (2014). *Myths and realities about crime and justice: What every American should know* (2nd ed.). Burlington, MA: Jones & Bartlett Learning.

Becker, H. (1963). *Outsiders: Studies in the sociology of deviance*. New York: Free Press.

Boero, N. (2012). *Killer fat: Media, medicine, and morals in the American "obesity epidemic."* New Brunswick, NJ: Rutgers University Press.

Bogdan, R. (1988). *Freak show: Presenting human oddities for amusement and profit*. Chicago: University of Chicago Press.

Bogdan, R. (with Elks, M., & Knoll, J.). (2012). *Picturing disability: Beggar, freak, citizen, and other photographic rhetoric*. Syracuse, NY: Syracuse University Press.

Bogdan, R., & Taylor, S. (1989). Relationships with severely disabled people: The social construction of humanness. *Social Problems, 36*, 135–148.

Brayne, S. (2014). Surveillance and system avoidance: Criminal justice contact and institutional attachment. *American Sociological Review, 79*, 367–391.

Brownmiller, S. (1984). *Femininity*. New York: Linden.

Brune, J. A., & Wilson, D. J. (Eds.). (2013). *Disability and passing: Blurring the lines of identity*. Philadelphia: Temple University Press.

Burke, P. J., & Stets, J. E. (2009). *Identity theory*. New York: Oxford University Press.

Buss, D. (1994). *The evolution of desire: Strategies of human mating*. New York: Basic Books.

Butera, F., & Levine, J. M. (2009). *Coping with minority status: Responses to exclusion and inclusion*. New York: Cambridge University Press.

Cahill, S., & Eggleston, R. (2005). Wheelchair users. In E. Rubington & M. Weinberg (Eds.), *Deviance: The interactionist perspective* (9th ed., pp. 26–41). Boston: Pearson/Allyn & Bacon.

Campbell, F. K. (2009). *Contours of ableism: The production of disability and ableness.* New York: Palgrave Macmillan.

Chiricos, T., Stupi, E. K., Stults, B. J., & Gertz, M. (2014). Undocumented immigrant threat and support for social controls. *Social Problems, 61,* 673–692.

Darling, R. B. (2013). *Disability and identity: Negotiating self in a changing society.* Boulder, CO: Lynne Rienner Publishers.

Davis, J. L. (2014). Morality work among the transabled. *Deviant Behavior, 35,* 433–455.

Edgell, P., & Tranby, E. (2010). Shared visions? Diversity and cultural membership in American life. *Social Problems, 57,* 175–204.

English, C. (1993). Gaining and losing weight: Identity transformations. *Deviant Behavior, 14,* 227–241.

Etorre, E. (2010). Bodies, drugs and reproductive regimes. In E. Etorre (Ed.), *Culture, bodies and the sociology of health* (pp. 155–172). Burlington, VT: Ashgate.

Felson, R. (1991). Blame analysis: Accounting for the behavior of protected groups. *American Sociologist, 22,* 5–23.

Fiske, S. (2012). *Envy up, scorn down: How status divides us.* New York: Russell Sage Foundation.

Fitzpatrick, K. M., & Myrstol, B. (2011). The jailing of America's homeless: Evaluating the rabble management thesis. *Crime & Delinquency, 57,* 271–297. (Originally published online August 25, 2008)

Flaherty, T. (1992). *Odd and eccentric people.* Alexandria, VA: Time-Life Books.

Ford, J. A., Schroeder, R. D., & Dotson, H. M. (2014). Weight strain and binge drinking among adolescents. *Deviant Behavior, 35,* 742–757.

Furst, R. T., & Evans, D. N. (2015). An exploration of stigma in the lives of sex offenders and heroin abusers. *Deviant Behavior, 36,* 130–145.

Garfinkel, H. (1956). Conditions of successful degradation ceremonies. *American Journal of Sociology, 61,* 420–424.

Garot, R. (2010). *Who you claim: Performing gang identity in school and on the streets.* New York: New York University Press.

Gladwell, M. (2000). *The tipping point: How little things can make a big difference.* Boston: Little, Brown.

Glass, C., Haas, S., & Reither, E. N. (2010). The skinny on success: Body mass, gender and occupational standing across the life course. *Social Forces, 88,* 1777–1806.

Goffman, E. (1952). On cooling the mark out. *Psychiatry, 15,* 451–463.

Goffman, E. (1959). *The presentation of self in everyday life.* Garden City, NY: Doubleday Anchor.

Goffman, E. (1963). *Stigma: Notes on the management of spoiled identity.* Englewood Cliffs, NJ: Prentice Hall.

Goffman, E. (1969). *Strategic interaction.* New York: Ballantine.

Goffman, E. (1971). *Relations in public: Microstudies of the public order*. New York: Harper & Row.

Goode, E. (2002). Sexual involvement and social research in a fat civil rights organization. *Qualitative Sociology, 25*, 501–534.

Goode, E. (2011). *Deviant behavior* (9th ed.). Upper Saddle River, NJ: Pearson/Prentice Hall.

Goode, E. (2013). *Justifiable conduct: Self-vindication in memoir*. Philadelphia: Temple University Press.

Goode, E. (2015). *Deviant behavior* (10th ed.). Upper Saddle River, NJ: Pearson.

Goode, E., & Vail, D. A. (Eds.). (2008). *Extreme deviance*. Thousand Oaks, CA: Pine Forge/Sage.

Gregersen, E. (1983). *Sexual practices: The story of human sexuality*. New York: Franklin Watts.

Grogan, S. (2009). Femininity and body image: Promoting positive body image in the "culture of slenderness." In R. Colls & K. Hörschelmann (Eds.), *Contested bodies of childhood and youth* (pp. 41–52). New York: Palgrave Macmillan.

Gruys, K. (2012). Does this make me look fat? Aesthetic labor and fat talk as emotional labor in a women's plus-size clothing store. *Social Problems, 59*, 481–500.

Gusfield, J. (1967). Moral passage: The symbolic process in public designations of deviance. *Social Problems, 15*, 175–188.

Guthman, J. (2011). *Weighing in: Obesity, food justice, and the limits of capitalism*. Berkeley: University of California Press.

Haenfler, R. (2013). *Goths, gamers, grrrls: Deviance and youth subcultures* (2nd ed.). New York: Oxford University Press.

Hamermesh, D. (2013). *Beauty pays: Why attractive people are more successful*. Princeton, NJ: Princeton University Press.

Herman, N., & Miall, C. (2005). The positive consequences of stigma. In E. Rubington & M. Weinberg (Eds.), *Deviance: The interactionist perspective* (9th ed., pp. 237–249). Boston: Pearson/Allyn & Bacon.

Hills, S. L. (1980). *Demystifying social deviance*. New York: McGraw-Hill.

Hitlin, S. (2008). *Moral selves, evil selves: The social psychology of conscience*. New York: Palgrave Macmillan.

Hogan, D. (2012). *Family consequences of children's disabilities*. New York: Russell Sage Foundation.

Huey, L. (2012). *Invisible victims: Homelessness and the growing security gap*. Toronto, Ont., Canada: University of Toronto Press.

Hughes, E. C. (1945). Dilemmas and contradictions of status. *American Journal of Sociology, 50*, 353–359.

Hughes, E. C. (1951). Work and the self. In J. Roher & M. Sherif (Eds.), *Social psychology at the crossroads* (pp. 313–323). New York: Harper & Brothers.

Interview with a vampirette. (1997, February 9). *New York Times Magazine*, p. 17.

Irwin, J. (1985). *Managing the underclass in American society*. Berkeley: University of California Press.

Jaeger, M. M. (2011). "A thing of beauty is a joy forever"? Returns to physical attractiveness over the life course. *Social Forces, 89,* 983–1004.

Jones, A., & Ratterman, N. (2009). Mate choice and sexual selection: What have we learned since Darwin? *Proceedings of the National Academy of Sciences of the United States of America, 106*(Supp. 1), 10001–10008.

Jong, E. (1990). *Any woman's blues.* New York: Harper & Row.

Kent, L. (2010). Fighting abjection: Representing fat women. In L. J. Moore & M. Kosut (Eds.), *The body reader: Essential social and cultural readings* (pp. 367–383). New York: New York University Press.

Kitsuse, J. (1962). Societal reactions to deviant behavior: Problems of theory and method. *Social Problems, 9,* 247–257.

Kitsuse, J. (1980). Coming out all over: Deviants and the politics of social problems. *Social Problems, 28,* 1–13.

Kosut, M., & Moore, L. J. (2010). Introduction: Not just the reflexive reflex. Flesh and bone in the social sciences. In L. J. Moore & M. Kosut (Eds.), *The body reader: Essential social and cultural readings* (pp. 1–26). New York: New York University Press.

Kwan, S. (2009). Framing the fat body: Contested meanings between government, activists, and industry. *Sociological Inquiry, 79,* 25–50.

Lasky, N., Jacques, S., & Fisher, B. S. (2015). Glossing over shoplifting: How thieves act normal. *Deviant Behavior, 36,* 293–309.

LeBel, T. P. (2012). Invisible stripes? Formerly incarcerated persons' perceptions of stigma. *Deviant Behavior, 33,* 89–107.

Lindegaard, M. R., & Jacques, S. (2014). Agency as a cause of crime. *Deviant Behavior, 35,* 85–100.

Lizardo, O., & Collett, J. L. (2013). Embarrassment and social organization: A multiple identities model. *Social Forces, 92,* 353–375.

Lyman, S., & Scott, M. (1989). *Sociology of the absurd* (2nd ed.). New York: General Hall.

MacKinnon, N. J., & Heise, D. R. (2010). *Self, identity, and social institutions.* New York: Palgrave Macmillan.

Maggard, S. R., & Boylstein, C. (2014). Changing masks: Identity maintenance and the role of marijuana among a small circle of marijuana growers. *Deviant Behavior, 35,* 593–610.

Maner, J., Gailliot, M., Rouby, D., & Miller, S. (2007). Can't take my eyes off you: Attentional adhesion to mates and rivals. *Journal of Personality and Social Psychology, 93,* 389–401.

Mankoff, M. (1976). Societal reaction and career deviance: A critical analysis. In W. Chambliss & M. Mankoff (Eds.), *Whose law? What order?* (pp. 240–256). New York: Wiley.

Mason, K. (2012). The unequal weight of discrimination: Gender, body size, and income inequality. *Social Problems, 59,* 411–435.

McClintock, E. A. (2014). Beauty and status: The illusion of exchange in partner selection? *American Sociological Review, 79,* 575–604.

McCray, K., Wesely, J. K., & Rasche, C. E. (2011). Rehab retrospect: Former prostitutes and the (re)construction of deviance. *Deviant Behavior, 32,* 743–768.

McHugh, P. (1970). A common-sense conception of deviance. In J. Douglas (Ed.), *Deviance and respectability: The social construction of moral meanings* (pp. 61–88). New York: Basic Books.

Menard, S., & Pollock, W. (2014). Self reports of being falsely accused of criminal behavior. *Deviant Behavior, 35,* 378–393.

Montanino, F., & Sagarin, E. (1977). Deviants: Voluntarism and responsibility. In E. Sagarin & F. Montanino (Eds.), *Deviants: Voluntary actors in a hostile world* (pp. 1–15). Morristown, NJ: General Learning Press/Scott, Foresman.

Moore, L. J., & Kosut, M. (Eds.). (2010). *The body reader: Essential social and cultural readings.* New York: New York University Press.

Mueller, L. (1996, November 19). Father of black-lipsticked girl arrested. *Lexington Herald-Leader,* pp. A1, A8.

Nash, J. R. (1982). *Zanies: The world's greatest eccentrics.* Piscataway, NJ: New Century.

Newman, D. (2008). *Sociology: Exploring the architecture of everyday life* (7th ed.). Thousand Oaks, CA: Pine Forge/Sage.

Nisbett, R. E., & Ross, L. (1991). *The person and the situation.* Philadelphia: Temple University Press.

O'Brien, J. (2006). Shared meaning as the basis of humanness. In J. O'Brien (Ed.), *The production of reality* (4th ed., pp. 64–82). Thousand Oaks, CA: Pine Forge/Sage.

Offer, A., Pechey, R., & Ulijaszek, S. (Eds.). (2012). *Insecurity, inequality, and obesity in affluent societies.* Oxford, UK: Oxford University Press.

Olzak, S., & Shanahan, S. (2014). Prisoners and paupers: The impact of group threat on incarceration in nineteenth-century U.S. cities. *American Sociological Review, 79,* 392–411.

Pager, D. (2007). *Marked: Race, crime, and finding work in an era of mass incarceration.* Chicago: University of Chicago Press.

Pitts-Taylor, V. (2007). *Surgery junkies: Wellness and pathology in cosmetic culture.* Brunswick, NJ: Rutgers University Press.

Pontikes, E., Negro, G., & Rao, H. (2010). Stained red. A study of stigma by association to blacklisted artists during the "Red Scare" in Hollywood, 1945 to 1960. *American Sociological Review, 75,* 456–478.

Rassin, M. (2011). Tactics of concealment among people living with HIV. *Deviant Behavior, 32,* 101–114.

Renfrow, D. G., & Rollo, E. A. (2014). Sexting on campus: Minimizing perceived risks and neutralizing behaviors. *Deviant Behavior, 35,* 903–920.

Richardson, N. (2010). *Transgressive bodies: Representations in film and popular culture.* Burlington, VT: Ashgate.

Ridley, M. (1993). *The Red Queen: Sex and the evolution of human nature.* New York: Penguin.

Ridolfo, H., & Ward, B. W. (2013). *Mobility impairment and the construction of identity.* Boulder, CO: Lynne Rienner Publishers.

Roberts, I., & Edwards, P. (2010). *The energy glut: Climate change and the politics of fatness*. New York: Zed Books.

Rocheleau, G. C., & Chavez, J. M. (2015). Guilt by association: The relationship between deviant peers and deviant labels. *Deviant Behavior, 36,* 167–186.

Ruane, J. M., & Cerulo, K. A. (2015). *Second thoughts: Sociology challenges conventional wisdom* (6th ed.). Thousand Oaks, CA: Sage.

Sabatello, M., & Schulze, M. (Eds.). (2014). *Human rights and disability advocacy.* Philadelphia: University of Pennsylvania Press.

Sagarin, E. (1975). *Deviants and deviance: An introduction to the study of disvalued people and behavior.* New York: Praeger.

Saguy, A. C. (2013). *What's wrong with fat?* New York: Oxford University Press.

Saguy, A. C., & Gruys, K. (2010). Morality and health: News media constructions of overweight and eating disorders. *Social Problems, 57,* 231–250.

Saguy, A. C., Gruys, K., & Gong, S. (2010). Social problem construction and national context: News reporting on "overweight" and "obesity" in the United States and France. *Social Problems, 57,* 586–610.

Sanders, C. (1996). Getting a tattoo. In E. Rubington & M. Weinberg (Eds.), *Deviance: The interactionist perspective* (6th ed., pp. 364–377). Boston: Allyn & Bacon.

Schafer, M. H., Ferraro, K. F., & Mustillo, S. (2011). Children of misfortune: Early adversity and cumulative inequality in perceived life trajectories. *American Journal of Sociology, 116,* 1053–1091.

Schroeder, R. D., & Mowen, T. J. (2014). "You can't eat WHAT?" Managing the stigma of celiac disease. *Deviant Behavior, 35,* 456–474.

Schur, E. (1971). *Labeling deviant behavior: Its sociological implications.* New York: Harper & Row.

Schur, E. (1983). *Labeling women deviant.* Philadelphia: Temple University Press.

Scott, M., & Lyman, S. (1968). Accounts. *American Sociological Review, 33,* 46–62.

Sender, K. (2012). *The makeover: Reality television and reflexive audiences.* New York: New York University Press.

Shanahan, M. J., Bauldry, S., Roberts, B. W., Macmillan, R., & Russo, R. (2014). Personality and the reproduction of social class. *Social Forces, 93,* 209–240.

Sherry, M. (2010). *Disability hate crimes: Does anyone really hate disabled people?* Burlington, VT: Ashgate.

Shippee, N. D. (2011). Gay, straight, and who I am: Passing within the frames for everyday life. *Deviant Behavior, 32,* 115–157.

Sifakis, C. (1984). *American eccentrics.* New York: Facts on File.

Silver, E., Silver, S. R., Siennick, S., & Farkas, G. (2011). Bodily signs of academic success: An empirical examination of tattoos and grooming. *Social Problems, 58,* 538–564.

Skvoretz, J. (2013). Diversity, integration, and social ties: Attraction versus repulsion as drivers of intra- and intergroup relations. *American Journal of Sociology, 119,* 486–517.

Slevin, K. F. (2010). "If I had lots of money . . . I'd have a body makeover": Managing the aging body. *Social Forces, 88,* 1003–1020.

Small, M. (1995). *What's love got to do with it? The evolution of human mating.* New York: Anchor.

Stein, J. (2015, June 29). Nip. Tuck. Or Else. Why you'll be getting cosmetic procedures even if you don't really want to. *Time, 185,* 40–48.

Steinmetz, K. F., & Gerber, J. (2014). "The greatest crime syndicate since the Gambinos": A hacker critique of government, law, and law enforcement. *Deviant Behavior, 35,* 243–261.

Stiles, B. L., & Clark, R. E. (2011). BDSM: A subcultural analysis of sacrifices and delights. *Deviant Behavior, 32,* 158–189.

Suran, B. (1978). *Oddballs: The social maverick and the dynamics of individuality.* Chicago: Nelson Hall.

Sykes, G., & Matza, D. (1957). Techniques of neutralization: A theory of delinquency. *American Sociological Review, 22,* 664–670.

Thomas, J. N., Crosby, L., & Milford, J. (2015). Gender differences among self-reported genital piercing stories. *Deviant Behavior, 36,* 441–462.

Thompson, W. E., & Thompson, M. L. (2014). Mature motorcyclists: Violating age norms and loving it. *Deviant Behavior, 35,* 233–242.

Trost, C. (1982). The blue people of Troublesome Creek. *Science, 82,* 34–39.

Turner, R. (1972). Deviance avowal as neutralization of commitment. *Social Problems, 19,* 308–321.

Vail, D. A. (2008). Tattoos are like potato chips . . . you can't have just one: The process of becoming and being a collector. In E. Goode & D. A. Vail (Eds.), *Extreme deviance* (pp. 5–14). Thousand Oaks, CA: Pine Forge/Sage.

Van Buren, A. (1981). *The best of Dear Abby.* Kansas City, MO: Andrews & McMeel.

Vecitis, K. S. (2011). Young women's accounts of instrumental drug use for weight control. *Deviant Behavior, 32,* 451–474.

Venkatesh, S. (2008). *Gang leader for a day: A rogue sociologist takes to the streets.* New York: Penguin. (e-book)

Wallace, I. (1957). *The square pegs: Some Americans who dared to be different.* New York: Knopf.

Wappett, M., & Arndt, K. (Eds.). (2013). *Emerging perspectives on disability studies.* Hampshire, UK: Palgrave Macmillan.

Way, L. B., & Patten, R. (2013). *Hunting for "dirtbags": Why cops over-police the poor and racial minorities.* Boston: Northeastern University Press.

Weeks, D., & James, J. (1995). *Eccentrics: A study of sanity and strangeness.* New York: Villard.

Yagil, D., & Luria, G. (2014). Being difficult: Customers' sensemaking of their deviant behavior. *Deviant Behavior, 35,* 921–937.

Young, R. L., & Thompson, C. Y. (2011). Gender, attributions of responsibility, and negotiation of deviant labels in small groups. *Deviant Behavior, 32,* 626–652.

3

Power, Social Networks, and Organizational Deviance

Power Corrupts, and Absolute Power Corrupts Absolutely

Social Structure and Self-Interest

Some people regularly act to feather their own nests instead of doing what is politically correct or morally just. Individuals may build up *criminal capital* in which they acquire knowledge and skills that allow them to commit crimes successfully (Loughran, Nguyen, Piquero, & Fagan, 2013). Some may head to shopping malls to steal things from department stores; others may embezzle funds from their employers, take automobiles that do not belong to them, or break into people's homes or businesses; and still others may rob hapless strangers at gun- or knifepoint. The principal reason is the lure of getting other people's money and other valuables in a quick and easy way. Other reasons are a sense of accomplishment, fun and excitement, and opportunities for control over people and the increased sense of power and potency that this can create (Tunnell, 1992). Sometimes taking other people's money and valuables is an act of resistance to mainstream culture and the values it contains, especially those that encourage hard work, delayed gratification, job stability, and responsibility (Tunnell, 2006).

If people have power because of their organizational positions or interpersonal networks, it is easier for them to get what they want regardless of whom it hurts, and then to portray their actions as reasonable and necessary (Prechel & Morris, 2010). These efforts at legitimation, when successful, help to free these powerful individuals from the kind of blame and derision that would befall thieves of lesser means. Organizational men and women are more likely to commit acts of deviance and crime when they believe that these kinds of trespasses are widespread among their business associates (Tavits, 2010).

Opportunity structure is an important variable in understanding what kind of deviance occurs and why (J. W. Coleman, 1987, 2006; Merton, 1938). Only police can engage in police brutality, only politicians can engage in political corruption, and only members of corporations can commit corporate crime. Organizational and institutional dynamics powerfully affect the attitudes and behaviors of individuals who work within them (Fullerton & Villemez, 2011). The existence of opportunities to commit deviance usually means that it will occur more often (Merton, 1938; Thio, 2010).

The simple and simplistic explanation that bad apples and bad barrels exist is useless when it comes to something as durable and complicated as organizational wrongdoing. Organizations can be *both* good and bad, just like the people in them. When organizational men and women make decisions about what to do and the legality or ethics of their plans, their decisions are often filled with confusion and contradictions; their decisions are based on information that is narrow and limited (Palmer, 2013). Even principled individuals can find that they are at risk of doing something illegal when they are in an organizational setting that encourages or overlooks any rule breaking that increases an organization's wealth.

The worldwide financial crisis, called the Great Recession, that started in late 2007, and as of this writing continues to generate worldwide problems is well known but still poorly understood despite a large number of books and other publications about it (Grusky, Western, & Wimer, 2011). One thing is beyond dispute: A significant variable was the too-cozy relationship between policy makers and regulators on the one hand and the financial community on the other (Barak, 2012; Smith, 2010). The Financial Crisis Inquiry Commission (2011) concluded in its final report, issued in January 2011, that the principal cause of the financial meltdown of 2008 and 2009 was the failure of federal regulators to exercise sufficient oversight and control of Wall Street's reckless profiteering. Problems with corporate governance and risk management were also cited. The report also strongly contradicted the claim (coming from Wall Street and parts of Washington) that the financial crisis could not have been predicted (Rooney, 2011).

The institutional drive in banking to make money—lots of it and as quickly as possible—created incredible financial growth, but it was almost entirely based on U.S. home mortgages. Home mortgages were increasingly based on predatory lending strategies that encouraged the emergence of a Darwinian social world in which it was the greediest, most ruthless, and least restrained who survived (Will, Handelman, & Brotherton, 2012).

> But while everything seemed to be falling apart at the same time, there was a common source: the reckless lending of the financial sector, which had fed the housing bubble, which eventually burst. (Stiglitz, 2010, p. 27)

While private profits of some individuals and the wealth of banks increased, most everyone else was injured in one way or another (Sherman, 2013; Smith, 2010). The declaration that the market is always rational was shown to be a mythical construction (Fox, 2009; Pacewicz, 2013; Werner, 2012).

Bankers acted recklessly and greedily because they had both opportunities and incentives to do so. Repeal of the Glass-Steagall Act (in 1999), a 1933 creation of the New Deal reform movement that had prohibited commercial banks, investment firms, and insurance companies from merging into one company, is one of the things that led to the economic meltdown. Its repeal made it possible for large banks to get even larger, reaching a point where they were in every sense of the term just too big to fail. This is a condition that Stiglitz (2010) labels *ersatz capitalism,* meaning fake or phony capitalism—an economic system that generates private gains without risk. Whatever losses occurred did not fall upon the individuals who were making the greatest profits. Executives could take whatever risks they wanted with other people's money, confident that whatever happened would not affect their own personal fortunes. This provided the incentive or motive for unbridled risk taking (Posner, 2010). The opportunity surfaced due to an economic climate of deregulation and lax governmental oversight. Additional factors were a housing bubble in which too many houses were built and risky lending practices in which too much money was given out too easily (Harvey, 2010; Rugh & Massey, 2010).

Money handed out by the U.S. Treasury under TARP (Troubled Assets Recovery Program), which was supposed to be used to recapitalize and provide credit to those who needed it, was used instead to pay out huge corporate bonuses. It was as if the record losses were not losses at all and that it would be business as usual thanks to taxpayers' generosity. Much of what was not used to pay bonuses was used to pay dividends to shareholders, a monetary way to share profits. In this case, however, no profits existed, only taxpayers' handouts. In fact, nine lenders that had combined losses of almost $100 billion were given $175 billion in bailout money from the government. Of this, they paid almost $33 billion in bonuses (which included giving $1 million to *each* of almost 5,000 employees, a total of nearly 5,000 *million* dollars) (Stiglitz, 2010, p. 80).

Power and Inequality

We cannot separate our understanding of the relativity of deviance from our understanding of *power*—who has it, how much they have, and how it affects the ebb and flow of social life (Davis, 1980; Kendall, 2008; Sherwood, 2010). Power over others is based partly on an individual's knowledge and skills—and in the case of a deviant, on his or her willingness to con or defraud others (Robbins, 2008). For example, in a game of three-card monte, a bettor must find the queen when it and two kings are thrown face down on a table and all three cards are mixed. Sometimes, it is not a game of chance at all because the card tosser uses sleight of hand to manipulate the cards so it is practically impossible for a bettor to win (Scarne, 1974). It would improve a bettor's chances if he or she did not even watch the cards being thrown and just randomly picked one. The card tosser, then, has power over bettors because the thief knows how to use sleight of hand to manipulate the cards. Some scams require greater skill and knowledge than others. It is more difficult, for example, to maintain one's composure during a high-stakes poker game while cheating others—bottom-dealing, holding out cards, stacking a deck, undoing the cut—than it is to master the throw used in the game of three-card monte (Prus & Sharper, 1977).

A more enduring and important source of power comes from an individual's social networks and opportunity structures that enable him or her to do things that affect the lives of others. Conan the Barbarian has a certain amount of power because he is big and strong; the chief executive officer (CEO) of General Motors (even in troubled economic times), however, has infinitely more power, even though the CEO may have small stature and be unable to lift a feather. When powerful people with interests in common unite to accomplish their objectives and establish ties to other powerful groups, they can move mountains. They can also use their power and resources in harmful or malicious ways.

[W]e live in a world in which hazards are produced as often by the action of complex organizations as by persons of flesh and blood, and where the scale of damage is often proportional to the size of the organizational actor. (Gray & Silbey, 2014, p. 132)

A fish rots from the head first, claims an ancient proverb (which originated in either China or Italy), reminding us to consider that it is those who have the *most* resources who are responsible for a substantial amount of deviance (Samuel, 2010).

We live in an *asymmetric society* in which the power of large organizations (e.g., corporations) far outweighs the power of the ordinary person (J. S. Coleman, 1982). Power, an important variable in the understanding of any kind of deviance, is particularly valuable in analyzing the organizational deviance that is regularly perpetrated by more privileged members of a society. Whether a company conforms to norms that demand lawful behaviors and socially responsible actions depends a lot on the expectations and examples set by its senior management (Dashwood, 2012).

A transnational class now exists, characterized by global interconnections. Just as corporate influence and mass communications are no longer confined to just one country, so too, this transnational class scours the globe in search of the most hospitable climate for its economic interests to flourish (Fairbrother, 2014). The power of this class comes from the spread of consumerism, new information technology, and the international electronic economy. Globalization has made it more difficult for national governments to deal with problems within their borders, and governmental power has eroded (Carroll, 2010; Rothkopf, 2012). Big Business manipulates what it can to work one country against another (and one region against other regions in the *same* country) to obtain lower taxes; looser regulations; and an abundance of low-cost, uncomplaining laborers (Schwartzman, 2013). Foreign investment actually impedes economic growth in a country, leading to economic stagnation, especially if it happens too quickly (Curwin & Mahutga, 2014).

Some of the individuals in large organizations use their organizational positions to commit deviance, having both the opportunity to do so and the resources and interests to hide their deviance from others. They may experience a more intense sense of *subjective* or *relative deprivation,* increasing substantially their motivations to take what doesn't belong to them. Differential opportunity and relative deprivation can coalesce to make it more likely that the powerful will engage in harmful acts of deviance more frequently than will the powerless (Thio, 2010). The powerful may deny that anyone was harmed by what they did, blame their deviance on some external factor over which they have no control, or convince themselves that they deserve the rewards that their deviance brought them (J. W. Coleman, 1987). They may use their resources to direct public attention to the deviances of others.

The powerful benefit from a *shield of elitist invisibility* (Simon, 2008, p. 38) or *cloak of immunity* (Box, 1983, p. 99), such that their rule breaking either is not uncovered or, if it is uncovered, it is accorded a milder penalty than it probably deserves. According to Box, "The process of law enforcement, in its broadest possible interpretation, operates in such a way as to *conceal* crimes of the powerful against the powerless, but to *reveal* and *exaggerate* crimes of the powerless against 'everyone'" (p. 5). The ruin caused by powerful individuals in powerful organizations has a good chance of being peddled as an accident, as an isolated event (and therefore less harmful), or as the result of the antisocial behaviors of just a few "bad apples" (Poveda, 1994). The bad apple narrative, blaming individuals instead of organizations, protects the economy and the state apparatus from a more sweeping condemnation (Cavender, Gray, & Miller, 2010). A study of accounting scandals in the United States from 1999 to 2006 (Benediktsson, 2010) reports that corporate boards did all they could to sever all ties with law-breaking executives, making them stand trial alone. This diverted attention away from the organization itself.

The Deviant Elite

Hightower (2003) declares the United States of the twenty-first century to be a *kleptocrat nation,* a nation ruled by thieves where money and power are consistently taken from the many to enrich the few. In this process, liberty, justice, political integrity, social equality, and opportunity for the many are continually threatened (Lobao, Adua, & Hooks, 2014; Lorenz, 2012). Little doubt exists that some economic elites are so prominent and powerful in the global economy that they are able to influence money flow, debt, and credit sufficiently that these core resources are manipulated to create private benefits and social costs (Lendman, 2011). Members of the elite class are able to successfully maintain relationships and occupy positions in organizations and voluntary associations that keep them in contact with one another while making it easier for them to control resources in a community (Cornwell & Dokshin, 2014).

Democracy and free markets are not inevitable traveling companions (Polillo, 2013). While they do at times play complementary roles, at other times they do not (Wherry, 2012). Markets have no morality, and they do not guarantee either social equality or individual well-being. Markets encourage whatever is the most profitable, which usually rewards size, and this generates a concentration of economic and political power in the hands of the relative few. Ultimately, this leads to an undermining of both democracy and free enterprise. Reining in the power of government is not always a victory for democracy and individual freedoms. What this may actually mean is that the most privileged and powerful among us find that their freedoms have indeed increased, enabling them to go practically anywhere and do practically anything they want to make the most money (Pollard, 2012).

Large businesses and some of the wealthiest individuals in U.S. society continue to prosper, but practically everyone else does not (Brady, 2009; Nau, 2013). Workers' share of national incomes in capitalist democracies has decreased during the last 40 years or so, due principally to the deterioration in their bargaining power in relationship to their bosses (Kristal, 2010; Mouw & Kalleberg, 2010). Working Americans, with no other option available, embraced the market with the hopes that it would benefit them and their families. However, this is not what happened (Martin, 2008). Economic inequality in the United States has increased over time, and it is higher than that found in most other developed nations (Clark, 2013; Gornick & Jäntti, 2013; Reich, 2010). Poorer households saw their average real incomes decline substantially between 2010 and 2013 (Bricker et al., 2014). A strong case can be made that a positive relationship exists between the levels of inequality in a society, particularly economic and racial, and rates of deviance and crime (Bernard, Snipes, & Gerould, 2010). Greater social and economic equality makes for stronger, more robust societies (Flavin, Pacek, & Radcliff, 2014; Ono & Lee, 2013; Stiglitz, 2012; Wilkenson & Pickett, 2010).

Collectivizing Risk

Risk has been shifted to the backs and shoulders of members of the working class, and laborers have found to their dismay that even a good education, hard work, and strong family ties no longer provide the protection from economic ruination that they once did (Gosselin, 2009). U.S. workers are being expected to do more and more for less and less, leading to both worker alienation and exploitation (Juravich, 2009). U.S. workers, especially when compared to laborers in other Western democracies with a strong history of capitalism and workplace democracy (e.g., Germany), experience greater levels of domination by their bosses and have fewer opportunities to contract and unionize. It is the workers in this country, rather than their bosses or flaws in the workplace, that are blamed for whatever lack of job success or restricted mobility they may experience (Frege & Godard, 2014; Sharone, 2013).

The turn to the financial market has not only been generally unrewarding for most of the people who hoped to benefit from it, but it has had other unfortunate consequences as well:

> Civic disengagement, health care and prisons for profit, the malling of suburban America, the epidemic of corporate advertising in public space, and the torrent of private money in public life all testify to a coarsening of American

politics and culture. Competition to get the price right may be the hallmark of our economic system, but competition to put a price on everything produces a war of all against all. In this wartime condition, race and class tightly circumscribe communities, and the capacity to empathize with other people is fragile or nonexistent. (Blau, 1999, p. 4)

When what matters most is how much money some policy or practice produces for its corporate owners, many unsavory things can occur. Our collective and individual fears are manipulated by some individuals to get them what they want and to create the kind of society that they see as better for them and their economic interests.

Employees are "liquidated"—fired or let go—to increase the value of corporate stocks and market control (Ho, 2009). A heavier use of contingent or temporary workers, a cost-cutting and profit-increasing measure, threatens full-time employees' sense of job security and well-being (Pedulla, 2013). An analysis of 185 large U.S. firms (from 1996 to 2005) indicates that top executives' salaries and other compensations (e.g., bonuses, stock options, stock grants) are lower when the bargaining power of labor is greater. This suggests that workers' power, measured by the percentage of unionized workers in the industry, directly reduces the pay gap between executives and everybody else (Shin, 2014).

Deindustrialization and the flight of industry to countries outside the United States make it harder and harder for U.S. workers to find jobs and, especially, to find *good* jobs (Kalleberg, 2011; Kollmeyer & Pichler, 2013). This means that more and more Americans are either unemployed or underemployed, being either without jobs or without jobs that pay a living wage (Prasad, 2012). Added to this are the high prices of practically everything (e.g., gas, food, health care, energy, education, entertainment). Some individuals' problems are, of course, related in part to character and personality structure in that some people do have poor work ethics or possess skills in low demand. However, many of the problems we now face can be traced in one way or another to the effects of globalization, free trade agreements, tax incentives for companies to move production out of the United States, deregulation, and privatization of more and more services that governments once provided for citizens (Goldsmith & Blakely, 2010).

The Rich Get Richer

What we are seeing in the United States is the emergence of a corporatist society in which the principal feature is a huge transfer of public wealth to private hands and a widening gap between the superrich and everyone else

(Carroll, 2010). Though the details and the data are at times quite complex, the central idea is not: The rich get richer because they can convert their wealth into long-term gains much faster than the rest of us who live on income, much of which goes every year to subsisting in a society. People who depend on income from their jobs for their daily bread will never be able to accumulate sufficient wealth to keep up with those who already have wealth and can generate increasingly greater returns on it. For this reason, inequality increases in a society unless workers are powerful enough to affect the kind of governmental policies (e.g., taxes on the wealthy) to hold inequality and the accumulation of wealth by elites in check (Piketty, 2014).

U.S. history during the last 50 years or so is not simply a reflection of failed policies due to political incompetence or self-serving behaviors of elected officials. It is also a result of policies that were designed and implemented to produce total corporate liberation from public accountability, along with the violence and totalitarianism that result from this (Jaffee, 2012). The wars being waged by the United States are described by the "talking heads" on the evening news as righteous struggles to bring freedom and democracy to nations that lack them. This plays better with the public than describing them as what they also are: wars for the advancement of capitalism, unfettered by public interference or political oversight (Klein, 2007).

Though great fortunes should not be condemned on principle alone (Kahan, 2010), we also should not allow ourselves to be bamboozled by public relations campaigns that portray the superrich as those who deserve the very best due to their strong characters, principled behaviors, hard work, and boundless energy. A few businesspeople do embody these principles, but most do not. Great success in business is based mainly on making great deals in which much comes from little in a short period of time and with little or no risk. Economic elites are in the best position to set their own salaries and then to avoid paying taxes by taking advantage of tax shelters and other tax-avoidance strategies. This means they are able to keep an increasingly greater share of their earnings for themselves (Piketty, 2014).

To accumulate great wealth almost always requires being at the right place at the right time, coupled with a willingness to exploit others. Using other people's ideas and talents to enrich oneself is at the heart of most personal fortunes, coupled with the interpersonal skills to keep these dishonorable activities as invisible as possible (Villette & Vuillermot, 2009). Advantage, deserved or not, once attained can lead to further advantage (called the *Matthew effect*) (Rigney, 2010). Though common sense might indicate that talent, hard work, and success all go together, the fact is that success comes from a complicated mix of social constraints, opportunities, individual choices, and plain old luck (Watts, 2011).

The "rugged individualism" and "frontier spirit" that are such a central part of U.S. culture are more an idealization of our history than an accurate reflection of it (Vela-McConnell, 1999). The West was tamed by people working together, not some lone gunslinger or high-kicking Texas Ranger (Charbeneau, 1992). Almost always, great success of the few only comes from group efforts and contributions of the many.

> In most job settings . . . any individual's performance—indeed, any individual's apparent skill—depends subtly on communication and collaboration with co-workers, including supervisors. Great dancers need supportive partners; great journalists lean on skilled editors. (Tilly, 1998, p. 101)

Even great athletes or successful performers would not have gone very far without a supportive team or an adoring public. The rich and powerful maintain social inequality because it benefits them in a number of ways (McCall, 2013), and wealthy parents are able to pass the benefits of privilege on to their kids (Duncan & Murnane, 2011).

Groysberg (2010) showed that successful financial analysts in any given Wall Street firm usually do not experience the same level of success when they move to a rival firm, *unless* they are able to take their crew or team with them. Apparently, talent and success are not entirely portable, and the claim that individual merit and success are closely and inevitably aligned is less fact than fancy (O'Flynn, 2009). The success of a corporate CEO is determined more often by factors extraneous to the organization, such as the overall success of the economy or the particular industry, than by any talents or skills of the CEO (Khurana, 2002). It practically goes without saying that what is valuable at one place and time may be valueless at some other. No matter what the distribution of wealth or other scarce resources might be in a society, this distribution *always* reflects a particular set of choices about what skills should be valued, what to tax or subsidize, and what rules to make and enforce (Watts, 2011).

The Carrier's Case: Other People's Belongings and the Crime of Theft

Though it may seem natural to want to own things and to protect them from others, laws protecting property as we know them were nonexistent before the fifteenth century. Their creation had practically nothing to do with a belief in the right of all persons to be safe and secure in their possessions. The laws regarding theft, which transformed taking other people's belongings into a crime, were established by powerful individuals for the purpose of further-ing their own interests. Any benefit that these laws may have had for others was purely coincidental. This reminds us once again of the relativity of devi-ance in that certain kinds of taking are considered appropriate and in the public interest (e.g., taxation), while other kinds are labeled as criminal and steps are taken to punish the perpetrators. Whenever "deviance" is reconfig-ured as "crime," an important social event has occurred. The perpetrator of the untoward act now has a different status—criminal—and what a criminal does can be formally and forcefully sanctioned with the full weight of government (Chambliss & Seidman, 1982).

The case that is responsible for the creation of the crime of theft occurred in England in 1473 and is known as the *carrier's case*. A man was hired to carry bales of cloth to Southampton. Instead of completing the job, he broke the bales open and took off with their contents, intending them for his own use. He was eventually caught and taken into a court of law for magistrate review. The judges were in total agreement about what the carrier had done in terms of the details of his act, and they were also in total agreement that what the carrier had done was entirely legal. Because the carrier had been given the bales lawfully by his employer, nothing that he did after he took possession violated any existing law. Theft at the time was defined in terms of illegal trespass, and nobody who had been given property by its owner could trespass against it. Legally, it was the owner who was at fault for not employing a more trustworthy carrier (Hall, 1952).

The judges were under great pressure, however, to craft the necessary legislation to transform what the carrier had done into something sinister and harmful. They decided that a crime *had* occurred after all. When the carrier broke open the bales, the judges figured, the property instantly reverted back to its owner. By absconding with the contents, the carrier was guilty of a form of trespass, and he could be treated as a criminal (Hall, 1952). Curiously enough, if the carrier had somehow known what the judges were going to do, he could simply have taken *all* of the bales without breaking them open (but then the law would probably have been crafted differently). The judges portrayed the new law and the new understandings of "crime" and "criminal" that it established as just one more example of the strict application of legal precedent.

Why would the judges in the carrier's case invent a new law? It was not because they felt sorry for this particular owner or even because they wanted to encourage this particular carrier to walk the straight and narrow. Feudalism and its system of relationships based on sentiments of fidelity and obligation between serf and master were evaporating, being replaced by mer-cantilism and a middle class that owed its livelihood to commerce and trade.

Any threat to the transportation of goods was a blow to this burgeoning economic system. King Edward IV, the ruling monarch at the time of the carrier's case, was highly supportive of trade, and he assiduously courted business interests. The owner of the property that the carrier stole was an Italian merchant who had been assured of safe passage for his cargo by King Edward himself. The bales contained wool (or some other cloth), merchandise of great importance to England's budding economy. The fact that the material was stolen while in transport to Southampton was even worse because it undermined business confidence in the security of a major English trading center and shipping port. As if that weren't enough, the goods were stolen by a professional carrier. Merchants were finding it increasingly difficult to use their own servants to transport goods and were being forced to rely more often on carriers. If carriers could not be trusted to deliver safely the cargo they were given, trade would be adversely affected.

When the carrier stole the contents of the bales, he was doing more than depriving a foreign merchant of his goods. He was threatening—or that's how it was conceptualized and understood by the court—the economic interests of the textile industry, one of the most powerful and important businesses in all of England. He was also challenging the interests of the Crown, both personally and as a warrantor of the safety of economic transactions in the British state. King Edward exerted a great deal of influence over public officials, so the courts were likely to adopt any legislation that he wanted. What the new law of theft did, enforced by the courts, was to make taking property without consent of the owner a felony so that guilty parties were subject to severe penalties. During the centuries following the carrier's case, laws of theft were expanded to the point that the taking of money or property by cashiers and clerks eventually became illegal (called embezzlement), as did the receiving of stolen property.

The law is a tool that powerful groups can use to give themselves superior moral as well as coercive power in their conflicts with others (Chambliss & Seidman, 1982; Norton, 2014). Law is symbolic: It sets the broad parameters of correct and incorrect ways of acting in a society. Whether the law is actually followed is less important than the fact that practically everybody knows it is *supposed* to be followed. Law is also instrumental: It encourages people to follow the rules under the threat of unpleasant penalties. The law of theft that was created in 1473 in Britain was a concession to powerful interests. It gave influential individuals who felt victimized a way to protect themselves from the trespasses of others. It also provided a new understanding about proper and improper ways of doing business. Merchants' interests were protected and reinforced, while the interests and self-serving behaviors of the carriers were singled out for control and correction.

The carrier's case suggests that anything could be made illegal—and the new rules and sanctions could be justified as customary and reasonable—if the groups that create and enforce laws want this to happen. A corollary is that nothing will be illegal unless groups of people with sufficient resources are willing to take the time and trouble to criminalize those things that they do not like. (At times, the poor or powerless can work together to advance their interests and influence what kind of laws and judicial routines are implemented [Routledge & Cumbers, 2009].) Social factors and cultural dynamics are the principal elements that account for what is defined as right and wrong, legal or illegal, at a given time and place. In this sense, rule creators are responsible for creating deviance and crime through the rules and laws that they make and enforce to advance their own social interests (Palmer, 2013).

White-Collar Crime and Elite Deviance

White-Collar Crime, Social Organization, and Differential Association

The American Sociological Society (ASS) held its thirty-fourth annual meeting jointly with the American Economic Society's (AES) fifty-second meeting in December 1939 in Philadelphia. The president of the AES, Jacob Viner (1940), addressed the audience first, talking about the relationship between public policy and economic doctrine. After he finished, Edwin Hardin Sutherland (1883–1950), the president-elect of the ASS, advanced to the podium and spoke about white-collar crime. (In 1959, the organization changed its name to the American Sociological *Association*, because it had become fashionable to use initialisms for professional organizations, and "ASA" seemed to its members to make a much better one.) Sutherland (1940) defined *white-collar crime* as any crime committed by a person or persons of respectability and high social status in the context of professional activities, occupations, or jobs. This included crooked practices in professions, businesses, corporations, and even politics. An "enduring legacy" of Sutherland is that he showed that organizational dynamics and culture in a legitimate company can create crime among its workers (Lilly, Cullen, & Ball, 2015).

Sutherland (1940) traced the causes of white-collar crime to the structure of a society. Differential social organization and differential association create a situation in which some people encounter group supports and the values, norms, motives, rationalizations, techniques, and definitions that make crime more likely. Sutherland believed that the demands of a business organization can create strong in-group loyalties that may lead to an indifference to the demands of legal or moral norms. This, in turn, can lead to an indifference to the interests or needs of outside groups, such as the public, customers, or other business organizations. A study of female involvement in white-collar crime indicates that women's opportunities to commit crimes in the corporate world are different from men's, which meant in this study that female executives played more of a subsidiary role in the commission of corporate crime. They were less responsible for planning the crimes and carrying them out, deriving fewer financial rewards from them than their male counterparts (Steffensmeier, Schwartz, & Roche, 2013).

The message of Sutherland's address was clear to his audience: White-collar crime is real crime, it causes tremendous destruction, the perpetrators have a wanton disregard for the consequences of their actions, and the victims are unaware of the severity of the damage it has caused them. White-collar crime rips the fabric of society, Sutherland believed, and its perpetrators deserve both scorn and punishment. More than scientific interest prompted his concern with white-collar crime. He was outraged by the egregious acts of corporate representatives, and his sense of social decency was offended (Green, 1997). White-collar crimes almost always result from the perpetrators' desire to increase their control of human events and reduce the economic uncertainties that they face (Schoepfer, Piquero, & Langton, 2014; Tittle, 1995).

Sutherland's own experiences in getting his ideas published support much of what he believed about the benefits of privilege and power (Geis & Goff, 1983). He had amassed a great deal of incriminating information about the collective and individual harms caused by some of the largest and most powerful companies on Earth. His writings about the predatory activities of these organizations were filled with the names and histories of the offending companies. However, his editors at Dryden Press balked at Sutherland's intention to describe the companies as criminal even though they had never been convicted of any crimes. The administrators at Indiana University in Bloomington, where Sutherland taught, were also made skittish by Sutherland's plan to reveal in writing the names of offending corporations. They apparently feared that donations from these companies might stop. Sutherland (1949) succumbed to the pressure and allowed his work to be published without the names of the offending companies. It was not until 1983 that a different publisher, Yale University Press, came out with an uncut version of Sutherland's book in which the names were finally revealed.

Many years after Sutherland's presidential address, Clinard and Quinney (1973) discerned two distinct types of crime covered by Sutherland's omnibus term: corporate and occupational. The crux of the distinction is who benefits from the antisocial activity. *Corporate criminal behavior* directly benefits an organization itself, even though agents of the corporation carry out the acts. *Occupational criminal behavior* is done by a person of respectability and high social status who is himself or herself the primary beneficiary. Even if the rule breaking takes place in a group setting, the deviant is acting primarily on his or her own to further his or her selfish interests. The organization is not responsible; in fact, the organization itself can be a victim (Belbot, 1995).

Organizational Crime, Corporate Skullduggery, and Political Racketeering

White-collar crime is not the prerogative of the corporate sector—it can be found in politics, the military, labor unions, medicine, law, churches, universities, and so on—so it may be wise to replace the words *corporate crime* with *organizational crime* (J. W. Coleman, 2006). We must also remember that organizations themselves do not operate in a social vacuum, and many instances of white-collar crime or elite deviance are made possible by supportive linkages between representatives of the corporate world and state functionaries (Kramer, Michalowski, & Kauzlarich, 2002). For example, at the end of the twentieth century, in Detroit, Michigan, 465 acres were cleared by the city to make space for a General Motors automobile plant to be built. This required the removal and relocation of more than 4,200 residents from an area informally known as "Poletown" (most of its residents were of Polish descent), along with the destruction and removal of the debris of 1,400 homes, 144 businesses, 2 schools, 1 hospital, and 16 churches. Without the linkages, both formal and informal, among the Detroit City Council, General Motors, the Roman Catholic Church, and the United Auto Workers, the plunder of Poletown would not have been possible (Wylie, 1989). Because the residents received no major institutional support, it was possible for their community to be taken from them.

In most of the white-collar crimes that have plagued us through the ages, the distinction between occupational and organizational crime has been irrelevant because *both* the organization and its employees have benefited from the ongoing deviances (Roy, 1997). These violations of norms help the organization and its employees compete in a system where survival is never guaranteed and where objective indicators of personal and professional success are few and far between. Large corporations have become both the sites of acts of major rule breaking and the instruments used to carry them out (Tillman & Pontell, 1995).

The text of Sutherland's (1940) speech shows that he believed that politicians presented a lesser threat than representatives of the business world. Would he still think that way if he were alive today? It is hard to be at all familiar with political scandals and not have a suspicion that far too many politicians view the government as their own private cash cow that can be milked whenever the need arises. If there is a difference between political rackets and other kinds of trespass, it is to be found in opportunity structures, levels of accountability, and organizational supports, not in the greater morality or integrity of politicians as compared to other kinds of crooks. In 2014, Transparency International rated 175 countries' or territories' level of public corruption. The country ranked as least corrupt—rankings are like golf scores in that the lower the score, the cleaner and less corrupt the country is considered to be—was Denmark; the countries ranked as most corrupt were Somalia and North Korea. The United States was ranked at position 17. Public opinion about U.S. corruption registered a 20-point increase from 2006 to 2013: Results showed 59% of respondents in 2006 believed governmental corruption was "widespread," which increased to 79% in 2013.

American political life is replete with corruption, duplicity, and excessive self-interest. An arrogance of power and a shield of elitist invisibility can work together to allow destructive acts to flourish, undefined and unchecked. (Gross, 1996; Rosoff, Pontell, & Tillman, 2004). The great irony in the study of deviance—no surprise to relativists—is that some individuals can cause great harm without being viewed as harmful individuals. The structure of relations in political organizations blurs responsibility, and it is difficult to know who did what. Top officials deny responsibility by claiming that they had no knowledge of how things were being implemented, and low-level employees deny responsibility by claiming that they were following orders. If blame is assessed, it is usually placed on this individual or that, not on organizational structure (Cavender, Jurik, & Cohen, 1993).

Some politicians are guilty of campaign corruption and the illegal raising of funds to run them, lying, indifference to the needs of voters, conceit, cronyism, ignorance, and mismanagement of the governmental apparatus (Franken, 2003). Their greatest sins may be their waste of valuable resources and their taking and squandering (with the full protection of the law) of other people's belongings. Almost every politician tries to reward certain constituents by throwing special projects their way (called "pork"). This practice is rampant and almost wholly unaccountable, an example of stealing without stigma. Politicians take our money from us, money we may very well not wish to give up, and they then use it in ways over which we have little to no control. How is this any different from the depredations of a garden-variety thief? If a difference can be found between pork and theft, it is primarily in who has the power to say what is legal and what is not.

Sutherland (1940) claimed in his presidential address that the "inventive geniuses" for many kinds of white-collar crime are attorneys (p. 11). If only he could see us now, he would realize how prophetic his words have turned out to be. Without the assistance of lawyers who know how to use legal procedures to benefit their clients, it is unlikely that the wealthy would have fared as well as they have (Lauderdale & Cruit, 1993). Attorneys make it possible for some people to take other people's belongings with little or no accountability (Nader & Smith, 1996).

Sutherland (1945) concluded that white-collar crooks are not viewed as real criminals by the general public or even by themselves. They may have done something technically illegal, but they do not believe that they are real criminals (Conklin, 1977). Even if corporate representatives are charged with a crime, their resources make it easier for them to rebuke the charges against them (Sharkey, 2014). A study of defendants charged with bribery in Swedish courts showed that these individuals attempted to make themselves look less blameworthy by constructing narratives that claimed they were not culpable because everyone in their same situation was breaking the law too. They insisted that they were highly moral people despite their trespasses (Jacobsson, 2012). White-collar offenders both excuse and justify their crimes by offering accounts that portray themselves as more sinned against than sinning by too-powerful and unsympathetic politicians or economic competitors. They believe it was permissible for them to have broken the law because of what they saw as the treachery of others (Azarian & Alalehto, 2014). Unsurprisingly, corporate representatives who break the law do all they can to keep themselves free from punishment for their wrongdoings (Sutherland, 1945).

Money, hype, and monotonous repetition are used to perpetuate a false image that corporations face a barrage of frivolous lawsuits and pay huge and undeserved fines. The truth is that corporations are *not* the target of a flood of lawsuits from consumers. If an increase in lawsuits against businesses does exist, it is due to businesses suing other businesses, a form of litigation that will undoubtedly continue. Juries are far from antibusiness, and they award punitive damages to an injured citizen only if it is clear that a corporation acted with glaring disregard for the consequences of its actions (Nader & Smith, 1996).

As Nader and Smith (1996) tell it, in 1992, Stella Liebeck, age 79, was a front-seat passenger in her grandson's car when they pulled into a McDonald's drive-up window in Albuquerque, New Mexico, so that Ms. Liebeck could order coffee. Once it was served, she tried to remove the lid from the cup to add cream and sugar—the vehicle was motionless—and the entire contents spilled on her lap. She experienced third-degree burns on her thighs, groin, and buttocks, and she was permanently scarred on 16% of her body. These injuries were serious, and it took more than 2 years for her to recover fully. Ms. Liebeck wanted some compensation for her emotional ordeal, some help with her medical bills, and some recognition by McDonald's of the dangers lurking in those cups of coffee for other unsuspecting customers. However, when she appealed to restaurant executives for help, they were unmoved by her pain and suffering. They refused to pay anything close to what her operations had cost (about $20,000). All they did was offer Ms. Liebeck $800. In desperation, she hired a lawyer, and a lawsuit was filed.

At the trial, at least initially, Ms. Liebeck faced a skeptical jury. Its members believed that a lawsuit over a cup of coffee was a waste of their time, being both frivolous and malicious. They certainly had no discernible animosity toward McDonald's. However, as the details of the case unfolded in the week-long trial, McDonald's reputation was tarnished. Testimony was introduced that corporate headquarters required the temperature of the coffee to be maintained at between 180 and 190 degrees Fahrenheit to make it taste better for longer periods. (Many other restaurants keep the temperature of their coffee at 160 degrees.) At this high temperature, severe burning and tissue destruction occur within seconds in the case of a spill. Making matters worse was the quality of the McDonald's cup. It has exceptional insulating properties, so coffee drinkers are unable to appreciate just how hot their coffee really is until they start drinking it (or spill it on themselves or on someone else). The jury concluded that McDonald's did keep the temperature of the coffee much too high for human consumption and that customers were given insufficient warnings about the potential dangers. The jury settled on compensatory damages of $200,000, which it then reduced to $160,000 because it believed Ms. Liebeck had to bear some of the responsibility for spilling the coffee on herself.

The jury awarded an additional $2.7 million in punitive damages to Ms. Liebeck. Why? The answer is simple: McDonald's had shown a wanton disregard for the well-being of its customers. It came to light that 700 other people had experienced a fate similar to Ms. Liebeck's between 1982 and 1992; this included some children who had been severely burned in accidents involving the too-hot coffee when adults accidentally knocked cups over or dropped them, and the contents spilled on the youngsters. Executives of the restaurant chain believed that no compelling reason existed to turn down the heat because, considering all the coffee that their restaurant chain served, 700 burns were insignificant to them. The jury concluded that anyone who ordered a cup of McDonald's too-hot coffee was a potential burn victim. The jury's principal objective was to get McDonald's attention and force its executives to reduce the temperature of the coffee. The jury came up with the $2.7 million figure because that is about how much McDonald's made from 2 days of selling coffee worldwide. The judge decided that the punitive damages were too high, so he reduced them to $480,000, three times greater than the compensatory damages. McDonald's had intended to appeal the $640,000 award, but it finally agreed to settle for an undisclosed amount if the details of the arrangement were kept silent forever by Ms. Liebeck and her attorney. (Ms. Liebeck died in 2004, but she and her story live on in the 2011 movie titled *Hot Coffee*.)

The Relativity of Terrorism

One Nation's Terrorist . . .

Terrorism is widely viewed as loathsome behavior—practically by definition, to call something terrorism is to condemn it as the ultimate evil—but disagreement still exists over the exact meaning of the term and to which specific acts or individuals the label is most appropriately applied (Feniger & Yuchtman-Yaar, 2010). The consensus view is that if the targets of violence are selected randomly and are nonmilitary, civilian targets, to generate fear in an entire population, it qualifies as "terrorism" (Jenkins, 2003). Though this definition is valuable, allowing some precision in regard to classifying acts of terrorism, the terms *terrorist* and *terrorism* do have a measure of relativity, representing both a socially constructed and a socially contested terrain (Stampnitsky, 2013). What looks like terrorism to one nation (or group or individual) may look like freedom fighting or martyrdom to some other nation (or group or individual). About 2 weeks after the attacks on September 11, 2001, on the United States, fans at a European Cup soccer game in Athens, Greece, were asked to observe a minute of silence for the victims. Instead, they jeered the United States and even tried to burn a U.S. flag (Nacos, 2007). Definitions of terrorism and terrorist, as well as understandings about terrorism, are not universal.

Some organizations (e.g., the British Broadcasting Company) avoid use of the term *terrorist* or *terrorism* to describe any individual or group, no matter how violent or savage the actions (Jenkins, 2003). We do not have to adopt this extreme view. Rather, we can acknowledge that reasonable people agree that certain violent incidents qualify as terrorism, while also conceding that disagreement exists over what terrorism is and to what it refers. Perceptions of the legitimacy of some political act go hand in hand with perceptions of how much terrorism it represents.

The word *terrorism* is often used by some governments to describe the actions of nations they do not like, but not to describe what seem to be similar actions of nations they *do* like (Chomsky, 1988; Ross, 2013). During the 1980s, President Ronald Reagan and members of his administration fully supported the activities of "insurgents" (or Contras) in Nicaragua, who were fighting to overthrow the Sandinista government of Daniel Ortega. Reagan compared the Contras to the U.S. Founding Fathers, opining that if they were, in fact, counterrevolutionaries, then so was he. This praise was curious because the Contras were responsible for acts of brutal violence against civilians—men, women, and children—in order to pressure their government (Peace, 2012). According to the consensus view of terrorism and terrorist, the Contras were terrorists, but they were not viewed that way (at least officially) by key players in the Reagan administration, including Reagan himself.

A study by Beck and Miner (2013) of who gets designated a terrorist by agents in the United States, the United Kingdom, and the European Union clarifies some of what is involved in defining terrorism. The chance of being labeled a terrorist organization is not dependent exclusively on the level of violent activity as measured by the number of attacks, the number of victims, or their recency. Islamic organizations, especially those that have attacked planes or airports, are the ones most likely to be called terrorist organizations. Both the United Kingdom and the European Union are significantly more likely to designate a group as terrorist when the United States has already done so. Suicide bombings had no significant influence on the likelihood of being labeled a terrorist prior to the attacks of September 11, 2001, but they did have a significant and positive influence after that. Increasing attention is now paid to Islamic militancy to the neglect of other forms of terrorism—a bias, because Islamic groups neither carry out a majority of the worldwide attacks nor harm a majority of the victims of terrorism.

Prejudice and discrimination against Muslims, especially those from the Middle East, have become more frequent and blatant with the passage of time (Goode, 2015; Helbling, 2014). Arab Muslim males are increasingly viewed as a security threat and Arab Muslim women as a cultural threat (Cainkar, 2009). Hate crimes against Muslims and Arabs went up following the attacks of 9/11, while hate crimes against other racial/ethnic minorities went down. Some Americans wrongly concluded that Islam had declared war on the United States, which justified in their own minds the commission of hate crimes against Muslims (Disha, Cavendish, & King, 2011; Santoro & Azab, 2015).

The "war on terror" provides an opportunity for authorities to instruct the U.S. public to be continually afraid *and* perpetually prepared for some future terrorist attack on U.S. soil (Blain, 2012). What this does is give U.S. citizens the responsibility for protecting themselves from future attacks amid a climate of surveillance and suspicion (T. Monahan, 2010). Terrorism may be uniquely susceptible to this form of distortion and exaggeration because the agencies that we rely on to provide valid and reliable information about terrorism have many reasons to not want to divulge all that they know (Jenkins, 2003). Sometimes, this involves powerful groups taking advantage of terrorist attacks against themselves or their home countries so that it will make any subsequent violent retaliations seem more justified, reasonable, and necessary (Kelman & Hamilton, 1989). In fact, this is what happened in 2011. In response to widespread protests in the Middle East against ruthless dictators and corrupt tyrants, the Syrian leader Bashar Assad found his power slipping. In response, he released many of the terrorists he had imprisoned, expecting—in fact, hoping— that they would join the fight *against* him. When they did, it served as a rationale for him to ruthlessly suppress dissent and political protest, which he justified as the only way he could reasonably deal with the terrorist threat.

Fact and Fancy

It is difficult to separate fact from fancy in regard to what happened during the terrorist attacks on the World Trade Center and the U.S. Pentagon on September 11, 2001 (Bonn, 2010). In the days following the attacks, new facts became harder to find, so reporters and journalists scrambled to find stories that regaled audiences with accounts that exaggerated the tragedy and pathos of events that were already filled with enough tragedy and pathos (B. A. Monahan, 2010).

The 9/11 events were not just attacks on Americans and America. They were organized and deliberate assaults on a constellation of U.S. cultural icons (i.e., the World Trade Center as the embodiment of business and consumption; the Pentagon as the embodiment of the military; and, had the plane forced down in Pennsylvania reached its probable target, the White House, as the embodiment of U.S. politics) (Ritzer, 2006). Although the United States is no stranger to terrorist attacks (Chomsky, 1988; Howard & Forest, 2008; Stritzke, Lewandowsky, Denemark, Clare, & Morgan, 2009), the enormity of the damage of the September 11 attacks was too much for most Americans to comprehend; certainly it was too much for them to forgive. The attacks seemed to be unprovoked and unprincipled, the taking of innocent life by a crazed terrorist group. While this is true, it is not the whole truth, and more is involved in what happened than meets the eye.

A study of the September 11 attacks by Ahmed (2002) suggests that "significant elements" in the U.S. government, the military, and the intelligence community had received "extensive" warnings about them. According to Ahmed, rather than moving vigorously to either stop the attacks or to lessen their damage, these significant elements remained silent, expecting to benefit from what happened. The attacks were ultimately used to justify an invasion of Afghanistan and Iraq, which was being planned in advance of September 11, in order to obtain strategic and economic advantages in the region. Although reasonable people can disagree over who or what was really responsible for the attacks of September 11, few people can disagree that they came at a good time for the Bush administration. They made it possible for George W. Bush's presidency to end the crisis of legitimacy that had threatened to topple it and to enter the world stage with a new sense of purpose and confidence.

A few things seem true about 9/11 that demand a measure of caution in accepting the official view that the attacks came out of nowhere. First, U.S. intelligence agencies apparently knew in advance that an attack from the air on key U.S. targets was likely; they even had a fairly good idea about when it would occur.

> It is a fact that the American intelligence community received multiple authoritative warnings, both general and specific, of a terrorist attack on the U.S. using civilian airliners as bombs, targeting key buildings located in the nation's capital and New York City, and likely to occur around early to mid-September. (Ahmed, 2002, p. 290)

On July 10, 2001, an FBI agent (Kenneth Williams) sent a message to FBI headquarters to alert his superiors that Middle Eastern students were enrolled in an Arizona flight school. He feared that al-Qaeda operatives could possibly be trying to infiltrate the U.S. aviation system. However, his warnings were ignored (Franken, 2003), even though by late June of that year, high-ranking officials in the Bush administration (e.g., Richard Clarke) and at the CIA (e.g., George Tenet) were certain that terrorist attacks were imminent (Clarke, 2004).

Second, it is very difficult to understand why standard operating procedures fell apart on September 11, allowing the attacks on the World Trade Center and the Pentagon to reach their deadly conclusion. Air traffic controllers followed the flights of the hijacked airliners from start to finish. They were certain that a hijacking had occurred by 8:20 AM, a full 15 minutes *before* the first plane (Flight 11) slammed into the North Tower of the World

Trade Center, 43 minutes before the second plane (Flight 175) slammed into the South Tower, and 80 minutes before the third plane (Flight 77) hit the Pentagon (Ahmed, 2002).

It seems incredible that fighter planes were not dispatched in time to intercept the hijacked planes and, if necessary, shoot them from the sky. Although presidential approval is required to shoot down a civilian aircraft, it is *not* required to scramble jets to intercept one. An F-15 Strike Eagle could have left McGuire Air Force Base in New Jersey and reached the World Trade Center in less than 3 minutes. Yet this did not happen. Why were no planes dispatched until 95 minutes *after* clear evidence existed that a hijacking of commercial airlines was in progress and only after destruction of the World Trade Center and a section of the Pentagon had already occurred?

The sluggish response of the U.S. Air Force to the terrorist attacks, in violation of standard operating procedures of the FAA and 95 minutes too late, was apparently due to decisions by the president and high-ranking members of his cabinet (Ahmed, 2002). This does *not* mean that U.S. officials staged the attacks or that hijackers were paid in U.S. dollars and told what to do by U.S. officials. This also does not mean that members of the Bush administration knew just how costly the attacks would be but were willing to sacrifice both lives and property to garner political capital. What it *does* mean—if Ahmed is right—is that "significant elements" in the United States must bear some responsibility for what happened on September 11 and its aftermath.

Faulty Intelligence

The organizations that were entrusted to protect U.S. citizens did not do so (National Commission on Terrorist Attacks, 2004). They failed to get information to the right place at the right time, and they failed to act more courageously to eliminate, or at least reduce, the threat of a terrorist attack (Clarke, 2004). The war on terror has made it possible to manage citizen complaints about U.S. foreign and domestic policies, while it has allowed a crackdown on civil rights, dissent, and free speech. The attacks of September 11 made it much easier for the Bush administration to justify the U.S. invasion of Iraq. The specter of international terrorists and the al-Qaeda network will continue to offer "significant elements" in the United States a golden opportunity to expand into other nations and extend U.S. military, political, and economic influence abroad. The war on terror is being used to justify intervention into regions of strategic and economic importance to the United States and to consolidate U.S. hegemony over them. By keeping the bona fide horrors of 9/11 and the need for increased security always in the public eye, "significant elements" in the United States are likely to reap a cornucopia of rewards in the years ahead.

When it came to foreign policy, the distinguishing feature of the presidency of George W. Bush was not so much what he would do as whom he would appoint to his war cabinet. His foreign policy advisors adopted a name for themselves, the Vulcans, based on the name of the Roman god of fire, metalwork, and the forge. This word embodied the precise image that Bush's advisors wanted to project: power, durability, and toughness (Mann, 2004). The most significant foreign policy decision of the Bush administration was the decision to invade Iraq in 2003. It resonated so well with the Vulcans' view of global events that it is unlikely it could have been averted. Members of this war cabinet had great respect for U.S. military power, believing that the United States personified what is good and right in global politics. They remained confident that America would prevail quickly and firmly in Iraq without outside help or interference.

The Vulcans' political astuteness in capitalizing on 9/11 was matched only by their political blindness in going to war in Iraq, using excessive means to accomplish limited ends. The true claim that a legitimate security threat to the United States—its interests and its values—is posed by terrorism was based on a simpleminded (and ultimately counterproductive) strategy. Its core premise was that to stop the spread of Middle Eastern terrorism, it required a U.S. military presence that would transform the entire social fabric of the Middle East (Mann, 2004). The U.S. intervention in Iraq was, according to Abu-Lughod (2010), "extraordinarily self-serving and arrogant" (p. 213). The U.S. media's treatment of Iraq and its people was distorted and simplistic because it did little more than parrot the official view that the war in Iraq was a fight to bring freedom and democracy to a troubled land, using terms that lack universally accepted meanings. One of the U.S. media's principal failures has been its disinclination to do stories about the richness of Iraqi society, the intelligence and humanity of the Iraqi people, and the destructiveness caused in the region by U.S. policies and programs.

The terrorist attacks of 9/11 should have made it clear to everyone that the United States needed to mobilize its vast resources to eliminate al-Qaeda, help strengthen any nation that was threatened by radical Islamic terrorists, and reduce as much as possible U.S. domestic vulnerabilities to further terrorist attacks (Clarke, 2004). Instead of using the apparatus of government and the full resources of the United States to deal with the terrorist threat in a reasoned and effective way, President George W. Bush (and his advisors) pursued a different strategy. Clarke succinctly describes what it was:

> September 11 erased memories of the unique process whereby George Bush had been selected as President a few months earlier. Now, as he stood with an arm around a New York fireman promising to get those who had destroyed the World Trade Center, he was every American's President. His polls soared. He had a unique opportunity to unite America, to bring the United States together with allies around the world to fight terrorism and hate, to eliminate al Qaeda, to eliminate our vulnerabilities, and to strengthen important nations threatened by radicalism. He did none of those things. He invaded Iraq. (p. 286)

The decision to wage war in Iraq, a country that had not sponsored much, if any, anti-U.S. terrorism, has arguably made the United States less safe and secure.

As our national debt increases to pay for the wars and continuing military/counterterrorist actions in the Middle East, so does the body count among both allies and enemies of the United States. U.S. credibility and status are both diminished. By invading Iraq initially, an oil-rich Arab nation that posed little threat to the United States, it made it practically impossible for other Arab nations to work alongside the United States to ferret out and eradicate the many legitimate terrorist threats that do exist (Feldkamp, 2014a). U.S. retaliation for 9/11 has not eliminated the threat of al-Qaeda, but it has increased Muslim contempt for the United States. Rather than acting like a superpower, the United States acted like a super-bully, ignoring or even criticizing policies and procedures that it would later need (Clarke, 2004). The United States has shown that it is fully capable of waging war in Iraq and removing ruthless dictators. What it has not done is show that it has the interests and abilities to construct something of enduring quality after it leaves.

Trying to control terrorism is much like trying to squeeze a balloon. Pressure applied in one place leads to an eruption somewhere else. As of this writing, the new player on the terrorist roster is the Islamic State of Iraq and Syria (or ISIS), which is also referred to by the names Islamic State of Levant (or ISIL, the name preferred by Barack Obama), Islamic State of Iraq and Greater Syria, or Islamic State of Iraq and al-Sham (al-Sham being the Arabic term for the geographical region including parts of southern Turkey, Syria Egypt, Lebanon, Israel, the Palestinian territories, and Jordan). Members of the terrorist organization now (as of this writing) call it the Islamic State, while critics and detractors, some of whom are prominent Muslims, prefer to call it the *un-Islamic* State because they think it is neither Muslim nor a state. Arab-speaking opponents of ISIS derisively refer to it simply as Daesh (meaning "one who crushes something underfoot" or "one who sows discord").

Regardless of which name is used, the faction's stated objective is to destroy all infidels and establish an Islamic state, or caliphate, wherever it can. ISIS was started in Iraq by a Jordanian radical named Abu Musab al-Zarqawi after the U.S. invasion of that country in 2003. It did not reach its current prominence until 2014 when al-Baghdadi, its current leader (as of this writing), declared its establishment and growing power in the Middle East. (Al-Zarqawi was killed in his hideaway in 2006 by U.S. smart bombs, and his two successors were killed in 2010.) A U.S. air strike in western Iraq in March 2015 seriously wounded al-Baghdadi, but not seriously enough to prevent him from leading.

Though the Islamic State did splinter from al-Qaeda, it is incorrect to view it as al-Qaeda's weaker partner or a jayvee team. The refusal or failure to recognize important differences between the two organizations makes it harder to understand global terrorism. The Islamic State grew out of the disorganization and chaos that was created by the U.S. occupation of Iraq and the continuing U.S. presence in the area (Wood, 2015). The Islamic State jihadists were able to occupy more and more parts of Iraq in 2014 not because they were a well-oiled fighting machine. It was principally because nobody they met really wanted to stop them. In place after place, they found civilians who were tired of the status quo and wanted to see some positive changes. The Islamic State fighters were embraced as champions (Drehle, 2015). The Islamic State has been successful in places characterized by shifting social norms, bad rulers, and sparse lands whose only value is the oil under the ground (Morell, 2015).

If the main objective of terrorists is to terrorize (Ganor, 2014), the Islamic State has done this as well as any terrorist group in recent history. They have used crucifixions and beheadings to kill their enemies, as well as slavery and kidnappings to scare and intimidate them. These are not actions by crazy or crazed terrorists in desperate attempts to find meaning in their lives. On the contrary, these practices are consistent with strategies of war in the Koran and the narratives of Mohammed the Prophet (Wood, 2015). In fact, crucifixion is the only sanctioned punishment for enemies of Islam, and Islamic State fighters are convinced that they are warriors for a holy cause. If crucifixion is impossible, then beheadings, poisonings, burnings, starvation, or running over enemies with motor vehicles is acceptable.

ISIS fighters upped the bar again during the fall of 2015. On October 31, a bomb planted on board a Russian plane brought it down over the Sinai Peninsula, killing all 224 persons on board. About two weeks later (November 12), suicide bombings in Beirut killed 43 people and wounded more than 239 others, the deadliest attack there in 25 years. On November 13, a Friday night in Paris was turned into an evening of slaughter. Killings, suicide bombings, and the taking of hostages occurred in restaurants, on streets and boulevards, and at concert halls. When the smoke had cleared, 130 people were dead and over 350 more were injured, the deadliest attack on French soil since World War II.

Terrorism is also a business (Feldkamp, 2014b). Successful terrorist organizations must recruit new members and raise sufficient capital to finance their programs and propaganda. Simply put, their product is terror, and to be successful at manufacturing it requires the ability to be as scary and threatening as possible. This is why destroying artwork that is thousands of years old, while seeming to have no purpose, ranks alongside kidnappings, beheadings, and crucifixions for ISIS fighters in showing that they are a singular threat that must be taken seriously. Humiliation of enemies is an effective terrorist strategy because it shows the impotence of authorities to protect that which they hold so dear. This generates even greater terror in the civilian population, producing a bonanza of rewards for terrorist groups. The number one supporter of a U.S.-led invasion into the territories now held by the Islamic State is the Islamic State itself (Wood, 2015).

National Insecurity

National security has always been both a curse and a blessing for U.S. presidents. It reveals the tensions and opportunities that exist between political practicality and lofty idealism. Presidents from Woodrow Wilson to Jimmy Carter to George W. Bush and to Barack Obama have been defined in part by how successfully they spread democracy and human rights throughout the world. These men faced criticism from the left and the right, as well as from idealists and pragmatists. Barack Obama campaigned in 2008 as an anti-Bush candidate regarding foreign policy and national security, and the effort was not without success. After Bush's shoot-from-the-hip approach, Obama's more calculated, deliberative approach seemed to be a better option.

Richard Clarke, an expert on counterterrorism and cybersecurity under many U.S. presidents, met with Barack Obama on May 16, 2007, at a dilapidated apartment in northeast Washington, D.C., months before Obama would become the forty-fourth president of the United States (Klaidman, 2012). Clarke was drawn to Obama, believing he might be able to offer the kind of wisdom and inspired policy initiatives that had been lacking for so long in U.S. counterterrorism work. As Clarke listened to Obama's analysis of global events, he found that he agreed with him on every point. The strongest area of agreement was on how foolish it had been to invade Iraq and how much damage had been done to U.S. interests and reputation all across the world. However, Clarke was not sure that Obama had the grit and determination to be an effective leader in the war on terror. Could he understand that as president he would be fighting an implacable and resolute foe for whom the only option would be to capture or kill? Clarke was eventually convinced that Obama did indeed have the mettle to make the fight and would use both soft and hard power to craft a counterterrorism strategy that was both effective *and* restrained (Clarke, 2004).

President Obama has used force when he thinks it will accomplish something of value in the war against terrorism (though some of his critics would like to see him use more than he has). Early on the morning of May 2, 2011, under orders from the president, U.S. Navy SEALS charged the residence of Osama bin Laden, in Abbottabad, Pakistan, where the mastermind of the 9/11 attacks had been living with members of his family (three wives and a dozen of his children and grandchildren). The sky was moonless, and the electricity in the compound had been made inoperable by the men who hunted bin Laden. The total darkness made a tense and confusing situation even more so. Members of the SEAL team made their way from floor to floor, dispatching anyone who stood in their way. Their ascent required them to blast open one metal gate, but they were prepared to do whatever was necessary to reach bin Laden (Bergen, 2012).

Instead of going for the weapons he kept in his bedroom to stage his last stand (an AK-47 and a Makarov machine pistol), bin Laden opened a metal gate to his room and stuck his head out to gauge the progression of his pursuers. He was spotted by members of the SEAL team. Bin Laden ducked behind the metal door but, surprisingly, did not lock it (Bergen, 2012). Members of the SEAL team burst into bin Laden's bedroom after moving down a short hallway. Amal, bin Laden's 29-year-old wife, threw herself at the feet of her husband. She was shoved aside by the first SEAL in the room, and another SEAL shot her in the calf. Bin Laden, though he was unarmed and offering no resistance, was still viewed as a threat that had to be eliminated. He was killed quickly by two shots, one through his left eye socket and the other to his chest. (A book by Owen and Maurer [2012] offered a slightly different rendition of the killing of bin Laden. Owen, whose real name is Matt Bissonnette, was a member of the SEAL team that killed the terrorist leader. He claims that bin Laden was shot immediately when he stuck his head out of his bedroom. Owen and another member of the team then finished the job.)

Bin Laden's remains were transported to the U.S.S. *Carl Vinson,* an aircraft carrier anchored in the Arabian Sea. His corpse was prepared for burial, and it was dropped overboard so that no gravesite would exist to be honored by his admirers. In February 2012, the complex in which he had lived in Pakistan was razed, and the ground on which it once stood is now the site of cricket matches played by people in the region. Modest fines ($110) and 45-day prison sentences were assessed to bin Laden's three widows and two of his daughters. Whether the killing of bin Laden furthered U.S. interests is still an open question. Martyrs' importance and influence usually increase after their deaths, so bin Laden may still reap rewards in the days ahead (though he will not be alive to enjoy them). Bin Laden's death (as of this writing) has not precipitated significant retaliatory attacks by members of al-Qaeda against the United States, perhaps because of a lack of funds sufficient enough to make a large and impressive terrorist operation possible (Gonzalez, 2014). (In a 2015 essay by Hersh, he alleges that the official version of the killing of bin Laden is wrong on practically every point, representing a massive cover-up.)

Sense and Nonsense

The terrorist attacks of 9/11 offered the opportunity or necessity—it is sometimes hard to know which is the primary motive—to expand counter-terrorist activities, rules (e.g., USA Patriot Act), and agencies (e.g., Department of Homeland Security). The attacks of 2001 were not the first time terrorists had staged an assault on the United States on U.S. soil (an attack on the World Trade Center in 1993 killed 7 and injured 103), but 9/11 was a watershed event. U.S. responses to the attacks showed that at least two styles of counterterrorist activities exist. One is a legalistic, criminal justice approach, which remains faithful to due process and defendants' rights, civil liberties, and individual freedoms, even while it acknowledges the distinctive nature of international terrorism. The second type of counterterrorism is militaristic, waging war against terrorists with little concern for legal restrictions, due process, or civil rights of suspected terrorists (Deflem, 2010). During the George W. Bush years, militaristic counterterrorism was the primary strategy (embodied in Bush's taunt to terrorists, "Bring it on"). In some respects, Barack Obama has moved closer to embracing a law-enforcement counterterrorism, but in other respects, such as the authorization of the killing of Osama bin Laden or the use of air strikes in the war on terror, he has not. Though Americans do voice strong support for human rights and due process, when faced with the threat of further terrorist attacks, most are fully prepared to look the other way when it comes to counterterrorist activities, even if they are both inhumane and illegal (Brooks & Manza, 2013).

It seems clear that a militaristic, Wild West approach to international terrorism is doomed to failure. It may accomplish the short-term goal of vengeance and seem to be just deserts to those wronged by an egregious act, but it is counterproductive in the long run if a safe, secure, sane world is our objective. Not only does it fail to eliminate terrorist organizations, but it also generates greater resistance and the counterviolence that this strategy often precipitates (Mullins & Young, 2012). In addition, it leads to the United States being viewed as an outlier nation by other countries in the world

(Deflem, 2010). Bush capitalized on the confusion caused by 9/11 and the anger over it to encourage U.S. military intervention in Iraq. He portrayed our intervention as not only necessary, but heroic, designed to rescue Iraqis from a toxic leader as well as protect them from themselves because they lived in a violent, undemocratic land (Messerschmidt, 2010). Bush's arrogance and ethnocentrism alienated both friends and foes alike.

One of the more embarrassing and damaging pieces of information to emerge from the war in Iraq has been evidence of U.S. torture and other human rights violations of Iraqis at Abu Ghraib prison. This facility, located about 20 miles west of Baghdad, started receiving detainees in 2003. Photographic evidence and two visits to the prison by the International Committee of the Red Cross documented the use of forced nudity of prisoners, sensory overloads, shackles, sleep deprivation, and engineered stress to break prisoners' wills in order to obtain confessions. Photographs provided (or seemed to) clear evidence of torture being administered by U.S. military personnel. They suggested an attitude of smugness, or at least indifference, among the soldiers as they participated in acts of brutality and cruelty that euphemisms such as "coercive interrogations," "permissible duress," or "stress positions" could no longer mask (Carrabine, 2011).

The U.S. military's initial response to accusations that soldiers were torturing detainees was filled with denials. When these denials were no longer credible due to press investigations and formal hearings that showed that widespread abuse had occurred in Iraq (and Afghanistan), the denials stopped. However, military spokespersons had little interest in coming clean and telling the whole and unvarnished truth about the role of torture in the war on terror. They worked, instead, to make the abuses of prisoners look cleaner, more reasonable, and more necessary than they probably were, making it more likely that as a political issue, "prisoner abuse" would go away as quickly as possible (Rosso, 2011). In congressional hearings on torture from 2007 to 2008, both supporters and critics of waterboarding agreed that ferocious use of state violence was un-American. Where they parted company was that supporters of waterboarding defined it publicly as a rational way (i.e., clinical and dispassionate) to wage war on terror when other strategies have been ineffective, and opponents defined it publicly as both cruel and ineffective (Rosso, 2014).

The Senate Select Committee on Intelligence's (2014) final report was highly critical of CIA activities in the detention and interrogation of detainees in CIA-controlled facilities in the years after the 9/11 terrorist attacks. The report concluded that the CIA's practices were improper, abusive, illegal, and inconsistent with American values. They were described by Senator Dianne Feinstein, chair of the committee, as cruel, inhuman, and degrading (p. 4). The evidence, she declared, for reaching this dismal assessment was overwhelming and incontrovertible. The report faulted the CIA—its operatives and contractors—for a litany of abuses and mistakes, as well as for lies galore about what was done to prisoners and for exaggerations of the benefits for national security that came from these practices. The principal conclusion of the report was that not only were the techniques excessive and inhumane, but they also were an ineffective way to get accurate information and cooperation from the detainees. When a carrot might have been far more effective, a rather large and painful stick was used. In some instances, the wrong people had been detained and subjected to horrific treatments to extract information that they never could have provided because, quite simply, they did not know it. Interrogators and torturers used a variety of techniques to extract information such as verbal abuse, beatings, sleep deprivation, physical duress (chaining prisoners to walls in stress positions), waterboardings, dousings in frigid water, walling (being thrown against a flexible wall), and rectal rehydration (where pureed food was rectally administered to inmates).

The war on terror, now a permanent feature of the global landscape, has cemented the alliances between the private sector and the public war-making apparatus of the United States (Rothe, 2009). Companies (such as Halliburton) have used the war in Iraq as an opportunity for systematic and significant overcharging for services and supplies. Under rules instituted by the George W. Bush administration, Halliburton was able to obtain no-bid contracts, even when it had a history of violating environmental, labor relation, and trade laws (p. 441). This allowed monumental war profiteering. The over-costs, overcharges, failure to provide goods and services that were charged and paid for, and kickback profits resulted principally from the cozy relationship between a handful of politicians and corporate boosters. This created the opportunity for private corporations to amass substantial profits in a war-torn nation. Amid all the death, injury, misery, stupidity, and waste found in the U.S. war with Iraq, Halliburton was still able to make a tidy profit. By the end of 2006, this energy giant had earned $20 billion in revenues since the war's start (Klein, 2007). A report in 2013 asserted that KBR (Kellogg, Brown, and Root), a subsidiary of Halliburton, made $39.5 billion from 2003 to 2013 from the war in Iraq (Fifield, 2013).

Privilege, Power, and Penalties

Sutherland's (1940, 1945, 1949, 1983) study of white-collar crime showed that its perpetrators were able to avoid the stigma and punishment accorded lesser offenders. The legal status of white-collar crime is ambiguous, and laws may be difficult to apply to the wrongdoings of the powerful (Gerber & Weeks, 1992). Irrespective of its moral or ethical status, behavior is illegal only if laws exist to criminalize it. Laws are crafted by lawmakers, and lawmakers can be influenced in all kinds of ways by powerful people who do what they can to control the content of law and how it applies to them (Livingston, 1996).

The arrogance of power can easily prompt individuals to believe that laws are inapplicable to them. This heightened sense of importance and invincibility can motivate and rationalize many disreputable activities. Richard Nixon, forced from the office of President of the United States for his role in the Watergate scandal, claimed—and probably believed—that whatever the president did, no matter how unsavory, was not against the law. Key players in the Iran–Contra scandal of the Reagan era—in which arms were sold to Iran, and monies from the sale were used to aid the Contras in Nicaragua—assumed that everything they did was legal.

> Organizations have their own versions of events and respond to accusations of deviance with accusations and assertions of their own. In the exchange of claims and counterclaims, whether an organizational action actually comes to be seen as deviant is fundamentally a matter of definition. (Ermann & Lundman, 2002, p. 27)

The confusion created by disputes over the legal status of this act or that act has great benefits for white-collar offenders, who capitalize on the ambiguity and turn it to their own ends. In this project, they are often able to take advantage of organizational resources to create and disseminate ideas that are the most beneficial to them and their interests.

On August 9, 2014, in the township of Ferguson, Missouri, on a section of Canfield Drive, Michael Brown, an unarmed African American teenager (Brown was 18), was shot dead by a white police officer named Darren Wilson. Some individuals concluded the officer was the aggressor; others concluded that the teenager had been both threatening and sufficiently defiant to the officer's commands that Brown was the one ultimately responsible for the officer's use of lethal violence. One question was whether the police officer racially profiled the suspect, a fundamental but controversial practice in police agencies in much of the country (Barkan & Bryjak, 2014). The FBI found no evidence that the officer had broken any criminal laws or was guilty of any civil rights violations, and the officer was neither indicted by a grand jury nor charged with any crimes by the U.S. Attorney General.

The killing and its aftermath, along with all the official investigations and conclusions about the killing of Brown, show that how deviance is to be understood and dealt with cannot be separated from organizational resources and interests. Supporters and critics of any particular police officer, any particular police action, or any particular police force hold different views of how "policeable" (i.e., amenable to successful police intervention and control) some event actually is (Roussell & Gascón, 2014). If Michael Brown had killed the officer or if Brown had been slain in a shoot-out with police or by a random drive-by shooting, the social construction of this event would have been very different. Interests and resources work together in systems of group conflict to decide what happened, what kind of penalties ought to be assessed, to whom they should be assessed, and exactly who ought to be responsible for assessing them. (Wilson no longer works as a police officer. He submitted a letter of resignation shortly after his grand jury testimony. He insists that he believes he acted properly in the events surrounding the killing of Brown.)

It is more difficult to apply sanctions to deviants who have organizational resources at their disposal that they can use to challenge others' definitions of them, making the rules seem less clear than they might otherwise be and negative sanctions less warranted. Unlike physicians, college professors, accountants, librarians, and most other occupational groups that never have to use force in their working lives, police officers must use it all the time. "Few people question the need for police to use necessary force in the performance of their duty, as many individuals they encounter will resist arrest, run from the officers, attack them, and on occasion, attempt to kill them" (Barkan & Bryjak, 2014, p. 222). Thus, the question is not whether force should be used by police but when, how much, and for what reasons. If force is necessary, was the minimum amount used to accomplish the job? Did more peaceful ways exist to accomplish the same ends? Some police violence is justified and justifiable, and some is not (e.g., the beating of Rodney King in 1991).

The fact that police must use force, sometimes of the lethal kind, on their jobs, coupled with their access to organizational resources and cultural legitimations, means that police can usually justify and explain away much of the violence they use. This usually works unless the violence is excessive and evidence exists that the officer (or officers) used force disproportionate to the situation at hand. This seems to be what happened in 2015 when Officer Michael Slager, of North Charleston, South Carolina, gunned down Walter Scott during what started as a routine traffic stop. As Scott tried to flee the officer, Slager shot him several times in the back. One of the main reasons for police violence is *contempt of cop*, where suspects show disrespect for both the badge and the officer(s) and are violently "corrected" for their insolence (Chevigny, 1995). (This does not seem to have been the motive for the killing of Scott, as a video taken by a concerned citizen shows.

It looks less like contempt of cop than a contemptible killing *by* a cop.) It is rare for official investigations to find no justification for the use of force by police officers, and police officers usually receive the benefit of the doubt, fairly or not, when their dealings with citizens erupt in violence, and citizens are injured or killed. (As of this writing, Slager has been indicted, but the case has not yet been resolved.)

Even when laws are firmly in place and no dispute exists that they were broken, it may still be difficult to detect white-collar crimes, arrest and convict white-collar criminals, and then hold the organizations for which they work accountable. Because victims may be unaware that they have been intentionally hurt by some misdeed, or because an offending corporation has neither a body to kick nor a soul to damn, it is more difficult to apply to white-collar misdeeds the same legal procedures and penalties that were invented to cover one-on-one harms of individuals (Belbot, 1995). The nature of law, the size and power of the corporation, the privileged status of white-collar offenders, and the diffuse nature of white-collar victimizations all mean that penalties for white-collar crime are likely to be relatively painless and ineffective (Sutherland, 1945). What seem to be huge fines of corporations for misdeeds are seldom large enough to deter their illegal behavior (J. W. Coleman, 2006). A fine of $3 million to a company like McDonald's, even if it had been paid, would have been little more than a slap on the wrist.

It would be an error to conclude that privileged and powerful people *always* fare better in a court of law than do the less powerful or prosperous. What is true, however, is that legal penalties are relative, being responsive to factors other than the degree of injury produced by some untoward act. This relativity can produce an inconsistency in how sanctions are dispensed, which can benefit high-status offenders and major organizations. Sometimes, high-status individuals are treated preferentially, receiving greater leniency than individuals of lower rank who are guilty of far less. At other times, however, they are treated more harshly (Rosoff et al., 2004).

What is important to remember about white-collar crime is not simply that high-status deviants can receive preferential treatment. We must also remember that some privileged and powerful individuals, usually acting through the organizations for which they work, do a great deal of harm to a society, not only in terms of the taking of other people's belongings, but also in terms of the number of people killed or injured by white-collar activities. These predatory acts generate both public resentment and political outrage, mostly because they are done by persons in positions of responsibility and trust in political and economic institutions. The fact that these people who are responsible for so much wanton injury receive *any* leniency in a court of law is a bitter pill to swallow.

Conclusions

Power plays a singularly important role in the social construction of deviance, and it must play a singularly important role in our understanding of it. Regardless of whether we are examining the plunder of a community or the game/swindle of three-card monte, power is implicated in much of what happens. It is true that bad apples exist. Some individuals will be able to take advantage of their access to positions of power or influence to break the rules so as to benefit themselves with no support from others. However, this deviance by individuals inside an organization to benefit themselves is just the tip of the iceberg.

Organizations themselves may be corrupt, encouraging bad apples to grow and develop. It is almost always a web of relationships and the power that this allows that account for the patterns of deviance that occur. Power corrupts, and absolute power has the tendency to corrupt absolutely. Power is also a critical variable in understanding how harmful acts are viewed, defined, and described. What is considered a crime and what penalties are prescribed for it almost always reflect the power and interests of specific groups. If you are a carrier, your taking will be dealt with harshly; if you are a General Motors, your taking may not be viewed as taking at all. It may even be viewed as a valuable renovation project for the city of Detroit.

The many incidents we examined in this chapter can be traced to the distribution of power and privilege, organizational dynamics, and social networks. Regardless of whether it is the carrier's case, occupational crime, corporate crime, elite deviance, international terrorism, or police violence, certain groups will use the power that organizational networks give them to do things that other people cannot and then to justify and excuse them as both valuable and necessary. The icing on the cake for powerful groups is that they will be able to influence the content of law (or other social norms), which legitimates and normalizes even further the activities and understandings based on them.

References

Abu-Lughod, R. A. (2010). Legitimacy of the war in Iraq: The role of the media in sorting fact from Foxtion. In R. L. Bing, III (Ed.), *Race, crime, and the media* (pp. 210–218). New York: McGraw-Hill.

Ahmed, N. M. (2002). *The war on freedom: How and why America was attacked, September 11, 2001.* East Sussex, UK: Institute for Policy Research and Development.

Azarian, R., & Alalehto, T. (2014). Patterns in account-giving among white collar criminals. *Deviant Behavior, 35,* 101–115.

Barak, G. (2012). *Theft of a nation: Wall Street looting and federal regulatory colluding.* Lanham, MD: Rowman & Littlefield.

Barkan, S. E., & Bryjak, G. J. (2014). *Myths and realities of crime and justice: What every American should know* (2nd ed.). Burlington, VT: Jones & Bartlett.

Beck, C. J., & Miner, E. (2013). Who gets designated a terrorist and why? *Social Forces, 91,* 837–872.

Belbot, B. (1995). Corporate criminal liability. In M. Blankenship (Ed.), *Understanding corporate criminality* (pp. 211–237). New York: Garland.

Benediktsson, M. O. (2010). The deviant organization and the bad apple CEO: Ideology and accountability in media coverage of corporate scandals. *Social Forces, 88,* 2189–2216.

Bergen, P. L. (2012). *Manhunt: The ten-year search for Bin Laden from 9/11 to Abbottabad.* New York: Random House/Crown.

Bernard, T. J., Snipes, J. B., & Gerould, A. L. (2010). *Vold's theoretical criminology* (6th ed.). New York: Oxford University Press.

Blain, M. (2012). *Power, discourse, and victimage ritual in the war on terror.* Burlington, VT: Ashgate.

Blau, J. (1999). *Illusions of prosperity: America's working families in an age of economic insecurity.* New York: Oxford University Press.

Bonn, S. A. (2010). *Mass deception: Moral panic and the US war on Iraq.* New Brunswick, NJ: Rutgers University Press.

Box, S. (1983). *Power, crime, and mystification.* London: Tavistock.

Brady, D. (2009). *Rich democracies, poor people.* New York: Oxford University Press.

Bricker, J., Dettling, L. J., Henriques, A., Hsu, J. W., Moore, K. B., Sabelhaus, J., et al. (2014). Changes in U.S. family finances from 2010 to 2013: Evidence from the Survey of Consumer Finances. *Federal Reserve Bulletin, 100,* 1–40.

Brooks, C., & Manza, J. (2013). *Whose rights? Counterterrorism and the dark side of American public opinion.* New York: Russell Sage Foundation.

Cainkar, L. A. (2009). *Homeland insecurity: The Arab American and Muslim American experience after 9/11.* New York: Russell Sage Foundation.

Carrabine, E. (2011). Images of torture: Culture, politics and power. *Crime, Media, Culture, 7,* 5–30.

Carroll, W. K. (2010). *The making of a transnational capitalist class: Corporate power in the 21st century.* New York: Zed Books.

Cavender, G., Gray, K., & Miller, K. W. (2010). Enron's perp walk: Status degradation ceremonies as narrative. *Crime, Media, Culture, 6,* 251–266.

Cavender, G., Jurik, N., & Cohen, A. (1993). The baffling case of the smoking gun: The social ecology of political accounts in the Iran–Contra affair. *Social Problems, 40,* 152–166.

Chambliss, W., & Seidman, R. (1982). *Law, order, and power* (2nd ed.). Reading, MA: Addison-Wesley.

Charbeneau, T. (1992). Ragged individualism: America's myth of the loner. *Utne Reader, 51,* 132–133.

Chevigny, P. (1995). *Edge of the knife: Police violence in the Americas.* New York: The New Press.

Chomsky, N. (1988). *The culture of terrorism.* Boston: South End Press.

Clark, R. (2013). Convergence in national income distributions. *Social Forces, 92,* 413–436.

Clarke, R. (2004). *Against all enemies: Inside America's war on terror.* New York: Free Press.

Clinard, M. B., & Quinney, R. (1973). *Criminal behavior systems: A typology* (2nd ed.). New York: Holt, Rinehart & Winston.

Coleman, J. S. (1982). *The asymmetric society.* Syracuse, NY: Syracuse University Press.

Coleman, J. W. (1987). Toward an integrated theory of white-collar crime. *American Journal of Sociology, 93,* 406–439.

Coleman, J. W. (2006). *The criminal elite: Understanding white-collar crime* (6th ed.). New York: Worth.

Conklin, J. (1977). *Illegal but not criminal.* Englewood Cliffs, NJ: Prentice Hall.

Cornwell, B., & Dokshin, F. A. (2014). The power of integration: Affiliation and cohesion in a diverse elite network. *Social Forces, 93,* 803–831.

Curwin, K. D., & Mahutga, M. C. (2014). Foreign direct investment and economic growth: New evidence from post-socialist transition countries. *Social Forces, 92,* 1159–1187.

Dashwood, H. S. (2012). *The rise of global corporate social responsibility: Mining and the spread of global norms.* Cambridge, UK: Cambridge University Press.

Davis, N. (1980). *Sociological constructions of deviance: Perspectives and issues in the field* (2nd ed.). Dubuque, IA: W. C. Brown.

Deflem, M. (2010). *The policing of terrorism: Organizational and global perspectives.* New York: Routledge.

Disha, I., Cavendish, J. C., & King, R. D. (2011). Historical events and spaces of hate: Hate crimes against Arabs and Muslims in post-9/11 America. *Social Problems, 58,* 21–46.

Drehle, D. V. (2015, March 9). The War on Isis. *Time, 185,* 24–29.

Duncan, G. J., & Murnane, R. J. (Eds.). (2011). *Wither opportunity: Rising inequality, schools, and children's life chances.* New York: Russell Sage Foundation.

Ermann, M. D., & Lundman, R. (2002). Corporate and governmental deviance: Origins, patterns, and reactions. In M. D. Ermann & R. Lundman (Eds.), *Corporate and governmental deviance: Problems of organizational behavior in contemporary society* (6th ed., pp. 3–49). New York: Oxford University Press.

Fairbrother, M. (2014). Economists, capitalists, and the making of globalization: North American free trade in comparative-historical perspective. *American Journal of Sociology, 119,* 1324–1379.

Feldkamp, J. L. (Ed.). (2014a). *Theory and politics of terrorism.* San Diego, CA: Cognella.

Feldkamp, J. L. (2014b). Foreword. In J. L. Feldkamp (Ed.), *Theory and politics of terrorism* (pp. xi–xvi). San Diego, CA: Cognella.

Feniger, Y., & Yuchtman-Yaar, E. (2010). Risk groups in exposure to terror: The case of Israel's citizens. *Social Forces, 88,* 1451–1462.

Fifield, A. (2013, March 18). Contractors reap $138bn from Iraq war. *Financial Times.* Retrieved March 1, 2015, from http://www.ft.com/intl/cms/s/0/7f435f04–8c05–11e2-b001–00144feabdc0.html#axzz3T9pNGDgW

Financial Crisis Inquiry Commission. (2011, January). *The financial crisis inquiry report: Final report of the National Commission on the Causes of the Financial and Economic Crisis in the United States.* Retrieved January 6, 2014 from http://www.gpo.gov/fdsys/pkg/GPO-FCIC/pdf/GPO-FCIC.pdf

Flavin, P., Pacek, A. C., & Radcliff, B. (2014). Assessing the impact of the size and scope of government on human well-being. *Social Forces, 92,* 1241–1258.

Fox, J. (2009). *The myth of the rational market: A history of risk, reward, and delusion on Wall Street.* New York: HarperCollins.

Franken, A. (2003). *Lies (and the lying liars who tell them): A fair and balanced look at the right.* New York: Dutton.

Frege, C., & Godard, J. (2014). Varieties of capitalism and job quality: The attainment of civic principles at work in the United States and Germany. *American Sociological Review, 79,* 942–965.

Fullerton, A. S., & Villemez, M. J. (2011). Why does the spatial agglomeration of firms benefit workers: Examining the role of organizational diversity in U.S. industries and labor markets. *Social Forces, 89,* 1145–1164.

Ganor, B. (2014). Terror as a strategy of psychological warfare. In J. L. Feldkamp (Ed.), *Theory and politics of terrorism* (pp. 43–47). San Diego, CA: Cognella.

Geis, G., & Goff, C. (1983). Introduction. In E. H. Sutherland, *White-collar crime: The uncut version* (pp. ix–xxxiii). New Haven, CT: Yale University Press.

Gerber, J., & Weeks, S. (1992). Women as victims of corporate crime: A call for research on a neglected topic. *Deviant Behavior, 13,* 325–347.

Goldsmith, G., & Blakely, E. J. (2010). *Separate societies: Poverty and inequality in U.S. cities.* Philadelphia: Temple University Press.

Gonzalez, E. (2014). The nexus between human trafficking and terrorism/organized crime: Combating human trafficking by creating a cooperative law enforcement system. In J. L. Feldkamp (Ed.), *Theory and politics of terrorism* (pp. 119–131). San Diego, CA: Cognella.

Goode, E. (2015). *Deviant behavior* (10th ed.). Boston: Pearson.

Gornick, J. C., & Jäntti, M. (Eds.). (2013). *Income inequality: Economic disparities and the middle class in affluent countries.* Stanford, CA: Stanford University Press.

Gosselin, P. (2009). *Highwire: The precarious financial lives of American families.* New York: Basic Books.

Gray, G. C., & Silbey, S. S. (2014). Governing inside the organization: Interpreting regulation and compliance. *American Journal of Sociology, 120,* 96–145.

Green, G. (1997). *Occupational crime* (2nd ed.). Chicago: Nelson-Hall.

Gross, M. (1996). *The political racket: Deceit, self-interest and corruption in American politics*. New York: Ballantine.

Groysberg, B. (2010). *The myth of talent and the portability of performance*. Princeton, NJ: Princeton University Press.

Grusky, D. B., Western, B., & Wimer, C. (Eds.). (2011). *The Great Recession*. New York: Russell Sage Foundation.

Hall, J. (1952). *Theft, law, and society* (2nd ed.). Indianapolis, IN: Bobbs-Merrill.

Harvey, D. (2010). *The enigma of capital: And the crises of capitalism*. New York: Oxford University Press.

Helbling, M. (Ed.). (2014). *Islamophobia in the West: Measuring and explaining individual attitudes*. New York: Routledge.

Hersch, S. M. (2015, May 21). The killing of Osama bin Laden. *London Review of Books, 37*, pp. 3–12. Retrieved July 10, 2015, from http://www.lrb.co.uk/v37/n10/seymour-m-hersh/the-killing-of-osama-bin-laden

Hightower, J. (2003). *Thieves in high places: They've stolen our country—and it's time to take it back*. New York: Viking.

Ho, K. (2009). *Liquidated: An ethnography of Wall Street*. Durham, NC: Duke University Press.

Howard, R., & Forest, J. (Eds.) (with Bahema, N.). (2008). *Weapons of mass destruction and terrorism*. New York: McGraw-Hill.

Jacobsson, K. (2012). Accounts of honesty: Refuting allegations of bribery. *Deviant Behavior, 33*, 108–125.

Jaffee, D. (2012). Weak coffee: Certification and co-optation in the fair trade movement. *Social Problems, 59*, 94–116.

Jenkins, P. (2003). *Images of terror: What we can and can't know about terrorism*. New York: Aldine de Gruyter.

Juravich, T. (2009). *At the altar of the bottom line: The degradation of work in the 21st century*. Amherst: University of Massachusetts Press.

Kahan, A. S. (2010). *Mind vs. money: The war between intellectuals and capitalism*. New Brunswick, NJ: Transaction Publishers.

Kalleberg, A. L. (2011). *Good jobs, bad jobs: The rise of polarized and precarious employment systems in the United States, 1970s to 2000s*. New York: Russell Sage Foundation.

Kelman, H., & Hamilton, V. L. (1989). *Crimes of obedience: Toward a social psychology of authority and responsibility*. New Haven, CT: Yale University Press.

Kendall, D. (2008). *Members only. Elite clubs and the process of exclusion*. Lanham, MD: Rowman & Littlefield.

Khurana, R. (2002). *Searching for a corporate savior: The irrational quest for charismatic CEOs*. Princeton, NJ: Princeton University Press.

Klaidman, D. (2012). *Kill or capture: The war on terror and the soul of the Obama presidency*. Boston: Houghton Mifflin Harcourt.

Klein, N. (2007). *The shock doctrine: The rise of disaster capitalism*. New York: Picador/Henry Holt.

Kollmeyer, C., & Pichler, F. (2013). Is deindustrialization causing high unemployment in affluent countries? Evidence from 16 OECD countries, 1970–2003. *Social Forces, 91,* 785–812.

Kramer, R., Michalowski, R., & Kauzlarich, D. (2002). The origins and development of the concept and theory of state-corporate crime. *Crime & Delinquency, 48,* 263–282.

Kristal, T. (2010). Good times, bad times: Postwar labor's share of national income in capitalist democracies. *American Sociological Review, 75,* 729–763.

Lauderdale, P., & Cruit, M. (1993). *The struggle for control: A study of law, disputes, and deviance.* Albany: State University of New York Press.

Lendman, S. (2011). *How Wall Street fleeces America: Privatized banking, government collusion and class war.* Atlanta, GA: Clarity Press.

Lilly, J. R., Cullen, F. T., & Ball, R. A. (2015). *Criminological theory: Context and consequences* (6th ed.). Thousand Oaks, CA: Sage.

Livingston, J. (1996). *Crime and criminology* (2nd ed.). Englewood Cliffs, NJ: Prentice Hall.

Lobao, L., Adua, L., & Hooks, G. (2014). Privatization, business attraction, and social services across the United States: Local governments' use of market-oriented neoliberal policies in the post-2000 period. *Social Problems, 61,* 644–672.

Lorenz, E. C. (2012). *Civic empowerment in an age of corporate greed.* East Lansing: Michigan State University Press.

Loughran, T. A., Nguyen, H., Piquero, A. R., & Fagan, J. (2013). The returns to criminal capital. *American Sociological Review, 78,* 925–948,

Mann, J. (2004). *Rise of the Vulcans: The history of Bush's war cabinet.* New York: Penguin.

Martin, I. W. (2008). *The permanent tax revolt: How the property tax transformed American politics.* Stanford, CA: Stanford University Press.

McCall, L. (2013). *The undeserving rich: American beliefs about inequality, opportunity, and redistribution.* New York: Cambridge University Press.

Merton, R. K. (1938). Social structure and anomie. *American Sociological Review, 3,* 672–682.

Messerschmidt, J. W. (2010). *Hegemonic masculinities and camouflaged politics: Unmasking the Bush dynasty and its war against Iraq.* Boulder, CO: Paradigm.

Monahan, B. A. (2010). *The shock of the news: Media coverage and the making of 9/11.* New York: New York University Press.

Monahan, T. (2010). *Surveillance in the time of insecurity.* New Brunswick, NJ: Rutgers University Press.

Morell, M. (2015). *The great war of our time: The CIA's fight against terrorism from al Qa'ida to ISIS.* New York: Hachette Book Group.

Mouw, T., & Kalleberg, A. L. (2010). Occupations and the structure of wage inequality in the United States, 1980s to 2000s. *American Sociological Review, 75,* 402–431.

Mullins, C. W., & Young, J. K. (2012). Culture of violence and acts of terror: Applying a legitimation-habituation model of terrorism. *Crime & Delinquency, 58,* 28–56.

Nacos, B. (2007). Terrorism as breaking news: Attack on America. In T. Badey (Ed.), *Annual editions: Violence and terrorism 07–08* (10th ed., pp. 110–125). New York: McGraw-Hill.

Nader, R., & Smith, W. (1996). *No contest: Corporate lawyers and the perversion of justice in America*. New York: Random House.

National Commission on Terrorist Attacks. (2004). *The 9/11 Commission Report: Final report of the National Commission on Terrorist Attacks Upon the United States*. (Authorized Ed.) New York: Norton.

Nau, M. (2013). Economic elites, investments, and income inequality. *Social Forces, 92*, 437–461.

Norton, M. (2014). Classification and coercion: The destruction of piracy in the English maritime system. *American Journal of Sociology, 119*, 1537–1575.

O'Flynn, M. (2009). *Profitable ideas: The ideology of the individual in capitalist development*. Leiden, The Netherlands: Brill.

Ono, H., & Lee, K. S. (2013). Welfare states and the redistribution of happiness. *Social Forces, 92*, 789–814.

Owen, M., & Maurer, K. (2012). *No easy day: The autobiography of a Navy SEAL*. New York: Dutton.

Pacewicz, J. (2013). Regulatory rescaling in neoliberal markets. *Social Problems, 60*, 433–456.

Palmer, D. (2013). *Normal organizational wrongdoing: A critical analysis of theories of misconduct in and by organizations*. Oxford, UK: Oxford University Press.

Peace, R. (2012). *A call to conscience: The anti-Contra War campaign*. Amherst: University of Massachusetts Press.

Pedulla, D. S. (2013). The hidden costs of contingency: Employers' use of contingent workers and standard employees' outcomes. *Social Forces, 92*, 691–722.

Piketty, T. (2014). *Capital in the twenty-first century* (A. Goldhammer, Trans.). Cambridge, MA: Belknap Press.

Polillo, S. (2013). *Conservatives versus wildcats: A sociology of financial conflict*. Stanford, CA: Stanford University Press.

Pollard, V. K. (Ed.). (2012). *State capitalism, contentious politics and large-scale social change*. Chicago: Haymarket.

Posner, R. A. (2010). *The crisis of capitalist democracy*. Cambridge, MA: Harvard University Press.

Poveda, T. (1994). *Rethinking white-collar crime*. New York: Praeger.

Prasad, M. (2012). *The land of too much: American abundance and the paradox of poverty*. Cambridge, MA: Harvard University Press.

Prechel, H., & Morris, T. (2010). The effects of organizational and political embeddedness on financial malfeasance in the largest U.S. corporations: Dependence, incentives, and opportunities. *American Sociological Review, 75*, 331–354.

Prus, R., & Sharper, C. R. D. (1977). *Road hustler: The career contingencies of professional card and dice hustlers*. Lexington, MA: Lexington.

Reich, R. B. (2010). *Aftershock: The next economy and America's future*. New York: Knopf.

Rigney, D. (2010). *The Matthew effect: How advantage begets further advantage.* New York: Columbia University Press.

Ritzer, G. (2006). September 11, 2001: Mass murder and its roots in the symbolism of American consumer culture. In G. Ritzer (Ed.), *McDonaldization: The reader* (2nd ed., pp. 240–252). Thousand Oaks, CA: Pine Forge/Sage.

Robbins, T. (2008). *The modern con man: How to get something for nothing.* New York: Bloomsbury/Macmillan.

Rooney, B. (2011, January 27). Financial crisis was avoidable. *CNNMoney.* Retrieved January 23, 2013, from http://money.cnn.com/2011/01/27/news/economy/fcic_crisis_avoidable/index.htm?hpt=T2

Rosoff, S., Pontell, H., & Tillman, R. (2004). *Profit without honor: White-collar crime and the looting of America.* Upper Saddle River, NJ: Pearson/Prentice Hall.

Ross, J. (2013). Conceptualizing the criminological problem of terrorism. In A. Thio, T. Calhoun, & A. Conyers (Eds.), *Deviance today* (pp. 281–288). Upper Saddle River, NJ: Pearson.

Rosso, J. D. (2011). The textual mediation of denial: Congress, Abu Ghraib, and the construction of an isolated incident. *Social Problems, 58,* 165–188.

Rosso, J. D. (2014). The toxicity of torture: The cultural structure of U.S. political discourse of waterboarding. *Social Forces, 93,* 383–404.

Rothe, D. (2009). War profiteering: Iraq and Halliburton. In P. Adler & P. Adler (Eds.), *Constructions of deviance: Social power, context, and interaction* (6th ed., pp. 433–445). Belmont, CA: Thomson/Wadsworth.

Rothkopf, D. (2012). *Power, inc.: The epic rivalry between big business and government—and the reckoning that lies ahead.* New York: Farrar, Straus & Giroux.

Roussell, A., & Gascón, L. D. (2014). Defining "policeability": Cooperation, control, and resistance in South Los Angeles community-police meetings. *Social Problems, 61,* 237–258.

Routledge, P., & Cumbers, A. (2009). *Global justice networks: Geographies of transnational solidarity.* Manchester, UK: Manchester University Press.

Roy, W. (1997). *Socializing capital: The rise of the large industrial corporation in America.* Princeton, NJ: Princeton University Press.

Rugh, J. S., & Massey, D. S. (2010). Racial segregation and the American foreclosure crisis. *American Sociological Review, 75,* 629–651.

Samuel, Y. (2010). *Organizational pathology: Life and death of organizations.* New Brunswick, NJ: Transaction Publishers.

Santoro, W. A., & Azab, M. (2015). Arab American protest in the terror decade: Macro- and micro-level response to post-9/11 repression. *Social Problems, 62,* 219–240.

Scarne, J. (1974). *Scarne's new complete guide to gambling* (Rev. ed.). New York: Simon & Schuster.

Schoepfer, A., Piquero, N. L., & Langton, L. (2014). Low self-control versus the desire-for-control: An empirical test of white-collar crime and conventional crime. *Deviant Behavior, 35,* 197–214.

Schwartzman, K. C. (2013). *The chicken trail: Following workers, migrants, and corporations across the Americas*. Ithaca, NY: Cornell University Press.

Senate Select Committee on Intelligence. (Declassification Revisions December 3, 2014). *Committee study of the Central Intelligence Agency's Detention and Interrogation Program. Findings and conclusions. Executive Summary*. Washington, DC: United States Senate.

Sharkey, A. J. (2014). Categories and organizational status: The role of industry status in the response to organizational deviance. *American Journal of Sociology, 119*, 1380–1433.

Sharone, O. (2013). Why do unemployed Americans blame themselves while Israelis blame the system? *Social Forces, 91*, 1429–1450.

Sherman, J. (2013). Surviving the Great Recession: Growing need and the stigmatized safety net. *Social Problems, 60*, 409–432.

Sherwood, J. H. (2010). *Wealth, whiteness, and the matrix of privilege: The view from the country club*. Lanham, MD: Lexington Books.

Shin, T. (2014). Explaining pay disparities between top executive and nonexecutive employees: A relative bargaining power approach. *Social Forces, 92*, 1339–1372.

Simon, D. (2008). *Elite deviance* (9th ed.). Boston: Allyn & Bacon.

Smith, Y. (2010). *ECONned: How unenlightened self interest undermined democracy and corrupted capitalism*. New York: Palgrave Macmillan.

Stampnitsky, L. (2013). *Disciplining terror: How experts invented "terrorism."* Cambridge, UK: Cambridge University Press.

Steffensmeier, D. J., Schwartz, J., & Roche, M. (2013). Gender and twenty-first-century corporate crime: Female involvement and the gender gap in Enron-era corporate frauds. *American Sociological Review, 78*, 448–476.

Stiglitz, J. E. (2010). *Freefall: America, free markets, and the sinking of the world economy*. New York: Norton.

Stiglitz, J. E. (2012). *The price of inequality: How today's divided society endangers our future*. New York: Norton.

Stritzke, W., Lewandowsky, S., Denemark, D., Clare, J., & Morgan, F. (Eds.). (2009). *Terrorism and torture: An interdisciplinary perspective*. New York: Cambridge University Press.

Sutherland, E. H. (1940). White-collar criminality. *American Sociological Review, 5*, 1–12.

Sutherland, E. H. (1945). Is "white-collar crime" crime? *American Sociological Review, 10*, 132–139.

Sutherland, E. H. (1949). *White-collar crime*. New York: Dryden.

Sutherland, E. H. (1983). *White-collar crime: The uncut version*. New Haven, CT: Yale University Press.

Tavits, M. (2010). Why do people engage in corruption? The case of Estonia. *Social Forces, 88*, 1257–1280.

Thio, A. (2010). *Deviant behavior* (10th ed.). Boston: Allyn & Bacon.

Tillman, R., & Pontell, H. (1995). Organizations and fraud in the savings and loan industry. *Social Forces, 73*, 1439–1463.

Tilly, C. (1998). *Durable inequality.* Berkeley: University of California Press.

Tittle, C. R. (1995). *Control balance: Toward a general theory of deviance.* Boulder, CO: Westview.

Transparency International. (2014). *Corruption Perceptions Index 2014: Results.* Retrieved June 21, 2015, from http://www.transparency.org/cpi2014/results

Tunnell, K. D. (1992). *Choosing crime: The criminal calculus of property offenders.* Chicago: Nelson-Hall.

Tunnell, K. D. (2006). *Living off crime* (2nd ed.). Lanham, MD: Rowman & Littlefield.

Vela-McConnell, J. (1999). *Who is my neighbor? Social affinity in a modern world.* Albany: State University of New York Press.

Villette, M., & Vuillermot, C. (2009). *From predators to icons: Exposing the myth of the business hero* (G. Holoch, Trans.). Ithaca, NY: ILR Press.

Viner, J. (1940). The short view and the long in economic policy. *American Economic Review, 30,* 1–15.

Watts, D. J. (2011). *Everything is obvious once you know the answer: How common sense fails us.* New York: Random House.

Werner, T. (2012). *Public forces and private politics in American big business.* Cambridge, UK: Cambridge University Press.

Wherry, F. (2012). *The culture of markets.* Cambridge, UK: Polity.

Wilkinson, R., & Pickett, K. (2010). *The spirit level: Why greater equality makes societies stronger.* New York: Bloomsbury Press.

Will, S., Handelman, S., & Brotherton, D. C. (Eds.). (2012). *How they got away with it: White collar criminals and the financial meltdown.* New York: Columbia University Press.

Wood, G. (2015, March). What ISIS really wants. *The Atlantic.* Retrieved March 2, 2015, from http://www.theatlantic.com/features/archive/2015/02/what-isis-really-wants/384980

Wylie, J. (1989). *Poletown: Community betrayed.* Urbana: University of Illinois Press.

4

Mental Disorders

Medicalization on 34th Street

A 1947 story by Valentine Davies, *Miracle on 34th Street,* and the beloved film of the same title, described what could have been the trial of the century: the time that Santa Claus was hauled into court and his sanity was questioned. The story really begins at the Maplewood Home for the Aged in Great Neck, Long Island. An elderly and kind gentleman, at the peak of health, whose name was Kris Kringle, spent his time there making toys and smoking his pipe. One November, the resident physician at Maplewood (Dr. Pierce) gave Kris the bad news that he was being evicted. The reason was that state laws and Maplewood's charter allowed only people who were in both good physical *and* mental health to live there. Kris's claim he was the one and only Santa Claus indicated that he was mentally ill, so he had to leave. He collected his belongings and left to make his way in the world. Luckily for him, he had a friend who lived and worked at the Central Park Zoo, and he made room for Kris at his place. It was a good arrangement because Kris had an uncanny ability with animals, especially the reindeer.

Mr. Kringle wanted to see the Macy's Thanksgiving Day Parade. That year, the fake Santa that Macy's had hired got drunk, too drunk to carry out his duties. When Kris saw the man, he was furious. He complained directly to the personnel director and organizer of the parade, Doris Walker. She was visibly upset, dispatched the phony Santa, and asked Kris to take his place. Kris consented only because he did not want to disappoint the children. He did so well that he was offered a job at Macy's as the permanent Santa, a position he reluctantly accepted.

Kris ran afoul of entrenched beliefs of other Macy's employees, continuing to insist (at least when asked) that Santa Claus did exist and that he was the one and only. In fact, Ms. Walker wondered if Kris was as harmless as he appeared. She consulted Macy's resident expert on psychology and vocational guidance, Mr. Albert Sawyer. He was an arrogant man who thought he knew practically everything about practically everything. He told Doris Walker that he would be pleased to interview Kris. Sawyer concluded without much to go on that Kris had a fixed delusion and could be dangerous, which he reported to Ms. Walker.

That December, Sawyer was scheduled to give a lecture titled "Exploding the Myth of Santa Claus." Kris attended because he believed he had something to contribute. At the lecture, Sawyer insisted that any adult who believed in Santa Claus revealed himself or herself to have an incomplete and neurotic personality. He opined that the "vicious myth" of Santa Claus had done more harm in the world than had opium. Kris's presence unnerved Sawyer. He became distracted and he garbled sentences. Sawyer demanded that the old "jackanapes" be removed from the room, but Kris refused to leave. Sawyer advanced on him. Kris raised his cane to protect himself, and Sawyer grabbed it and tugged, making Kris lose his grip. Sawyer hit himself in the cheek with the cane, but he accused Kris of attacking him. The altercation with Sawyer (along with Kris's claim that he was Santa Claus) worried others. Steps were taken to have a hearing to determine if Kris should be committed to Bellevue Psychiatric Hospital for his own good and for the safety of the people around him.

The commitment hearing was under the charge of Judge Henry X. Harper. Thomas Mara represented the state of New York, and Fred Gailey represented Kris Kringle. The first witness Mr. Mara called was the defendant, Mr. Kringle. Kris was a right sprightly old elf, and Judge Harper smiled when he saw him in spite of himself. Mara got right to the point and asked Kris if he believed that he was Santa Claus. "Of course!" was the reply. The courtroom erupted. The old gentleman didn't even try to hide his craziness! Mara rested his case and sat down, confident that he had proved that the old man was insane. Gailey was desperate as he sat in court. He was trying to prove by a preponderance of the evidence that Kris Kringle was mentally healthy, but things were not going well. It looked as if Kris might be committed to Bellevue after all. However, a fortuitous turn of events kept this from happening.

Gailey was summoned from the courtroom by a security officer and shown bundles and bundles of letters, each one addressed to Santa Claus.

(Every letter addressed to Santa Claus that was in the local post office had been bundled up and delivered to Kris at the courthouse.) Struck by an idea, Gailey returned to the courtroom and reminded the court that it was a serious offense to deliver mail to the wrong party. He then produced three letters from his jacket, each one addressed simply to "Santa Claus, USA." Their delivery to Kris proved (or so Gailey claimed) that Kris was recognized by a competent authority (i.e., the U.S. Post Office) to be the one and only Santa Claus. The court was unimpressed. Three letters were hardly enough to make such a strong claim, but Gailey had further exhibits. Judge Harper insisted that they be put on his bench. Gailey complied, and the judge was eventually covered by a mountain of mail. Judge Harper ruled that if the United States government believed Kris Kringle was Santa Claus, his court would not disagree, and the case was dismissed. Kris was deeply moved. Smiling happily, he rushed to the bench and wished the judge a Merry Christmas. Then Kris disappeared into the night. After all, it was Christmas Eve.

Davies's book about the *fictional* trial of Santa Claus illustrates something factual: Mental illness is a social construction. Claiming to be Santa is no different in important respects from claiming to be Judge Harper, Fred Gailey, or Thomas Mara. The rendering of a judgment that a mental disorder exists comes from the determination that an individual is not what he or she claims to be and that he or she should not be thinking, feeling, or doing what he or she *is* thinking, feeling, or doing. The dispute over the sickness or wellness of Kris's so-called delusion, or even the determination that he had one in the first place, cannot be separated from the social context in which that decision is made. A pivotal issue seems to be whether a "competent authority" will state for the record that an individual is sick or well, insane or sane, or abnormal or normal.

The Medicalization Process

Different narratives exist to describe and evaluate human conditions or experiences. Sometimes, none of the narratives is viewed as more legitimate or correct than any of the others. An intellectual division of labor exists in which each narrative has its own turf, and its supporters stay within their own borders. For example, it would be possible for a killing of one human being by another to be considered a legal matter, major depression to be considered a medical matter, sin to be considered a religious matter, and poverty to be considered a social matter. At other times, however, turf wars are frequent, and skirmishes and battles to expand one's power and influence are ongoing (Whooley, 2013). Some groups are more successful than others in the process of defining "deviance" and tagging "deviants."

> Although negotiations may occur, more powerful interests in society are better able to implement their version of reality by creating and legitimating deviance definitions that support their interests. (Conrad & Schneider, 1992, p. 25)

Certain groups can come to "own" particular problems (e.g., religion's relationship to sin, medicine's relationship to disease), and members of these groups will then be widely viewed as the only real experts on the problems in question (Gusfield, 1981). Until that happens, it can still be a highly contentious issue whether a specific attitude, behavior, or condition is best viewed as sin, sickness, crime, or something else altogether. Narratives change all the time, and new ones are invented on a continual basis.

When a physician diagnoses a patient as having measles, mumps, or chicken pox, we really don't need to spend much time trying to figure out whose interests are served or why this ailment received medical attention. Medicalization is both reasonable and helpful. Sometimes, however, the institution of medicine is used principally to control people, perpetuating the status quo and helping physicians to expand their power and privilege. In 1851, the physician Samuel Cartwright first diagnosed and so invented the "illness" of *drapetomania*. It referred to the "disease" of slaves in the South running away from the plantations of their white owners (Conrad & Schneider, 1992, p. 35). It is easy enough to see that a diagnosis of drapetomania is different in fundamental ways from a diagnosis of chicken pox, measles, or mumps. The determination that running away from a plantation qualifies as a disease is both arbitrary and political. It was a disease only because someone who had the authority to define a human condition as a medical problem said it was. In the early 1970s in the former Soviet Union, psychiatrists diagnosed political dissidents as having *sluggish schizophrenia,* a so-called medical condition characterized by symptoms of wanting to change a social system and having actual ideas about how to go about it. This medical diagnosis made it possible to control political dissidents by sending them to special mental hospitals that were established exclusively for them, run in conjunction with the KGB (Gosden, 2003). There was a time in the past when masturbation was medicalized, and things were blamed on it that seem laughable by today's standards (e.g., homosexuality or masturbatory insanity). In like fashion, erectile dysfunction, attention-deficit hyperactivity disorder (ADHD), menopause, posttraumatic stress, alcoholism, withdrawal from caffeine, and the inability to do arithmetic have been medicalized as well. Things that seem to facilitate medicalization include support from the medical profession, a convincing and empirically supported theory of the origin and prognosis of the illness, the existence of profitable therapies, willingness of insurance companies to pay for treatments, and the inclination of individuals who have the condition to accept medicalization of it (Conrad, 2007).

With increasing regularity, conditions that were once viewed as crime, sin, incompetence, or bad manners (e.g., incivilities) are now being viewed as medical diseases in need of cure. Part of this transformation from badness to sickness can be attributed to medical crusades by physicians to expand their sphere of influence, but not all of it. In some cases, patient collectivities, or even individual sufferers, have been insistent that their conditions be treated as diseases. The corporate sector, especially the pharmaceutical industry and medical insurers, has been playing a more significant role in the medicalization process (Frances, 2013). Some human conditions (e.g., childbirth, senility, pregnancy, AIDS, Alzheimer's) have been thoroughly penetrated by medical interpretations. Others, such as alcoholism, menopause, baldness, or suicide, have been partly medicalized. Still others, such as hypersexuality or compulsive gambling, have been only slightly medicalized.

Pharmaceutical companies do what they can to invent and then peddle *diseases* for which they have curative drugs or to exaggerate the medical nature of conditions that had heretofore not been viewed as medical problems (Watters, 2010). GlaxoSmithKline pathologized anxiety by "selling" the idea that shyness was a medical problem that should and could be cured (Conrad, 2007). Its advertising campaigns changed consumers' views of "social anxiety disorder" and "generalized anxiety disorder," which expanded the market for Paxil, its anxiety-reducing drug. Manipulation of consumers is easier in the United States because it is, according to Frances (2013), the only country in the world that allows drug companies to advertise directly to consumers. (He failed to acknowledge that New Zealand does, too.)

Psychiatry, as the medical profession that is granted the most authority to deal with *mental* illness, is in a unique position. It can deal with *anything* defined as an abnormality, especially if the abnormality is defined as lacking rhyme or reason. In this way, psychiatry has been able to extend its authority over a terrain that was coveted by other professionals and groups (e.g., lawyers, social workers, clinical psychologists, counselors) (Foucault, 2003).

[Organized psychiatry] develops media relationships, hires PR firms, develops its medical image, holds press conferences to publicize its products, lobbies on behalf of its interests, and issues "scientific" reports that protect its members from malpractice suits by lending legitimacy to brain-damaging technologies. (Breggin, 1991, pp. 366–367)

Many human conditions exist as medical diseases principally because they have powerful lobbies, consisting of physicians, politicians, and consumers, that authenticate or legitimate constellations of syndromes or complaints as genuine mental disorders (Frances, 2013; Sharkey, 1997). Although it is not at all clear when "normal" psychology becomes "abnormal," it is clear that more and more problems in living are being medicalized.

The trend in medicine has been to more thoroughly embrace a model whose linchpin is biomedicalization (A. E. Clarke, Shim, Mamo, Fosket, & Fishman, 2003). Psychiatry has shifted much of its attention away from the use of psychotherapy and group therapy and toward genetic explanations of mental disorders and drug-based cures (Grob & Horwitz, 2010). This movement has been encouraged by insurance companies, most of which will pay for drugs used for the treatment of mental illness but practically no other kind of therapy. The choice today is not whether to use a talk-based therapy or a therapeutic drug; it is which type of drug works best and should be prescribed (Conrad, 2007).

Increasingly, medicine is insurance driven, insurance is quick-treatment driven, and quick treatments are drug driven. If medicine is not exactly addicted to drugs, it is true that medical treatments are heavily dependent on them (Shorter, 2013). Drugs give physicians both the ability to cure some diseases and the appearance of competence (warranted or not). In a situation that looks much like putting the cart before the horse, treatment options may determine medical diagnoses. For example, supplemental serotonin reuptake inhibitors (SSRIs) are drugs classified as antidepressants, but they could just as correctly be classified as antianxiety drugs. Physicians are more likely to define diseases they treat with SSRIs as forms of depression rather than as forms of anxiety (Grob & Horwitz, 2010).

It has become faster and easier for drug companies to get new drugs approved and to market. Speeding up the approval process, which was claimed to be in the best interest of patients because it fostered innovation, actually decreased whatever safety and security existed in the traditional system of drug approval. Information about the safety and efficacy of a drug now usually comes *after* the drug is already approved and in use. Drug companies usually do a shoddy job in testing their drugs and in exposing the health risks of them. This means that expensive, unsafe, ineffective, and unnecessary drugs can be peddled as effective, safe, innovative, and beneficial. Speeding up of the drug-approval process increased neither public health nor patients' well-being (Davis & Abraham, 2013).

Manufacturing Madness

Diversity Into Disease

The medical manufacture of the idea of mental illness (or madness) spans a period of more than 2,000 years, and its development has been an uneven one, characterized by starts, stops, and side trips (Conrad & Schneider, 1992; Foucault, 1965). Social and cultural factors play a pivotal role in creating those attitudes, behaviors, and conditions that are diagnosed as mental illness (Schieman & Glavin, 2011). They also play a key role in establishing the criteria or decision rules that allow given constellations of attitudes, behaviors, and conditions to be diagnosed as mental illness instead of something else (King & Bearman, 2011).

Being strange (or being defined that way by others) or acting strangely does not automatically qualify an individual as sick and in need of medical cure. No specific attitude, behavior, or condition universally and uniformly indicates the presence of a mental illness, and mental illness—as condition and as category—varies from place to place and time to time. Feeble minds can be understood only in the context of a matrix of relationships in which certain pursuits become so central—material success, upward mobility, intellectual superiority—that anyone who does not display the appropriate levels of self-interest, emotional maturity, and cognitive ability will be branded as mentally defective (Trent, 1994).

Before the Industrial Revolution in the United States, deviants—criminals, the poor, delinquents, the dependent, the insane—were cared for at the local level by family or friends or, when these significant others were unavailable, the local community. Families, friends, and communities became increasingly ineffective as the population grew, the number of deviants increased, and deviance changed so that it seemed to be more dangerous and threatening (Rafter, 1997). Large-scale institutions were built for housing deviants of all types, leading eventually to the segregation of the insane into special institutions designed to hold only them (Rothman, 1974; Sutton, 1991).

Psychiatric Segregation

The first general hospital in the United States was built in Philadelphia by the Quakers (in 1756). It was the first U.S. hospital to care explicitly for the sick poor. Some of the sick who were admitted were diagnosed as mad and were the target of a great deal of prejudice and discrimination, even inside the institution. These patients were confined to the cellar of the hospital. Their scalps were shaved, and a blister-inducing powder was applied to them. These patients were even periodically chained to the walls. Members of the community could pay money to be permitted to visit the hospital to view them, which served both to remind the patients of their stigmatized status and to celebrate the virtues of mental normality and psychic conformity (Conrad & Schneider, 1992).

Mental health reformers of the nineteenth century were initially quite optimistic. They believed that treatment of the mentally ill inside a specialized institution (i.e., the asylum) would lead to their eventual cure and return to a normal life, free from psychic distress (Horwitz, 2002). The dominant view was that most mental patients were normal persons who had temporarily lost both their way and their reason because of exposure to social pressures, stresses, and temptations. A therapy was invented called *moral therapy*. It consisted of companionship for patients, analyses of their difficulties by caring and compassionate therapists, and meaningful activities for them to do. Caregivers of the time hoped their patients would learn more effective ways of coping that would protect them from the corrupting influences of society once they were released from the asylum.

Moral therapy eventually fell into disfavor because the view of mental disorders changed. A medical perspective was growing in power and popularity, and its supporters increasingly argued that mental disorders were the result of physical disease, not stressful social environments. The mad were conceptualized more and more as sick individuals in need of therapies based on science. At the same time, the growth of capitalism in the United States (and Britain) altered in significant ways whatever sense of mutual responsibility and trust that might have existed between rich and poor, challenging substantially whatever lingering paternalism the poor (and powerless) might have received (Scull, 1977b).

A formal view of mental illness developed that conceptualized abnormality as a physically based condition that could be treated, or even cured, through medical interventions. Psychiatrists and the asylums within which they did their treatment work were inseparable, and each reinforced the apparent value of the other. Separating the mad from other kinds of deviants (e.g., the bad or the lazy), as well as from the general population, came to be viewed as the only approach that would have any chance of success. Asylums developed into *total institutions* in which large numbers of individuals were confined together for long periods of time, sometimes for life, and all their activities—work, sleep, play—were organized and regulated (Goffman, 1961). Although these large, bureaucratic asylums were costly, what they provided seemed worth the investment. They authenticated the claim that mental problems were medical problems, while they allowed management and control of the mentally ill under a centralized authority.

Asylums initially received a great deal of positive press that portrayed them as an effective way to deal with abnormality. However, the rosy assessments were more rhetoric than reality. "Even a superficial acquaintance with the functioning of nineteenth century mental hospitals reveals how limited was the asylum's concern with the human problems of its inmates" (Scull, 1977b, pp. 346–347). By the end of the nineteenth century, asylums were little more than holding pens for people who either would not or could not adjust to a changing society. They became a repository for the most deranged and abnormal, and asylums were tainted terrain. Families would only send even grossly disabled members to them if no other option existed. Asylums were dreary places, bereft of optimism and characterized by huge buildings, rigid routine, and a stifling monotony.

Psychiatrists and paraprofessionals within the asylums, while still affirming the importance of treatment and rehabilitation, were little more than custodians for the wayward. Cure had been replaced by caretaking, and a creeping hereditarianism challenged the earlier optimism that mental illness and insanity could be cured by medical treatments. If disease was inborn, originating in the genes, what could any kind of talk-based therapy hope to do? In reality, psychiatrists could not cure the mentally ill because they lacked a coherent system of classification, empirically based theories of the etiology of diseases of the mind, and effective therapies.

Expanding Definitions

Psychiatrists were able to salvage psychiatry a bit by finding a new population of patients to treat: the mentally sick in the general population who could be treated outside of asylums in community-based clinics. The chronic and severely disabled were abandoned whenever possible, left in asylums to be managed by those lower on the professional food chain (e.g., superintendents or hospital aides). Psychiatrists dropped the old term for their profession, *alienist*, in favor of *psychiatrist*, committing themselves more thoroughly to the idea of prevention, instead of cure, for people outside of asylums. They developed a renewed sense of optimism and confidence, expecting to be able to find mental illnesses in their early stages and cure them. The outcome, they believed, would be a healthier, happier, more successful society (Rafter, 1997).

The use of asylums declined dramatically after World War II, and more and more patients were moved out of mental hospitals in a process of *decarceration* (Scull, 1977a). The community mental health movement became the new cure-all. Its stated goals were to promote the reintegration of the patient into the home and community and to foster positive mental health (Leifer, 1969, p. 210). Small institutions replaced large ones; professional personnel replaced custodial personnel; and mental patients were moved out of institutions and into community centers, halfway houses, or even their own homes (Dunham, 1976).

Decarceration could not have occurred without the development of psychoactive drugs. The development and availability of these drugs made it possible for therapists to control disordered behaviors of former patients outside of hospitals, starting in the 1950s (Scull, 1977a).

> The discovery of tranquilizing drugs permitted the elimination of physical restraints such as the straightjacket, chloroform, and the "sick needle." Almost overnight, tranquilizers transformed the madhouse and made possible the introduction of psychotherapy and activity programs for patients who had previously been regarded as hopeless. (Sommer, 1976, pp. 155–156)

These drugs were far from a perfect solution. They did not cure. They only suppressed the more overt signs and symptoms of certain disorders, making patients easier to control in a nonhospital setting. They did not ensure the development of the kind of behaviors a former patient would need in the outside world. Most patients stopped taking their tranquilizers shortly after their release from the institution (Scull, 1977a).

Most former mental patients faced a bleak existence after their release from mental hospitals, with the more disordered faring the worst, as inadequate or nonexistent services for them were the order of the day (Klein, 2009). U.S. prisons and jails became holding pens for many of those who had been decarcerated (Adams & Ferrandino, 2008; Lamb, Weinberger, & Gross, 2004; Torrey, 1995). The United States has effectively removed the mentally ill from state psychiatric hospitals, but it has not as effectively provided them with the resources and services that they would need in order to live successfully in the outside world (Torrey & colleagues, 2012).

Decarceration was encouraged by the passage of state laws that mandated periodic review of a mentally ill individual's confinement in a mental hospital to determine if it was warranted (Walker, 2011). Decarceration of the mentally ill began in earnest in California with the passage of the *Lanterman-Petris-Short Act*, which went into full effect in 1972. This law made it illegal to hold anyone in a hospital against his or her will for longer than 72 hours unless clear and convincing evidence existed of the individual's danger to others or the self (Scheff, 2014). The law was crafted by a California legislator (Jerome Waldie) and his chief of staff (Arthur Bolton), though their names appear nowhere on it. These two men realized that one outcome of the law would be that former mental patients without families or friends to care for them would end up in prisons, jails, or out on the streets. Waldie and Bolton wrote the law to keep this from happening. The monies saved from the closing and downsizing of hospitals were supposed to be used to build county mental health clinics to take care of the released patients who had nowhere else to go. This didn't happen, however, because the governor of California at the time, Ronald Reagan, line vetoed the clinic funding.

Psychiatrists formulated an ever-expanding definition of mental illness, and all types of problems in living became a target of psychiatry (e.g., alcoholism, children's school adjustment problems, sleep disorders, marriage problems, drug addictions, impotence, excessive smoking, children's defiance of authority, caffeine withdrawal, job loss). Nowadays, it is even possible to be diagnosed as having *anosognosia*: when a person with an illness seems unaware that he or she has the illness (American Psychiatric Association [APA], 2013). With a few *medical* illnesses, a diagnosis like this might be defensible (e.g., an individual has cancer but doesn't know it because the disease is asymptomatic). With *mental* illnesses, however, things are different. A diagnosis like anosognosia maximizes the chances that the disease is only in the eyes of the physician.

In the 1960s and 1970s, not only did psychiatry medicalize an increasing number of human conditions, but psychiatrists also reported they had found increasingly high rates of untreated mental disorders in U.S. communities. This finding, however, rather than showing that U.S. society was undergoing a psychic meltdown, was actually an artifact of how the information was collected. Community surveys exaggerate the number of mentally ill individuals that they find. The questions are incapable of distinguishing expectable and reasonable reactions to life's troubling events from those reactions that make no sense at all (Horwitz & Wakefield, 2008). The interviewers almost always lack the clinical training and professional expertise to be able to decide whether the problems in living that are the target of concern qualify as bona fide mental illnesses. No epidemic of mental illness exists in the United States. What we have is more elasticity in definitions, leading to diagnostic inflation, which makes it harder and harder for *anyone* to be defined as mentally healthy (Frances, 2013).

Mental illnesses that were once said to be restricted to adults are today being said to exist among youngsters, too. Boosters and cheerleaders for the psych sector claim that it is possible for even infants and toddlers to be afflicted by major depression, posttraumatic stress disorder (PTSD), insomnia, social-anxiety disorder, and bereavement (Kluger, 2011). Any objections to the expansion of psychiatry into unchartered waters are dismissed by psychiatrists as unreasonable and uninformed, founded on a lack of medical knowledge about what to look for in these youthful sufferers. It may be true that the young are now being afflicted with the same ailments as adults, but it may also be true that this is one more way for therapists to do what they have done before: find a new population of humans to treat for individual dysfunctions and personal maladjustments. Apparently, the population of treatable beings does not even have to be human. Members of the psych sector have turned their therapeutic gaze onto nonhuman animals, particular the kind that we humans call pets. Increasingly, dogs, cats, and birds are said to be suffering from human-like psychological disorders that are treatable (Kluger, 2015). We can only wonder when this medical evangelism and disease mongering will end.

Psychiatry has experienced an impressive level of success in its efforts to control its turf and define its subject matter. This monopoly, like all monopolies, can have a life of its own, seeming no longer to be nourished directly by the groups or organizations that it benefits most. Psychiatry's claim that some errant hereditary factor or chemical imbalance is responsible for a dysfunction in the brain, which produces sick minds, seems now to be beyond dispute and thus practically impossible *to* refute (Foucault, 2003). Every newly discovered (or invented/diagnosed) ailment is blamed on a new hereditary factor or brain pathology. The fact is that psychiatry has no valid and reliable understanding of how individual factors lead to most of the mental disorders it deals with or of what cures could possibly be used to heal a sick mind (Frances, 2013). What makes a medical intervention morally permissible to psychiatry is not that it is therapeutic, but that it is something a patient wants (Szasz, 1973). Not all individuals with problems in living willingly accept medicalization of their conditions. Former patients—they call themselves "psychiatric survivors"—regularly protest at American Psychiatric Association meetings to publicize what they believe are injuries inflicted by their treatments.

The Myth of Mental Illness

Madness and Metaphors

One of the more influential scripts for classifying human attitudes, behaviors, and conditions is the *Diagnostic and Statistical Manual of Mental Disorders (DSM),* published by the American Psychiatric Association (APA). The fifth edition of the manual (APA, 2013) is the current one, and it is the longest and most inclusive of all the *DSMs. DSM-5* is 947 pages long and has 19 major diagnostic categories, plus three more categories: Other Mental Disorders, Medication-Induced Movement Disorders and Other Adverse Effects of Medication, and Other Conditions That May Be a Focus of Clinical Attention. The only thing that the hundreds of disorders in the manual have in common is that they all appear in *DSM-5;* any other similarity is purely coincidental. Allen Frances (2013), himself a distinguished and experienced psychiatrist, excoriates *DSM-5* and the way it was developed. He insists that the manual was carelessly written and guilty of the most blatant form of diagnostic inflation: turning ordinary, everyday experiences (e.g., nervousness, forgetting, anxiety, bad eating habits, confusion) into mental disorders. Moreover, it slights individuals who are truly impaired and in need of psychiatric assistance. The manual erodes the meaning of "normal" and lays a foundation that will make it easier for psychiatrists to overprescribe drugs and overmedicate patients with the enthusiastic assistance of profit-hungry drug companies. The manual did more for the pharmaceutical industry and the medical profession than it could ever do for patients (pp. xiv–xv).

The manual is not a coherent framework for understanding and explaining mental disorders (but it does not attempt to be). Instead, it is an exhaustive list of clusters of signs and symptoms that the architects of the *DSM* think characterize one mental disorder or another. It simply provides a long (extremely) list of things that a therapist *might* encounter at some point in his or her career. The manual is excruciatingly descriptive and completely atheoretical. In fact, it is best viewed as a compilation of officially sanctioned diagnoses rather than a list of diseases that patients might actually have (Szasz, 1994). The *DSM* represents a strange mix of cultural values, political compromises, scientific research, and human ailments or complaints that can be legitimately recorded on insurance claim forms (Kutchins & Kirk, 1997). Each new edition of the *DSM* expands the number of thinking, feeling, and behaving patterns that it medicalizes and diagnoses as mental disorders.

What does it mean to lose a mind? You can lose weight, you can lose your hair, you can lose an earring, you can lose your money, and you can even lose your life. But how can you lose your mind? One of the best and most lucid accounts of "mind" was written by a social behaviorist named George Herbert Mead. *Thinking, mind,* or *reflexive intelligence*—Mead (1934) used these terms interchangeably—is an inner conversation through the use of symbols or significant gestures (p. 47). Mead concluded that mind and brain are not the same. The brain is a biological organ, and without it, the mind is impossible. However, the existence of a brain does not necessarily mean that an organism has a mind, and it is possible to have mental processes that may appear odd to others but that are not caused by any brain dysfunction or abnormality.

Psychiatrists conceptualize patients as having experiences that could only be understood by proceeding *as if* their states of mind were diseased and responsible for their trespasses. Central to this project has been the sustained reconceptualization by psychiatry of disorders of the *mind* as disorders of the *brain* (Insel & Wang, 2010). The utilization of explanations of mental illnesses based on genetics, epigenomics (which specializes in the molecular effects of human experience), and neuroscience has strengthened psychiatry's claim that its explanations and treatments are scientific and therefore reliable and true (Kiehl, 2014; Rose & Abi-Rached, 2013).

To say that a person's mind is sick is like saying the economy is sick or that a joke is, meaning it is more metaphorical than factual (Szasz, 1973). A metaphor is a figure of speech wherein two things are contrasted to present a new way of thinking about an old concept. "The moon is a ghostly galleon" and "she has abdominal muscles of steel" are both metaphors. These words paint pictures that help us understand the ideas, but we must not confuse a metaphor with a scientific description or a truth statement. The moon is not a boat, and no human can have abdominal muscles made of metal. When a metaphor is mistaken for reality, used to advance some group's interests more than others', then we have the makings of myth. The *mythical* nature of the claim that minds can be sick was eventually forgotten, and it came to be accepted as truth (Conrad & Schneider, 1992; Szasz, 1994).

Individual Dysfunction or Social Deviance?

Psychiatrists have crafted a definition of mental illness that makes "losing a mind" look entirely individualistic, objective, and uniformly debilitating. In the *DSM-5*, a definition of *mental disorder* appears (the term "mental *illness*" rarely does), preceded by the claim that,

> [a]lthough no definition can capture all aspects of all disorders in the range contained in DSM-5, the following elements are required: . . . a syndrome characterized by clinically significant disturbance in an individual's cognition, emotion regulation, or behavior that reflects a dysfunction in the psychological, biological, or developmental processes underlying mental functioning. Mental disorders are usually associated with significant distress or disability in social, occupational, or other important activities. (APA, 2013, p. 20)

The authors of this definition emphasize that these syndromes or patterns absolutely *cannot* be an "expectable" or "culturally sanctioned" response to a particular event (p. 20). The disorder must be a manifestation of a *dysfunction* in an *individual* (behavioral, psychological, or biological). Neither deviant behavior (political, religious, or sexual) nor conflicts between an individual and society are mental disorders *unless* they are a symptom of some individual dysfunction. This conceptualization of mental illness creates a false separation between those people whose life experiences make no sense and everybody else.

Psychiatrists' desire to separate deviance, interpersonal conflicts, and all the rest from an individual dysfunction or mental disorder is based on little more than wishful thinking. They really have no way to know an individual dysfunction when they spot one or separate it from "expectable" and "culturally sanctioned" responses (Caplan, 1995; Fernando, 1991). The disorders in the *DSM* are themselves disordered, being neither internally consistent nor mutually exclusive.

> Some mental disorders describe short-term states, others life-long personality; some reflect inner misery, others bad behavior; some represent problems rarely or never seen in normals, others are just slight accentuation of the everyday; some reflect too little self-control, others too much; some are intrinsic to the person, others are culturally determined; some begin early in infancy, others emerge only late in life; some affect thought, others emotions, behaviors, or interpersonal relations; some seem more biological, others more psychological or social; some are supported by thousands of research studies, others by a mere handful; some may clearly belong in the *DSM*, others could have been left out and perhaps should be eliminated; some are clearly defined, others not; and there are complex permutations of all of these possible differences. (Frances, 2013, p. 17)

Mental disorder is a vague, ambiguous, and confusing term. Human behaviors, thoughts, and feelings are just too diverse to be neatly separated into the two categories of "sick" or "healthy." According to Frances (2013), none of the existing definitions of mental illness is "the slightest bit helpful either in determining which conditions should be considered mental disorders and which not, or in deciding who is sick and who is not" (p. 17).

It may come as a surprise to learn that psychiatry was disinclined to define mental disorder in early editions of the *DSM*. In one respect, this reluctance makes sense. It made it possible for psychiatrists to diagnose and then treat practically anything they wanted. The only requirement was that the thing being treated not be entirely normal. Ultimately, it became both embarrassing and potentially injurious to the success of psychiatry to be unable to offer a definition of mental illness. So, over 135 years after the founding of the American Psychiatric Association and after going through two editions of the manual (in 1952 and 1968), *mental disorder* was finally defined in *DSM-III*, published in 1980. The definition of mental illness really didn't do much to help clear up the mystery of exactly what mental illness is or how to separate it from related deviances. It did, however, offer a definition that could be used by the APA as one more tool in its quest to amass more and more patients (Kirk & Kutchins, 1992). (The American Psychiatric Association started in 1844 as the Association of Medical Super-intendents of American Institutions for the Insane; it changed its name in 1892 to the American Medico-Psychological Association, and changed its name again in 1921 to the current one.)

Individuals both inside and outside of the mental health field are skeptical that disorders can be differentiated from non-disorders or that *mental* prob-lems can be neatly separated from problems that are physical, behavioral, social, or moral (Kirk & Kutchins, 1992). In fact, what the architects of a previous edition of the manual, *DSM-IV-TR,* confess remains true for the current edition, namely, that

> there is no assumption that each category of mental disorder is a completely discrete entity with absolute boundaries dividing it from other mental disor-ders or from no mental disorder. There is also no assumption that all individu-als described as having the same mental disorder are alike in all important ways. (APA, 2000, p. xxxi)

This is quite a remarkable statement! It acknowledges that mental disorders cannot be separated from each other or even from a condition called "no mental disorder." According to this excerpt, individuals who have been given the same diagnostic label are not even necessarily alike in terms of the defining features of the diagnosis, let alone in terms of other biological, psychological, or social factors. The authors of the current manual do admit that "the current diagnostic criteria for any single disorder will not necessarily identify a homo-geneous group of patients who can be characterized reliably with all of these validators" (APA, 2013, p. 20). If psychiatrists, who have a strong incentive to formulate a definition of mental disorder that is beyond reproach, can do no better than they have done, then it probably cannot *be* done.

Diagnostic Dilemmas and Difficulties

It defies common sense, logic, and all that we know about human atti-tudes, behaviors, and conditions to believe it is possible to distinguish the socially acceptable from the socially unacceptable by targeting some indi-vidual characteristic or trait. Determining mental illness is an ineradicably social process of deciding who is normal and who is not that has little to do with a diagnosed individual's physical characteristics or individual dysfunc-tions (Turner & Edgley, 1996). What wayward chemical or brain pathology could possibly exist to differentiate all those individuals who hear socially *acceptable* voices, such as God's or Allah's, from all those individuals who hear the socially *un*acceptable voices of space invaders or some dead relative? What wayward chemical or brain pathology could possibly distinguish the socially *acceptable* pretending of children, adolescents, actors, magicians, defense attorneys, lovers, parents, and false flatterers from the socially *un*acceptable pretending of people who claim to be (and may believe that they are) Napoleon, Jesus Christ, or Santa Claus? It is easy to see how a society could make clear distinctions between the sick and the well or between the acceptable and the unacceptable; it is much more difficult to see how neurochemistry could (Turner & Edgley, 1996). Any effort to define mental disorder in some objective and uniform way is doomed to failure. Despite huge sums of money being thrown at the matter, psychiatry has failed to find convincing evidence that *any* mental disorder is a uniform illness with a single cause (Frances, 2013).

When the primary diagnostic strategy of a medical specialty is to create diseases through naming and proclaiming, as psychiatry is prone to do, it can produce all kinds of difficulties and dilemmas for its practitioners, as well as for its patients. This can be seen with the example of autism, called *autism spectrum disorder* in the *DSM-5*. This is a heterogeneous constellation of signs and symptoms that is usually diagnosed early in a child's life (before the age of 3). It includes difficulties in interacting or communicating with others or the presence of repetitive behaviors (e.g., throwing a wooden stick up in the air again and again to watch it bounce on the ground over and over).

The APA narrowed how autism would be diagnosed in the *DSM-5,* lumping it in with *Asperger's disorder, childhood disintegration disorder, Rett's syndrome*, and *pervasive developmental disorder not otherwise specified* (p. 809). Families that have a member who has been diagnosed with autism are understandably alarmed by the change and defend the previous diagnosis as both necessary and beneficial (Barker & Galardi, 2015). They fear that the change will influence the available research monies, government funding in schools to help with troubled children, and payments made by insurance companies. The APA claims that it made the changes to remove inconsistencies and misunderstandings (Rochman, 2012). If history is any guide, it is unlikely that greater consistency and clarity will be the outcome of the APA's diagnostic prestidigitations.

Finding and diagnosing mental illness is problematic, because mental illness is not itself a *specific* type of attitude, behavior, or condition. Mental illness is a name that is attached to a constellation of signs and symptoms, a constellation that is both wide and heterogeneous (Goode, 2015). Szasz

(1973) nicely illustrates the variable and relative nature of mental illness while showing the folly of searching for chemical or inborn causes of it:

> If you believe that you are Jesus, or have discovered a cure for cancer (and have not), or the Communists are after you (and they are not)—then your beliefs are likely to be regarded as symptoms of schizophrenia. But if you believe that the Jews are the Chosen People, or that Jesus was the Son of God, or that Communism is the only scientifically and morally correct form of government—then your beliefs are likely to be regarded as reflections of who you are: Jew, Christian, Communist. This is why I think that we will discover the chemical cause of schizophrenia when we will discover the chemical cause of Judaism, Christianity, and Communism. No sooner and no later. (pp. 101–102)

Psychiatry has tried to calm its critics by convincing them that it is doing both good science and good medicine and that mental illnesses are really no different from physical illnesses. The factual basis of this claim is suspect (Szasz, 1994). A human cadaver can have physical illnesses that are no different from what living humans can have, such as cancer, pneumonia, or a myocardial infarction. However, a cadaver most certainly cannot have a mental illness (Szasz, 1973).

Sharp lines between the normal and the abnormal cannot be drawn in the murky world of right/wrong, legal/illegal, proper/improper, healthy/sick, moral/immoral—that is, in the complex and ever-changing world of relationships, rules, and rule breaking—and when lines are drawn, they have more to do with sociocultural settings, languages, meanings, and interpersonal conflicts than with an individual's body chemistry or brain structure. Any psychological disorder tells us not only about the anguish of an individual, but also about patterns of interaction: what they are and how they unfold over time (Banton, Clifford, Frosh, Lousada, & Rosenthall, 1985).

Despite a multitude of uncertainties and disagreements in regard to what qualifies as a mental illness and who exactly has one, it is beyond dispute that a large number of groups have a vested interest in what the *DSM* says about mental illness—how it is defined and what it covers (Kupfer & Regier, 2010). This includes physicians, patients, hospitals, drug companies, psychologists, social workers, nurses, medical insurers, and taxpayers. If any way exists to further one's economic, political, or social interests by invoking the psychiatric nomenclature in the manual, someone will find a way to do it (Frances, 2013).

Declaration that an individual has a mental illness, rather than being based on sophisticated knowledge of disease, is really a judgment about one individual's personal, social, and ethical problems in living, offered by others who do not share or subscribe to the same understandings (Szasz, 1974; see also Szasz, 1960, 1994). A basic struggle in the human kingdom is a struggle over *words:* name or be named, define or be defined (Szasz, 1973). The only way that a judgment could be rendered that an individual who claims to be Santa Claus (or to be Jesus Christ or to be persecuted by the FBI or the communists) is mentally sick is for the definer to conclude that this claim is false by comparing it to other claims that he or she believes are healthier. Mental illness is a practical accomplishment of people acting together. It cannot be understood apart from the methods and procedures that we use to make the phenomenon describable (Blum, 1970). In order to find witches and identify them, we must already believe in witchcraft. The same goes for mental illness (Szasz, 1970).

Psychiatric Imperialism

Transcultural psychiatry (and global mental health) is the new growth industry for psychiatry. Its stated objective is to develop treatments to improve the lives of the mentally disordered wherever they may be found (Patel & Prince, 2010; Watters, 2010). One outcome of the transmission and diffusion of an American conceptualization of mental health and illness to other countries is that it has changed the way people there experience and express mental diseases (Watters, 2014). Depression, posttraumatic stress disorder, anorexia, and a host of other illnesses are spreading all across the planet, replacing local forms and expressions of human suffering.

> Mental health professionals in the West, and in the United States in particular, create official categories of mental disease and promote them in a diagnostic manual that has become the worldwide standard. American researchers and institutions run most of the premier scholarly journals and host top conferences in the fields of psychology and psychiatry. Western drug companies dole out large sums for research and spend billions marketing medications for mental illnesses. In addition, Western-trained traumatologists often rush in where war or natural disasters strike to deliver "psychological first aid," bringing with them their assumptions about how the mind becomes broken by horrible events and how it is best healed. (Watters, 2014, p. 383)

The *DSM-5* is an 800-pound gorilla that is harder and harder for the world's citizens to ignore.

In the appendix at the back of the *DSM-5,* the authors present a Glossary of Cultural Concepts of Distress. There, we are told about *dhat syndrome* (a range of diverse symptoms that are due to semen loss); *kufungisisa* (anxiety, depression, panic attacks, and irritability caused by thinking too much); and *susto* (an illness precipitated by a frightening event that causes the soul to leave the body, producing loss of appetite, excessive sleep, sadness, and low self-worth). On page 264, a condition related to *dhat* is described called *koro* (curiously, a term not included in the glossary noted above, but it should be). *Koro* is an intense anxiety in a male over the fear that his penis will withdraw into the body, causing death; in a female, it is a fear that her vulva and nipples will recede into her body, also with lethal consequences.

Cross-cultural mental illnesses undercut a fundamental plank of the APA's definition of abnormality that specifies that a mental disorder exists *only if* it is an individual dysfunction and *only if* it is not "merely" an expectable and culturally sanctioned response to a particular event. Cross-cultural mental illnesses prove by their very existence that mental illnesses vary by geographical region and cultural expectations. "The current formulation acknowledges that *all* forms of distress are locally shaped, including the DSM disorders" (APA, 2013, p. 758). So, by the APA's own admission, mental illness may not be an individual dysfunction characterized by uniform and universal signs and symptoms.

More and more individuals (professional and nonprofessional) are concluding that Western psychiatry (and the *DSM*) is particularly inapplicable, inappropriate, ineffective, and incomplete in cross-cultural settings. What is required is a more culturally sensitive definition of mental illness, along with therapies that can be applied cross-culturally, in order for psychiatry to have any relevance for global issues (Wedenoja, 2006). The APA's (2013) discussion of the cultural formulation of illness and its Cultural Formulation Interview does little of value. The manual is too sterile and formulaic, as well as being too heavily influenced by the medical model, to be able to display enough cultural sensitivity to avoid ethnocentrism.

Although certain attitudes, behaviors, and conditions are recognized as mental disorders, in most places and times, these disorders are conceptualized in a multitude of ways. No human characteristic has universal significance or meaning; time, place, and situation always exert an influence. *Eudysphoria* is dysphoria (i.e., anxiety or distress) that is viewed positively and as worthwhile. In the Mediterranean region, displays of suffering and misfortune are valued and valuable, being both functional and admired. Those who are able to suffer are viewed as no different from individuals who have been divinely blessed, and the ability to experience suffering and sadness demarcates the mature personality. For Buddhists, eudysphoria occurs because thoughts of worthlessness or meaninglessness are considered to be indicative of insight and spiritual maturity (Gaines, 2006).

The anthropological literature on cross-cultural variations in mental illness does permit a few conclusions. First, a relatively small percentage of people in societies across the globe are severely and chronically disordered due to high levels of irrationality and their inability to fulfill even the minimal requirements of participation in social life. A second conclusion is that most people who act in strange ways do not do so in an extreme or chronic fashion, and the labeling of people as mentally ill is a complex matter, influenced by a wide range of regional factors (Goode, 2015).

The United States is a nation of immigrants, and the existence of so much diversity and differential experiences based on race, ethnicity, national origin, religion, class, and geography poses substantial challenges for any therapeutic approach founded on an assumption of inherent pathology and homogeneity of experience (Garcia & Petrovich, 2011). An open society with diverse and often conflicting cultural messages and competing group loyalties and allegiances makes the formation of self-identity and individual personality difficult to achieve and sustain. Unsuccessful identity formation, rooted in the forces of nationalism and modernity, can produce problems for individuals who become overwhelmed by the cultural demands to become independent and self-reliant (Greenfield, 2013).

One thing that would help transcultural psychiatry would be the addition of the idea of *intersectionality*, an understanding of the ways that an individual's statuses and cultural factors affect one another and how social and individual factors work together (or intersect) to influence individuals and their lived experiences (Garcia & Petrovich, 2011). The value of considering how society and culture work together to influence individuals is, of course, well understood by social scientists, but it undercuts the core requirement of psychiatry that mental illnesses are individual dysfunctions. Rather than some poorly defined objective of promoting mental health, cultural competence and resilience may be more reasonable treatment objectives. Though *DSM-5* does acknowledge that it is important to be sensitive to the influence of race and ethnicity on health outcomes, the brief discussion of them on page 749 in the manual is woefully inadequate. It lacks enough substance and insight to do anybody any good. (In fact, the words "race" and "ethnicity" don't even appear in the manual's index.)

Mental Health Buccaneers and Social Control

The number and type of wayward events to which the label mental illness is attached has increased over time, principally because of changing social conditions and the emergence of so many groups that define and treat mental illnesses.

The variety of conditions currently regarded as mental illnesses, the large number and wide distribution of people who presumably suffer from these illnesses, and the great number of professionals who treat them are unprecedented. (Horwitz, 2002, p. 208)

Though many groups and professions benefit from a society-wide interest in being mentally healthy (Herman, 1995), psychiatry sits at the top of the heap. It has a near monopoly over definitions of mental health and mental illness, and its practitioners have a disproportionate influence over the treatment and cure of mental disorders. It is impossible to talk about mental illness without discussing the structure and function of psychiatry and the central role it plays in the definition and treatment of it.

Psychiatrists claim that they, just like all other physicians, specialize in the discovery and treatment of pathological body structures that just happen to cause diseased minds. When psychiatrists were unable to find structural abnormalities in the brain and trace them to particular signs and symptoms of mental illness, they were not discouraged. They merely *invented* mental diseases through the simple but effective strategy of proclaiming that certain specific attitudes, behaviors, and conditions were sick and in need of cure (Phillips, 2013). "For more than a century, psychiatrists constructed diagnoses, pretended that they are diseases, and no one in authority challenged their deceptions. The result is that few people now realize that diagnoses are not diseases" (Szasz, 1994, p. 36). Psychiatrists hoped that they would eventually find some biochemical or genetic abnormality to go along with each named disease (Kutchins & Kirk, 1997; Szasz, 1974).

Scheff (1984) asserts that the mentally ill have actually violated a *residual rule,* a rule associated with the label of mentally ill because no other label seems to fit. It is as if some of the violations of rules prompt humans to quickly go through names for normative departures, searching for the one that fits best. If individuals break the law, they are criminals; if they drink to excess, they are drunkards; if they misuse drugs, they are addicts; if they don't use good manners when eating, they are boors. However, if individuals think they have bee hives in their stomachs or that their ideas turn into butterflies, things are different. It is clear that something is wrong, but it is not entirely clear what it might be. At this point, a residual rule has been violated, and so the residual label of "crazy," "mad," "insane," or "just plain nuts" is most likely. The label of mental illness can be called into service as a wastebasket or default category to cover all those distressing attitudes, behaviors, and conditions that have no specific label of their own.

Critics of psychiatry deplore the arbitrary and pseudoscientific way that psychiatrists determine what is sick and what is not. Armstrong (1993) took psychiatrists to task for using what she calls the *Peter Pan method* to create and validate diagnostic categories: Clap if you believe in fairies. In this case, the "fairies" are conditions like schizophrenia, simple phobia, and posttraumatic stress disorder. Only the hopelessly naive or extremely gullible could believe that high consensus among psychiatrists is the same thing as the scientific discovery of mental disease. Peter Breggin (1991), himself a psychiatrist, criticized his colleagues in the profession: "Only in psychiatry is the existence of physical disease determined by APA presidential proclamations, by committee decisions, and even, at times, by a vote of the members of APA, not to mention the courts" (p. 141).

Mental disorders are inseparable from the language that names and defines them (Kovel, 1988; Szasz, 1994). Modern psychiatry has achieved the enviable position in which proclamations are taken as truth, wishes can become achievements, and propaganda is taken as science (Breggin, 1991, p. 182). Psychiatrists have tried to align themselves more closely with specialists in brain abnormalities, laboring to convince the public, health insurance companies, and the federal government that psychiatry is a bona fide medical science, no different from other branches of medicine (Szasz, 1985). Psychiatrists have enough power and influence to be able to ratify their claims as correct and declare their critics' claims to be delusional (Szasz, 1994).

Psychiatric intervention is used at times to handle unruly or errant populations, such as the insane, the deranged, the idle, the ignorant, or even the deprived. The psychiatrization of more and more problems in living makes it quite likely that what are actually manifestations of *social* problems are being refurbished as individual problems of adjustment (Szasz, 1997). Caplan (1995) provides an excellent example of this. At a clinic where she was employed early in her career as a clinical psychologist, she was told by her supervisor that her job was *not* to attempt to find better jobs or additional welfare monies for the poor families who came to the clinic for help (even though that is what Caplan believed they really needed). Her charge was to find some appropriate psychiatric label that would fit her clients' complaints and then to suggest some appropriate medical treatment—such as psychotherapy—that was an established part of traditional mental health care (p. 280).

One of the populations that psychiatry has controlled is children, almost always under the guise of helping them. The psych deck, however, has been stacked against them. Not only are they young and powerless, but they are also defined by psychiatrists as having individual dysfunctions, and they have probably alienated central figures in their families, their schools, and their communities (Potter, 2014). The claim that some children have serious mental disorders can serve as a convenient smokescreen.

Poverty was let off the hook. Social injustices were let off the hook. Parents were let off the hook. Lousy schools and dysfunctional teachers were let off the hook. There was simply something biologically wrong with these children that accounted for all the things that teachers, parents, and Boy Scout leaders did not like about a whole panoply of childhood behaviors: not sitting still, not paying attention, not learning to read correctly (on time), butting in. (Armstrong, 1993, p. 196)

Psychiatrists cannot determine in any scientific way how many of children's problems in living are individual dysfunctions and how many are actually normal responses to abnormal situations. Psychiatrists cannot even agree on exactly *who* would benefit from psychiatric treatment. Are we talking about behavioral misfits, the emotionally ruined, the angry, the unmotivated, the irresponsible, the intractable, the socially deprived, the abused, the maladjusted, the promiscuous, the frigid, the rigid, the amoral, the immoral, the insane, the depressed, the hyperactive, or all of the above?

The psychiatric diagnosis given to children most often today is *attention-deficit/hyperactivity disorder* (ADHD). The *DSM-5* (APA, 2013) puts the prevalence of ADHD in "most cultures" at approximately 5 percent of children and 2.5 percent of adults (p. 61). Though it is a diagnosis that is suspect—how could U.S. psychiatry have any knowledge of most cultures of the world even if the diagnosis were a bona fide illness?—it is also a diagnosis with more sinister characteristics. It is the reason that countless numbers of children and teenagers are put on prescription drugs every year all across the world (Schubert, Hansen, & Rapley, 2014). ADHD exists as a disease primarily because enough powerful and influential people have convinced enough other people that children's not paying attention, impulsivity, and moving around a lot constitute a disease that should be included within the boundaries of medicine and medical research.

Unlike a bona fide medical disease (e.g., tertiary syphilis or tuberculosis) in which a known pathogen or abnormal body lesion produces a consistent constellation of signs and symptoms (i.e., a demonstrable pathology), ADHA is best viewed as a hypothetical construct or a definitional disease. Even the APA (2013) confesses as much when it reports, "No biological marker is diagnostic for ADHD" (p. 61). The absence of physiological, metabolic, or neurological markers for individuals diagnosed with ADHD means no medical basis exists for considering it as a disease. (Some differences are reported to exist between ADHD kids and their peers in total brain volume, but the differences are not diagnostic [APA, 2013].) "ADHD is not . . . a scientifically discovered disorder, but rather a concept created via the discourse of [psychiatry] to police behaviors that are socially unacceptable" (Schubert et al., 2014, p. 362).

What gets a child defined as mentally ill is almost always a persistent conflict or disagreement with some adult authority figure. Most of these children usually have little difficulty getting along with their peers in situations of their own making. To call a lack of fit between children and adults a mental illness of the child is at best a distortion and at worst an outright lie. Too much is blamed on the child and not enough on the people with whom he or she must cope or situations the child must handle successfully. Practically any characteristic of children that irritates, interferes with, or troubles adults can be medicalized and used to justify psychiatric interventions into children's lives. A child's inappropriateness may be little more than a method of adapting to what seems to the child to be an intolerable or undecipherable situation (Breggin & Breggin, 1994).

In some cases, it is certainly true that psychiatrists have used a great deal of restraint in their dealings with problem behaviors of patients. Some parents have children who are markedly disordered, being a threat to themselves and to others, and parents have done all they could to understand and correct them, all to no avail. They know something must be done with their self-destructive, violent, troubled youngsters, but they don't know what to do. The problem in these cases is not too much medicine, cognitive therapy, or psychiatric intervention; it is too little (J. Warner, 2010). Ethical and experienced psychiatrists, when confronted with patients who want to better themselves, can sometimes offer successful treatments. In these cases, the lives of patients can be changed for the better (Frances, 2013).

Sense and Nonsense in the Psychiatric Enterprise

A script for human experience that is formal, shared, and viewed as correct gives the impression that certain experiences are far more reasonable, healthy, necessary, normal, and uniform than they really are. Unsurprisingly, people who have taken a great deal of time and trouble to master a particular script—learning its language, coming to believe in its importance and value, appreciating its logic—have trouble accepting that it is just one script among many. People march to a different beat because they hear a different drummer, but ideal scripts tend to make it appear that only one parade exists. Psychiatric nomenclature, along with the medicalization of problems in living that it creates and legitimates, is characterized by ethnocentrism and the imposition of standards of health and normality on people for whom they are inadequate (Bartholomew, 1997). A growing tendency exists in U.S. society to find psychological abnormality where there is only pathos and to believe that problems in living can be cured by attaching a medical diagnosis and a code number to each one (Kutchins & Kirk, 1997).

The authors of the *DSM* claim that logic, science, and well-conducted research have all worked together to tell them what is normal and what is not. However, the *DSM* has little to do with science. In fact, according to Caplan (1995), it is "shockingly unscientific" (p. 31). The contents of the manual are determined primarily by the gatekeeping efforts of the small number of influential psychiatrists who have the directive to decide which disorders will be allowed to appear and which will not. The *DSM* was constructed primarily to benefit psychiatrists (and other mental health professionals), not their patients (Kovel, 1988). A handbook of mental disorders gives psychiatrists many benefits. It gives them a sense of competency and control, professional respectability, and legitimacy and credibility. If psychiatrists cannot reliably and correctly diagnose a patient's mental illness, how can they treat it? It also allows them to know which diagnoses will result in compensation from health insurers (Grob & Horwitz, 2010; Kirk & Kutchins, 1992).

As the *DSM* has gone through its many revisions, it has expanded its list of mental disorders and lost both its sense of proportion and its utility as a guidebook that could reasonably help people to overcome some debilitating human afflictions.

> A comprehensive medically oriented diagnostic manual could be helpful for some purposes, but only if it were much narrower in scope, included only clearly distinguishable mental disorders that entail severe consequences and didn't pander to insurers, drug companies and therapists by medicalizing so many social problems. (Kirk & Kutchins, 1994, p. A17)

If architects of the *DSM* had packaged their document as what it is—a sourcebook of diagnoses based on a sampling of studies of unknown validity and reliability, as well as on ethics, values, hunches of psychiatrists (and others in the mental health field), reflecting political pressures, tradition, and economic/business decisions—it could be honestly accepted or rejected. As it stands now, it is an ailing document. Though reasonable people can disagree over what should or should not be included in a manual of mental disorders, they must agree that definitions of terms and ailments in the *DSM* are fuzzy and that people—therapists and non-therapists—use them without much precision (Kirk & Kutchins, 1992).

The fuzziness of many of the terms used in the manual can be appreciated by examining some of the disorders that appear on its pages. One of these is *specific learning disorder with impairment in written expression* (APA, 2013, pp. 66–67). The essential feature of this disorder is that a person's writing skills (as measured by standardized tests) are "substantially below" those "expected" given the individual's chronological age, measured intelligence, and age-appropriate education and have been for at least 6 months. The presence of this disorder is indicated by such things as grammatical or punctuation errors within sentences, poor paragraph organization, multiple spelling errors, and excessively poor handwriting. What is wrong with this picture? Though a few students may be poor writers because they have sick minds or bad brains, the manual provides no clue about how to separate these dysfunctional writers from those who are poor writers because they were badly trained or were unresponsive to writing instruction. The *specific learning disorder with impairment in mathematics* (p. 67) covers individuals who are unable to learn multiplication tables, to carry numbers correctly, to decode word problems, to obey mathematical signs, or to copy numbers or figures correctly. Once again, something that can have many causes (and is really only a problem in places where math skills are necessary for daily living or success in school) is transformed into an individual pathology through the process of naming and proclaiming.

The *DSM-IV-TR*, the previous edition, included Appendix B, a list of proposed disorders that required further study (APA, 2000). Each of the proposed disorders, the authors claimed, was subjected to a careful empirical review, and wide commentary was solicited from the field. Each one had failed to receive the kind of support necessary to warrant making it a bona fide disorder in the body of the text. One of these was *caffeine withdrawal*. The diagnostic criteria of caffeine withdrawal are heavy caffeine use; some physical withdrawal symptoms from abrupt cessation of caffeine (headaches, marked fatigue or drowsiness, marked anxiety or depression, nausea or vomiting); and clinically significant distress or impairment in social, occupational, or other important areas of functioning. In the current edition, the diagnosis of *caffeine withdrawal disorder* appears (APA, 2013, p. 507), based almost exclusively on one particular symptom: headaches occurring when heavy caffeine users discontinue their caffeine use. (The document is mute on the details of how this disorder moved from a provisional status in the previous edition to a bona fide mental illness in the current one.)

The important question is not whether some people have troubles with caffeine; it is whether the APA has any legitimate scientific reasons to apply vague terms (e.g., "impaired control," "risky use," "social impairment") to a cluster of signs and symptoms that could result from the use of a chemical substance and then to declare the cluster to be an indicator of a mental disorder. The APA has overstepped the boundaries of common sense, logical analysis, and scientific evidence in constructing the diagnoses in the book regarding the use of caffeine.

The kind of disorders we have been examining—learning disorders or caffeine withdrawal—seem to lack enough rigor and precision to be considered serious entries in a manual of mental disorders. Still, we would expect the classic disorders, such as schizophrenia, to be the model of objectivity and scientific precision. However, research into the causes and nature of schizophrenia is both extensive and contradictory (Boyle, 2002). A dazzling array of symptoms and signs is exhibited by schizophrenics, and about 20 distinct explanations have been proposed to make sense of the disorder (Gallagher, 2002). In 1993, Heinrichs reviewed 70 years of research on schizophrenia. His main conclusion was that very little is known or understood about it and that it suffers from a *heterogeneity problem,* a polite way of saying that the term is used in so many different ways to cover so many different things that it has lost much of its meaning. Things have changed little, according to Feldman (2009). He concludes that people diagnosed with schizophrenia show "significant differences" in their constellation of signs and symptoms, even when they are labeled with the same diagnostic category (p. 469). The APA (2013) seems to recognize this when it says that individuals with schizophrenia will "vary substantially on most features, as schizophrenia is a heterogeneous clinical syndrome" (p. 100).

Whatever schizophrenia is, it is not pure abnormality, and, if it is a disease, it is one of the most peculiar around. As Strauss (1991) commented, "Schizophrenia is very different from an illness like a broken leg. You cannot break a leg, take off the cast in order to play football, and then, after the game, put on the cast again and be an invalid" (p. 82). An individual who displays mentally disordered behaviors under some situations (e.g., stress or social isolation) may be perfectly normal or healthy under different situations (e.g., less stressful conditions or when social support networks are strong) (Goode, 2015). Schizophrenics can alternate back and forth between normality and abnormality on a moment-to-moment, hour-to-hour, or day-to-day basis (Strauss, 1991). Schizophrenia has been branded a defective, deficient, disrupted, and disorganized construct (Wiener, 1991).

Schizophrenia in Third World countries is neither as debilitating for sufferers nor as disruptive of their relationships as it is in the Western world (R. Warner, 2014). Where the hallucinations and delusions that regularly accompany schizophrenia are credited to supernatural forces, not blamed on some individual dysfunction, the mentally ill may actually experience *less* alienation, rejection, and stigma. Many times in Third World countries, the signs and symptoms of schizophrenia actually *elevate* the status of any individual who has them. "In non-industrial cultures throughout the world, the hallucinations and altered states of consciousness produced by psychosis, fasting, sleep deprivation, social isolation and contemplation, and hallucinogenic drug use are often a prerequisite for gaining shamanic power" (R. Warner, 2014, p. 376). In nonindustrial societies of the Third World, human labor power is valued for its contributions to the well-being of the community, even if it is done by a mentally ill individual. A consistent finding is that schizophrenics in the nonindustrial world do better over time than they do in industrial societies (Watters, 2014, p. 385).

Even the APA (2013) acknowledges the existence of culture-related diagnostic issues with schizophrenia. Ideas delusional in one culture, it observes (e.g., witchcraft), are common in another, and hallucinations in one culture, such as hearing God's voice, are an ordinary part of religious devotion in another. Even disorganized or incoherent speech can be a result, the APA concludes, of linguistic variation in narrative styles across cultures. This is also true for variations in emotional expression, body language, and eye contact. It is even possible for individuals to have hallucinations and overvalued ideas (i.e., unreasonable beliefs their possessors know are untrue) that look psychotic but are normative for their subgroups (p. 103). It seems reasonable to conclude from reading between the lines in the APA discussion of schizophrenia that schizophrenics in the United States are not sick at all. They are simply in the wrong country.

Social isolation of the schizophrenic, both before and after a flare-up of the disorder, is found consistently to be one of the best predictors of poor treatment outcomes. The way that schizophrenia is treated in the West has all the elements necessary to exacerbate the problems of the mentally ill. "In the Third World, it appears, the person with a psychotic disorder is more likely to retain his or her self-esteem, a feeling of value to the community and a sense of belonging" (R. Warner, 2014, p. 251). The schizophrenic must be given genuine responsibilities, usually in the form of important work, that are neither too much nor too little for him or her to handle. The schizophrenic must also not be exposed to the extremes of emotional contagion (i.e., either smothering or condemnation). Psychoactive drugs, shock therapy, surgery, hospitalization, MRIs, CT scans, and the rest of what is at the disposal of Western medicine fail to accomplish any of these integrative, assimilative functions often enough for us to have much confidence in their long-term efficacy.

Depressive symptoms are also influenced by sociocultural factors. The increase in depressive symptoms as individuals age is due principally to poor physical health, loss of one's spouse, and lack of meaningful employment (specifically, unemployment's adverse impact on lifestyle, finances, and feelings of self-worth). If individuals stay married, productive, socially involved, financially well-off, and healthy, mental health improves with advancing age (P. Clarke, Marshall, House, & Lantz, 2011). Young adults are able to cope with disappointments in their lives, along with whatever depression these disappointments can produce, if they have sufficient levels of *adaptive resilience*. This is a willingness to try again after some failure or the inclination to find something positive in the fact that they did not accomplish all that they wanted (Reynolds & Baird, 2010). When depression is found among the young, one reason is that depressed teenagers are inclined to withdraw from relationships over time, meaning they have few friends to help them overcome their episodes of depression (Schaefer, Kornienko, & Fox, 2011). Depression makes it harder for people to act deliberately (Remster, 2014).

Meltdown in the *DSM*

The APA has occasionally messed with the wrong group and then found itself the target of unwanted attacks. Sometimes these conflicts are little more than skirmishes, but other times they are outright wars over the validity and reliability of some of the mental disorders that psychiatrists include in the manual. For example, the gay community successfully pressed its claim that homosexuality is not a mental illness, and it was eventually removed from the manual (Bayer, 1981). No doubt, similar battles would have been fought over many more of the disorders in the manual if other offended groups had been able to muster the resources to challenge organized psychiatry's monopoly over determining what is normal and what is not. One group that the APA has consistently offended, or even outraged, is women. Women's battles with psychiatry show that tension and discord are at the heart of any effort to pigeonhole behavior and people, especially if those people prefer to be left alone and have the resources and abilities to defend themselves. When psychiatrists took on women, they had a tigress by the tail.

In the *DSM*'s third, revised edition (*DSM-III-R*; APA, 1987), an appendix appeared that included three disorders that were classified as needing further study: sadistic personality disorder, self-defeating personality disorder, and late luteal phase dysphoric disorder (LLPDD). The first two were cast out of *DSM-IV/DSM-IV-TR*, but the last was renamed premenstrual dysphoric disorder (PDD) and included in Appendix B. *Premenstrual dysphoric disorder* essentially transforms women's more extreme premenstrual experiences—anxiety, depression, irritability, despondency, anger—into a mental disorder. The APA apparently did not really consider PDD a *proposed* diagnosis that requires further study (the logic of appearing in Appendix B), because it *did*

appear in the body of the text as a "depressive disorder not otherwise specified" (APA, 2000, p. 381). A disorder that is relegated to a provisional
appendix can apparently be called into service as a bona fide mental disorder
when the need arises.

In the *DSM-5*, the APA (2013) reports that after careful scientific review
of the evidence, PDD was moved from the appendix of the fourth edition to
Section II of the current edition as a bona fide disorder. Twenty years of
research on PDD, the APA insists, confirmed that it is a depressive disorder
found in women at some point after ovulation, having a "marked" and
adverse impact on their abilities to function. In the 1950s, Katherine Dalton,
a British physician, concluded that women's raging hormones were responsible for their mood swings and antisocial behaviors that became especially
prevalent during premenstrual periods. Dalton and an associate called this
constellation of hormonally caused afflictions "premenstrual syndrome," or
PMS (Francoeur, 1996, p. 44). PMS is a diagnosis that ratifies a nineteenth-
century belief that women are uncontrollably swayed by sex hormones
produced by their ovaries. These hormones are blamed for premenstrual
tension, and premenstrual tension is blamed for women's apparent inability
to work and to carry out other social activities and responsibilities when
they are afflicted (Frank, 1931; Rittenhouse, 1991).

Even if significant monthly changes can be found in premenstrual women,
they may have more to do with social relationships and how women interpret their physical changes than with raging hormones and ovarian dysfunctions. Some women do experience a debilitating syndrome of maladies on a
cyclical basis, but this can hardly be typical for most women or even for a
substantial minority of them. No consistent biological markers have been
found to separate PMS women from non-PMS women, and practically all
women handle what they must handle—jobs, children, households, relationships—regardless of how they feel during or before their menstrual periods.
A woman's mood swings may have more to do with the quality of her life.
Representatives of different *social domains*—groups of people who share
views, concerns, and commitments—continue to contest the status of PMS
as a mental illness, and PMS continues to be a different construct to different
audiences: women, health and mental health practitioners, and scientists
(Figert, 1995).

Premenstrual changes—physical, mental, emotional—may occur in
women (to a greater or lesser degree), but these altered states are not necessarily mental disorders. Women who report the most acute problems live in
situations that are characterized by high levels of stress, poverty, insecurity,
and abuse. The treatments that seem to help these women the most are participation in self-help groups, changes in diet, and increases in exercise

(Caplan, 1995). According to Caplan, some women may feel depressed, angry, or irritable all the time, but they may notice it more during their periods or believe that it is more legitimate for them to give expression to their feminine fury when they are premenstrual (p. 162).

Women's growing independence and assertiveness, as well as their anger over persistent gender inequality, can be inauthenticated or delegitimized by attributing them to PMS. This social transformation of the political into the biological helps to defuse and redirect interpersonal tensions and social conflicts. Women may be less likely to vent their fury—or to unite with others to identify mutual problems and work to eradicate them—when they define the turbulence in their lives as physical, abnormal, and transitory (Laws, 1983). Martin (1992) reported that PMS is branded a serious individual problem at those points in time when it is necessary to keep women out of the labor force and in the home. When women were needed to assist in the war effort, little attention was paid to PMS. However, when men returned from war and needed jobs, women were nudged back into more traditional roles by the discovery (or rediscovery) of the crippling effects of PMS. When women's participation in the labor force is seen as a threat, PMS is more likely to be construed as a liability.

Some of the same disease mongering and diagnostic imperialism that psychiatry has shown with women and female conditions is being found increasingly with men and male conditions. Men's aging experiences, along with some features of male sexuality, have been medicalized, making them look more undesirable as they are portrayed as treatable. Many men do feel anxious over some of the physical changes they undergo, and some would like to slow them down or stop them altogether. In this medicalization of male conditions, one of the biggest winners may well be the pharmaceutical industry, which supplies the pills to make many of the promised transformations possible.

> Concerns with aging and performance are propelling men to seek medical solutions for declining signs of masculinity. The perception of these physical changes as threats to traditional characteristics of manliness is not universal, but it seems to be increasing as pharmaceutical and medical entrepreneurs seek to establish markets, amplify male anxieties, and provide solutions to the problems of aging men. . . . The partial medicalization of andropause and hair loss and the huge success of Viagra may be only the beginning. (Conrad, 2007, p. 45)

The question really isn't whether men should be upset by the physical changes that occur as they age. The question is whether psychiatrists are acting properly to define these changes as abnormal and in need of a cure.

Most every male will experience unreasonable pressure to regain his youth in light of the promises and propaganda. When natural and often inevitable biological changes can be linked together and portrayed as a "syndrome" of unwanted but treatable conditions, it pathologizes ordinary and expectable human conditions.

Because of the close association among virility, sexuality, and masculinity, one of the more troubling experiences for some men—and one that psychiatry has felt the best equipped to medicalize—is erectile dysfunction. Inspired by a 1992 National Institute of Health conference and a 1994 study on the condition, the diagnosis has been expanded from the rather strict criterion of inability to get an erection to the more elastic and subjective criterion of inability to get or maintain an erection adequate for completion of sexual activity, which causes "significant distress" for a male. (The APA [2013] places *erectile disorder* on its list of sexual dysfunctions.) Aggressive marketing of drugs such as Viagra, Cialis, and Levitra only adds more fuel to men's anxieties over their masculinity. This intensifies pressures to seek a "cure" in an atmosphere that is powerfully influenced by the economic interests of drug companies and medical practitioners.

As psychiatrists use the "marked distress" criterion more and more, baldness may find itself listed on the pages of the *DSM,* too. The effort to medicalize and pathologize hair loss is gaining momentum, especially as more drugs (e.g., Rogaine, Propecia) and new surgical techniques (scalp reduction, hair implants) become available. A *baldness dysphoric disorder* would be no stranger, no less reasonable, or no less scientific than some of the others that now appear in the book (either as bona fide disorders or as conditions for further study): *Internet gaming disorder* (i.e., using the Internet so much that school performance drops, jobs are lost, or relationships are impaired); *hoarding disorder* (i.e., inability to discard items regardless of value and regardless of the clutter this creates); *premature ejaculation* (you're on your own with this one); *rumination disorder* (i.e., repeated regurgitation of food over the period of at least 1 month to then be chewed again and swallowed or spit out); *disruptive mood dysregulation disorder* (i.e., throwing enough tantrums of sufficient ferocity that it bothers enough people that it eventually leads to the individual being diagnosed as mentally ill).

Conclusions

The efforts to define mental disorders in some uniform and objective way, though understandable, are doomed to failure. Terms such as *mental disorder* or *mental illness* are just too fuzzy and unscientific to be used in systematic and reliable ways to differentiate among people for what they say, think, feel, and do. Mental disorders do not exist in a social vacuum, and they tell us more about the nature and quality of life in a society than they do about individual dysfunctions. Sharp lines cannot be reliably drawn between the sick and the well in the complex and ever-changing world in which we live.

Whatever good a manual such as the *DSM* does is hardly compensated for by the great harm it does to our understanding of human diversity. Mental illness is less an objective medical condition than something that is socially constructed and socially sustained. Representatives of organized psychiatry further their interests by crafting an ideal script to define human abnormality that seems beyond dispute. The proffering of an image of inherent order and incontrovertible individual normality, as wrongheaded as it may be, is probably the major accomplishment of the *DSM*.

Mental disorders flesh out our understanding of the relativity of deviance. They show us that even private, personal experiences (such as "losing one's mind") are also public, social events. Power, conflict, and the social construction of reality all play a part in the manufacture of madness. Psychiatry, an organized and influential medical specialty, has mustered sufficient resources to craft understandings of sick and well that directly benefit it. Medicine generates meanings about the human condition that are given life through the words and deeds—the concrete actions and reactions—of people who use what they have learned to judge, evaluate, and classify certain attitudes, behaviors, and conditions as sick or abnormal.

Deviance is in the eyes of the beholders, it is true, but these beholders are not always lone moral crusaders. We may be upset by what we believe are odd qualities of others: appearances, eccentricities, quirks, and attributes. However, more and more, the definitions of deviance depend on the actions, interests, outlooks, and resources of representatives of formal organizations or professions (such as psychiatry) who can draw on a vast arsenal of meanings in their dealings with troublesome and maybe troubled individuals. Institutions and formal organizations are important centers of social activity, and they provide rules and understandings about proper and improper ways of acting, thinking, feeling, and being.

References

Adams, K., & Ferrandino, J. (2008). Managing mentally ill inmates in prison. *Criminal Justice and Behavior, 35,* 913–927.

American Psychiatric Association. (1952). *Diagnostic and statistical manual of mental disorders.* Washington, DC: Author.

American Psychiatric Association. (1968). *Diagnostic and statistical manual of mental disorders* (2nd ed.). Washington, DC: Author.

American Psychiatric Association. (1980). *Diagnostic and statistical manual of mental disorders* (3rd ed.). Washington, DC: Author.

American Psychiatric Association. (1987). *Diagnostic and statistical manual of mental disorders* (3rd ed., rev.). Washington, DC: Author.

American Psychiatric Association. (1994). *Diagnostic and statistical manual of mental disorders* (4th ed.). Washington, DC: Author.

American Psychiatric Association. (2000). *Diagnostic and statistical manual of mental disorders* (4th ed., text rev.). Washington, DC: Author.

American Psychiatric Association. (2013). *Diagnostic and statistical manual of mental disorders* (5th ed.). Washington, DC: Author.

Armstrong, L. (1993). *And they call it help: The psychiatric policing of America's children*. Reading, MA: Addison-Wesley.

Banton, R., Clifford, P., Frosh, S., Lousada, J., & Rosenthall, J. (1985). *The politics of mental health*. New York: Macmillan.

Barker, K., & Galardi, T. R. (2015). Diagnostic domain defense: Autism spectrum disorder and the *DSM-5*. *Social Problems, 62,* 120–140.

Bartholomew, R. (1997). The medicalization of the exotic: Latah as a colonialism-bound "syndrome." *Deviant Behavior, 18,* 47–75.

Bayer, R. (1981). *Homosexuality and American psychiatry: The politics of diagnosis.* New York: Basic Books.

Blum, A. (1970). The sociology of mental illness. In J. Douglas (Ed.), *Deviance and respectability: The social construction of moral meanings* (pp. 31–60). New York: Basic Books.

Boyle, M. (2002). *Schizophrenia: A scientific delusion* (2nd ed.). London: Routledge.

Breggin, P. (1991). *Toxic psychiatry: Why therapy, empathy, and love must replace the drugs, electroshock, and biochemical theories of the new psychiatry.* New York: St. Martin's Press.

Breggin, P., & Breggin, G. R. (1994). *The war against children.* New York: St. Martin's Press.

Caplan, P. (1995). *They say you're crazy: How the world's most powerful psychiatrists decide who's normal.* Reading, MA: Addison-Wesley.

Clarke, A. E., Shim, J. K., Mamo, L., Fosket, J. R., & Fishman, J. R. (2003). Biomedicalization: Technoscientific transformation of health, illness, and U.S. biomedicine. *American Sociological Review, 68,* 161–194.

Clarke, P., Marshall, V., House, J., & Lantz, P. (2011). The social structuring of mental health over the adult life course: Advancing theory in the sociology of aging. *Social Forces, 89,* 1287–1314.

Conrad, P. (2007). *The medicalization of society: On the transformation of human conditions into treatable disorders.* Baltimore: Johns Hopkins University Press.

Conrad, P., & Schneider, J. (1992). *Deviance and medicalization: From badness to sickness* (Exp. ed.). Philadelphia: Temple University Press.

Davies, V. (1947). *Miracle on 34th Street.* San Diego, CA: Harcourt Brace Jovanovich.

Davis, C., & Abraham, J. (2013). *Unhealthy pharmaceutical regulation: Innovation, politics, and promissory science.* New York: Palgrave Macmillan.

Dunham, H. (1976). *Social realities and community psychiatry.* New York: Human Sciences Press.

Feldman, R. (2009). *Essentials of understanding psychology* (8th ed.). New York: McGraw-Hill.

Fernando, S. (1991). *Mental health, race and culture.* New York: St. Martin's Press.

Figert, A. (1995). The three faces of PMS: The professional, gendered, and scientific structuring of a scientific disorder. *Social Problems, 42,* 56–73.

Foucault, M. (1965). *Madness and civilization: A history of insanity in the age of reason.* New York: Pantheon/Random House.

Foucault, M. (2003). *Abnormal: Lectures at the Collège de France, 1974–1975* (V. Marchetti & A. Salomoni, Eds.; G. Burchell, Trans.). New York: Picador/ St. Martin's Press.

Frances, A. (2013). *Saving normal: An insider's revolt against out-of-control psychiatric diagnoses, DSM-5, big pharma, and the medicalization of ordinary life.* New York: William Morrow/HarperCollins

Francoeur, R. (1996). Introduction. In R. Francoeur (Ed.), *Taking sides: Clashing views on controversial issues in human sexuality* (5th ed., p. 44). Guilford, CT: Dushkin.

Frank, R. T. (1931). The hormonal causes of premenstrual tension. *Archives of Neurology and Psychiatry, 26,* 1053–1057.

Gaines, A. (2006). Eudysphoria. In H. J. Birx (Ed.), *Encyclopedia of anthropology* (pp. 870–871). Thousand Oaks, CA: Sage.

Gallagher, B. J., III. (2002). *The sociology of mental illness* (4th ed.). Upper Saddle River, NJ: Prentice Hall.

Garcia, B., & Petrovich, A. (2011). *Strengthening the DSM: Incorporating resilience and cultural competence.* New York: Springer-Verlag.

Goffman, E. (1961). *Asylums.* Garden City, NY: Anchor/Doubleday.

Goode, E. (2015). *Deviant behavior* (10th ed.). Upper Saddle River, NJ: Pearson.

Gosden, R. (2003). The medicalisation of deviance. In D. Kelly & E. Clarke (Eds.), *Deviant behavior* (6th ed., pp. 402–409). New York: Worth.

Greenfeld, L. (2013). *Mind, modernity, madness: The impact of culture on human experience.* Cambridge, MA: Harvard University Press.

Grob, G. N., & Horwitz, A. V. (2010). *Diagnoses, therapy, and evidence: Conundrums in modern American medicine.* New Brunswick, NJ: Rutgers University Press.

Gusfield, J. (1981). *The culture of public problems.* Chicago: University of Chicago Press.

Heinrichs, R. W. (1993). Schizophrenia and the brain: Conditions for a neuropsychology of madness. *American Psychologist, 48,* 221–233.

Herman, E. (1995). *The romance of American psychology: Political culture in the age of experts.* Berkeley: University of California Press.

Horwitz, A. (2002). *Creating mental illness.* Chicago: University of Chicago Press.

Horwitz, A., & Wakefield, J. (2008). The epidemic in mental illness: Clinical fact or survey artifact? In J. Goodwin & J. Jasper (Eds.), *The contexts reader* (pp. 345–352). New York: Norton.

Insel, T. R., & Wang, P. S. (2010). Rethinking mental illness. *Journal of the American Medical Association, 303,* 1970–1971.

Kiehl, K. A. (2014). *The psychopath whisperer: The science of those without conscience.* New York: Crown.

King, M. D., & Bearman, P. S. (2011). Socioeconomic status and the increased prevalence of autism in California. *American Sociological Review, 76,* 320–346.

Kirk, S., & Kutchins, H. (1992). *The selling of DSM: The rhetoric of science in psychiatry.* New York: Aldine de Gruyter.

Kirk, S., & Kutchins, H. (1994, June 20). Is bad writing a mental disorder? *New York Times,* p. A17.

Klein, G. C. (2009). *Law and the disordered: An exploration in mental health, law, and politics.* Lanham, MD: University Press of America.

Kluger, J. (2011, March 21). Small child, big worries. *Time, 177,* 38–39.

Kluger, J. (2015, March 9). Dog interrupted. *Time, 185,* 40–43.

Kovel, J. (1988). A critique of *DSM-III.* In S. Spitzer & A. Scull (Eds.), *Research in law, deviance and social control* (Vol. 9, pp. 127–146). Greenwich, CT: JAI.

Kupfer, D., & Regier, D. A. (2010). Why all medicine should care about *DSM-5. Journal of the American Medical Association, 303,* 1974–1975.

Kutchins, H., & Kirk, S. (1997). *Making us crazy: DSM, the psychiatric bible and the creation of mental disorders.* New York: Free Press.

Lamb, H. R., Weinberger, L. E., & Gross, B. H. (2004). Mentally ill persons in the criminal justice system: Some perspectives. *Psychiatric Quarterly, 75,* 107–126.

Laws, S. (1983). The sexual politics of pre-menstrual tension. *Women's Studies International Forum, 6,* 19–31.

Leifer, R. (1969). *In the name of mental health: The social functions of psychiatry.* New York: Science House.

Martin, E. (1992). *The woman in the body: A cultural analysis of reproduction.* Boston: Beacon.

Mead, G. H. (1934). *Mind, self, and society: From the standpoint of a social behaviorist.* Chicago: University of Chicago Press.

Patel, V., & Prince, M. (2010). Global mental health: A new global field comes of age. *Journal of the American Medical Association, 303,* 1976–1977.

Phillips, J. (2013). The conceptual status of DSM-5 diagnoses. In J. Paris & J. Phillips (Eds.), *Making the DSM-5: Concepts and controversies* (pp. 143–157). New York: Springer.

Potter, D. A. (2014). Acting up and acting out: Conduct disorder and competing media frames. *Deviant Behavior, 35,* 152–172.

Rafter, N. (1997). *Creating born criminals.* Urbana & Chicago: University of Illinois Press.

Remster, B. (2014). Self-control and the depression–delinquency link. *Deviant Behavior, 35,* 66–84.

Reynolds, J. R., & Baird, C. L. (2010). Is there a downside to shooting for the stars? Unrealized educational expectations and symptoms of depression. *American Sociological Review, 75,* 151–172.

Rittenhouse, C. A. (1991). The emergence of premenstrual syndrome as a social problem. *Social Problems, 38,* 412–425.

Rochman, B. (2012, February 6). The end of an epidemic? Why a proposed new definition of autism has parents and advocates worried. *Time, 179,* 16.

Rose, N., & Abi-Rached, J. M. (2013). *Neuro: The new brain sciences and the management of the mind.* Princeton, NJ: Princeton University Press.

Rothman, D. (1974). *The discovery of the asylum.* Boston: Little, Brown.

Schaefer, D. R., Kornienko, O., & Fox, A. M. (2011). Misery does not love company: Network selection mechanisms and depression homophily. *American Sociological Review, 76,* 764–785.

Scheff, T. (1984). *Being mentally ill: A sociological theory* (2nd ed.). Chicago: Aldine.

Scheff, T. (2014). A note on the origins of deinstitutionalization. *Deviant Behavior, 35,* 475–476.

Schieman, S., & Glavin, P. (2011). Education and work–family conflict: Explanations, contingencies and mental health consequences. *Social Forces, 89,* 1341–1362.

Schubert, S., Hansen, S., & Rapley, M. (2014). "There is no pathological test": More on ADHD as rhetoric. In R. Heiner (Ed.), *Deviance across cultures: Constructions of difference* (2nd ed., pp. 361–370). New York: Oxford University Press.

Scull, A. (1977a). *Decarceration: Community treatment and the deviant.* Englewood Cliffs, NJ: Prentice Hall.

Scull, A. (1977b). Madness and segregative control: The rise of the insane asylum. *Social Problems, 24,* 337–351.

Sharkey, J. (1997, September 28). You're not bad, you're sick. It's in the book. *New York Times,* pp. E1, E5.

Shorter, E. (2013). The history of DSM. In J. Paris & J. Phillips (Eds.), *Making the DSM-5: Concepts and controversies* (pp. 3–19). New York: Springer.

Sommer, R. (1976). *The end of imprisonment.* New York: Oxford University Press.

Strauss, J. (1991). The meaning of schizophrenia: Compared to what? In W. Flack Jr., D. Miller, & M. Wiener (Eds.), *What is schizophrenia?* (pp. 81–90). New York: Springer-Verlag.

Sutton, J. (1991). The political economy of madness: The expansion of the asylum in progressive America. *American Sociological Review, 56,* 665–678.

Szasz, T. (1960). The myth of mental illness. *American Psychologist, 15,* 113–118.

Szasz, T. (1970). *The manufacture of madness.* New York: Harper & Row.

Szasz, T. (1973). *The second sin.* Garden City, NY: Anchor.

Szasz, T. (1974). *The myth of mental illness* (Rev. ed.). New York: Harper & Row.

Szasz, T. (1985, September 28). Psychiatry: Rhetoric and reality. *Lancet, 2,* 711–712.

Szasz, T. (1994). Mental illness is still a myth. *Society, 31,* 34–39.

Szasz, T. (1997). Idleness and lawlessness in the therapeutic state. In L. Salinger (Ed.), *Deviant behavior 97–98* (2nd ed., pp. 214–219). Guilford, CT: Dushkin/Brown.

Torrey, E. F. (1995). Jails and prisons—America's new mental hospitals. *American Journal of Public Health, 85,* 1611–1613.

Torrey, E. F., & colleagues. (2012). Documenting the failure of deinstitutionalization. In L. M. Salinger (Ed.), *Social deviance* (pp. 349–351). San Diego, CA: Cognella.

Trent, J., Jr. (1994). *Inventing the feeble mind: A history of mental retardation in the United States.* Berkeley: University of California Press.

Turner, R., & Edgley, C. (1996). From witchcraft to drugcraft: Biochemistry as mythology. In H. Pontell (Ed.), *Social deviance: Readings in theory and research* (2nd ed., pp. 432–441). Englewood Cliffs, NJ: Prentice Hall.

Walker, S. (2011). *Sense and nonsense about crime, drugs, and communities* (7th ed.). Belmont, CA: Wadsworth.

Warner, J. (2010). *We've got issues: Children and parents in the age of medication.* New York: Riverhead Books/Penguin.

Warner, R. (2014). Schizophrenia in the Third World. In R. Heiner (Ed.), *Deviance across cultures: Constructions of difference* (2nd ed., pp. 371–380). New York: Oxford University Press.

Watters, E. (2010). *Crazy like us: The globalization of the American psyche.* New York: Free Press.

Watters, E. (2014). The Americanization of mental illness. In R. Heiner (Ed.), *Deviance across cultures: Constructions of difference* (2nd ed., pp. 381–387). New York: Oxford University Press.

Wedenoja, W. (2006). Psychiatry, transcultural. In H. J. Birx (Ed.), *Encyclopedia of anthropology* (pp. 1961–1964). Thousand Oaks, CA: Sage.

Whooley, O. (2013). *Knowledge in the time of cholera: The struggle over American medicine in the nineteenth century.* Chicago: University of Chicago Press.

Wiener, M. (1991). Schizophrenia: A defective, deficient, disrupted, disorganized construct. In W. Flack, Jr., D. Miller, & M. Wiener (Eds.), *What is schizophrenia?* (pp. 199–222). New York: Springer-Verlag.

5

Predatory Violence

The Social Construction of Murder and Violence

Definitions of Murder and Violence

One fact of the human condition is that people die. Some of these deaths are caused by factors that are unrelated to human intent. These deaths are officially classified in the United States as either "accidental" or "natural." Other deaths, however, are viewed as deliberate human acts that are malicious and unnecessary. The individuals held responsible for them are subjected to punishments for what they have done. *Murder* is defined by the Federal Bureau of Investigation (FBI, 2014) as the willful (nonnegligent) killing of one human being by another. Murder is the most serious, but rarest, of all the *violent crimes* (any crime that involves force or the threat of force) defined by this federal agency. Rates of violence, especially lethal violence, are high in the United States when compared to other Western, industrialized nations (Beeghley, 2003; Winslow & Zhang, 2008). Messner and Rosenfeld's (2013) comparison of murder rates in 16 Western nations reported that the U.S. rate of murder was the highest in the sample, being more than five times greater than the average of all the other nations (p. 21).

Killing and murder are related, but they are not identical. It is possible for a killing to not be a murder (but not the other way around), as when a police officer shoots a felon in the line of duty or when a condemned criminal is lawfully executed for a crime. Murder and manslaughter are the two types of illegal killing identified by U.S. law. A killing in which an offender plans out the murder *(premeditation)* and then deliberately carries it out (with *malice aforethought,* indicating that criminal intent existed) is a *first-degree murder. Second-degree murder* lacks the element of premeditation, but malice afore-thought is still present. *Manslaughter* is an illegal killing that lacks both premeditation and malice aforethought (Hall, 2002). Some killings are excluded from the FBI's definition of murder. These include suicides (being self-inflicted, suicides are not killings of one human by *another* human), acci-dental deaths, and traffic fatalities (these latter two because they are not viewed as intentional). If a person dies of a heart attack as the result of being robbed or witnessing a crime, it would not be classified as a murder either.

A psychiatric diagnosis used to explain individual violence is that of *antiso-cial personality disorder* (APA, 2013). This diagnosis describes someone who is self-centered and uncaring about others, willing to do anything that will benefit him or her, even if it involves extreme acts of violence (Kiehl, 2014). The ambiguity of the term "antisocial personality"—it is also called psychopathy, sociopathy, or dyssocial personality disorder—is paralleled by confusion over its meaning. Despite strenuous efforts to make the term more precise, it is still used as a catch-all to describe bad people and bad behaviors that seemingly cannot be explained in any other way. The diagnosis is a way to understand why seemingly normal people could do seemingly abnormal things: They have a mental disorder that has afflicted their moral development. The trouble is that the term is circular—individuals get labeled as having antisocial personali-ties because they do antisocial things. The unrestrained pursuit of self-interest, the principal sign that identifies antisocial people, may be found in too many people for the diagnosis to have much value. Sociopathic traits are not necessarily bad for an individual who possesses them and, kept within limits, they are not bad for others either (Regoli, Hewitt, & DeLisi, 2010).

The Elasticity of Violence

No act is universally defined as violent and then negatively sanctioned in all human societies. In one setting, people may be negatively sanctioned for too much violence; in another setting, they may be sanctioned for too little violence; and in still another setting, they may be sanctioned for committing the wrong type of violence (Edgerton, 1976).

> What audiences label as violence is not dependent on the harm that is inflicted. Instead, what observers regard as instances of violence are illegiti-mate, unjustified, inexcusable—or *deviant*—actions taken by one person or a set of persons against another. In other words, violence is a loaded, biased, socially constructed concept. (Goode, 2008, p. 150)

In some places, for some people, certain acts of violence are viewed as normal and reasonable—as evidence of courage and bravery—and at other times, for other people, what appear to be similar acts are viewed as serious public health emergencies (Koop & Lundberg, 1992).

The killing of one human being by another can elicit a wide range of social reactions, influenced not only by time and place, but also by characteristics of the victim and the offender and the nature of the relationship between the two (Cooney, 2009). Killers have been lynched, brutally killed by outraged mobs, executed by the government, imprisoned for life, banished from the society, fined, scorned, or even admired and rewarded for their violent acts. Different groups in a society may have very different views of the *same* killing (or killer), with some groups being outraged by the killing and others being delighted that it occurred. Some individuals communicate to others how horrific or brutal they find whatever violence they have witnessed or experienced, while others do what they can to normalize or dismiss it (Six-Hohenbalken & Weiss, 2011).

Centuries ago, Roman holidays involved the slaughter of thousands of combatants in gladiator shows. After Spartacus's uprising, the crucified bodies of 6,000 slaves lined the road from Rome to Capua like lampposts. In Christian Europe, executions replaced the Roman circuses. Criminals were beheaded publicly; they were hanged, with their intestines drawn out and their bodies quartered; they were elaborately tortured and guillotined in front of enthralled crowds; and their severed heads were exposed on spikes, their bodies hung in chains from gibbets (gallows). The public was amused and excited, more delighted than shocked. An execution was like a fun fair, and for the more spectacular ones, even apprentices got the day off (Alvarez, 1972, pp. 53–54). If an Ashanti woman of West Africa calls a man a fool, it is considered a violent act, and she can be killed for it. However, if an Ashanti child dies before puberty, he or she is given no funeral rites. The body is simply ditched in the community garbage dump. In that culture, the death of a child is no big deal, nor is the killing of an insulting woman; however, insulting a man is a very serious matter indeed (Service, 1963). In slave-owning societies, if a slave kills an owner, it is dealt with harshly. However, if a slave owner kills a slave, it is treated leniently or may even be overlooked (Cooney, 2009).

Wayne Wilson (1991) separated what he called "good" from "bad" murders. The distinction is based on the premise that individuals distinguish those who deserve to die (a *good murder*) from those who do not but are killed anyway (a *bad murder*). It seems to be true that the nastier the killer, the more ghastly the killing, and the purer the victim is perceived to be, the greater the likelihood that the killing of the victim will be viewed as bad and the killing of the offender (if it occurs) as good (p. 2). Some violence may reach the point where it is viewed as so normal and justified that it doesn't even look like violence anymore. In 1911, an accused rapist was bound on the stage of an opera house in Livermore, Kentucky, and tickets were sold to see him. Ticket holders were allowed to shoot at the rapist as they sat in their seats (Lane, 2003). Decisions about who should live and who should die are fundamentally social decisions that cannot be separated from issues of race, ethnicity, class, gender, geography, or organizational dynamics (Baumer & Martin, 2013; Roy, 2009).

No doubt exists that some individuals are prepared to use brutality and violence to get what they want and that they produce untold misery for everybody else. Consider the following account, written by Ms. Kuzmaak, describing the anguish caused by the murder of her daughter Donna. It is an example of a "bad murder" if anything is.

> I keep searching for the right descriptive words to convey the emotional impact our daughter's murder made on us. "Devastating" just doesn't make it—"ravaged" is closer, engulfed, overwhelmed, drowning in sadness, numb, oblivious to EVERYTHING else, totally immersed in the horror, the why, the who, what she had to go through in the closing minutes of her short life, how terrified she must have been, did she scream for help and no one came, did she fight, the pain, how it felt to be strangled, what her dying thoughts were, how she must have held out hope until the last that she would be rescued, her shock and disbelief that this was happening, and as the information unfolded itself to us in bits and pieces that first day, the anguish of hearing how badly she was beaten, then a couple of hours later crying out when I heard that she had been repeatedly stabbed. Then, the ultimate horror to learn that the cause of death was strangulation. To be deprived of breath—lungs bursting—"Oh, God, oh God," I would wail, tears streaming, hands clenched and imploring.
>
> That is how I remember the day, March 21, 1979. A decade has passed, but the emotions go on, the anger, the sorrow, and the loss. (Hickey, 1997, pp. 125–126)

If the killer were ever to be caught and executed for murdering Donna, the execution would fit W. Wilson's (1991) idea of a "good murder" (though it would no longer be called murder because, as noted, murder by definition is an *illegal* killing). However, a genuine dilemma exists in applying good murder/bad murder definitions to real-world events. The unique qualities of a victim—how innocent, pure, or kind he or she is (or is considered to be)—cannot reasonably be used to determine a killer's level of criminal responsibility or what his or her penalty should be (Lesser, 1993).

In the Eye of the Beholder

We must be familiar with social context and cultural understandings, or it will be impossible to know what an act means or how it should be understood (Schoon, 2014). Police officers use "roughness" in their jobs, and so do football players, wrestlers, and animal trainers. In Brownstein's (2000) words, "We do not have any precise or simple measure of violence in our society. We do not even have agreement on how to define violence, or when and how to identify particular acts or actions as violent" (p. 169). Most people commit acts of violence at some point in their lives—most of them more than once—and practically everyone has the opportunity to use violence in a variety of ways and for a variety of reasons. The boundary that separates violence from nonviolence is fuzzier and more permeable than most people think (Eller, 2006).

The relativity of violence is easy enough to see by examining something that at first blush would seem to be straightforward: figuring out how many individuals died during the terrorist attack on the World Trade Center, September 11, 2001, and then how to classify them. The number who died as a result of being on the two planes that slammed into the North and South Towers could be accurately determined from both airline records and reports from surviving family members. Figuring out how many died in the Twin Towers, however, proved to be more challenging. On September 24, 2001, the number of casualties was estimated to be 6,453. As the days passed, however, the list got shorter. Some victims had been counted multiple times, which had incorrectly inflated the number of presumed casualties; some people classified as dead (or missing) were actually found to be alive; and some people fraudulently claimed that they had lost family members, hoping to receive survivors' benefits. A year after the attack, the authoritative list of estimated deaths due to the World Trade Center attack stood at 2,801, less than half of the initial estimate (Best, 2004, pp. 109–111). The FBI's Uniform Crime Reports (UCR) for 2001, which also included in its estimate the deaths at the Pentagon and on the plane that crashed in Pennsylvania, reported the body count from 9/11 to be 3,047.

If estimating the number of individuals killed was difficult, classifying them was too. The killings fit perfectly the FBI's definition of murder: They were willful; they were done *by* human beings; and they were done *to* human beings. How much clearer could it be that these killings were murders? The FBI (2001), however, decided *not* to count these approximately 3,000 deaths as murders, so the murder and nonnegligent manslaughter figures for 2001 did not increase at all despite the thousands of killings that occurred the day of the attacks. What is most curious is that the FBI stated that it did not know what to call the killings because so much disagreement and dispute existed over what they should be called (e.g., an act of war, a local crime, an international conspiracy, or terrorism). The FBI apparently knew enough, however, to decide they weren't going to be counted as murders.

Some individuals, groups, or organizations will use violence to get what they want (e.g., terrorists using violence to terrorize) (Schinkel, 2010). Individuals, groups, and organizations can also construct narratives or ideas about violence that they then use in their conflicts with others, depicting these others' attitudes, behaviors, and conditions as forms of violence, and thereby justifying their condemnation and control. Having the authority to decide what and who is violent has great symbolic value (Brownstein, 2000). The violence of professional boxing, hockey, rugby, wrestling, rodeos, or cage fighting is not defined as a social problem, but the violence of school shootings or Halloween sadism is. Some violence that was once viewed as a serious problem (e.g., wilding) has gone the way of the buggy whip, and some violence that was once ignored is now viewed more seriously (e.g., road rage or cruelty to animals). Some groups will manipulate our fears of violence to advance their interests.

Arbitrary Meanings

Definitions of deviance, including violence, develop and grow in specific locations or arenas in a society, such as government, mass media, research communities, social action groups, professional organizations (e.g., in medicine and law), and religious organizations. It is at the intersections of these different arenas that notions of risk are created, massaged, and manipulated; they are also where remedies or solutions for the problems we face are constructed and presented for review (Bing, 2010; Ghatak, 2011). Best (1999) refers to media, government, experts (e.g., from medicine or law), and activists as the *iron quadrangle,* because these four arenas are (or can be) central in promoting an interest in some troubling event in mutually reinforcing ways (even while disagreement can and does exist). Influential politicians and cultural leaders must do the symbolic work necessary for the suffering of individuals to be defined and commemorated as something that is a significant problem for the entire nation (Eyerman, Alexander, & Breese, 2013).

Social reactions to violence can develop into a *moral panic* in which the response is so extreme that it is disproportionate to the threat posed (Goode & Ben-Yehuda, 1994). This is what happened when the "devil came to day care" and refused to leave for almost a decade. In the 1980s, individuals (how many is a matter of dispute) in the United States came to believe that day care centers were the site of horrendous violence against children, done by the very people entrusted to care for them (DeYoung, 2014). The new buzzwords of "satanic ritual abuse" emerged as a shorthand way to describe these terrifying acts, and the McMartin Preschool in Southern California (located in the town of Manhattan Beach) was defined as the epicenter of it all.

In 1983, Judy Johnson was in a bind. She needed affordable, quality child care at the exact point in time when the societal demand was great but the supply was not. She tried to enroll her 2-year-old son at McMartin, but the center was full and no openings were anticipated. Nonetheless, one day she simply dropped the child off at the center and went to work. Employees arrived and found him playing all alone in the center's yard. They took pity on him (and on his mother) and made room for him. The rest of what happened should be placed in the "no good deed goes unpunished" file, because the staff's willingness to care for the child and help the mother eventually led to catastrophe for the center and for all the people who owned and worked in it.

One day in August after her son was back home from school, Johnson decided on the flimsiest of evidence and with little substantiation that her son had been sexually assaulted by someone at the school (in her opinion, the child had a reddened anus). During a drawn-out process of questioning her son, filled with leading questions, repeated again and again, Johnson extracted the kind of information she needed to convince herself that her initial suspicions were true. Her son had been sodomized, and she knew by whom: Raymond Buckey, the only male staff member (and grandson of the founder of the day care center). Though her son had said that Buckey had done nothing to him, Johnson was not convinced. In response to her insistent questioning, the boy eventually relented, claiming that Buckey had taken his temperature. The mother had her smoking gun. She concluded that the "thermometer" was really Buckey's penis, which he had used to anally penetrate her child.

Johnson had her son examined by a physician (the physical was inconclusive), and she then went to the police. Other parents who had used the day care center learned of the complaint against it, and they started quizzing their children, too. Aggrieved parents were encouraged in letters from the police to take their children to the Children's International Institute (CII), a nonprofit treatment facility, to be interviewed by the resident social workers. Social workers subsequently talked to more than 400 McMartin youngsters, concluding that 369 of them had been victims of satanic ritual abuse. The way that CII social workers questioned them led the children to realize that truth statements about any conscientious and compassionate care they had received at the center were not what the social workers wanted to hear.

And so they told . . . tales—tales about the ritualistic ingestion of feces, urine, blood, semen, and human flesh; the disinterment and mutilation of corpses; the sacrifices of infants; and the orgies with their day care providers, costumed as devils and witches, in the classrooms, in tunnels under the center, and in car washes, airplanes, mansions, cemeteries, hotels, ranches, gourmet food stores, local gyms, churches, and hot air balloons. (DeYoung, 2014, p. 129)

The greater the degree of strangeness in the children's tales, the more convinced the social workers—and practically everyone else—became that the children were telling the truth about what had happened. Due process went out the window, along with both truth and reason. The social workers played a central and powerful role in the construction of a reality that they believed they played no role in at all. In February 1984, seven of the day care center's staff were indicted on multiple charges.

Two trials were held in the McMartin Preschool case, and all charges against the seven defendants were eventually dropped. However, the damage had already been done. The accused individuals had no way to reclaim what they had lost. Judy Johnson had a nervous breakdown and was institutionalized for a time with a diagnosis of paranoid schizophrenia. (She told police detectives that her ex-husband had anally penetrated her son and that an unknown intruder had done the same thing to the family dog.) She died in 1986 of liver failure due to the effects of alcohol, but her legacy lived on as more and more day care centers fell under the suspicion of parents, police, prosecutors, politicians, social workers, and the media. The story was told and retold of a massive network of organized predators who victimize children in day care centers all across the United States. The moral panic ended almost a decade after it started, in 1992, with the arrest and conviction of day care center owner Fran Keller (who owned Fran's Day Care in Austin, Texas) and her husband (Dan). They were both convicted of aggravated sexual assault on a child and each received a sentence of 48 years for the crime.

Once some event, group, or individual is defined as menacing, this definition and the reactions based on it become part of how the event (or group or individual) is identified and understood (Young, 2011). The process of demonization is furthered often enough by media coverage, which usually offers distorted or even false images of some deviant happening (Bjornstrom, Kaufman, Peterson, & Slater, 2010; Covington, 2010; Farrall, Jackson, & Gray, 2009). It is difficult, if not impossible, to figure out if the social response is reasonable or if it is an exaggerated response to some earlier disproportionate *reaction* to some event. Moral panics have the ability to create their own reality (Heiner, 2014).

Patterned Violence

Subcultures of Violence

Violence can occur in a variety of ways, depending on the opportunities to learn and express it and the cultural understandings about it (Goetting, 1995). At certain times, violence is both normal and normative: It occurs frequently, is well-integrated with other parts of society and culture, and is defined as legitimate and reasonable. This kind of violence is legal, socially supported, and rational. It is *organized violence*. Other violence, however, does not flow from any clear or discernible social conditions or cultural issues. It is illegal, antisocial, and irrational (Yablonsky, 1990). This is *raw violence*. Raw violence is more often done by the kinds of people who are considered immoral, insane, or evil; these individuals will be labeled more often as psychopaths, as sociopaths, or as having antisocial (or dyssocial) personalities. They are usually hostile toward, and suspicious of, others, and their predatory activities usually come from their aberrant or warped personalities or character structures (Kiehl, 2014). The distinction between "raw" and "organized" violence is not a hard and fast one. It is functional for some groups to portray the violence of other groups (or individuals) as rawer than it really is, and people can disagree over the degree of organization in some violent event.

In a society characterized by diversity and heterogeneity (as is found in the United States), a number of subcultures exist. The wealthy may associate primarily with the wealthy, the poor primarily with the poor, and people from different ethnic and racial groups may interact primarily with people who share a similar identity and social history. This diversity of subcultures produces a diversity of life experiences, opportunities, learning experiences, and outcomes. People from some subcultures consistently do better in achieving their dreams than people from other subcultures. They have more money, more control over their lives, and better jobs. They generally feel good about what they do and who they are. In other subcultures, however, there is misery and degradation, and people who live within them are frustrated and angry much of the time (Blau & Blau, 1982). This defective social environment can stimulate interpersonal conflicts and individual tensions from which interpersonal violence can result (Linsky, Bachman, & Strauss, 1995). For example, African American males in U.S. cities are reported to have high levels of anger and defensiveness, mainly because of what they see as their mistreatment at the hands of the police. This is a principal reason that they become involved in riots more often than do other racial and ethnic groups (Santoro & Broidy, 2014).

When a tradition of neighborhood support for violence exists, along with the presence of actual groups that champion aggression, then violence is a subcultural happening (Felson, Liska, South, & McNulty, 1994). A *subculture of violence* provides opportunities to observe, learn, and act out the kinds of violence that would shock, upset, or baffle individuals from other subcultures (Wolfgang & Ferracuti, 1967). In a subculture of violence, it is not some personal defect that explains what happens. Rather, it is the internalization of a subculture's values and norms that is the principal cause. In some communities, fighting to protect one's honor is a core value for both males and females (Ness, 2010). Research suggests that those individuals who are the most predisposed to develop an angry, aggressive, hostile view of the world when they are surrounded by brutalizing social conditions are the very same individuals who are most likely to develop a nonviolent, peaceable outlook on life if they are in a serene social environment (Simons et al., 2011).

Dueling is a good example of how violence can become both normative and normalized (Kiernan, 1988). At one time, duels were disorderly gatherings, with witnesses and spectators often joining in the fight. However, duels eventually became more ritualized and formalized. Each duelist selected someone to serve as a *second*, who ensured that the rules were enforced and the duel was fair. If swords were used, they had to be the same length. If pistols were used, they had to carry the same charge or be of the same caliber. Neither duelist was supposed to be at a disadvantage by, for example, having to face the sun or shoot into the wind. In France and England, the main weapon was the sword, whereas in the United States it was the pistol. In some places, a duel was ended at the drawing of first blood, but in other places, the dueling code required death. Though a large number of incidents, some quite petty, could precipitate a duel—personal insults, arguments over property, affronts to personal honor, cheating at cards—failing to respond to a challenge, no matter how ridiculous it was, meant disgrace and dishonor. Individuals who were arrested by police for dueling (it became a federal crime in the United States in 1877) almost always lacked remorse or shame because they were duty bound to duel if challenged. The participants viewed the violence as both justified and justifiable regardless of its legal status.

Social Inequality, Community Disadvantage, and the Code of the Street

Elijah Anderson (1999) paid attention to a neighborhood characteristic that he believed plays a central role in patterns of African American violence: the code of the street. His *code of the street thesis* indicates that violence in African American neighborhoods is caused by a subculture (i.e., a code) that allows those who share its understandings to know how to use violence and when, primarily to maintain personal status and respect. The code is found most often in inner-city areas characterized by poverty, a scarcity of legitimate jobs, unemployment, guns, drugs, crime, declining welfare payments, hopelessness, and despair (Burgason, Thomas, Berthelot, & Burkey, 2014; Kirk & Papachristos, 2011). It encourages both a positive evaluation of violence in the abstract ("Tough guys are to be admired") and a willingness to use violence whenever necessary ("If someone starts trouble, I will finish it"). Youth who adopt the code of the street think that they are more vulnerable to becoming targets of violence, though they generally express fearlessness regarding its use (Baron, 2011; White, 2013). (Not all parents, even in a violent neighborhood, teach their kids to use violence to defend themselves and their honor [Crawford, Whitbeck, & Hoyt, 2011].)

A study of over 2,500 census tracts in 13 U.S. cities over a 10-year period found reciprocal effects between neighborhood characteristics and violence (Hipp, 2010). Those neighborhoods with the greatest amount of poverty had experienced a long-term increase in crime, and neighborhoods with higher rates of violent crime had experienced the greatest increase in poverty, disadvantage, and normlessness. An increase in crime rates can change a neighborhood's characteristics (e.g., retail outlets are replaced by bars and liquor stores) and reduce its attractiveness as a place to live. This leads to the influx of lower-income families. "Neighborhoods with more crime tend to experience increasing levels of residential instability, more impoverished residents, a worsening retail environment, and more racial/ethnic minorities and heterogeneity" (p. 224). Some neighborhoods can generate a sense of hopelessness and unhappiness among their residents, so these individuals have no optimism that their situations and opportunities will ever improve (Griffiths, 2013; Peterson & Krivo, 2010). This sense of despair is a factor that leads to both an adoption of the code of the street and involvement in the higher rates of violence that the code reinforces (Contreras, 2013; Drummond, Bolland, & Harris, 2011; Zimmerman & Messner, 2010).

Areas characterized by community disadvantage in an unequal society, with subcultures of violence and a code of the street, have an additional liability: weak social capital. *Social capital* (Coleman, 1988; Putnam, 2000) describes the existing network of relationships. When it is strong, it makes it possible for community members to work together to achieve common goals. They will have a sense of community spirit, along with a sense of mutual trust and responsibility. This increases their level of *collective efficacy* so that community residents are able to control the public space within which they live and move (e.g., streets, street corners, parks, playgrounds) and maintain order (Sampson & Raudenbush, 1999; Sampson, Rauden-bush, & Earls, 1997). They may call police to report crimes in their com-munities, or they may even take responsibility themselves for what goes on in the places they live. High levels of social capital and collective efficacy lead to a reduction in rates of crime and delinquency (Dufur, Hoffmann, Braudt, Parcel, & Spence, 2015; Lyons, Vélez, & Santoro, 2013). Even the rates of serious crime (e.g., homicide) go down as collective efficacy goes up (Morenoff, Sampson, & Raudenbush, 2001). Most research shows that economic inequality and homicide are positively related (Bernard, Snipes, & Gerould, 2010; Hipp, 2011).

Dehumanizing Others

Violence is facilitated by the existence of a socially constructed "other": an individual who is defined as a legitimate target of aggression and deserving of whatever injury he or she receives. This dehumanization process helps to neutralize any lingering moral inhibitions against violence that might still exist among aggressors, which makes it possible for rather ordinary people to commit acts of extraordinary evil (F. Katz, 1994). People may even develop justifications and excuses for violence that become part of their cultural tradi-tion, being passed on to others. This makes certain kinds of violence seem more necessary, more reasonable, and less in need of correction than other kinds of violence done by other kinds of people. If these excuses and justifica-tions are persuasive enough, some individuals will be able to commit acts of extreme cruelty with very little social prompting, even when they are given many opportunities to renege without penalty or embarrassment (Browning, 1992). The "other" may even be blamed for things over which he or she could have had no control whatsoever. In 1923, thousands of Koreans were massacred by the Japanese in Tokyo because they were held responsible for the earthquake that had occurred that year (Baudrillard, 2002).

Philip Zimbardo (2007) explored how seemingly good people could do seemingly bad things. The *Lucifer effect*—the transformation of ordinary men and women into beings who are capable of committing reprehensible atrocities against their fellows—is something that can occur practically any-where if the conditions are right. Zimbardo concluded that evil is something of which we are all capable, depending on the time and circumstances. (By evil, Zimbardo means intentionally behaving in ways that harm, abuse, demean, dehumanize, or destroy innocent people—or using one's authority and systemic power to encourage or permit others to do so on one's behalf.) He may have overstated his case: Some people would forfeit their own lives before they would do anything to hurt another living thing, nonhuman animals included. However, he is on firm ground when he argues that the dividing line between good and bad, between evil and honor, is nebulous and permeable. The cause of the Lucifer effect is found mainly in systems of power and how authorities use propaganda to scapegoat outsiders so that insiders will come to define them as legitimate targets of aggression. Insiders can reach the point where they will not only willingly victimize the dehumanized others, but they are happy to do so.

A study of more than 900 lynchings of black males, between 1882 and 1929 in 10 southern U.S. states, showed that the victims had been at the social margins of the communities that lynched them. They were targeted because of their marginality and separation, not because of their occupational, social, or educational accomplishments (e.g., literacy). Being an "uppity" or successful black man was far less important to lynch mobs than the fact that he was an outsider (Bailey, Tolnay, Beck, & Laird, 2011; Hagen, Makovi, & Bearman, 2013). Lynching became a method of social control of blacks by whites at a point in time when other methods of control were weakening or disappearing altogether. Southern whites were fearful about their economic future, anxious over the fate of southern women in the climate of emancipation, and concerned about the consequences of increasing racial equality. These worries found expression in a lynch culture that targeted blacks more than it did whites (I. Evans, 2011).

Groups will use violence to get what they want, but they develop—or try to—ideologies that legitimate their violent activities as necessary and reasonable, while branding the violence of other people as dangerous and unreasonable. Sometimes, one particular group's *ideology of violence* will be internalized by a majority of people in the society; at other times, support for this ideology will be very limited. It is even possible for members of a group to be seduced by their own ideology about the value of violence, coming to believe what it says without question. If an ideology of violence is firmly in place, the violence of the group that adheres to it will appear more normal, more legitimate, more necessary, and less in need of correction than other groups' violence.

The *thugs* were a group of violent criminals who lived in India centuries ago. They murdered and robbed their victims in honor of Kali, the Hindu goddess of destruction. Her followers believed that if they worshipped her and carried out her bidding, she would bestow great power and riches upon them (Hutton, 1981). The weapons the thugs used in their murders were represented as parts of Kali herself: The pickaxe was imaged as one of her teeth; the knife was imaged as one of her ribs; and the cloth that thugs used to strangle their victims (called a *roomal*) was imaged as a piece of her garment. The thugs believed that their robberies and murders were not only moral, but also admirable and completely justified (Hollick, 1840).

The favorite victims of the thugs were native soldiers on leave, men of nobility and bearing, and treasure carriers (Ahmad, 1992). Sometimes, the thugs brought along their children, partly so that they could learn how to kill, and partly to help disguise the thugs' true mission. The thugs would journey along with their intended victim until the time was ripe for the killing. One member of the gang would wrap a rope or cloth several times around the victim's neck and hold one end tightly, and a second thug would hold the other end. The rope or cloth would be drawn tight. The two thugs would push the victim's head forward to guarantee that suffocation occurred quickly. To make certain that the job was rightly done, the thugs would kick and hit the immobile victim to damage vital organs (Thornton, 1837). Victims were sometimes dispatched with weapons other than a rope or cloth: A pickaxe could be used to bludgeon and disembowel a victim, or a knife could be used to stab and cut. Sometimes, the thugs would travel several days with their intended victim to allay any suspicions.

The thugs believed that if they carefully followed the wishes of Kali, they would receive great riches and earn supernatural points that could pay off in a subsequent life. This is one reason that they showed so little guilt or remorse over their violence. Murder was defined by them as good and necessary, and thugs who did it in the proper way were thought of by their associates as heroes. Their killings were acts of worship and reverence that would allow them one day to attain a state of grace and a close affinity with Kali. However, their murderous ways were not at all acceptable to the British, who began a drive in 1831 to end *thuggee*. However, what if the thugs had been more successful at spreading their religious beliefs and violent customs to others? What then?

Righteous Slaughter and Violentization

Jack Katz's (1988) attention to the meanings of crime, its moral and sensual attractions, provides a valuable contribution to our understanding of it. One central feature of the typical murder, which Katz calls *nonpredatory*, is that the killer views the killing as a reasonable and meaningful act, and the victim is usually a family member, friend, or acquaintance. The killer usually feels comfortable in the setting in which the murder takes place. Nonpredatory murders are not carefully planned, coldly executed acts of violence, such as political assassinations, serial murders, or terrorist attacks. Casual life, Saturday nights out drinking and cruising Main Street, day-to-day activities with family members and friends, and the search for escape from the routines of ordinary life are the cradle for the occurrence of nonpredatory homicidal violence.

The average nonpredatory killing is done by someone who thinks the killing actually *supports* important and widely held values. Even though the murder can appear irrational or foolish to everyone else—and may even appear that way to the killer after its completion—it does not seem that way to the killer during its commission or in the events leading up to it. What may appear to be irrational violence to outsiders may seem very reasonable and justified to the person doing it (Black, 1993; Heimer, 1997). In the killer's view, a *righteous slaughter* has occurred. Most nonpredatory killers lack premeditation or even a well-developed motive; they really don't plan on becoming killers until the murders actually occur.

Some killings, however, are cold-blooded *predatory murders*. Examples (unfortunately) are not hard to find. Predatory murders occurred in Tucson, Arizona, on January 8, 2011, when Jared Loughner, wearing sunglasses and a hoodie, took a taxi to a Safeway grocery store. He went inside to get change to pay the cab driver, and then he calmly proceeded to a parking lot where he used his Glock 19 pistol to kill 6 people and wound 13 others (one of whom was Gabrielle Giffords, Democratic representative). Another example is the mass murder by James Holmes. On July 20, 2012, he entered a movie theater in Aurora, Colorado, and used an AR-15-type semiautomatic assault rifle to open fire in the crowded theater. When the smoke had cleared, 12 were dead and another 70 wounded. On December 14, 2012, Adam Lanza killed his mother in her home and then went to Sandy Hook Elementary School (in Newtown, Connecticut). He was heavily armed. Over the span of about 15 minutes, he killed 20 children and 6 adults before taking his own life with a shot to the head. On April 15, 2013, the Tsarnaev brothers (Dzhokhar and Tamerlan) planted two bombs near the finish line of the Boston Marathon. The eventual explosions led to the death of 3 individuals and the injury of over 260 others. Tamerlan, the older brother, was eventually killed in a shootout with police, and the younger brother was arrested and taken into police custody. In 2015, he received the death penalty for his brutal crimes. On June 17, 2015, Dylann Roof, a 21-year-old white male, entered a traditionally black church (the Emanuel African Methodist Episcopal Church) in Charleston, South Carolina, and attended a bible study session. After about an hour of sitting calmly with the parishioners, he opened fire, killing three men and six women, all strangers to him. One of the victims was the pastor (Clementa Pinckney), who was also a state senator. On July 16, 2015, Mohammad Youssuf Abdulazeez, who was born in Kuwait but was a naturalized U.S. citizen, killed four marines in Chattanooga, Tennessee, and wounded three others. He then traveled about 7 miles and fired on individuals at a U.S. Navy facility. Abdulazeez himself was killed by police officers. On October 1, 2015, Chris Harper Mercer went to Umpqua Community College in Roseburg, Oregon, in body armor and with six firearms. He ended up killing nine people at the college and wounding eight others, eventually taking his own life. On December 2, 2015, the husband and wife team of Syed Rizwan Farook and Tashfeen

Malik armed themselves—they had previously dropped off their 6-month-old daughter at her grandmother's—and entered the Inland Regional Center at San Bernardino, California. The pair opened fired on people attending an employee banquet, killing 14 and injuring an additional 22. (Farook had been at the party himself earlier but left abruptly, returning with his wife so they could do the killings.) The two killers fled the scene in their vehicle and were killed hours later in a shootout with police officers.

It is easy to understand why an immediate response to the horrific violence these murders embody is that the perpetrator is insane, mentally ill, or the embodiment of evil. (Roof's murders had clear racial overtones, and Mercer's murders targeted Christians, making them easier to portray as signs of wickedness than of illness. The FBI declared the San Bernardino killings to be an act of terrorism, carefully planned and efficiently executed.) Murders like these seem to have been done without rhyme or reason, bringing the killer no advantage, and so they are likely to be called "insane" (unless they can be classified as domestic terrorism or as racially motivated). This claim that the killers are insane, however, is almost always an incorrect assessment of most predatory murders (Declercq & Audenaert, 2011; J. Katz, 1988; Leyton, 1986).

Multiple murderers, Leyton (1986) concludes, are not insane. They kill others to make a statement through the fundamental insult of killing the innocent. They are individuals who have no interest in continuing the dull lives that they see no way of escaping. Their killings alleviate both their alienation and their boredom by giving them a cornucopia of rewards: revenge on what they view as an uncaring society, celebrity status, a new identity, and a measure of excitement and pleasure. The killings are a way for the killer to get attention while transforming himself or herself into something that he or she desperately wants to be: a ferocious individual who must be taken seriously.

Predisposing factors to mass murder exist: having a personal history of violence; having been the victim of bullying (if the killer is an adolescent) or having been rejected by female intimate partners, family members, or people at work (if the killer is an adult); preoccupation with firearms and war; and a fantasy life revolving around violence and revenge. Adolescent mass murderers turn "hot shame into cold anger" (Meloy et al., 2004, p. 297). The bullying and accompanying humiliation that they experienced lies dormant as these killers-to-be try to manage the intolerable shame and loss of self-respect by withdrawing into a fantasy world. Adult mass murderers embody a compensatory fantasy that culminates in a "warrior mentality," which promotes an inflated sense of power and superiority.

Rarely is mass murder an eruption of an act of excited, agitated fury. It is almost always an unemotional, intentional, premeditated act that is methodically executed. Mass murderers are inclined to *externalize* responsibility for their real or imagined failures, placing the blame squarely on the shoulders of others. Not only do they long to escape this world that they believe has hurt them deeply, but they also seek to overcome their feelings of worthlessness and inadequacy by being remembered for their cunning and boldness in being able to carry out a massacre of individuals who have hurt them so much (Murray, 2015). The principal emotions of the killer are relief and exhilaration, and the principal outcome is a sense of peace or calm (Declercq & Audenaert, 2011).

To predatory murderers, conformity is the real problem, especially what they view as a numbing conformity, and their extreme violence is their road to salvation and moral transcendence. Cold-blooded killing gives the killer an edge. According to J. Katz (1988), "As the deviant increasingly appreciates the moral dangers of conformity to conventional rules and reasons, he may simultaneously appreciate the transcendent power he might attain through a 'senseless' killing" (p. 297). A primary anxiety of cold-blooded killers is that they are—or will be viewed by others as—individuals who go straight because they are afraid to be deviant. Cold-blooded killings establish killers as individuals who are like no others, people who are so much in control of their lives and so powerful that it is unnecessary for them to follow even rudimentary principles of human decency.

Lonnie Athens (1980) theorizes that some violent men and women have gone through a developmental process of *violentization* in childhood during which they were brutalized by adults in their families, and so were their siblings (and even their friends). At some point, an individual decides to stop being a victim and takes command of situations whenever possible, both violently and definitively. The individual develops the capacity to be comfortable using violence in different situations to get what he or she wants (e.g., using a weapon to intimidate others). If successes come from using violence, the individual's self-concept and personal identity both change. He or she is increasingly defined by others and also by himself or herself as a violent person. As the individual plays this role more and more, he or she becomes increasingly engulfed by the new identity and comfortable with it. The individual is now ready, willing, and able to use violence in all kinds of situations and for all kinds of reasons: as protection, to defend personal honor, to get something of value, or to punish someone defined as deserving it. The individual has become someone—and is viewed this way by others—who is fully capable of committing barbaric violence with little provocation (Athens, 2015).

Vocabularies of Motive and Interpersonal Accounts

Motives are usually treated as inner factors that cause individuals to act in certain ways. "He hit his brother because he was angry" identifies anger as the

motive for the assault. Motives, however, are more than this. They are vocabularies or verbal statements used by people in a social encounter to explain,
define, and interpret social action as it unfolds and develops (Mills, 1940).
Motives are provided in response to the question, "Why did you do that?"
(p. 907). People use motives to understand and sometimes to explain what
they do; they also use motives to interpret and make sense of what others do.
Motives are themselves part of a social scene, and they can determine how
social relationships unfold and how they are understood by others.

Just as individuals learn the proper ways of acting, they also learn a finite
number of proper motives *for* acting. In some instances, individuals will abandon entirely what they plan to do, or they will choose a different course of
action, if they are unable to find appropriate motives for their planned activities (or motives that others will accept). Individuals can disagree over which
motives are operating in a particular situation, and they can be confused over
what motivated others just as they can be unsure over their own motives. They
may offer motives for their actions that are disbelieved and challenged by
others. A corrupt politician may insist that he or she was forced to go above
the written law for the good of the country. Others may believe it was the politician's greed, arrogance, or stupidity—not the good of the country—that was
the real motivating factor. Self-defense is a motive for violence that is easier for
most people to accept than is the claim that violence is being used to serve the
goddess Kali. If the motives seem reasonable enough, the activity may not even
be defined as a form of violence in the first place.

How does it help us to know that motives are verbal constructions that
are situationally specific? Let us consider an example. Professional killers—
individuals who are paid money to kill other people—have a vocabulary of
motive that makes it possible for them to kill people with neither guilt nor
regret. They organize their murders in such a way that their violence appears
routine and necessary, and their victims appear deserving of whatever happens to them. "Routine kill of targets for money" is a motive that allows
professional killers to ignore the fact that they are ruthlessly killing real
human beings; this motive helps them to maintain the degree of coldness,
detachment, and daring required by their professional activities (Levi, 1989).

Accounts (see Chapter 2) are interjected into social relationships by
individuals who want to influence perceptions about their motives. If an
individual who did a violent act successfully uses an account, he or she has
been able to convince others that the violence that occurred is excusable
(unintentional) or justified (necessary and unavoidable). Accounts are sometimes so standardized within specific cultures or subcultures that they are
routinely expected when conduct departs too much from what is supposed
to happen. For example, a police officer may handcuff a suspect without

offering any account. Handcuffing is part of the job, and it is expected. However, if a suspect is brought to the police station bruised and battered, some account will have to be offered by the arresting officer. He or she might give the "standardized account" that the suspect was "resisting arrest." If this account is believed by others, it will convince them that the police officer did not really want to hurt the suspect but was forced to by the suspect's failure to comply with the officer's commands.

A study of 73 incarcerated felons (in 11 different correctional facilities in Colorado) who were found guilty of gun-related crimes that produced either death or injury for their victims reveals the power of accounts (Pogrebin, Stretesky, & Unnithan, 2009). These inmates offered either excuses to deflect responsibility for the violence from themselves (e.g., by blaming external factors) or justifications (in which responsibility was accepted for the crime, but its deviancy was discounted by insisting that violence was necessary). The most common excuse offered by members of the sample for using their guns was that they were not thinking clearly or were forced to act violently by others. The most common justification used by members of the sample was denial of the victim, embodied in their claim that the victims deserved to be shot. These prisoners used many different excuses or justifications, sometimes simultaneously, to account for their gun violence.

Research indicates that in cases of domestic violence, "intimacy repels law" (i.e., familiarity between offender and offended leads to some confusion for police about what to do) (Black, 1980). The likelihood of an offender being arrested for assaulting another individual is lower if the victim and victimizer are romantically involved or related by family ties than if they are acquaintances or strangers. Factors that operate to change this association between intimacy and the likelihood of arrest are drug use by the perpetrator, a perpetrator's use of a weapon, or physical injury to a victim. Males who assault females, regardless of relational distance (i.e., stranger, acquaintance, or family/intimate), are more likely to be arrested than are males who assault males (or than females who assault others). What seems to be operating is that the closer the relationship, the greater is the inclination of police to conclude that other mechanisms of informal control and regulation will kick in and start working. They believe they do not have to arrest an assaulter in incidents of intimate partner violence unless clear indicators are present that show the situation might get worse rather than better. The "amount of formal control, in this case enforcement, applied in any given situation is inversely proportional to the amount of informal control perceived present" (Lally & DeMaris, 2012, p. 116). While some women do assault or even kill their male partners, most violence in intimate relationships is done by men (DeKeseredy, 2011).

A worldwide shift in attitudes toward intimate partner violence has occurred. It is increasingly rejected as a correct or proper way for males and females to relate to one another. These changing attitudes have been associated with greater public attention to domestic violence, as well as greater media coverage of it. A dramatic increase has occurred in the number of countries that implemented legislation to stop violence against women (Pierotti, 2013). (The passage in the U.S. Violence Against Women Act of 1994 and its recertification in subsequent years showed police officers who needed to learn it that spousal violence is a matter for them to take seriously.)

Peralta and Cruz (2006) were interested in how a sample of university students viewed and interpreted (i.e., attached meanings to) alcohol-related violence. It is clear from their study that drinking a lot and often is viewed as both an indicator of masculinity and as a way to justify and excuse some of the violent things that drinking men are inclined to do.

> [T]he general belief some males "naturally" become violent after drinking helps to shape and inform the gendered world of drinking behavior within the context of college culture. What is more, these common expectations may reduce a student's ability to recognize harmful behavior as damaging and undesirable if these behaviors are assumed to be natural byproducts of gender. (p. 117)

From their interviews with 78 respondents, the authors found that these individuals were inclined to believe that alcohol plays a major role in patterns of violence, especially for young males, and that alcohol-related violence represents a form of "macho" behavior ("beer muscles"). These definitions and understandings normalize violent behavior while they motivate it. It seems clear from a wealth of data that alcohol use and interpersonal violence are related, and drinking patterns and risk of victimization are, too. Simply put, in areas where alcohol is both available and accessible, higher rates of youth violence exist, and one's chance of becoming either a victimizer or a victim increases (Berthelot, Brown, Drawve, & Burgason, 2015; Parker & McCaffree, 2013).

A study by Faris and Felmlee (2011) of high school students' violent behavior shows that violence is not necessarily the province of marginal, psychologically deranged, out-of-control individuals. In fact, these researchers uncovered a link between relatively high levels of status in a social hierarchy and aggressive behaviors. Moving up in status in the school hierarchy and being able to maintain it requires a willingness to use violence when necessary. Students at the very bottom of the status hierarchy lack a capacity for using violence to increase their status, and those at the very top refrain from using it because they have no reason to employ it. However, "for the vast majority of adolescents, increases in status are, over time, accompanied by increases in aggression toward their peers" (p. 67). The researchers also found evidence of an expressive use of violence, especially with same-sex aggression. Some individuals torment others only because they find it pleasurable to hurt them and think that they can get away with it. Other studies indicate that violence occurs, at least in online college relationships (i.e., those that aren't face-to-face), because it is defined by its perpetrators as a form of entertainment (Rafferty & Ven, 2014).

The Curious Case of Jack the Ripper

Murder Most Foul

In 1888, a killer who came to be known as Jack the Ripper prowled the streets of London's East End. Although the identity of this killer was never uncovered in a court of law, a consensus view evolved that the killer was a male who acted alone to murder five women (known as the "canonical five"), all of whom were prostitutes, from the end of August until the beginning of November. He killed his victims through asphyxiation and/or cutting and stabbing. The loss of blood was extensive. Robbery did not seem to be a primary motive, and body cavities had been cut open and body parts removed for some specific reason by the killer. All but the last known victim (Mary Jane Kelly) were killed and mutilated on the street, probably close to where they met their killer. Except for one killing that occurred in the City of London (Catherine Eddowes), the rest were confined to districts in the East End known as Whitechapel and Spitalfields, which lay just outside the city's northeastern boundary. The identity of the killer was a matter of speculation and dispute in 1888 and still is to this very day.

Douglas and Olshaker (2001) claim that when it comes to serial killers, Jack the Ripper is ground zero, the point at which both history and discussion begin. In fact, curiosity about the killings, the killer, and the victims has increased with the passage of time.

> Interest in the Jack the Ripper murders is probably greater today than at any time since the killer himself actually stalked the streets of London's East End. In recent years we have been all but deluged in a swelling tide of books, articles, films, plays and comics inspired by the case, and aficionados can now debate their theories and exchange views via Internet sites, at annual conferences and in the columns of specialist magazines. (Sugden, 2002, p. xi)

The murders and murderer continue to be the object of investigative reports, board games, computer games, wax museum exhibits, trading cards, songs, operas, comic books, movies, television shows, baseball caps, and even alcoholic drinks (e.g., the Ripper Tipple, containing blood-red spirits). One of the most interesting features of the Ripper's killings is the enduring interest in the case.

It is not hard to accept as truth some of what contemporaries of the killer believed. He had physical strength, both daring and coolness, and perhaps special knowledge and skill to be able to do what he did. He probably acted alone and was either very lucky or very accomplished to be able to vanish without leaving any trace of evidence as to who he was. In fact, it is probably Scotland Yard's most famous unsolved crime. The number of suspects remains large, and nobody is widely accepted as *the* killer. Russo's (2004) examination of 71 possible suspects led him to conclude that we are no wiser about the true identity of Jack the Ripper than we ever were. Even Lewis Carroll (whose real name was Charles Dodgson), famous author of children's books like *Alice's Adventures in Wonderland,* was included on the list, supposedly killing in tandem with a lifelong friend from Oxford, Thomas Bayne (Wallace, 1996). Other suspects who were suggested at the time of the murders are a "sunstroked" physician, a cattle drover, a Malay, a slaughterhouse employee, a Frenchman who dabbled in the supernatural, and an American anatomist (Fisher, 1997, p. 213). Eddie Victor (the Duke of Clarence), grandson of Queen Victoria, has also been identified as possibly being the infamous killer (Abrahamsen, 1992; Russo, 2004). In 2014, DNA testing was conducted on bloodstains on the shawl of Catherine Eddowes, the fourth Ripper victim. Two strands of DNA from the shawl were tested against a descendant of the sister of a man named Aaron Kosminski, a long-time favorite among many Ripperologists as Jack the Ripper. One of the strands was a perfect match, and the second was a 99.2% match (Fox News, 2014).

Folk Devils and Moral Panics

Jack the Ripper has become larger than life, a concrete example of a folk devil. *Folk devils* embody evil, and they symbolize in a clear and consistent way, free from distractions and ambiguities, something despicable and ugly (S. Cohen, 1972). They are "unambiguously unfavorable symbols," stripped of any positive qualities and imbued with the ultimate evil (p. 41).

London has been, in its time, the largest city in the world. It is well over two thousand years old, and has stood at the heart of an empire that spanned the globe. Of all the blood that has been shed, the violence and the secrecy, the rise and fall of dynasties, five murders in the autumn of 1888 have cut more deeply into the memory of horror than any others. (Perry, 2006, p. 182)

Importantly, in such a symbolization process, "images are made much sharper than reality" (S. Cohen, 1972, p. 43).

Newspapers (of which there were hundreds in the area) did what they could to promote or even inflame residents' fears and anxieties at the time of the killings. The media either improvised rumors or manipulated and massaged the available ones to make each murder seem more sensational and barbaric than the previous one. Because fear sold more newspapers, editors and reporters had a vested interest in making the crimes look as horrific as possible and the theories as outlandish as they could (Fisher, 1997).

Moral panics—and the public reaction in 1888 to the Ripper's killings is a good example—by their very nature identify, condemn, and work to eliminate folk devils (Goode & Ben-Yehuda, 1994). A moral panic involves forecasts about possible disasters, increased sensitivity to signs of danger, exaggerated reactions, rumors, false alarms, and possibly even mass delusions (S. Cohen, 1972). As Fisher (1997) says,

> A community will attempt to contain the threat by attributing it to an outsider or someone from another part of society, or by ultimately finding the victims themselves responsible for their own misfortune. Social distancing, finding fault, and laying blame are a community's classic defense. (pp. 217–218)

The Ripper's killings chipped away at the structure of the community, at least temporarily, weakening whatever bonds might have existed and intensifying ethnic and religious animosities. Residents became less trusting and more suspicious of one another. With each murder, the level of police patrol went up and citizen presence on the streets of the East End went down. Sporadic violence broke out in which groups of vigilantes would beat up any man walking the streets of Whitechapel who brought suspicion upon himself.

A roaming, brutal, relentless murderer, killing at will and with impunity, was perfectly fit to demonstrate to residents of the East End in 1888—and people elsewhere forevermore—the dangers of public life and the risks of trusting others. "The blacker the villain," A. Cohen (1974) instructs, "the more useful he is to the ordinary man, who might otherwise be hard put to produce the desired contrast effect" (p. 17). The tale of Jack the Ripper was spread by newspapers and word of mouth, and given substance by letters to authorities, supposedly from the killer himself. Rather than prompting a generalized sense that something was wrong, a tangible threat like the Ripper made it possible for the East End inhabitants to deal with their anxieties in what seemed to be a deliberate and meaningful way.

News stories, editorials, and even cartoons in the popular press nudged Victorians in the direction of defining the East End, and especially Whitechapel, as a site of both political unrest and inherent pathology (Gray, 2011). To many Victorians, the East End itself was the real Ripper (Ackroyd, 2008). It was portrayed in both the popular press and in the oral tradition as grimy, sordid, and degenerate, populated by both the morally and physically unclean, people who were thoroughly committed to idleness instead of work. The East End was widely viewed as a strange and foreign land, a locale beyond the reach of both morality and law (Marriott, 2008). The East End became a synonym for danger and social decay. It became known by the fall of 1888 as the "abyss," "murderland," "plague spot," or "evil quarter-mile" (Ross, 2008, p. 181). It was conceptualized as "outcast London" (Rumbelow, 1988). Without the trappings of the East End, the Ripper case is just another slasher story (Bloom, 2008).

Constructing Jack

The social construction of the Ripper as a folk devil rests on three "planks." None of them is necessarily true, and each one is open to dispute. If any one of them were to be proven false, it would change substantially how this classic example of predatory violence is understood.

1. *One man was responsible for the series of murders in the East End in 1888.* The belief that one individual was responsible for each and every murder of the "canonical five" (Nichols, Chapman, Stride, Eddowes, and Kelly) is the core of the social construction of the Ripper. However, this may just be smoke and mirrors, a belief generated more by official responses and media attention than by any characteristics of the killings themselves. Street thugs and ruffians prowled the East End in search of cash and valuables. Some of the victims blamed on the Ripper could just as easily have been killed by these marauding gangs. These crooks used violence both to make prostitutes pay extortion money and to punish them if they refused. This sent a clear message to any others who might have been inclined to keep the money they had earned for themselves (Cornwell, 2002; Fido, 1993; Rumbelow, 1988). Stride, mainly because her murder was different from that of the other victims (i.e., no mutilations and no parallel incisions in the throat), is a good candidate as someone who was killed by a gang. In fact, one police

view, eventually rejected for reasons that are unclear, was that a gang of blackmailing ruffians was responsible for the string of murders in 1888 (Jackson, 2008).

During their lives, the canonical five had interpersonal difficulties (i.e., fights and disagreements) with husbands, ex-husbands, boyfriends, adult children, bosses, apartment owners, acquaintances, and friends. Where life is miserable, nasty, and brutish, little reluctance exists to act violently toward others. Even the fear of arrest and incarceration is an insufficient deterrent to override the brutalizing impact of desperate social conditions. Moreover, cutting throats was not an unusual way to murder people in 1888, especially in cases of domestic violence (Cornwell, 2002, p. 126). Furthermore, it is almost an article of faith among criminal profilers that stabbing a person multiple times in the region of the face is a very personal act. When it is found, it is taken as strong circumstantial evidence by police and medical examiners that victim and killer knew each other. More than one killer could have been operating in the area, and the canonical five could have been slain by other than a canonical one Jack the Ripper.

2. *The Ripper killed many women.* Estimates of the number of Ripper victims fluctuate over time and from writer to writer, going as low as 2 and as high as 11 (or higher in some accounts). These are widely divergent estimates and produce very different images of this nineteenth-century murderer. In fact, if it were to be true that the Ripper killed but two women—the consensus definition of serial killing requires that three or more people be killed with a lengthy cooling-off period after each murder (Homant & Kennedy, 2006, p. 190)—it would mean that Jack the Ripper, the most famous serial killer in the annals of crime, was not a serial killer at all (though the FBI [2013] defines serial murder as the unlawful killing of *two* or more victims by the same offender(s) in separate events).

S. Evans and Rumbelow (2006) consider but then reject the prevailing view that Jack the Ripper killed five and only five women. They note that there is very little hard evidence and no certainty available about which killings were done by whom. Because no murderer was arrested and convicted for the crimes, they concluded that it is impossible to know which victims fell to the Ripper. They whittle the list down to three on the basis of how the killings were done. Nichols (victim #1), Chapman (victim #2), and Eddowes (victim # 4), they conclude, were victims of the same killer. It is less likely that Stride (victim #3) and Kelly (victim #5) were (p. 260). This probably should have been the end of the discussion, but it was not. On page 268, in the "Authors' Epilogues," Rumbelow states the following: "Here I find myself agreeing with Superintendent Arnold that there were only four victims."

The press at the time of the killings concluded that a series of murders was occurring, when it was no series at all. Two women had been killed in the general vicinity of Whitechapel, Emma Smith in April and Martha Tabram in August. When Mary Ann Nichols was also slain in August, the three deaths were lumped together and blamed on the same person. "The three Whitechapel murders were immediately identified as a 'series' and the press proclaimed that a homicidal maniac was on the loose" (S. Evans & Skinner, 2001, pp. 2–3). This conclusion was reached in spite of the fact that very few people in the area actually believed that the three victims were killed by the same hand. The seriality was established on the flimsiest of evidence: All three women had been cut and stabbed, and murder was not common in the district.

The Federal Bureau of Investigation coined the term *linkage blindness* to describe the *failure* of members of the public to recognize that the same killer is responsible for multiple murders occurring at different places and times (Jenkins, 1994, p. 6). This is a legitimate concern with killers like Theodore "Ted" Bundy, executed in Florida by electric chair on January 24, 1989, for killing a preteen female by the name of Kimberly Diane Leach. When the killer is mobile and the victims are many—Bundy killed women in many different states—linkage blindness may impede both efforts to nab the killer and efforts to understand all that happened. With Jack the Ripper, however, we may have a mirror image of this phenomenon, a *linkage quest*. This term describes the inclination to link murders together that are neither connected nor done by the same individual. This usually leads to a perception that a surge has occurred in the actual rate of serial murder rather than what it really is: an artifact of how the data are being reported and understood.

3. *The Ripper was a sexually sadistic killer.* If these murders were, in fact, sexually motivated, they were unusual. Not a lot of evidence of sexual mutilation existed in the 1888 murders, as most of the damage was done to the throat, abdomen, and internal organs. C. Wilson's (1988) proof for his claim that Jack the Ripper inaugurated the age of sex crime is no proof at all. The only objective indicator he offers for classifying the killings the way he does is that "nightmarish mutilations" were inflicted upon the victims on their genital areas (p. 2). Just because the killer stabbed women in body parts that can be used for reproduction does not mean he was a sex criminal any more than the idea that because he stabbed victims in their abdomens, he had a sexual attraction to stomachs (called *alvinolagnia*). A quest to sexualize violence against women, when nothing comparable is done with violence against men, may impair our ability to understand serial murder (Monckton-Smith, 2010). The victim who comes closest to having been

assaulted by a sexually sadistic killer is Emma Smith. She was assaulted on April 3 with a blunt object that was inserted into her vaginal vault, dying a day later in the London Hospital. She has been discounted, however, as a Ripper victim.

Researchers at the FBI (Morton, Tillman, & Gaines, 2014) compiled a document to assist in the investigation of serial murders and the apprehension of individuals who commit them. It was based on 480 cases of serial murder in the United States (committed by 92 offenders), spanning the 46-year time period from 1960 to 2006. A majority of these killers (91.6%), all of whom were male, had killed three or more victims. A killing was classified as sexually motivated if any type of sexual interaction whatsoever had occurred between victim and killer. Even the presence of sexual fantasies alone—it is unclear how the FBI determined their existence—was sufficient for a murder to be defined as sexually motivated (p. 10). It is no surprise that when the brush sweeps this wide, a lot of sexually motivated murders will be found. The FBI concluded that sex was the principal motivation in 81.5% of the murders (p. 18) and that 69% of the victims (329 of the 480) were killed by someone who was deemed to have been sexually motivated (p. 43). Though their numbers don't agree, the mistake doesn't change their overall conclusion that most of the serial murder cases that law enforcement officers investigate are sexually motivated.

Medical specialists in 1888 could find no evidence of any sexual contact between the killer and the killed when they autopsied the victims. For example, Dr. Frederick Gordon Brown, the surgeon for the City of London police, reported at the inquest to determine the cause of death of Catherine Eddowes that no secretions of any kind were on the deceased's thighs, leading him to conclude that no traces of recent "connection" existed. Fido (1993) finds this conclusion significant. It indicates that nineteenth-century medical men seem to have been well aware that a serial murderer like Jack the Ripper might copulate with his victims (or masturbate on the body). The medical examiner looked for evidence of this but could find none. It is true that forensic science in 1888 was in its infancy and had not yet developed tests for crime scene investigators to determine the presence of semen in or on a victim's body. It is *not* true, however, that they were ignorant of the possibility that murders were sometimes done for sexual reasons.

None of the indicators used by Warren, Hazelwood, and Dietz (1996) in their study of 20 sexually sadistic serial killers was found in *any* of the Ripper murders. These researchers found binding, blindfolding, or gagging in 100% of the 20 murders studied; none of these occurred in the Ripper murders. They found torture in 100% of the 20 murders; no torture occurred in the Ripper murders. They found careful planning of the offenses in 95% of the 20 murders. The murders in the East End in 1888 were more a product of luck or opportunity than of careful planning. These researchers found sexual bondage in 95% of the 20 murders; no sexual bondage was found in the Ripper murders. They found evidence of penile penetration in 95% of the 20 murders; no evidence of sexual connection was uncovered by medical examiners in any of the Ripper murders. They found evidence of sodomy (e.g., anal or oral sex) or object penetration in 90% of the 20 murders; nothing like this occurred in the Ripper murders.

Some evidence—or more than was found—should have been present at the crime scenes or uncovered at the autopsies if Jack the Ripper was, in fact, a sexually sadistic serial killer. The Ripper may simply have wanted to generate as much fear and outrage as possible in the general public and concluded that brutal murders and horrific mutilations were the way to do it. It would probably be wise to err on the side of caution and not assert confidently that Jack the Ripper was a sexually sadistic serial killer, inaugurating the age of sex crime. One thing certainly is true: Not all serial murderers are sexually sadistic murderers (Holmes & Holmes, 2010; Ioannou, 2010; Purcell & Arrigo, 2006). Serial murderers are motivated by things other than, or in addition to, sex, such as attention seeking, anger, thrills, or even financial gain (U.S. Department of Justice, 2008).

The Radford/Florida Gulf Coast University serial killer database (Radford/FGCU) gives information on 3,873 serial killers, each of whom had killed 2 or more victims from 1992 until September 6, 2014, (Aamodt, 2014). It reports that 46% of the killings were for lust, thrill, or power, while the remainder were for financial gain (32%), anger (8%), gang activities (3%), to avoid arrest (1.21%), to get attention (0.62%), for convenience (0.73%), due to hallucinations (0.41%), or as part of cult violence (0.21%). This database was put together by Radford University students from a survey of the Internet, prison records, court transcripts, media sources, and true crime books. It seems true that serial murderers search for victims who are vulnerable and thus easier to isolate and control, even while some of their killings seem to reflect a compulsive, aberrational quality (Alvarez & Bachman, 2008; Beard, Hunter, Kern, & Kiley, 2014; Vronsky, 2004).

The Ripper's Legacy

If some doubt exists that the Victorians actually gave us the first sexually sadistic serial killer, no doubt should exist that an important legacy originated in the fog-shrouded streets of the East End in 1888. The crimes and the Victorians' treatment of them gave concrete meaning to the idea of *seriality*. These five killings (related or not) gave sustenance and nourishment to the developing view that separate crimes *could* be linked together. "Serial" came to mean something other than *repeated*. It indicated sinister characteristics of an offender, such as irrationality, compulsiveness, and extreme violence. Actual killers could draw inspiration from the idea of seriality and pattern their murders on the idea of stalking and repetition. Some individuals in the United States during the time of the murders devoured reports from abroad about the killings (Larson, 2003). A Whitechapel Club formed in Chicago. The club's president held the title of "The Ripper," and members, mostly journalists, both revered and sensationalized murder and mayhem. Their meetings consisted of a sharing of tales about murders that had occurred on the streets of Chicago. Weapons used in actual murders, supplied by the police, adorned the walls of the clubhouse. Skulls supplied by a nearby asylum did, too (pp. 31–32).

The Ripper murders established—or seemed to—that serial killers' level of violence escalates over time. Sugden (2002) shows this way of thinking when he describes the murder of Mary Jane Kelly, generally believed to be the last victim of the series, as "certainly his [the Ripper's] most extensively mutilated victim" (p. 112). The only way, however, that escalating violence could be confirmed in the East End killings is if they were all done by the same individual, and if the slow, methodical, private killing of Mary Kelly could be scientifically proven to be more violent than the savage blitz attack and frenzied mutilations, done in the open, of Catherine Eddowes. The claims about how many women Jack the Ripper killed, still a matter of dispute, get hopelessly confused with claims about whether the violence went up, went down, or stayed about the same.

The Ripper and his murders were a watershed event for the study of predatory violence. Not only was the East End in the nineteenth century perfectly suited to produce a killer like Jack the Ripper, but it was also perfectly suited to socially construct the murders in the way that they have been understood and remembered. Social context always matters. A good explanation of the Ripper would give a convincing account of why he killed whom he did, how he was able to escape again and again, and why he stopped killing when he did (Fisher, 1997). An even better explanation would give convincing evidence about the *meanings* these murders had for the killer, as well as the role played by social organization and cultural dynamics in how these murders have been conceptualized and why interest in Jack the Ripper has persisted for so long.

Variable Violence

Killing the Young

The prevailing standards in the United States today with regard to when life begins and when it can be taken away, though ambiguous, are clear in one respect: It is totally unacceptable for anybody to intentionally kill or abuse an infant or child. Even the most adamant proabortionist believes that once a child is born, he or she is a person and has the right to live and grow, and antiabortionists would no doubt agree. The killing or abuse of an infant or child is viewed as inexcusable—a monstrous act by either a very sick or a very sadistic individual (Kantrowitz, 1998). However, *infanticide*—killing of babies and small children—has not always been considered a heinous act.

Infanticide occurs among nonhuman primates (Rees, 2009), and it was once a fairly common human practice (deMause, 1974). Childhood used to be considered a brief period of development during which children were expected to acquire adult skills and capabilities as quickly as possible, and they were viewed as ungrateful dependents or even as parasites (McCoy, 1992). Middle- and upper-class parents believed that having too many children interfered with their lifestyles and their pursuit of pleasure. Working- and lower-class families also had their reasons for not wanting too many children. A new child meant another mouth to feed and another person to care for in a family where resources were limited. Time spent in the birth and care of a child pulled the mother away from important duties that contributed to the survival of the entire family. Prior to the late 1800s, as the American Medical Association formed in 1847, regular physicians still suffered from much ignorance about how to deliver healthy babies. If the mother were to die in childbirth—a distinct possibility given the low level of medical knowledge and skill—a valuable family member would be gone. Illegitimate children, deformed children, babies born to parents who did not want them, and infants born to families who were too poor to afford them were regularly killed outright or simply allowed to die through abandonment or neglect.

Improvement in economic conditions, new civil liberties for all people, healthier living conditions, and better medical care served to change attitudes about children and childhood. Children came to be seen as more valuable. By the late 1600s and early 1700s, child-rearing practices were already starting to change throughout the world. The Puritans, for example, elevated the status of children to new heights. They believed strongly in the value of the family, especially family cohesion and integration (Pleck, 1987). By the late 1700s, more women had access to birth control techniques, allowing some choice in regard to pregnancy. Because having a child was more voluntary, it meant that more parents had children because they wanted them. Children came to be defined more as rewards than as burdens, and a new closeness developed between parents and their children. Parents were more affectionate toward children and more indulgent of them than they had ever been (Zelizer, 1994).

Children came to be increasingly viewed as persons who needed to be protected from the risks and hazards of life. Child labor laws were passed in most Western nations to ensure that youngsters were no longer economically exploited by adults. During the twentieth century in the United States, children came to be viewed less as economic assets and more as priceless human beings. Their principal value was found in the pleasure that they brought to others and their capacity for learning and future success. Children had attained a sentimental value in the Western world that was unheard of and unimagined at other times and places. New laws, new criminal procedures, and new criminal justice institutions were crafted in 1899 in the United States just for them, largely as a result of a group in Chicago, Illinois, called the Child Savers. These reformers wanted youthful offenders removed from the corrupting influences of urban life and put into places that were supervised by people who cared enough to teach them right from wrong (Platt, 2009; Ward, 2012).

At times, in some places, infanticide has been defined as an expression of parental duty and love, not a retreat from it. The Netsilik Eskimo (Inuit) are a native group who live on the Arctic coast of North America. They hunt seals, caribou, and salmon with harpoons and spears. They were once nomadic and lived in tents in the summer and snow houses (igloos) in the winter that were heated by soapstone lamps. They were well-known for their custom of infanticide (Balikci, 1970/1989).

> Once when there was a famine Nagtok gave birth to a child, while people lay around about her dying of hunger. What did that child want here? How could it live, when its mother, who should give it life, was herself dried up and starving? So she strangled it and allowed it to freeze and later on ate it. (Rasmussen, as quoted in Balikci, p. 151)

The Netsilik considered infanticide as a way to increase their chances of survival in a harsh environment.

Female children were killed more often than male children. Why kill girls instead of boys? The Netsilik defined females as both poor hunters and big eaters, so their loss from society was considered less objectionable than the loss of males. They believed that female infanticide increased the entire community's chances for survival by reducing the number of people who ate food but were deemed less able to hunt for it. If a woman gave birth to a daughter and cared for her, it was considered time poorly spent; the mother could have given birth to a son and raised him in an equal amount of time. Thus, a daughter might be killed to make it possible for the family to bring forth a son.

Infants were killed in several ways. If a birth occurred during the winter, the newborn was placed at the entrance to the igloo. The child's screams only lasted a few minutes because the infant froze to death. In summer, a newborn was placed in a small grave, dug near the family's dwelling. The infant usually cried several hours before dying. A third method was used for all seasons: A furry skin was placed over the infant's face until the baby suffocated.

The Netsilik were either unconcerned with, or unaware of, the grave dangers that female infanticide posed to community survival. The custom produced powerful tensions and a great deal of disharmony. It caused an imbalance in the sex ratio, thereby reducing the number of marriageable females. This increased the pressure on men to find and hold mates. The community divided itself into many small, mutually suspicious groups. Sometimes, husbands were murdered by envious men who coveted their wives.

In 1936, a Catholic missionary established a mission near the Netsilik. As a result of his preaching and ongoing personal involvement with them, he was able to suppress the practice of female infanticide. This eventually restored the balance in the sex ratio. Men were able to find wives more easily, and they were less likely to murder each other to obtain mates. Monogamy became the rule. Very quickly, according to Balikci (1970/1989), the Netsilik started acting like "good Christians" (p. 250).

Killing the Not-So-Young

In some places, the idea of killing a person who is legally determined to "deserve it" because of some injury he or she has visited on the community receives great support. Such a killing—called *capital punishment* or the *death penalty*—may not even be viewed as an unnecessarily violent act because of its legitimacy in the eyes of the beholders. Unlike dueling violence, which skirted the official apparatus of control, the killings produced by capital punishment occur according to strict rules and formalized procedures and are carried out by representatives of the government itself. Specific due-process requirements must be followed for an individual to be sentenced to death and then executed, and the convict is legally permitted to appeal the sentence, many times in the usual case.

Amnesty International (2014) reported that 22 nations executed a total of 778 criminals in 2013 (China is excluded because it refuses to divulge any information about its executions.). This represented a decrease from a decade earlier when 31 countries carried out executions. Amnesty International concluded that the worldwide trend is toward abolition of use of the death penalty with over two-thirds of the world's countries terminating its use in law, in practice, or both. (Almost 80% of the executions in 2013 were confined to three countries: Saudi Arabia, Iraq, and Iran.) A more recent report (Amnesty International, 2015) indicates that the same number of countries executed people in 2014 as in 2013 (22 countries). However, the number of executions worldwide, 607 (excluding China, once again), was 22% lower than the 2013 figures. Saudi Arabia, Iraq, and Iran were responsible for over 70% of the reported executions in 2014.

Not all states in the United States have the death penalty, and different people have different opinions about its propriety, especially with subpopulations, such as juveniles, those with mental retardations (i.e., intellectual disabilities), the insane, or the mentally ill (Koch, Wark, & Galliher, 2012; Kubiak & Allen, 2011). Attitudes about capital punishment in the United States have shifted during the last 45 years or so from weak support (42% favored it as a punishment for murder in 1966) to the strong support of the 1980s and 1990s (71% favored it in 1996) (Maguire & Pastore, 1998, p. 141). Support for capital punishment declined a bit as the United States moved into the twenty-first century (60% favored it as a punishment for murder in 2013 [Bureau of Justice Statistics, 2013, Table 2.51]). However, a survey of college freshmen shows that they have become more supportive of the death penalty with the passage of time. In 1969, a total of 56% of them agreed ("strongly" or "somewhat") that the death penalty should be abolished; in 2006, only 35% of them felt the same way (Bureau of Justice Statistics, 2006, Table 2.93).

Ancient executions were savage affairs, characterized by a great deal of community rage and anger, in which the offender was expected to die slowly and in great misery. The entire community participated, either as executioners or as witnesses (Johnson, 1990). The bodily organs of some offenders were mutilated to increase their punishment even more. Intestines, hearts, and kidneys have been ripped out of condemned criminals by angry crowds, sometimes while the condemned was still alive, and their hands, noses, tongues, and ears have been either cut off or mutilated. In some cases, it was done because the body parts were viewed as the organs responsible for the crimes. Other times, offenders were mutilated simply to hurt them more or to humiliate them further (Newman, 1978).

The identifying features of modern, government executions, at least in the United States, are their bureaucratic nature and their isolation from the community. Community feelings of rage are supposed to be absent or at least suppressed. What was once an act by a community on its own behalf has become the province of prison officials, who are expected to approach executions with professionalism and detachment. The last government-sponsored *public* execution in the United States occurred in Owensboro, Kentucky, in 1937, where a young black man (named Rainey Bethea) was hanged for assaulting a 70-year-old woman. Twenty thousand people attended, and they were a coarse, unruly crowd (Prejean, 1989, p. 101).

Murderers not only take lives needlessly and ravage the families and friends of the victim, but also violate the sentiments of trust and affiliation that serve as the foundation of social life. The anger, the hurt, and the desire for revenge are easy enough to understand (Berns, 1982). However, not everyone who has had a family member murdered is in favor of the death penalty.

> I was eight years old when my father was murdered. It is almost impossible to describe the pain of losing a parent to a senseless murder. And in the aftermath, it is similarly impossible to quiet the confusion: "Why him? Why this? Why me?" But even as a child one thing was clear to me: I didn't want the killer, in turn, to be killed. . . . I saw nothing that could be accomplished in the loss of one life being answered with the loss of another. And I knew, far too vividly, the anguish that would spread through another family—another set of parents, children, brothers, and sisters thrown into grief. (M. K. Kennedy, 1989, p. 1)

The author of this statement is M. Kerry Kennedy, the daughter of Robert F. Kennedy. Her father was gunned down in Los Angeles in June 1968 during his bid for the Democratic nomination for the presidency of the United States. Why was Ms. Kennedy so strongly opposed to capital punishment, even as a child, and even after the murder of her father, when other people, whose lives have not been as dramatically changed by a violent crime, are in favor of it? Do they have greater concern for the victims of violence than does Ms. Kennedy, or is something else operating?

Elements can be found in an execution of a convicted felon to suggest that it is—or could be interpreted as—a premeditated, violent act. Johnson (1990) describes an execution he witnessed of a felon named Jones. The man was strapped into the electric chair, electrodes were attached to his head and leg, and a tight mask was placed over his face. Only his nose was visible. At the legally designated time, the electric switch was thrown, and 2,500 volts of electricity, at 5 to 7 amps, coursed through Jones's body, starting at his head and ending at the electrode on his ankle. Here, Johnson describes the details:

> Jones sat perfectly still for what seemed an eternity but was in fact no more than thirty seconds. Finally, the electricity hit him. His body stiffened spasmodically, though only briefly. A thin swirl of smoke trailed away from his head, then dissipated quickly. (People outside the witness room could hear crackling and burning; a faint smell of burned flesh lingered in the air, mildly nauseating some people.) The body remained taut, with the right foot raised slightly at the heel, seemingly frozen there. A brief pause, then another minute of shock. When it was over, the body was inert. (p. 111)

An execution is characterized by harm (death of the convicted felon), intent to kill (the execution is meticulously planned and carefully rehearsed to ensure a smooth and successful operation), and a deliberate taking of an individual's life by state representatives. In all those characteristics, a "murder" and an "execution" are identical (M. C. Kennedy, 1976). M. C. Kennedy argues that it is one group's superior power that creates and sustains the belief that punishment and crime are different from one another, belonging to mutually exclusive categories. It is peculiar, he thinks, that some groups will go to great lengths to stop the violence of murder but will allow, or even encourage, the violence of capital punishment.

Most people view executions as less violent than the killings that offenders committed that got them sent to the death chamber in the first place. Executions seem to be activated by proper motives, such as retribution and protection of innocent victims. Executioners are able to portray their acts as necessary and beneficial for protection of social order, both a professional duty and a legal obligation. It is widely believed that individuals who cannot live peacefully in an open, free, and prosperous society, deserve what they get, even if it is the death penalty. The heightened fear of violent crime, coupled with media coverage of criminal violence, no doubt plays a role when people's support for capital punishment increases (Mandery, 2012; Rankin, 1979). The U.S. Supreme Court, along with a majority of state legislatures, reformed the death penalty in the 1970s so that it seemed moral enough to justify its continued use—less arbitrary, less racist, and less brutal (because lethal injections replaced electrocutions and gassings) (Garland, 2005).

One thing that has made some difference in how executions are viewed is that the U.S. Supreme Court rendered decisions that restricted their use with certain populations. In *Atkins v. Virginia* (2002), the Court declared that individuals with mental retardation (i.e., intellectual disabilities) could no longer be executed (due primarily to the diminished capacity that can accompany such a disability). In *Roper v. Simmons* (2005), which extended similar logic about capacity to the young, the Court ruled by a vote of 5 to 4 that executing individuals who at the time of their offense were juveniles (anyone under the age of 18) was in violation of the Eighth and Fourteenth Amendments. Executions of juveniles were declared to be cruel and unusual punishments. (Repeal of the death penalty for juveniles has had no impact on rates of murder committed by them because its use had no deterrent effect on murder for offenders under age 18 anyway [Flexon, Stolzenberg, & D'Alessio, 2011].)

Supporters of the death penalty are traditionally more conservative than liberal, more concerned with public safety than with individual rights, and more focused on the malevolence of humans than on their benevolence or possibility for redemption (Garland, 2005). Curiously, some *extreme* supporters of the death penalty express their rage over violent crime by wanting murderers killed—as painfully as possible—along with anyone who *opposes* the death penalty (and the opponents' families, too) (Vandiver, Giacopassi, & Gathje, 2002). For individuals who see an execution as a reasonable, or even necessary, retribution for serious crimes, the desirability of the death penalty is a core value, and core values are unlikely to change much if at all (Mandery, 2012).

Public attitudes about the death penalty do change, however. Just as many factors work together to determine the likelihood of an individual being executed (Petrie & Coverdill, 2010), so do many factors work together to determine public opinions about the death penalty. Evidence of the conviction and execution of innocent individuals, political decisions to commute sentences, examples that the penalty is racist and discriminatory, and growing awareness that the United States is out of step with other countries in the global environment—all of these can intensify pressures to change the law to abolish the practice. Public support for the death penalty seems to rise when the public is convinced that it is administered fairly, free from prejudice and discrimination, and where innocent individuals are unlikely to be executed (Mandery, 2012). Changes in the actual use of capital punishment, as well as public attitudes about it, are influenced by changing views of its morality, constitutionality, reliability, irrevocability, and fairness (Garland, 2005; Mbionwu, 2010; Walker, 2011).

Conclusions

Violence—or social acts called violence—is a regular feature of most societies, and much of it is done by ordinary people who view their use of violence as practical and necessary, a form of self-help when legal authorities either will not or cannot help. These individuals seek their own brand of justice, and they seem to care little that they might be arrested and imprisoned for what they have done. Some of the individuals who commit murder may even wait for police to arrive or report the crime themselves. Important factors in the relativity of violence are the ability to offer appropriate motives for what one has done and to offer accounts if one's rationale for using violence is called into question.

Infanticide, capital punishment, dueling, thuggee, mass murder, nonpredatory violence, and serial murder are not individual random events, precipitated by stress and frustration. They are socially created and socially sustained, reflecting patterns of social organization rather than negations of it. What are the differences among the deaths caused by capital punishment, dueling, thuggee, predatory murder, nonpredatory murder, or infanticide and other violent happenings in some society? Are there any objective, intrinsic, or inherent qualities of killings *themselves* that would allow a dispassionate observer to know which deaths are legitimate and which are not? Even serious deviances, like the different kinds of violence described in this chapter, vary a great deal from place to place, time to time, and situation to situation. Individual motives and intentions are important to know about to understand predatory violence, as are social dynamics and cultural meanings.

References

Aamodt, M. G. (2014, September 6,). *Serial killer statistics.* Retrieved March 28, 2015, from http://maamodt.asp.radford.edu/serialkillerinformationcenter/projectdescription.htm

Abrahamsen, D. (1992). *Murder and madness: The secret life of Jack the Ripper.* New York: Donald Fine.

Ackroyd, P. (2008). Jack the Ripper and the East End. In A. Werner (Ed.), *Jack the Ripper and the East End* (pp. 7–29). London: Chatto & Windus.

Ahmad, I. (1992). *Thugs, dacoits, and the world-system in nineteenth century India.* Unpublished doctoral dissertation, State University of New York at Binghamton.

Alvarez, A. (1972). *The savage god: A study of suicide.* New York: Random House.

Alvarez, A., & Bachman, R. (2008). *Violence: The enduring problem.* Thousand Oaks, CA: Sage.

American Psychiatric Association. (2013). *Diagnostic and statistical manual of mental disorders* (5th ed.). Washington, DC: Author.

Amnesty International. (2014). *Death sentences and executions 2013*. Retrieved March 11, 2015, from http://www.amnestyusa.org/research/reports/death-sentences-and-executions-2013

Amnesty International (2015). *Death sentences and executions 2014*. Retrieved June 2, 2015, from http://www.amnestyusa.org/pdfs/DeathSentencesAndExecutions 2014_EN.pdf

Anderson, E. (1999). *Code of the street: Decency, violence, and the moral life of the inner city*. New York: Norton.

Athens, L. (1980). *Violent criminal acts and actors: A symbolic interactionist study*. Boston: Routledge/Kegan Paul.

Athens, L. (2015). Violentization: A relatively singular theory of violent crime. *Deviant Behavior, 36*, 625–639.

Atkins v. Virginia, 536 U.S. 304 (2002).

Bailey, A. K., Tolnay, S. E., Beck, E. M., & Laird, J. D. (2011). Targeting lynch victims: Social marginality or status transgressions? *American Sociological Review, 76*, 412–436.

Balikci, A. (1989). *The Netsilik Eskimo*. Prospect Heights, IL: Waveland. (Original work published 1970)

Baron, S. W. (2011). Street youths' fear of violent crime. *Deviant Behavior, 32*, 475–502.

Baudrillard, J. (2002). *The spirit of terrorism and other essays* (C. Turner, Trans.). London: Verso.

Baumer, E. P., Martin, K. H. (2013). Social organization, collective sentiment, and legal sanctions in murder cases. *American Journal of Sociology, 119*, 131–182.

Beard, V., Hunter, S., Kern, L., & Kiley, B. (2014). Death-related crime: Applying Bryant's conceptual paradigm of thanatological crime to serial homicide. *Deviant Behavior, 35*, 959–972.

Beeghley, L. (2003). *Homicide: A sociological explanation*. Lanham, MD: Rowman & Littlefield.

Bernard, T. J., Snipes, J. B., & Gerould, A. L. (2010). *Vold's theoretical criminology* (6th ed.). New York: Oxford University Press.

Berns, W. (1982). The morality of anger. In H. A. Bedau (Ed.), *The death penalty in America* (3rd ed., pp. 331–341). New York: Oxford University Press.

Berthelot, E. R., Brown, T. C., Drawve, G., & Burgason, K. A. (2015). The southern pub crawl and brawl: An examination of the alcohol–violence nexus in a southern city. *Deviant Behavior, 36*, 605–624.

Best, J. (1999). *Random violence: How we talk about new crimes and new victims*. Berkeley: University of California Press.

Best, J. (2004). *More damned lies and statistics: How numbers confuse public issues*. Berkeley: University of California Press.

Bing, R. L., III (Ed.). (2010). *Race, crime, and the media*. New York: McGraw-Hill.

Bjornstrom, E., Kaufman, R. L., Peterson, R. D., & Slater, M. D. (2010). Race and ethnic representations of lawbreakers and victims in crime news: A national study of television coverage. *Social Problems, 57,* 269–293.

Black, D. (1980). *The manners and customs of police.* New York: Academic Press.

Black, D. (1993). *The social structure of right and wrong.* San Diego, CA: Academic Press.

Blau, J., & Blau, P. (1982). The cost of inequality: Metropolitan structure and violent crime. *American Sociological Review, 47,* 114–129.

Bloom, C. (2008). Jack the Ripper: A legacy in pictures. In A. Werner (Ed.), *Jack the Ripper and the East End* (pp. 229–267). London: Chatto & Windus.

Browning, C. (1992). *The path to genocide: Essays on launching the final solution.* New York: Cambridge University Press.

Brownstein, H. (2000). *The social reality of violence and violent crime.* Boston: Allyn & Bacon.

Bureau of Justice Statistics. (2006). *Sourcebook of criminal justice statistics online.* Retrieved March 11, 2015, from http://www.albany.edu/sourcebook/pdf/t2932006.pdf

Bureau of Justice Statistics. (2013). *Sourcebook of criminal justice statistics online.* Retrieved March 11, 2015, from http://www.albany.edu/sourcebook/pdf/t2512013.pdf

Burgason, K. A., Thomas, S. A., Berthelot, E. R., & Burkey, L. C. (2014). Gats and gashes: street culture and distinctions in the nature of violence between youth and adult offenders. *Deviant Behavior, 35,* 534–554.

Cohen, A. (1974). *The elasticity of evil: Changes in the social definition of deviance.* Oxford, UK: Oxford University Penal Research Unit.

Cohen, S. (1972). *Folk devils and moral panics: The creation of the mods and rockers.* London: MacGibbon & Kee.

Coleman, J. (1988). Social capital in the creation of human capital. *American Journal of Sociology, 94,* 95–120.

Contreras, R. (2013). *The stickup kids: Race, drugs, violence, and the American dream.* Berkeley: University of California Press.

Cooney, M. (2009). *Is killing wrong? A study in pure sociology.* Charlottesville: University of Virginia Press.

Cornwell, P. (2002). *Portrait of a killer: Jack the Ripper—case closed.* New York: Putnam.

Covington, J. (2010). *Crime and racial constructions: Cultural misinformation about African Americans in media and academia.* Lanham, MD: Lexington Books.

Crawford, D. M., Whitbeck, L. B., & Hoyt, D. R. (2011). Propensity for violence among homeless and runaway adolescents: An event history analysis. *Crime & Delinquency, 57,* 950–968.

Declercq, F., & Audenaert, K. (2011). Predatory violence aiming at relief in a case of mass murder: Meloy's criteria for applied forensic practice. *Behavioral Sciences and the Law, 29,* 578–591.

DeKeseredy, W. W. (2011). *Violence against women: Myths, facts, controversies.* Toronto, ON, Canada: University of Toronto Press.

DeMause, L. (Ed.). (1974). The evolution of childhood. In L. DeMause (Ed.), *The history of childhood* (pp. 1–74). New York: Psychohistory Press.

DeYoung, M. (2014). The devil goes to day care: McMartin and the making of a moral panic. In R. Heiner (Ed.), *Deviance across cultures: Constructions of difference* (2nd ed., pp. 125–134). New York: Oxford University Press.

Douglas, J., & Olshaker, M. (2001). *The cases that haunt us.* New York: Simon & Schuster.

Drummond, H., Bolland, J. M., & Harris, W. A. (2011). Becoming violent: Evaluating the mediating effect of hopelessness on the code of the street thesis. *Deviant Behavior, 32,* 191–223.

Dufur, M. J., Hoffmann, J. P., Braudt, D. B., Parcel, T. L., & Spence, K. R. (2015). Examining the effects of family and school social capital on delinquent behavior. *Deviant Behavior, 36,* 511–526.

Edgerton, R. (1976). *Deviance: A cross-cultural perspective.* Menlo Park, CA: Cummings.

Eller, J. (2006). *Violence and culture: A cross-cultural and interdisciplinary approach.* Belmont, CA: Thomson/Wadsworth.

Evans, I. (2011). *Cultures of violence: Racial violence and the origins of segregation in South Africa and the American South.* Manchester, UK: Manchester University Press.

Evans, S., & Rumbelow, D. (2006). *Jack the Ripper: Scotland Yard investigates.* London: Sutton.

Evans, S., & Skinner, K. (2001). *Jack the Ripper: Letters from hell.* London: Sutton.

Eyerman, R., Alexander, J. C., & Breese, E. B. (Eds.). (2013). *Narrating trauma: On the impact of collective suffering.* Boulder, CO: Paradigm.

Faris, R., & Felmlee, D. (2011). Status struggles: Network centrality and gender segregation in same- and cross-gender aggression. *American Sociological Review, 76,* 48–73.

Farrall, S., Jackson, J., & Gray, E. (2009). *Social order and the fear of crime in contemporary times.* New York: Oxford University Press.

Federal Bureau of Investigation. (2001). Special report: The terrorist attacks of September 11, 2001: A compilation of data. In *Crime in the United States, 2001* (pp. 302–313). Washington, DC: Government Printing Office.

Federal Bureau of Investigation. (2013). Serial killers, Part 1: The FBI's role takes shape. Retrieved March 28, 2015, from http://www.fbi.gov/news/stories/2013/september/serial-killers-part-1-the-fbis-role-takes-shape

Federal Bureau of Investigation. (2014). *Crime in the United States, 2013.* Retrieved March 11, 2015, from http://www.FBI.gov

Felson, R. B., Liska, A. E., South, S., & McNulty, T. L. (1994). The subculture of violence and delinquency: Individual vs. school context effects. *Social Forces, 73,* 155–173.

Fido, M. (1993). *The crimes, detection, and death of Jack the Ripper.* New York: Barnes & Noble.

Fisher, J. (1997). *Killer among us: Public reactions to serial murder.* Westport, CT: Praeger.

Flexon, J. L., Stolzenberg, L., & D'Alessio, S. J. (2011). Cheating the hangman: The effect of the *Roper v. Simmons* decision on homicides committed by juveniles. *Crime & Delinquency, 57*, 928–949.

Fox News. (2014, September 8). *DNA testing reportedly reveals identity of Jack the Ripper.* Retrieved May 20, 2015, from http://www.foxnews.com/science/2014/09/08/dna-testing-reportedly-reveals-identity-jack-ripper

Garland, D. (2005). Capital punishment and American culture. *Punishment & Society, 7*, 347–376.

Ghatak, S. (2011). *Threat perceptions: The policing of dangers from eugenics to the war on terrorism.* Lanham, MD: Lexington Books.

Goetting, A. (1995). *Homicide in families and other special populations.* New York: Springer-Verlag.

Goode, E. (2008). *Deviant behavior* (8th ed.). Upper Saddle River, NJ: Pearson/Prentice Hall.

Goode, E., & Ben-Yehuda, N. (1994). *Moral panics: The social construction of deviance.* Oxford, UK: Basil Blackwell.

Gray, D. (2011). *Contextualizing the Ripper murders: Poverty, crime and unrest in the East End of London, 1888.* Paper presented at Jack the Ripper Through a Wider Lens: An Interdisciplinary Conference, Drexel University, Philadelphia, October 28–29.

Griffiths, E. (2013). Race, space, and the spread of violence across the city. *Social Problems, 60*, 491–512.

Hagen, R., Makovi, K., & Bearman, P. (2013). The influence of political dynamics on southern lynch mob formation and lethality. *Social Forces, 92*, 757–787.

Hall, K. (Ed.). (2002). *The Oxford guide to American law.* New York: Oxford University Press.

Heimer, K. (1997). Socioeconomic status, subcultural definitions, and violent delinquency. *Social Forces, 75*, 799–833.

Heiner, R. (2014). Crime scares. In R. Heiner (Ed.), *Deviance across cultures: Constructions of difference* (2nd ed., pp. 135–142). New York: Oxford University Press.

Hickey, E. (1997). *Serial murderers and their victims* (2nd ed.). Belmont, CA: Wadsworth.

Hipp, J. R. (2010). A dynamic view of neighborhoods: The reciprocal relationships between crime and neighborhood structural characteristics. *Social Problems, 57*, 205–230.

Hipp, J. R. (2011). Violent crime, mobility decisions, and neighborhood racial/ethnic transition. *Social Problems, 58*, 410–432.

Hollick, F. (1840). *Murder made moral.* Manchester, UK: A. Heywood.

Holmes, R., & Holmes, S. (2010). *Serial murder* (3rd ed.). Thousand Oaks, CA: Sage.

Homant, R., & Kennedy, D. (2006). Serial murder: A biopsychosocial approach. In W. Petherick (Ed.), *Serial crime* (pp. 189–223). Burlington, MA: Academic Press/Elsevier.

Hutton, J. (1981). *Thugs and dacoits of India.* New Delhi, India: Gian.

Ioannou, M. (2010). Serial murder. In C. Ferguson (Ed.), *Violent crime: Clinical and social implications* (pp. 300–326). Thousand Oaks, CA: Sage.

Jackson, L. (2008). Law, order, and violence. In A. Werner (Ed.), *Jack the Ripper and the East End* (pp. 99–139). London: Chatto & Windus.

Jenkins, P. (1994). *Using murder: The social construction of serial homicide.* New York: Aldine de Gruyter.

Johnson, R. (1990). *Death work: A study of the modern execution process.* Pacific Grove, CA: Brooks/Cole.

Kantrowitz, B. (1998). Cradles to coffins. In L. Salinger (Ed.), *Deviant behavior 98–99* (3rd ed., pp. 53–54). Guilford, CT: Dushkin.

Katz, F. (1994). *Ordinary people and extraordinary evil: A report on the beguilings of evil.* Albany: State University of New York Press.

Katz, J. (1988). *Seductions of crime: Moral and sensual attractions of doing evil.* New York: Basic Books.

Kennedy, M. C. (1976). Beyond incrimination: Some neglected facets of the theory of punishment. In W. Chambliss & M. Mankoff (Eds.), *Whose law? What order?* (pp. 34–65). New York: Wiley.

Kennedy, M. K. (1989). Foreword. In I. Gray & M. Stanley (Eds.), *A punishment in search of a crime: Americans speak out against the death penalty* (pp. 1–3). New York: Avon.

Kiehl, K. A. (2014). *The psychopath whisperer: The science of those without conscience.* New York: Crown.

Kiernan, V. G. (1988). *The duel in European history: Honor and the reign of aristocracy.* New York: Oxford University Press.

Kirk, D., & Papachristos, A. V. (2011). Cultural mechanisms and the persistence of neighborhood violence. *American Journal of Sociology, 116,* 1190–1233.

Koch, L. W., Wark, C., & Galliher, J. F. (2012). *The death of the American death penalty: States still leading the way.* Boston: Northeastern University Press.

Koop, C. E., & Lundberg, G. D. (1992). Violence in America: A public health emergency. *Journal of the American Medical Association, 267,* 3075–3076.

Kubiak, S. P., & Allen, T. (2011). Public opinion regarding juvenile life without parole in consecutive statewide surveys. *Crime & Delinquency, 57,* 495–515.

Lally, W., & DeMaris, A. (2012). Gender and relational-distance effects in arrests for domestic violence. *Crime & Delinquency, 58,* 103–123.

Lane, R. (2003). Murder in America: 1865–1917. In M. Silberman (Ed.), *Violence and society: A reader* (pp. 49–57). Upper Saddle River, NJ: Prentice Hall.

Larson, E. (2003). *The devil in the White City: Murder, magic, and madness at the fair that changed America.* New York: Crown.

Lesser, W. (1993). *Pictures at an execution.* Cambridge, MA: Harvard University Press.

Levi, K. (1989). Becoming a hit man: Neutralization in a very deviant career. In D. Kelly (Ed.), *Deviant behavior* (3rd ed., pp. 447–458). New York: St. Martin's Press.

Leyton, E. (1986). *Compulsive killers: The story of modern multiple murder.* New York: New York University Press.

Linsky, A., Bachman, R., & Strauss, M. (1995). *Stress, culture, and aggression.* New Haven, CT: Yale University Press.

Lyons, C. J., Vélez, M. B., & Santoro, W. A. (2013. Neighborhood immigration, violence, and city-level immigrant political opportunities. *American Sociological Review, 78,* 604–632.

Maguire, K., & Pastore, A. (Eds.). (1998). *Sourcebook of criminal justice statistics 1997.* Washington, DC: Government Printing Office.

Mandery, E. (2012). *Capital punishment in America: A balanced examination* (2nd ed.). Sudbury, MA: Jones & Bartlett.

Marriott, J. (2008). The imaginative geography of the Whitechapel murders. In A. Werner (Ed.), *Jack the Ripper and the East End* (pp. 31–64). London: Chatto & Windus.

Mbionwu, L. E. S. (2010). Media frames: The impact of public opinion on the death penalty. In R. L. Bing III (Ed.), *Race, crime, and the media* (pp. 177–186). New York: McGraw-Hill.

McCoy, E. (1992). Childhood through the ages. In K. Finsterbusch (Ed.), *Sociology 92–93* (21st ed., pp. 46–49). Guilford, CT: Dushkin.

Meloy, J. R., Hempel, A. G., Gray, G. T., Mohandie, K., Shiva, A., & Richards, T. C. (2004). A comparative analysis of North American adolescent and adult mass murderers. *Behavioral Sciences and the Law, 22,* 291–309.

Messner, S. F., & Rosenfeld, R. (2013). *Crime and the American dream* (5th ed.). Belmont, CA: Wadsworth.

Mills, C. W. (1940). Situated actions and vocabularies of motive. *American Sociological Review, 5,* 904–913.

Monckton-Smith, J. (2010). *Relating rape and murder: Narratives of sex, death and gender.* Hampshire, UK: Palgrave Macmillan.

Morenoff, J. D., Sampson, R. J., & Raudenbush, S. W. (2001). Neighborhood inequality, collective efficacy, and the spatial dynamics of urban violence. *Criminology, 39,* 517–559.

Morton, R. J., Tillman, J. M., & Gaines, S. J. (2014). *Serial murder: Pathways for investigations.* Behavior Analysis Unit 4. National Center for the Analysis of Violent Crime. Washington, DC: Federal Bureau of Investigation. Retrieved October 30, 2015, from https://www.fbi.gov/news/stories/2014/october/serial-killers-part-8-new-research-aims-to-help-investigators-solve-cases/serial-murder-pathways-for-investigations

Murray, J. L. (2015). Suicidal-homicidal ideation in mass killers and transcendence. *Deviant Behavior, 36,* 581–588.

Ness, C. D. (2010). *Why girls fight: Female youth violence in the inner city.* New York: New York University Press.

Newman, G. (1978). *The punishment response.* Philadelphia: J. B. Lippincott.

Parker, R. N., & McCaffree, K. J. (2013). *Alcohol and violence: The nature of the relationship and the promise of prevention.* Lanham, MD: Lexington Books.

Peralta, R., & Cruz, J. (2006). Conferring meaning onto alcohol-related violence: An analysis of alcohol use and gender in a sample of college youth. *Journal of Men's Studies, 14,* 109–125.

Perry, A. (2006). Why we will never forget Jack the Ripper. In P. Begg (Ed.), *Ripperology* (pp. 182–183). New York: Barnes & Noble.

Peterson, R. D., & Krivo, L. J. (2010). *Divergent social worlds: Neighborhood crime and the racial–spatial divide*. New York: Russell Sage Foundation.

Petrie, M. A., & Coverdill, J. E. (2010). Who lives and dies on death row? Race, ethnicity, and post-sentence outcomes in Texas. *Social Problems, 57,* 630–652.

Pierotti, R. S. (2013). Increasing rejection of intimate partner violence: Evidence of global cultural diffusion. *American Sociological Review, 78,* 240–265.

Platt, A. (2009). *The Child Savers: The invention of delinquency*, with an introduction and critical commentaries compiled by Miroslava Chávez-Garcia, the expanded 40th anniversary edition. New Brunswick, NJ: Rutgers University Press.

Pleck, E. (1987). *Domestic tyranny: The making of American social policy against family violence from colonial times to the present*. New York: Oxford University Press.

Pogrebin, P. B., Stretesky, & Unnithan, N. P. (2009). *Guns, violence, and criminal behavior: The offender's perspective*. Boulder, CO: Lynne Rienner.

Prejean, Sister H. (1989). A pilgrim's progress. In I. Gray & M. Stanley (Eds.), *A punishment in search of a crime: Americans speak out against the death penalty* (pp. 93–101). New York: Avon.

Purcell, C. E., & Arrigo, B. A. (2006). *The psychology of lust murder: Paraphilia, sexual killing, and sexual homicide*. Boston: Academic Press.

Putnam, R. (2000). *Bowling alone: The collapse and revival of American community*. New York: Simon & Schuster.

Rafferty, R., & Ven, T. V. (2014). "I hate everything about you": A qualitative examination of cyberbullying and on-line aggression in a college sample. *Deviant Behavior, 35,* 364–377.

Rankin, J. (1979). Changing attitudes toward capital punishment. *Social Forces, 58,* 194–211.

Rees, A. (2009). *The infanticide controversy: Primatology and the art of field science*. Chicago: University of Chicago Press.

Regoli, R. M., Hewitt, J. D., & DeLisi, M. (2010). *Delinquency in society* (8th ed.). Sudbury, MA: Jones & Bartlett.

Roper v. Simmons, 543 U.S. 551 (2005).

Ross, E. (2008). "Deeds of heroism": Whitechapel's ladies. In A. Werner (Ed.), *Jack the Ripper and the East End* (pp. 81–217). London: Chatto & Windus.

Roy, B. (2009). *41 shots . . . and counting: What Amadou Diallo's story teaches us about policing, race, and justice*. Syracuse, NY: Syracuse University Press.

Rumbelow, D. (1988). *Jack the Ripper: The complete casebook*. New York: Berkley Books.

Russo, S. (2004). *The Jack the Ripper suspects: Persons cited by investigators and theorists*. Jefferson, NC: McFarland.

Sampson, R. J., & Raudenbush, S. W. (1999). Systematic observation of public spaces. *American Journal of Sociology, 105,* 603–651.

Sampson, R. J., Raudenbush, S. W., & Earls, F. (1997). Neighborhoods and violent crime: A multilevel study of collective efficacy. *Science, 277,* 918–924.

Santoro, W. A., & Broidy, L. (2014). Gendered rioting: A general strain theoretical approach. *Social Forces, 93,* 329–354.

Schinkel, W. (2010). *Aspects of violence: A critical theory.* New York: Palgrave Macmillan.

Schoon, E. W. (2014). The asymmetry of legitimacy: Analyzing the legitimation of violence in 30 cases of insurgent revolution. *Social Forces, 93,* 779–801.

Service, E. (1963). *Profiles in ethnology.* New York: Harper & Row.

Simons, R., Lei, M., Beach, S., Brody, G., Philibert, R., & Gibbons, F. (2011). Social environment, genes, and aggression: Evidence supporting the differential susceptibility perspective. *American Sociological Review, 76,* 883–912.

Six-Hohenbalken, M., & Weiss, N. (2011). *Violence expressed: An anthropological approach.* Burlington, VT: Ashgate.

Sugden, P. (2002). *The complete history of Jack the Ripper.* New York: Carroll & Graf.

Thornton, E. (1837). *Illustrations of the history and practices of the thugs.* London: W. H. Allen.

U.S. Department of Justice. (2008). *Serial murder: Multi-disciplinary perspectives for investigators.* Washington, DC: Behavioral Analysis Unit, National Center for the Analysis of Violent Crime.

Vandiver, M., Giacopassi, D., & Gathje, P. (2002). I hope someone murders your mother! An exploration of extreme support for the death penalty. *Deviant Behavior, 23,* 385–415.

Vronsky, P. (2004). *Serial killers: The method and madness of monsters.* New York: Berkley Books.

Walker, S. (2011). *Sense and nonsense about crime, drugs, and communities* (7th ed.). Belmont, CA: Wadsworth.

Wallace, R. (1996). *Jack the Ripper: Light-hearted friend.* Melrose, MA: Gemini Press.

Ward, G. K. (2012). *The black child-savers: Racial democracy and juvenile justice.* Chicago: University of Chicago Press.

Warren, J., Hazelwood, R., & Dietz, P. (1996). The sexually sadistic serial killer. *Journal of Forensic Science, 41,* 970–974.

White, R. (2013). *Youth gangs, violence, and social respect.* Hampshire, UK: Palgrave Macmillan.

Wilson, C. (1988). Introduction. In D. Rumbelow, *Jack the Ripper: The complete casebook* (pp. 1–17). New York: Berkley Books.

Wilson, W. (1991). *Good murders and bad murders.* Lanham, MD: University Press of America.

Winslow, R., & Zhang, S. (2008). *Criminology: A global perspective.* Upper Saddle River, NJ: Pearson/Prentice Hall.

Wolfgang, M., & Ferracuti, F. (1967). *The subculture of violence.* London: Tavistock.

Yablonsky, L. (1990). *Criminology* (4th ed.). New York: Harper & Row.

Young, J. (2011). Moral panics and the transgressive other. *Crime, Media, Culture, 7,* 245–258.

Zelizer, V. (1994). *Pricing the priceless child: The changing social value of children.* Princeton, NJ: Princeton University Press.

Zimbardo, P. (2007). *The Lucifer effect: Understanding how good people turn evil.* New York: Random House.

Zimmerman, G. M., & Messner, S. F. (2010). Neighborhood context and the gender gap in adolescent violent crime. *American Sociological Review, 75,* 958–980.

6

Sexual Violence

Defining Rape

Rape is the term that is used to refer to acts of sexual violence or coercive sexuality. The term is derived from the Latin word *rapere,* a verb meaning to seize or obtain by force. Initially, the word had no sexual meaning at all, and it can still be used in a more general sense as in the "rape" of the land or the environment. The term eventually came to be used to refer to a type of violent crime or violent sexual trespass.

The Federal Bureau of Investigation for much of its history defined *forcible rape*—now referred to as the legacy definition—as carnal knowledge (vaginal intercourse) of a female, forcibly and against her will. Though this definition seems clear and direct, it was not applied clearly and directly. In actuality, legal authorities thought of rape in a narrower way: "It is deemed a rape only if the assailant is a violent stranger, if the victim reports the rape immediately after it occurred, and if she can provide evidence of the attack and of her active resistance" (Weis & Borges, 1973, p. 71). The determination that rape has occurred is really an outgrowth of the give-and-take among individuals who have different interests, resources, and understandings about what happened and why (Allison & Wrightsman, 1993; Meadows & Kuehnel, 2005).

Rape is not a set of concrete actions that can be objectively and uniformly identified no matter what. Its definition—the construction or interpretation of it—varies from one observer, audience, or group to another; from one society to another; and from one historical time period to another

(Gilmartin, 1994). Simply put, different audiences define rape in different ways, and it matters a great deal exactly *who* is doing the defining (Goode, 1996). Victims of sexual violence may even fail to realize or acknowledge that they are indeed victims of it. Rape is both interpersonal conduct *and* a legal/social category with shades of meaning.

In 2012, a firestorm of controversy raged among U.S. politicians over the meaning of rape, principally because of disagreements over right-to-choice and right-to-life issues. Richard Mourdock (Republican), during his bid to be elected as an Indiana state senator, expressed his view that abortions should not be allowed in cases where a rape leads to a pregnancy (unless the mother's life is in jeopardy). His rationale was that he believes that in these cases, it was "something that God intended to happen" (Madison, 2012, n.p.). Mourdock, in response to the criticisms he received for the insensitivity of his remarks, clarified (with the help of Rick Santorum, former GOP presidential candidate) that the "something" to which he was referring was the human life in the woman's womb, not the rape itself. In August 2012, Todd Akin (a Republican from Missouri) opined that "legitimate rape" was unlikely to result in pregnancy. His poorly chosen words (which indicate a profound ignorance of both human biology and human sexuality) generated the reaction from more informed individuals that sperm and egg can get together regardless of whether a rape is deemed by politicians to be legitimate or illegitimate. Even then–vice presidential candidate Paul Ryan (a Republican from Wisconsin), who had coauthored an antiabortion bill with Akin, felt compelled to distance himself from Akin's words by stating, "Rape is rape. Period. End of story" (Siddiqui, S., 2012). Barack Obama responded to a question from Jay Leno when he appeared as a guest on NBC's *Tonight Show* by declaring, "Rape is rape, and rape is a crime." If Obama's or Ryan's declarations were supposed to clarify matters, they didn't help much. What all the political wrangling and verbal miscues do show is that different understandings of rape exist. Law in action, as Roscoe Pound (1910) observed, is different from law on the books.

On January 6, 2012, Attorney General Eric Holder announced that a new definition of rape—referred to as the revised definition—was going to be used by the FBI to allow for a more comprehensive national reporting of the crime. The new definition of rape is the following: "The penetration, no matter how slight, of the vagina or anus with any body part or object, or oral penetration by a sex organ of another person, without the consent of the victim" (FBI, 2012). The revision is based on an evolving understanding of rape that acknowledges that both males and females can be raped; that both males and females can be rapists; and that rape is an attack on a person's identity, not specifically on a female's vagina. By shifting more attention *to* lack of consent and *away* from the use of force—the word "forcible" has been removed from the revised definition—it lessens the obligation of victims to prove beyond a reasonable doubt that they have actively resisted (FBI, 2014). The new emphasis on "without the consent" is supposed to make it easier to consider individuals as victims who are so incapacitated by alcohol or other drugs that they are unable to refuse the sex that they otherwise would have refused. Little doubt exists that the FBI's new definition of rape will pressure states that have not already done so to adopt a similar definition of this crime. Only time and data will tell us if the FBI's change in the definition is a good one. (It is very likely that victims of rape will continue to view it as a forced act despite the FBI's terminological changes.)

Another type of coercive sexuality is *sexual harassment,* because it, like rape, objectifies and depersonalizes victims, while it controls and hurts them (Fitzgerald, 1993; MacKinnon, 2003; McKinney, 1994). Unsurprisingly, men and women may not agree on exactly what qualifies as harassment. Where females may see harassing behavior directed toward them, men may see the same behavior as complimentary, harmless seduction, or horseplay (i.e., clowning around). Men who believe strongly in a sexual double standard and who have had traditional masculine upbringings are more likely to see what women would define as sexual harassment to be both normal and normative (Quinn, 2003).

Rape is no longer a capital crime in the United States, although it had been for much of U.S. history. (Ronald Wolfe was the last man executed in the United States for the crime of forcible rape, in 1964.) The U.S. Supreme Court decided in 1977 in *Coker v. Georgia* that the raping of an adult female was no longer serious enough to warrant a penalty of death (although in Coker's case, the "adult female" was only 16 years old). An execution was deemed to be a grossly disproportionate and an excessive penalty, representing a form of cruel and unusual punishment (Bedau, 1982; Mandery, 2012). Think how the 455 men who have been executed for rape in the United States (Barlow, 1996) would feel if they learned that it was not so much what they did, who they were, or the region of the country in which they raped that got them executed; it was mainly *when* they did it. And think how rape victims must *now* feel. Many—perhaps most—rape survivors view rape as much more than an assault on their bodies; they view it as a death of the self (Carosella, 1995). These women must find it incomprehensible that an experience so harmful to them is no longer considered serious enough to warrant the ultimate penalty.

Sexual violence is a principal cause of anxiety, fear, injury, and sometimes even death for women, especially for those who become direct victims of it

(Ferraro, 1996; Goodman, Koss, Fitzgerald, Russo, & Keita, 1993; Koss, 1993). This "female fear" is a special burden that women carry that is not shared with men who have not themselves been raped. Some of the fear exists because women believe—incorrectly, as it turns out—that a substantial number of rape victims are murdered by their assailants (Gordon & Riger, 1989; Monckton-Smith, 2010). In those murders in which circumstances were known (between 1976 and 1994), 1.5% involved rape or some other sex offense (Greenfeld, 1997, p. 3). Rape does have a *shadow effect* in that women, especially young ones, are apprehensive about *any* victimization because they always fear that it could lead to a rape (Ferraro, 1996).

The Symbolic Organization of Sexual Violence

Cultural Scripts and Group Understandings

Some individuals enhance their own feelings of power and control, release feelings of anger, and satisfy sadistic urges by persuading, manipulating, or directly forcing other people to engage in unwanted sexual acts (Groth, 1979; Pelka, 1995). Few nonhuman animals can accomplish a mating without the cooperation of *both* partners (Gregersen, 1983), but both the human female and the human male are susceptible to rape. *Every* rape fuses together elements of manipulation, power, control, anger, and sadism into one brutal sexual act, even while the extent of each one of these can vary from rape to rape. Even though *all* rapes are sadistic to a degree, some are far more so than others.

Holmes and Holmes (2009) give an example of a sadistic rapist in their description of the "Four-Poster Rapist." Like all sadistic rapists, he eroticized violence and aggression. After gaining entrance to an unsuspecting victim's home (and subtly determining that she had needle and thread in the house), he would become violent. He would force her into a bedroom and tear off her clothing while using vile and humiliating words. He would hit and slap her while committing acts of anal, oral, and vaginal rape. He would bite and scratch his victim. He would even rip out clumps of her hair. As a final degradation, he would force his victim at gunpoint to stand so that a bedpost was between her breasts. He then used the needle and thread to sew the woman's nipples together so they encircled the bedpost.

The kinds of acts that qualify as sexual violence and the determination that sexual violence has occurred are conditioned by a large number of social and cultural factors (Palmer, 1989). No society has yet developed a purely objective way to measure the amount of force or the degree of consent that is present during an act of sex, nor has any society developed a purely objective way to determine at what point sex becomes coercive enough to qualify as rape. "The act must be interpreted as rape by the female actee, and her interpretation must be similarly evaluated by a number of officials and agencies before the official designation of 'rape' can be legitimately applied" (Svalastoga, 1962, p. 48). A female who reports to police that she has been raped will find that her account of what happened will be scrutinized for consistency and believability by criminal justice personnel, and so will her character and reputation. If she is a woman who is deemed to be of low social standing, and therefore not a "good witness," she may find that her complaint is dismissed or trivialized by police (Frohmann, 2005). Cross-cultural comparisons of rape rates are practically useless, because nations use different definitions of rape and have differential or varying abilities to find and measure it. Even within the same society or community, the study of rape is filled with difficulties and complications.

Bourque (1989) interviewed a sample of 126 white and 125 black Los Angeles County residents to determine how they defined rape. She found that her respondents used information about the assailant's degree of force and the victim's degree of resistance to decide if a rape had occurred, but they did not all reach the same conclusion. Some respondents focused on what the female victim did and were prone to blame her for what happened. They believed that rape could be avoided if a woman resisted strenuously enough. These respondents tended to view rape in sexual terms. Other respondents, by contrast, looked primarily at the assailant. If he used any force to achieve his sexual goals, they believed a rape had occurred. These respondents tended to view rape as a form of violence. The rest of Bourque's sample used information about force and resistance, but also about location, acquaintanceship, ethnicity, prior sexual history, and socioeconomic status of the participants in deciding what had happened. White females were the most likely to use information on the degree of force as their principal cue and were the ones most likely to define a sexual encounter as rape; black males were the most likely to use information on resistance, and they were the least likely to label sexual encounters as rape. Buddie and Miller (2000) report that rape victims are more likely to be blamed for their own victimizations if they are raped by acquaintances in a dating situation rather than by a stranger and if they fail to quickly resist the sexual advances of their partners. Women who are sexually experienced are also more likely than those who are not to be held responsible for what happens to them (p. 140).

What kinds of decision rules do women use to decide that they have been raped? A study by Williams (1984) of 246 female rape victims who had obtained help from a Seattle rape relief center uncovered a number of reasons why victims report their rapes to police. Reporting, of course, is different from defining, but this study does give valuable information about how women understand rape. The women who were most likely to report their rapes were those who had endured what Williams called *classic rapes*: They had been forcibly raped in their own homes, cars, or public places by strangers, and the rapes caused them a great deal of serious injury. Women who were sexually assaulted in a social situation (e.g., at a party or on a date) by people they knew (acquaintances, friends, or relatives) were much less likely to report the incidents to police. Part of the reason was that a prior relationship between the rapist and his victim meant that the rape was usually less violent, causing less physical damage to the victim and requiring less immediate medical aid. However, even if a woman was severely injured during a rape, she was still less likely to report the crime if she had been raped by someone she knew. Williams concluded that when the elements of a classic rape are present, they provide the victim with the evidence that she needs to convince herself that she is indeed a true rape victim (p. 464).

We cannot know for sure if Williams's interpretation is the correct one. All women who are raped may know it regardless of how classic it is, but they may feel confident that police authorities will believe their accusations *only* if their rapes show the classic elements. Victims of *unclassic rapes*— forced sex by a man who has some prior relationship to them and who does not beat them or use a weapon—may see themselves as true victims, but they may not see themselves as credible complainants who can get justice in a court of law. Prior-relationship rapes are more likely to be viewed by others (e.g., police and prosecutors) as private matters, the rapist is more likely to be viewed as less blameworthy, and the victim is more likely to be held partly responsible (Buddie & Miller, 2000; Estrich, 1987).

A study of 40 intimate-partner rapes (Tellis, 2010) that were reported to authorities (Miami, Florida, in 1997) shows that the majority of them were both violent and coercive. The rapists used both physical force (victims received physical injuries in 88% of the assaults) and verbal threats (in 80% of the assaults). Relational distance between victim and offender also has an influence on the probability of arrest (at least in cases of domestic violence where physical battery occurs). The closer the relationship between offender and victim, the less chance there is that the rapist will be arrested (Lally & DeMaris, 2012). Rape victims themselves report that when they do not tell police about their victimizations, the main reason is that they view them as private or personal matters (Bureau of Justice Statistics, 2008, Table 102). In the absence of the elements of a classic rape, some women will decide that they have not been raped at all. Studies of spousal rape find that wives are reluctant to use the word *rape* to describe their sexual experiences with their husbands, even if a great deal of force was used by the men to get what they wanted (Bergen, 1996).

Rape and Popular Culture

Rape-revenge films (e.g., *Lipstick, Extremities, I Spit on Your Grave, Sudden Impact*) highlight some of the elements of the changing images of men, women, and rape. Films like these both contribute ideas to popular culture and mirror it. Though different from each other in both setting and savagery, these films share a set of unifying ideas that is reflective of changing social norms and sexual attitudes of the twentieth and twenty-first centuries: Rape requires a certain and severe retaliation, itself of a savage nature; the victim, usually a female, must become the aggressor, serving as her own redeemer and avenger; and we live in a rape culture where every man is implicated in the rape of any given woman (Clover, 1992).

Despite the differences among the films in this genre, the common element is a graphic depiction of excessive violence visited upon the female, leading to her pain and humiliation. She is proxy for *every* woman who has ever been harassed, humiliated, or sexually victimized by men. The female victims in rape-revenge films may even turn to vigilantism, going so far as to provoke specific men into initiating violence against them. Retaliation by a female for an act of sexual violence against her develops into sweeping violence against all men, sometimes of the most savage kind. Even men who do not directly participate in the rape are viewed as legitimate targets of aggression. Rape-revenge films are a concrete example of the *spillover hypothesis* of interpersonal violence. Spillover exists when violence to an individual causes him or her to become more violent in return. For example, domestic violence by a husband against his wife could interfere with her parental skills, increasing the likelihood that she will abuse her own children (Haskett, Portwood, & Lewis, 2010).

Rape-revenge films, like academic and popular discussions of rape in the closing decades of the twentieth century, moved away from viewing rape as personal and pathological and toward viewing it as social and political, an *intentional* act of violence and domination. On the silver screen, rape was portrayed more and more as a deliberate act designed to pleasure a man (or more often *men*) while it degraded and subjugated a woman, making her fearful of leading the life she had once led successfully. The sexual violence did not kill her physical body, but it did something worse: It killed her spirit, quashing her self-confidence, along with her sense of direction and purpose. Rape rendered her life far less meaningful and rewarding than it had once been. Rape-revenge films offer a primitive insight into the dangers to women that can come from sexual inequality and male dominance.

The relationships between rape and popular culture are complex and dynamic. During the colonial period in the United States, narratives and stories alleged widespread Native American savagery in the kidnapping of, and sexual attacks on, Anglo females. These captivity narratives were both distorted and inaccurate, leaving little room for exploration of Anglo attacks on Native American women or the existence of positive relationships across the ethnic divide. Rape was portrayed as one of the weapons that the uncivilized used against white colonists. White men's anxieties intensified because they feared that they were unable to protect their wives and daughters from sexual attacks (Bailey, 2010).

During the days of U.S. slavery, before the Civil War, the narratives changed but the themes did not. Though some awareness existed that whites sexually exploited blacks, it was little more than dust in the wind. Racial stereotypes capitalized on the popular view that African women were either asexual "mammies" or seductive and wanton "Jezebels." White men were able to rape black women, practically with impunity, by claiming either that the woman was a seductress and wanted to be raped or that her lascivious nature meant she could not be injured by any kind of sex. Female slaves were property with no rights of their own. Male slaves were also stereotyped. They could be traditional and loyal to white slave owners ("Uncle Toms"); lazy but uncomplaining field hands ("Sambos"); or both violent and sexual, willing to do anything for freedom while lusting after white women ("Nats") (Bailey, 2010, pp. 11–12).

Rape and Social Conflict

Power, Rape, and Social Control

Sexual inequalities exist in most human societies, which produce power differences between males and females (Iversen & Rosenbluth, 2010; Scott, Crompton, & Lyonette, 2010). These power differences can lead to tensions and antagonisms in male–female relationships, which can breed contempt. Males can come to hate females (and vice versa). Some men are in a position to express their contempt for women through forcible rape (Smith & Bennett, 1985). The research is clear in showing that the lower the status of females in comparison to males, the higher is the rate of forcible rape (Baron & Straus, 1987, p. 481; Schwendinger & Schwendinger, 1983). Rape is one indicator of females' low status and a way that their low status is maintained and reproduced (Baron & Straus, 1987; Baron & Straus, 1989; Eller, 2006; Funk, 1993; Higgins & Silver, 1991; MacKinnon, 1982; Sanday, 1981). Reiss's (1986) research on rape in many countries found that a belief in female inferiority is positively correlated with the occurrence of rape (pp. 191–192).

Susan Brownmiller (1975) argued that rape is a deliberate (she uses the word *conscious*) process of intimidation that *all* men use to keep *all* women in a state of fear and intimidation. In her analysis, *every man* is either a rapist or beneficiary of rape, and *every woman* is vulnerable, living her life in fear of being raped. Though her conclusions are arguable, what is beyond dispute is that cultural understandings about rape can actually help to produce and then shape it (Buchwald, Fletcher, & Roth, 1993). For example, the belief that an impetuous male sex drive causes men to lose control of themselves is partly responsible for the occurrence of rape (Sanday, 1996b). This belief allows rapists to neutralize forces of social control by disclaiming personal responsibility for what they have done (Jackson, 1995). It also makes it possible for observers to excuse more readily a rapist's violence. Not all cultures view rape as a naturally impulsive sex act (MacKellar, 1975). The Minangkabau peoples of West Sumatra have a fairly rape-free society that is partly due to their cultural belief that rape is neither impulsive nor uncontrollable (Sanday, 1990). Because humans are capable of exerting conscious control over many impelling bodily urges or drives—hunger, thirst, defecation, urination—it is probable that they can control their violent sexuality as well.

Defining women as property to be possessed fosters a sense of entitlement. *Entitlement* in this context is a cultural belief that men are within their rights to demand goods and services from women *as a class* (Bart & O'Brien, 1985). Some men rape women because they believe that sex is something to which they are entitled whenever they want it. If it is not given freely, then they believe it is entirely proper for them to take it.

> [Sexual] violence has deep roots in sociocultural constructions of gender and heterosexuality, constructions that promote male entitlement and social and political inequality for women. Cultural norms and myths, sexual scripts and social roles link various forms of violence and deny assistance to its victims. (Koss et al., 1994, p. 17)

A study of the sexual violence experienced by street prostitutes traced it directly to cultural beliefs about them. According to prostitutes themselves, the men who raped them were acting out core beliefs: Women who are sexually experienced cannot be harmed by sexual violence; all prostitutes are alike; and prostitutes deserve whatever happens to them (Miller & Schwartz, 1995).

Any woman can become a target of sexual violence if a rapist defines her as belonging to a class of individuals whose members are promiscuous and valueless. In order for a man to sexually assault a woman, he must not only think that he will get things of value from the attack. He must also be able to overcome or neutralize any inhibitions he might have that would prevent the rape from occurring (Felson, 2003). Neutralizations are easier for a man to muster if a potential rape victim belongs to a class that he dislikes and depersonalizes (Scully, 1990).

Rape itself may be used as a form of social control because it can transform a female into a powerless victim, an individual who has no capacity to stop what is being done to her (Collins, 2010). It may also be a way to punish a woman who is perceived to have deviated from important gender norms. Consider the Cheyenne Indians, one of the major tribes of the Great Plains. The Cheyenne were famous for their chastity, and they took marriage very seriously. At puberty, a female donned a chastity belt, a thin piece of rope that was knotted around her waist and then passed between her thighs. It was always worn at night, and night and day when the woman was away from home. If a man trifled with a woman's belt, it was considered a very serious matter. He could be beaten or even killed by female or male relatives of the offended woman. His goods would be destroyed and his horses killed. Even his parents could have their property ravaged (Llewellyn & Hoebel, 1941).

If a female Cheyenne yielded to a man, allowing him to seduce her, she was permanently disgraced. Her trespass would never be forgotten, and she would be scorned wherever she went. It would be almost impossible for her to marry because no man would have her (unless she were to be ritually purified by a shaman). If a wife was unfaithful to her husband, it was proper for him to administer what was called the *free woman penalty* or *on the prairie*. The husband would invite all of the unmarried men in his soldier band and all of his male cousins (except for his wife's relatives) to a spot on the prairie for a "feast." He would then turn his wife over to them, and she would be raped by 40 to 50 men. From then on, she was a woman apart who lived in permanent shame and disgrace. Some disagreement existed among the Cheyenne over the propriety of using a gang rape to punish an unfaithful wife, but the custom persisted and continued to be defined, at least officially, as a husband's right to use when sanctioning an unfaithful wife (Llewellyn & Hoebel, 1941).

In some cultures, rape is used to punish women for things other than participation in extramarital sexual relationships. The Mehinaku of central Brazil strictly segregate the sexes, and women are forbidden to enter the sacred and private communal house of men. If women spy on the men or their sacred rituals or artifacts, they can be punished with a gang rape (Gregor, 1982). Even in the United States, rape can be one of the possible consequences for women for doing things that are defined by some men as too unconventional, untraditional, or unfeminine (e.g., staying out too late, hitchhiking, being out alone, dressing and acting provocatively, being stoned or drunk, or running away from home). In the nineteenth-century United States, women were able to get protection from violent husbands only if they fit the Victorian image of a proper woman: respectful, dependent, and obedient. Those women who refused to follow feminine standards were more vulnerable to sexual attack, and they had few avenues for obtaining redress if they were raped (Pleck, 1979). Even today, sexual violence is viewed by some men as a way for them to control disobedient, disrespectful, or disreputable women (True, 2012).

Rape and War

Close connections exist between violence against females and world processes (Hudson, Ballif-Spanvill, Caprioli, & Emmett, 2012). Rape has played a role in all wars and most revolutions, ethnic conflicts, and geographic expansions. Sexual violence is a way for some men as a *gender collective* to demonstrate their power and dominance over both women and other men (Bahun-Radunovic' & Rajan, 2008; Collins, 2010). During the American Revolution, British troops raped colonial women. In the 1830s, Mormon women were raped by Missouri men in order to get them to leave the state. Southern black female slaves were raped throughout the slave era, and free black women were raped during Reconstruction. Native American women were raped during the white expansion westward.

> Sexual violence in warfare is among the darkest legacies of the twentieth century, and it continues to ravage societies in the new millennium. Instances of widespread use of sexual violence include: the 1915 Armenian genocide by Ottoman Turkey; the Japanese assault on the Chinese in Nanking during World War II, and in the Chinese civil war; the partition of India and creation of Pakistan; and Bangladesh's 1971 war of liberation. Sexual violence has been prevalent in many other conflicts during the Cold War and after, including the Korean War, Vietnam War, and Cambodia; in the wars and conflicts in Central and Latin America, and in Haiti; and in many African conflicts, such as Angola, Djibouti, Liberia, Mozambique, Sierra Leone, Somalia, and Sudan. In Asia, war rapes are found in East Timor, Sri Lanka, Burma, Kashmir (India), Papua New Guinea; and in wars and conflicts in Central Europe and Eurasia, including Afghanistan, Turkey, Kuwait, Georgia, Bosnia, and Kosovo. No part of the world has been unaffected by wartime sexual violence. (Leatherman, 2011, p. 2)

Soldiers use rape to show their enemies the contempt with which they are held. It demoralizes the defeated side, because these men can no longer protect wives and daughters, while it punishes the women for being in the wrong place at the wrong time (or simply for being at all). Rape has other benefits during war for a rapist: It demonstrates the rapist's masculinity to himself and to his peers; it is a reward for having fought hard and long; it demonstrates the impotence (political and sexual) of the vanquished; and it is a tangible way to show who has won and who has lost the war. Throughout human history, soldiers have viewed forced sexual intercourse with the wives and daughters of their enemies as one of the spoils of war (Winslow & Zhang, 2008).

During the "ethnic cleansing" in Bosnia in 1992, Serbian soldiers sexually victimized and terrorized Muslim women. The women were herded together like cattle into concentration camps where they were tortured, raped, and sodomized by a multitude of attackers. For those women who survived the sexual torture, the ordeal did not end. Their victimization was viewed as unbearably shameful by their husbands, and these women were treated as damaged goods, lacking both value and purpose. Some were barred by their husbands from what were once their homes or even were killed by them (Farr, 2009).

During wars, more men than women die, but more women than men are raped and sexually tortured (Alvarez & Bachman, 2008). However, men can be sexually victimized by their captors during wartime, too. Usually, male sexual assaults are hidden, unknown to all but a few. Occasionally, news reports and photographs (e.g., the sexual violence against Iraqi males at Abu Ghraib prison or male rape in the Congo) surface that show that male prisoners have been victims of anal rape and other forms of sodomy (Carlson, 2006). Males are raped during war for many of the same reasons that females are raped: to frighten, intimidate, control, traumatize, and silence a marginalized population (Stemple, 2009).

Wartime rapes are no longer, if they ever were, the sole province of a few sexually sadistic males who rape women because they enjoy it and can get away with it. More and more, rape is strategic and used in order to advance the military goals of sovereign nations. Rape is, quite literally, a weapon of war: "In today's wars, rape is . . . often a strategy of warfare, intended at the least to terrorize, disrupt and uproot civilian communities thought to be aligned with an enemy group" (Farr, 2009, p. 4). Rape is now officially designated as a war crime, and violence against women, both nationally and internationally, is viewed more than ever before as a crime against humanity.

As a strategy of war, rape is being used purposefully to humiliate families and destroy communities by ravaging women's bodies and destroying their spirits. Wartime rape is a way to take possession of an enemy population's resources and to make it necessary for them to leave their homes and all that they have. The sexual violence perpetrated against women in armed conflicts in today's world is vicious (Farr, 2009). It devastates women, their families, and communities—even nations—not only while the sexual violence is occurring, but also long after it has stopped (Jayaraman, 2008). Extreme war rape is systematic and systemic, not unfortunate collateral damage as much as a central tactic of modern conflicts (*PLoS Medicine* Editors, 2009).

Wartime rape is a central part of genocidal programs, and sperm, quite literally, is used as a biological weapon. Orchestrated and systematic rapes, of the same women, carried out over an extended period of time, along with the enforced pregnancy that this often entails, can destroy the morale and will to fight of an entire region. This strategy of wartime rape may hasten a people's departure from a geographical region, and it may lead to the birth of a generation of children that is unwelcome and unloved. These children are the responsibility of a community and parents who do not want to be burdened with them (Card, 2008). A generation such as this, born in terror and trauma, unwanted and disliked, a burden that can neither be wished away nor ignored, may make women in this region never want to have children again. In this way, rape during war is not only a way to "ethnically cleanse" an area, but it is also a way to intentionally destroy a population by symbolically polluting its next generation.

Rape Scenes

Some violence can be initiated by the individual who ultimately ends up as its victim. Wolfgang (1958) classified a homicide as *victim precipitated* if an individual initiated through word or deed the fight that caused his or her own death (p. 252). Can there be victim-precipitated *rape?* Amir (1971) certainly thought so. He classified a rape as victim precipitated if in his opinion a woman said or did something to cause her own rape (or *failed* to do or say something that might have prevented it):

> The term "victim precipitation" describes those rape situations in which the victim actually, or so it was deemed, agreed to sexual relations but retracted before the actual act or did not react strongly enough when the suggestion was made by the offender(s). The term applies also to cases in risky situations marred with sexuality, especially when she uses what could be interpreted as indecency in language and gestures, or constitutes what could be taken as an invitation to sexual relations. (p. 266)

Amir concluded that 19% of the 646 rapes he studied were victim precipitated. However, *any* estimate of the number of victim-precipitated rapes is open to dispute, and the higher the estimate, the less credible it is. We have neither consistent definitions of rape nor incontrovertible ways to determine a rape has occurred. How can we know for certain how many (or if any) are victim precipitated?

The term *victim precipitated,* though it has some value in heightening our understanding of certain types of predatory violence (e.g., murder), is woefully inadequate, or even sinister, when it comes to forcible rape (Meadows, 2004). It can serve as a self-fulfilling prophecy (Meloy & Miller, 2011). That is, the belief that rape can be victim precipitated can *itself* be a precipitant of rape. Some rapes are motivated and then rationalized by rapists through the technique of neutralization that blames the victim for all that happened (Gilmartin-Zena, 1988). When a victim of rape is blamed for her victimization, it can reduce whatever sympathy or charity she might otherwise have received (Dunn, 2010).

Blaming the victim lets both actual rapists and potential rapists off the hook (Tieger, 1981). Men who rape are more likely than men who do not rape to blame women for what has happened, even if the sexual encounter was openly violent (Garrett-Gooding & Senter, 1987). The belief in victim-precipitated rape not only can motivate sexual aggression toward women, but it also makes it easier for rapists to excuse or justify to themselves and others what they have done (Berkowitz, Burkhart, & Bourg, 1994; Scully & Marolla, 1984). Victim blaming also makes the kinds of changes that would be necessary to prevent rape more difficult to achieve (e.g., sociocultural changes in how men and women interact or changes in how rapists are punished or treated).

"Victim-precipitated rape" is a notion that has another damaging effect: It makes it easier to confuse cause and blame. Some victims of rape do things that are risky, making them more susceptible to victimization by others. However, this does not mean that they should be *blamed* for their own victimization. Golda Meir, former Israeli prime minister, had to respond to an outbreak of nighttime sexual assaults on women. One of the ministers asserted that the way to stop the assaults was to impose a curfew on women, forbidding them to be out after dark. Prime Minister Meir declined. Because it was men who were doing all the attacking, she concluded, it is men who should be restricted after dark, not women (Medea & Thompson, 1974). Meir would certainly have admitted that women's travel in public places after dark was part of the *cause* of what happened. She just was not going to *blame* them for something that men were responsible for doing.

It is of some value to have terms that allow us to consider that certain victims of violent crimes do things that facilitate (or cause) some of what happens to them without blaming them for it. Terms like *victim vulnerability* (Geis,

1977) or *victim contribution* (Kanin, 1984), though not perfect, are closer to what is needed. They make it easier to separate cause from blame, while allowing that some victims of rape do risky things while other rape victims do not.

Scully and Marolla (1984) studied the accounts of 114 incarcerated rapists in a Virginia prison who had been convicted of rape or attempted rape. Most men in the sample accounted for their rapes by discrediting their female victims and blaming them for what happened. They claimed that the women were promiscuous, seductive, or sexually aroused, and they portrayed the encounter as a consensual sex act. Even those rapists who did confess to a rape still tried to make themselves look better by blaming what had happened on their use of alcohol or other drugs, a temporary relapse, or on a simple misunderstanding of the women's wishes. Practically everybody offered some account for what he had done. Even a rapist who had raped five women at gunpoint and then stabbed each one to death attempted to make himself look good (or at least better).

> Physically they enjoyed the sex. Once they got involved, it would be difficult to resist. I was always gentle and kind until I started to kill them. And the killing was always sudden, so they wouldn't know it was coming. (p. 541)

The length to which some rapists will go to account for what they have done is truly amazing!

Bonnycastle (2012) interviewed 14 men incarcerated in a maximum-security prison in Canada. Each man was a high-risk sex offender who had attacked and raped or raped and killed an adult female who was a stranger to him on one or more occasions. Though these men had violently raped strangers—all rapes are violent in one way or another—they did not view themselves as monster rapists or even brutal individuals. The physical and emotional abuse that they had experienced growing up meant they had learned to remain emotionally distant from others and physically strong and aggressive in their dealings with them. They viewed masculinity as good and femininity as bad and weak. These rapists had hurt far more men than women during their lives, but their violence was gendered. They beat up men to show them that they could and to prove who was best. They raped women because they found it pleasurable and defined it as a right to which they were entitled.

Rapists don't have to go through a violentization process in order to do what they do or to be aggressive with women. An adolescent male may initially have great ambivalence about the propriety of sexually coercive behavior. In time, however, he may acquire group-based vocabularies of motive and techniques of neutralization that are sufficient for him to overcome any victim resistance he may encounter.

> In a rape-supportive culture, attitudes and values that degrade women and make rape possible are in existence and learned at some level by all men. . . . Some men choose to accept these values, integrating them into their own, and create neutralizations that allow them both to maintain their self-image as law-abiding citizens and also to victimize women. (Miller & Schwartz, 1995, p. 17)

Some males transform women into sex objects by defining them as "loose," "teases," or "sexually experienced" (Sanday, 2007).

Peer group support for sexual violence against women may make it more likely (Kanin, 1967b), but men who are not tightly integrated into male peer groups may come to believe that some women can be legitimately raped (Gebhard, Gagnon, Pomeroy, & Christiansen, 1965). This is clear in the case of Fred (Lowney, Winslow, & Winslow, 1981). He was standing at a bus stop in Arizona when a woman, age 35, picked him up in her car, which by that very fact indicated to him that she was "asking for it." He pulled a knife on her, forced her to drive 30 miles out into the desert, raped her, stole her car and clothes, and abandoned her in the 120-degree sun, all without guilt or remorse. In fact, he reported that he enjoyed the whole experience quite a lot. A while later, he saw the woman out in public. He approached her, telling her that he could not change what had happened and that she should never see him again. For some reason, their relationship grew, and Fred was able to report that "[e]ver since then I've sent her a Christmas card, she sends me one too, and now we're good friends." Rapes are violent acts that brutalize and humiliate victims. Even if Christmas cards are exchanged afterward, it does not change this fact.

Men may cobble together their own vocabularies of motive and rationalization from parts of culture or may simply create them on their own from personal experiences. In some cases, rape is simply a way for men who lack sufficient levels of personal control to achieve immediate gratification of their own sexual desires (Larragoite, 1994). An individual who is prepared to rape ignores some clear social cues, while making other cues far more significant than they actually are. Rape can move a rapist away from boredom and toward a more involved, more exciting phase of existence (Katz, 1988). Each successful rape or sexual assault that a man commits reinforces the original definition of the situation that some women can be legitimately raped.

Normalizing Sexual Violence

At certain times, in certain places, sexual violence against women is expected, encouraged, or even trendy. Consider Ingham, a small town in the countryside of Australia. In the 1970s, Schultz (1978) identified three characteristics of this community that made sexual violence against women a common occurrence. First, women were viewed as men's possessions. Every woman was expected to lead a virtuous life under her father's roof until she married, whereupon she was expected to assume the duties of faithful wife and devoted mother under her husband's roof. Second, women were never supposed to do or say anything that might bring shame on their families. Third, women were devalued. They were placed into one of two mutually exclusive categories, virgin or whore, depending almost entirely on how sexually experienced they were perceived to be. The virgin received some grudging respect for her chastity, but she was still resented because she spurned the sexual advances of men. The whore—a woman perceived to be sexually promiscuous—was considered contemptible by both the men and women of the town.

Factors worked in concert in Ingham to make it likely that women would be raped by men. Because women were viewed as men's possession and devalued, men had little reason *not* to treat them as sex objects. This depersonalization was especially likely with any woman who was defined as a whore. Because women were expected to protect their families from any kind of humiliation, any woman who was raped was under strong pressure to keep it to herself and suffer in silence. Rape victims were unlikely to tell even their closest friends or members of their families, and they were even less likely to tell police. The women of Ingham were in an extremely difficult situation. Their upbringing encouraged them to blame themselves and to handle the shame and guilt alone if they were raped (Schultz, 1978).

Rape on Campus

Rape-Prone Campuses and Sexual Relative Deprivation

The Ingham case shows that social dynamics and cultural factors can work together to make sexual violence against women more likely. However, we do not have to travel all the way to Australia to see these processes in operation. Consider the fraternity gang rape described by Sanday (1990). It occurred in February 1983, at a large university in the eastern United States, at the end of one of the weekly parties of a Greek organization identified as Fraternity XYZ. (In the second edition of Sanday's book on the incident, published in 2007, she revealed the location of the gang rape to be a fraternity house at the University of Pennsylvania, and a reviewer of the 1990 book identified the fraternity as Alpha Tau Omega [Lewin, 1991].)

According to Sanday (1990), a woman named Laurel, inebriated and semiconscious in one of the bedrooms in the fraternity house, was viewed by some of the fraternity brothers as a legitimate sexual target. She was vaginally penetrated by at least five of them while others stood by and watched and cheered. It was not until 5 days later that Laurel told a university administrator that she had been raped by several men at the XYZ house. She claimed that she had not reported the rape immediately because she believed she could handle the matter alone. However, she found that she could not. This delay in reporting was taken by some people on campus to mean that she did not really believe she had been wronged and that nothing really serious had happened.

The brothers of Fraternity XYZ thought Laurel was being cruel and vindictive in an effort to get them into trouble. They defined themselves as the injured party, and most of them thought that they had done nothing wrong. They were astounded anyone would consider what happened as a rape, and most of the fraternity brothers refused to believe anything out of the ordinary had occurred with Laurel. They branded her as the one who was really at fault because she drank too much and offered no resistance to their sexual advances. She was vilified as a "nympho," "fish," and "red meat." This attack on Laurel, coupled with the fraternity brothers' legitimation of what they had done to her, renewed the bonds of brotherhood among those men who directly participated in the rape, as well as among those who derived some vicarious enjoyment from it (Sanday, 1990, p. 109). Most of the members of the fraternity continued to believe that what had happened was all Laurel's fault and that all the participants were too drunk to know any better. Members of the fraternity who voiced an objection to the victimization of Laurel ran the risk of being called "wimps," "gays," or "faggots."

A special report by the U.S. Department of Justice (Sinozich & Langton, 2014) stated that for the years 1995 to 2013, females ages 18 to 24 had the highest rate of rape and sexual assault victimizations of any of the age categories studied. (The data exclude females under age 12.) It reported that the rate of rape and sexual assault was higher for nonstudents than for students (7.6 per 1,000 compared to 6.1 per 1,000), but students were less likely than nonstudents to report their victimizations to police (only about 20% were reported). However, other data show that females who attend universities and colleges are at a *greater* risk of rape and other forms of sexual assault than are women of comparable ages in the wider population (Alvarez & Bachman, 2008).

Date rapists usually suffer from *sexual relative deprivation* (Kanin, 2003). That is, they are dissatisfied with their sexual accomplishments, because they compare themselves to their peers who put a high value on such accomplishment and confer high prestige for sexual success. The more females that a male can brag about having sexually "snagged," the higher is his status

(Sanday, 2007, p. 7). In this atmosphere, men's inclination for their sexual reach to exceed their grasp is group-based and something that puts their dates at risk of being the target of sexual violence (Kanin, 1967b). Date rapists are somewhat predatory but *very* opportunistic.

Kanin (1967a) concluded from his study of coercive sexuality on a university campus that fraternities attracted sexually aggressive males and then supported or even championed a conquest mentality toward women. The fraternities contained a social dynamic that encouraged their members to accumulate as many sex acts with females as possible with less concern shown for how they were achieved. If persuasion failed, some males felt comfortable in using force to get what they wanted. These men did not have trouble finding sexual outlets; they had trouble finding authentic sexual fulfillment, principally because their sexual desires and wishes always outstripped their actual sexual achievements. Fraternities create a climate in which the use of coercion to reach sexual goals is normative, and few restraints exist to curb this exploitation of women for sexual purposes (Yancey & Hummer, 1989).

Some of the same social factors that cause sexual violence to occur in the fraternity setting are—or can be—found in the colleges and universities of which they are a part. Sanday (1996a) concluded that some colleges and universities are more "rape-prone" than others. *Rape-prone campuses* have both ideational and relational elements that make male sexual violence toward women more likely. A rigid inequality and institutionalized double standard are coupled with the encouragement (or at least tolerance) of heavy drinking by males. Males view females as sex objects and boosters for male interests and needs, and males are encouraged to be both hypermasculine and hypersexual. These social structural elements work together to create rigid norms of male dominance that make some men prepared to take sexual advantage of women, especially those who are intoxicated. An intolerance of sexual minorities (e.g., gays) also characterizes rape-prone campuses, and the penalties for sexual violence against women are mild or even nonexistent.

Acquaintance rapes are the bulk of all rapes, and date rape is a type of acquaintance rape that can grow out of a social or romantic situation (Hall, 1995). Just about 80% of females aged 18 to 24 who are raped or sexually assaulted know the person or persons who did it (Sinozich & Langton, 2014, p. 7). Kirkpatrick and Kanin (1957) sampled 291 college females at a midwestern university in the 1950s, and they found that over half of them (55.7%) reported that they had been sexually offended at some point during the academic year (by being the target of unwanted kissing, fondling, or vaginal penetration). A follow-up study by Kanin and Parcell (1981), done approximately 20 years later, found similar results (though the data were collected at a different large midwestern state university): A total of 50.7% of the 282 university females who participated reported that they had been offended at some level of erotic intimacy during the academic year.

Data on the prevalence of rape on campus should not cloud an important-to-remember finding: Not all college men are rapists. A relatively small cohort of males on college campuses is responsible for a disproportionate number of rapes. These men have found that institutions of higher learning are excellent places to find women to rape and then to avoid punishment for what they have done. Lisak and Miller (2002) assessed a sample of 1,882 college males (at a mid-size, urban commuter university) and found that offenders among them were responsible for 3,698 violent acts (rape, attempted rape, sexual assault, battery, as well as child physical and sexual abuse). This sample included a subsample—120 men, or 6.4% of the original sample—whose self-reported acts met the legal definition of rape or attempted rape. None of these 120 rapists had ever been reported to authorities for what he had done, and none of them had received any punishments for it either. Seventy-six (76) of the 120 men were repeat rapists, responsible for a combined total of 439 rapes or attempted rapes, with an average of 5.8 rapes each (p. 78). This means that 4% of the overall sample of 1,882 men accounted for 28% of the rapes, attempted rapes, or other acts of interpersonal violence (p. 80). Rapes that these men committed were not an outgrowth of sexual miscues or ambiguities in the dating experience. They were purposeful, planned, and deliberate acts of sexual violence by men who had raped before (and probably would again).

Coercive Sexuality and Shadow Cultures

Colleges and universities are legally obligated to ensure that students on their campuses are free from the threat and occurrence of sexual assault. Though institutions of higher learning cannot be expected to develop the kinds of investigative skills or penalties for rape that are found in the criminal justice system, they can help victims of sexual assault by trying to determine what happened, offering counseling services, and restricting contact between victims and offenders (e.g., class restrictions, suspensions of guilty parties, or expulsions). In 2011, the U.S. Department of Education sent letters (known as the "Dear Colleague Letter") to colleges and universities, informing them that a failure on their part to eliminate sexual violence violated Title IX and could be the basis for denial of their federal funding. This also meant that students who felt they had a case could file complaints. An important part of this letter was that it required that a different standard of proof be adopted than had heretofore been used in campus adjudications of alleged rapes. Instead of "absolute certainty" or "beyond a reasonable doubt," the new standard was to be "by a preponderance of the evidence." For this new standard to be met, after a review of the evidence, it must seem more likely than unlikely that a complainant's charges are true.

Time's cover story on May 26, 2014, was entitled "Rape: The Crisis in Higher Education" (Gray, 2014). It highlighted a visit to the University of Montana (Missoula) by Thomas Perez, the then-U.S. Assistant Attorney General for Civil Rights, to announce that the university, city police, and the county attorney and his office were all in the federal crosshairs. The university had a problem, and so did those who could have fixed the problem (i.e., police and prosecutors). During the 3 years prior to Perez's visit, 80 rapes had been reported in Missoula (Gray, 2014). (In fact, this figure was way off the mark. The U.S. Department of Justice informed County Attorney Fred Van Valkenburg that 350 sexual assaults had been reported to the Missoula police department between January 2008 and May 2012 [Krakauer, 2015, p. 325].) Missoula was dubbed by the media as the rape capital of America. However, the author of the *Time* article concluded that this condemnation was not entirely fair. The University of Montana was fairly average in its rape rate, not some outlier oasis of sexual assault and battery. Gray concluded that many of America's campuses are dangerous places for young women. On May 1, 2014, a list was made public of 55 colleges and universities that the federal government was reviewing because of the inept, insensitive, and biased way that they dealt with complaints of rape and sexual assault. The list grew to include more than 90 colleges and universities, many of which were high-profile, prestigious institutions (e.g., Princeton, Harvard, University of California at Berkeley, the University of Chicago, Vanderbilt).

Sexual assaults sometimes are allowed to occur on campuses because of negligence on the part of college and university administrators (Bohmer & Parrot, 1993). They find it easier—and better public relations—to stick their heads in the sand than to deal directly with sexual violence on campus. One practical piece of advice for campus administrators from Sanday's assembled works is that creating a rape-free campus will require the setting in motion of social dynamics that can transform the social structural elements that make up the foundation for sexual violence toward women. A *rape-free campus* will have a culture that both reflects and contributes to sexual equality between males and females and between straights and gays; no double standard, so that women are viewed by men as equals; abolition of heavy drinking; and direct and immediate punishment at the institutional level of sexual assaults, whenever they occur. If it is warranted, evidence of sexual assaults on campus should be turned over to criminal justice system representatives for review and punishment of offenders if crimes have occurred.

A study via questionnaire, translated into different languages to accommodate the particular locale, of 13,877 students, in 32 countries, attending 68 universities, reported that *both* males and females use violence to obtain sex from their dating partners, though males use it more often (Gámez-Guadix, Straus, & Hershberger, 2011). The use of verbal coercion to achieve sexual goals was reported by 26.7% of male students and 19.6% of female students, while the use of physical force to obtain sex was reported by 2.4% of males and 1.8% of females. One cause of the coercive sexuality that was found in this international sample was that these students had themselves been victimized as children, reporting that they had been neglected, spanked, slapped, or sexually abused.

The search for both fun and status in the campus setting can work to the disadvantage of females and to the advantage of sexually predatory males. At fraternity parties, where alcohol flows freely and the situation is controlled by the men who give the party, elements are present that can lead to sexual violence. Much of what happens takes place behind closed doors and with little accountability to outside agents of social control. Norms exist at parties that structure them in such a way that everyone is supposed to have a good time (or at least act like it), and partygoers are supposed to like and trust one another. Hosts, especially, are to be trusted, and they, in turn, are expected to treat their guests with courtesy and respect. The real situation at parties, however, can depart from the ideal. What may actually exist is a *shadow sexual culture* that makes it possible for some men to ensnare an inebriated, vulnerable female who is unable to comport herself well enough to avoid being sexually victimized (Sanday, 2007).

Women may find themselves in a highly gendered situation in which they are objectified and depersonalized. They may find that by fulfilling the expectations of what a "proper" partygoer is supposed to do, they put themselves in a situation that can be risky, making them more vulnerable to sexual violence. However, it only *becomes* sexual violence if men are willing to take advantage of a woman's dependent situation.

Party rape is accomplished without the use of guns, knives, or fists. It is carried out through the combination of low level forms of coercion—a lot of liquor and persuasion, manipulation of situations so that women cannot leave, and sometimes force (e.g., by blocking a door, or using body weight to make it difficult for a woman to get up). These forms of coercion are made more effective by organizational arrangements that provide men with control over how partying happens and by expectations that women let loose and trust their party-mates. This systematic and effective method of extracting non-consensual sex is largely invisible, which makes it difficult for victims to convince anyone—even themselves—that a crime occurred. Men engage in this behavior with little risk of consequences. (Armstrong, Hamilton, & Sweeney, 2009, p. 495)

Alcohol (or some other drug) can be used as a weapon by some men to sexually assault women, and it is an effective one. It undermines a woman's capacity to resist, her clarity and recollection about what actually happened, and her inclination to report any sexual victimization that took place (Martin & Hummer, 2003). The majority of sexual assaults that happen to college women occur when they are incapacitated due principally to their use of alcohol and by men they know and trust (Krebs, Lindquist, Warner, Fisher, & Martin, 2007).

A party culture, along with party routines, exists at most colleges and universities, although not all students are committed partiers. Weiss's (2013) study at the one "party school" that served as her sample (a large state school with over 20,000 undergraduates) reports that a majority of her respondents were either extreme partiers (14%), drinking nine drinks on a typical night, four or more nights a week, or using other drugs; or heavy partiers (40%), drinking five to eight drinks on a typical night, two to three nights a week. The rest of her sample classified themselves as either light partiers or abstainers. The university's party culture made it easier to justify and excuse high levels of irresponsibility, injury, or abuse: blackouts, hangovers, missed classes, failed exams, physical assaults, rapes, sexual assaults, litter, falls, vandalism, and excessive noise. Crimes in this climate, even violent ones, go unrecognized or unreported for what they are, adversely affecting the quality of life at the school and in the surrounding community.

Sexual Miscues and Contentious Definitions

Disputes and disagreements over date rape—what it is, how many occur, how it should be handled—sometimes reflect the ambiguity that can characterize dating relationships (Ward, Dziuba-Leatherman, Stapleton, & Yodanis, 1994). "Sexuality is messy, passionate, unclear, tentative, anxiety-producing, liberating, frightening, embarrassing, consoling, appetitive, and cerebral. In other words, sexuality is contradictory, it is different for different people, and it is even different for the same person at different times" (Schwartz, 1995, p. 35). This ambiguity is one of the principal justifications for the formulation of what came to be called the "Antioch policy" (at Antioch College in Yellow Springs, Ohio), adopted in 1993. (Since then, many other colleges and universities have adopted the language and procedures of Antioch College to deal with sexual violence on their campuses.)

The *Antioch policy* required that each new level of intimacy be verbally consented to by a partner. Without this consent, any subsequent sex was viewable as forced, and it could be penalized through one of several sanctions, such as expulsion, suspension, mandatory therapy, or restrictions on class scheduling (Antioch College Community, 1995). The Antioch policy is founded on the premise that consent cannot be presumed or inferred to be present. It must be freely given and clearly understood. Males, in particular, were expected to take steps to be certain that they were not forcing their dating partners to engage in sex acts that they did not want and that any sex that occurred was mutually rewarding. Active verbal consent was the foundation of the efforts to establish a college sexual culture that was less exploitative and dangerous for dating partners. (Antioch College closed its doors on June 30, 2008, due to financial reasons, but it reopened in October 2011.)

Does a rape crisis currently exist at colleges and universities? The answer partly depends on what is meant by "rape" and what is meant by "crisis." Some researchers use such a broad definition of sexual violence that the real difference between the brutality of rape and the disappointment of bad sex gets lost in the shuffle.

> We all agree that rape is a terrible thing, but we no longer agree on what rape is. Today's definition has stretched beyond bruises and knives, threats of death or violence to include emotional pressure and the influence of alcohol. (Roiphe, 1995, p. 75)

The belief that a rape crisis exists on college and university campuses may be caused in part by a new way of interpreting data. Broadening the definition of rape to include any bad or regretted sex—Cathy Young (1992) calls this *definitional shenanigans*—may actually lead to the unintended and unwanted outcome of trivializing severe forms of sexual violence, as well as finding rapists where none exists.

Some people see no difference between the crime of rape and sexual intercourse. Andrea Dworkin (1987) presented her views of the sexed world of dominance and submission in her book entitled *Intercourse*. Practically *every* instance of heterosexual intercourse is portrayed in the book as just one more example of the sexual violence perpetrated by the class of men against the class of women. According to Dworkin, the only real difference between rape and sexual intercourse is that the latter occurs so often that few people are able to see it for the sexual violence it really is. In a later preface to the 1987 book, Dworkin (1995) claimed years after *Intercourse* was published that she did not say that all men are rapists or that all intercourse is rape. However, if she believed a distinction exists between sexual intercourse and rape, it is difficult from reading her book to know what that might be. (Dworkin passed away on April 9, 2005.)

The failure or refusal to draw a distinction between the brutality of rape and the misfortune of bad or regretted sex not only leads to misunderstandings and flawed knowledge about forcible or nonconsensual sex, but it can also lead to allegations and charges being lodged against innocent individuals, causing irreparable damage to their lives, reputations, and resources. Some parents report that they worry more about sending their sons off to college, where they might be falsely accused of raping someone, than they do about sending their daughters (Kaiser, 2014; Sommers, 2014). It does not help victims of rape or efforts to reduce the harm done by campus rape to ignore the damage that can be done to individuals who are falsely accused of rape. While one rape is one too many, one false accusation is also one too many.

In the November 19, 2014, issue of *Rolling Stone,* a rape of a student at the University of Virginia at Charlottesville (UVA) was recounted in stark detail by the author, Sabrina Erdley (2014). Erdley blasted the university, as well as members of the Phi Kappa Psi fraternity, for what her news gathering had led her to believe had happened in 2012 to an 18-year-old female referred to only as "Jackie" (not her real name). The reporter concluded that Jackie had been brutally gang raped at the Phi Kappa Psi fraternity house. According to the article, based almost exclusively on Jackie's first-person account of what had happened to her, the woman had been asked out on a date by a student named Drew (not his real name), a man she worked next to as a lifeguard at the university pool. He invited her to dinner and then to a social function at his fraternity. At some point after they reached the fraternity house, Jackie told the reporter, Drew took her into a bedroom and closed the door. It was totally dark, but Jackie knew she and her date were not alone. For the next 3 hours, she recalled, she was held down, punched, and raped by several men while her date encouraged and supported the rapists. Jackie was forced to perform oral sex on some of the men, and one man even sodomized her with a glass beer bottle. She finally passed out. When she awoke, it was after 3:00 AM, and she was alone in the room. She was bloody, beaten, and bruised. She left the room, barefoot, and exited the house by descending a staircase and leaving by a side door. She called friends to come and get her.

The president of UVA, Teresa Sullivan, in response to Erdley's article and the rape of Jackie, suspended Greek organizations and their social activities (until January 9, 2015), while the university reviewed how it handles sexual assaults on campus. The university requested the Charlottesville police to look into the gang rape of Jackie, and the fraternity conducted its own internal investigation. It was fully expected that the men who had sexually victimized Jackie would soon be identified and the appropriate punishments handed out to them. Then Jackie's account of what had happened to her, as well as Erdley's reporting of it, started to come apart at the seams. It became increasingly clear that Jackie's account was mistaken, confused, or deceitful, and Erdley's article was either incompetent or irresponsibly one-sided and incomplete.

An assessment of Erdley's story (Coronel, Coll, & Kravitz, 2015) concluded that she relied too heavily on what Jackie told her, never trying hard enough to get information from the men who were identified as the rapists or from the friends who came to get her. According to Coronel et al., the failures evidenced in Erdley's reporting could have been avoided. The reporter should have tempered her trust of Jackie with efforts to verify or corroborate what she learned from the woman. A managing editor of *Rolling Stone*, Will Dana, one month after the article appeared added introductory comments to the online version, first explaining why Jackie's case was reported the way it was and then apologizing to readers for inaccuracies in it. The editor said the accused men were not interviewed out of concern for Jackie, who professed a fear of retaliation from them. He claimed that Jackie was convincing enough that what she had said seemed credible enough to report.

The magazine accepted full responsibility for the mistakes, refusing to implicate Jackie in any wrongdoing, coupled with a promise to continue to investigate the story. Spokespersons for the national headquarters and local branch of the fraternity were contacted. While they would neither confirm nor deny Jackie's account, they did express doubts about its accuracy and honesty. The *Washington Post*, as well as other news outlets, conducted its own investigation and reported on the many discrepancies that existed in Jackie's account of what happened to her (Farhi, 2014; Hartmann, 2015; Wemple, 2014). An investigation by Charlottesville police found "no basis" to conclude that the rape of Jackie described in the *Rolling Stone* had actually occurred at the fraternity house (Hartmann, 2015).

None of the published reports (that I've found) about this complex and involved event has cleared up one of its most perplexing mysteries. Why would Jackie make the charges that she did? Was she the victim of some horrible sex crime in her life but became confused over when and where it happened? Did she imagine the whole thing? Chief of the Charlottesville police, Timothy Longo, stated that the conclusions from the police investigation do not mean that something terrible did not happen to the woman (but they did not happen the way she claimed). It is hard to fathom what might have been Jackie's objective. Her allegations did a great deal of damage to her own life, not to mention to Erdley and her reputation, as well as to the university, the fraternity, and the men she accused.

Men and women do, or at least can, have different views of the world of sex and intimacy. Research has found that most males who commit date rape do not define it as rape (Capraro, 1994). Male college students and males in general tend to believe that a woman's refusal to engage in sex is usually nothing more than a required part of the dating ritual (Celes, 1991). They rarely view a "no" from their dates as being as definite or as firm as it is meant. A "no" is even more likely to be meaningless to an individual who truly believes that sex should be the outcome of any male–female relationship. Females might not be viewed by their dates as equal sexual partners with the same right as males to say "no" to sex (Sanday, 2007). Krakauer's (2015) examination of rape and justice in Missoula, Montana, should give pause to anyone who believes that lots of women are falsely charging rape in order to get attention or to cause trouble for men they do not like. When a female is raped in the United States, he reports, over 90% of the time the offender gets away with it (p. 10). Most of the men who rape are never adjudicated for their crimes, and most rape victims suffer in silence.

An asymmetry may exist in how interactants view the same relationship. A study of 41 women who had been followed by males indicated that the victims and their stalkers did not agree on the dynamics of what was happening. The women believed that little or no relationship existed between them and their stalkers; the stalkers, however, believed (or said they did) that a strong, close relationship existed (or would one day) between them and the individuals they were following. What was most alarming to the victims was not that they were being stalked, but that the stalkers wanted them to know how vulnerable and susceptible they actually were (Emerson, Ferris, & Brooks, 1998).

New(er) technologies in regard to communication and information storage have made it possible for stalkers to intrude into the lives of their victims by using e-mail, texting, tweets, and instant messaging. These technologies also make it possible for stalkers to gather information online about people they intend to stalk that at one time would have been impossible to obtain (e.g., e-mail addresses). The electronic culture not only makes *cyberstalking* possible, but it also makes it possible for cyberstalkers to repeatedly victimize others without fear of either punishment or retribution. Even though most cyberstalkers know their victims at some level, they are more likely to be strangers to their victims than are stalkers who track their victims in more traditional ways (i.e., directly or physically, without the use of electronic gadgets) (Reyns, Henson, & Fisher, 2012).

Sex and Violence in Gusiiland

It is possible to have a great deal of sexual violence in a relationship without the encounter automatically being defined as forcible rape. LeVine

(1959) studied sexual relationships between the men and women of Gusii, a small agricultural community in the highlands of southwestern Kenya. Every relationship between males and females in this community was filled with hostility, and even marriage brought no relief from sexual antagonisms. All it did was bring together a man and a woman from different and probably warring clans and unite them in a continually stormy relationship. Women were especially ambivalent about marriage. They needed to marry because marriage and the birthing of sons were the only ways that women could gain status and respect. However, marriage forced them to sever ties with their own families and to live with a clan that might be cruel and mean-spirited. Practically every Gusii bride was fearful of what would happen to her when she left the protection of her own home and family.

Even though a woman's parents had granted permission for the marriage to proceed, and the woman herself had adjusted to the prospect, the bride-to-be strongly resisted when her husband-to-be sent escorts to get her. Part of the resistance was obligatory. She could not look too willing, or she might be considered a whore. However, much of it was genuine and born out of anxiety over just what would become of her in her future husband's clan. She might run away and hide. Her parents might have to find her and convince her to go. She might have to be dragged out of her house by her friends and relatives, all the while kicking and screaming. She might even go to her new home in tears, with her hands on top of her head in a gesture that combined sorrow, regret, and fear of the unknown.

The wedding night sexual encounter was an ordeal for both husband and wife, and it displayed the kinds of sexual conflicts that plague all Gusii marriages. The bride put her new husband's sexual abilities to the test. She did everything that she could to ensure his failure at intercourse. She might use magical charms. These included such things as chewing a small piece of charcoal, placing a piece of knotted grass under the marriage bed, or twisting the phallic flower of the banana tree. She might tie her pubic hairs together so that they covered her vaginal opening. She might constrict her vaginal muscles so tightly that any penetration by her husband would be impossible. She might even refuse to get onto the bed at all. Her resistance to his advances persisted throughout the entire wedding night, and wives took great enjoyment in being able to keep their husbands from achieving intercourse for an indefinite period of time.

The new husband, however, did all he could to guarantee his own success and to overcome his wife's resistance. He made certain that he was well fed by eating special herbs, as well as large quantities of coffee beans, valued as an aphrodisiac. He was cheered on by his brothers and male cousins, who stayed close to the wedding-night dwelling and sang and danced while the events unfolded. The man's relatives might become more than onlookers. If the new groom was young (under 25) and his new bride was particularly uncooperative, some of these men might offer some assistance. They would grab the woman, undress her, throw her on the bed, and hold her down until her husband could penetrate her. The husband wanted to cause his new bride as much physical pain as possible. In fact, his status was greatly enhanced if she were unable to walk the next day. "Legitimate heterosexual encounters among the Gusii are aggressive contests, involving force and pain-inflicting behavior which under circumstances that are not legitimate could be termed 'rape'" (LeVine, 1959, p. 971). Even though husbands obtained sex from their wives through force and wives strenuously resisted, the sex was not defined as rape.

The Rape of Males

The multiple ways that society and culture impact both rape and our understandings of it are clear with a relatively neglected topic: the rape of males.

> Men have been abused and sexually humiliated during situations of armed conflict, such as the highly publicized Abu Ghraib scandal in Iraq. Childhood sexual abuse of boys is alarmingly common; in fact, the vast majority of those abused at the hands of Roman Catholic clergy in the United States were boys. And sexual assault against gay men remains unchecked due to assumptions that, as was once commonly assumed about women, gay men who have been raped must have "asked for it." (Stemple, 2009, p. 605)

Males are raped both inside and outside of prisons and jails. In fact, male-on-male rape *inside* of penal institutions is more frequent than is male-on-female rape *outside* of penal institutions, even though far more women than men are raped in a given society (Gilligan, 1996; Thio, 2010). Stemple concludes that not only is inmate-on-inmate rape a serious human rights abuse, but it is also a major public health problem.

The first-ever National Former Prisoner Survey provides information on sexual victimization of incarcerated individuals (both male and female). It reports that approximately 10% of former state prisoners claimed they had been victims of one or more incidents of sexual victimization during their most recent period of incarceration (Beck & Johnson, 2012). About half were victimized by another inmate, and about half by a member of the facility's staff. The rate of inmate-on-inmate sexual victimization was higher for females than it was for males. The majority (72%) of the victims of inmate-on-inmate victimizations reported feelings of shame or humiliation, and over half (56%) reported experiencing some guilt.

When males are raped, it is usually done by other males, even when the rape occurs outside of penal institutions. The rape usually occurs in social situations that are similar to those in which females are raped: The men are alone, isolated, and vulnerable. Male-on-male rape has a strong symbolic message in that it tells the victim he is an object or thing. In this sense, *all* victims of rape have a shared plight: "[N]ot women, but the weak, become the second sex, subordinate, submissive, subject to rape" (Janeway, 1975, p. 10). Sex can be a way to show who has power and who does not.

Some of the dynamics and identifying features of the rape of males can be seen in what is called the "Penn State child sex abuse scandal" or the "sex scandal at Penn State." The epicenter of this scandal was Jerry Sandusky, a former defensive coordinator under Joe Paterno, long-time head football coach at the university. (Paterno died January 22, 2012, at the age of 85.) Sandusky was arrested in November 2011 for sexually abusing and raping boys in sexual encounters that went back to the 1970s and 1980s. An investigation conducted by Louis Freeh, former director of the FBI, concluded that university administrators were aware of Sandusky's sexually predatory activities but failed to acknowledge their severity or take effective steps to stop them. Sandusky founded The Second Mile (in 1977), a nonprofit charity to assist and encourage at-risk and underprivileged youth. Whether this was a genuine effort to help the young or simply Sandusky's way to find youngsters to groom and then sexually victimize is impossible to know with any certainty. The jury, however, concluded that Sandusky planned to sexually exploit the boys in his care.

Sandusky was charged with 52 counts of sexual abuse of 10 boys extending over a 15-year-period. Four of the charges were eventually dropped (bringing the total to 48). In June 2012, Sandusky was found guilty of 45 of the charges. His victims testified—they ranged in age at the time of the trial from 18 to 28—that the coercive sexuality included kissing, fondling, joint showering, oral sex, and anal sex. Sandusky did not restrict his sexual encounters to the university's shower room; they also occurred in hotel rooms and even in his own home. Mike McQueary, a former graduate assistant coach, testified that he had witnessed Sandusky sodomizing a boy in a shower at the university. Even one of Sandusky's adopted children claimed that he, too, was sexually abused by the man. (The son was prepared to testify in court if his father had testified in his own defense.) Sandusky was sentenced to 30 to 60 years in prison for his crimes.

This scandal had a ripple effect the size of a tsunami. Paterno was fired as head football coach, and Graham Spanier, Penn State's president at the time, was also fired. (Paterno did bring the abuse to the attention of his superiors, but he did not contact police, which is what led to his dismissal.) Charges were also brought against Vice President Gary Schultz and former Athletic Director Tim Curley for failing to report the abuse and lying under oath. Along with all the injury Sandusky caused for his victims (and their families and friends) and everything that Sandusky himself lost—his reputation, his freedom, his financial standing—one other thing can be chalked up to his predatory acts: his image. His likeness was removed from a mural of Penn State greats. The painted image of Dora McQuaid, a poet who uses her linguistic talents to condemn domestic violence and sexual assault, has replaced the space that once belonged to Sandusky.

In July 2012, the other shoe dropped for the Penn State Lions, and it was a heavy shoe indeed. The university had the 900-pound bronze statue of Paterno removed from the sidewalk outside Beaver Stadium and secluded somewhere inside the building. A day later (July 23, 2012), the president of the National Collegiate Athletic Association (NCAA), Mark Emmert, announced the details of a consent decree that had been reached with the university: no postseason play for 4 years; the loss of several scholarships; removal of 111 of Paterno's 409 coaching victories, dropping him to twelfth on the all-time wins list (vacated because they were earned during the 14 years since it was known that Sandusky was preying on youngsters); and a $60 million fine (to serve as an endowment to help victims of child sexual abuse). The Big Ten (football conference division) levied additional punishments. The NCAA placed the university's athletic department on probation for 5 years (Wolff, 2012). Penn State eventually agreed to pay the 26 victims (16 in addition to the 10 involved in the case) of Sandusky a total of $59.7 million. (In 2015, the university reinstated some of Paterno's legacy. All of his wins that had been taken away were restored, putting him back on top as the winningest coach of all time. Scholarships were reinstated, and the restriction on post-season play was removed. Whether the statue of Paterno should be displayed once again became a subject of discussion with a decision pending as of this writing.)

Though Sandusky cannot be excused for his crimes—without him and his sexual predations, no scandal would have occurred—the fact is that the culture at Penn State, if not a cause of what happened, certainly played a pivotal role in its cover-up. The intense sense of loyalty found in the football program, both to the game and to Paterno, coupled with the incredible wealth that big-time football generates, led to an arrogance of power in which Paterno pulled the strings and most others danced. (The Freeh report branded it a "culture of reverence" [Freeh Sporkin & Sullivan, LLP, 2012].) In this climate, a disinterest and disinclination existed to scrutinize

Sandusky's behavior and allegations against him very closely for fear that it would hurt the university, the football program, and the coaches.

Males who rape males are more likely than males who rape females to be strangers to their victims and to use a great deal of force and violence to overpower and sexually assault their victims. However, the motives for the rape of males are not so different from the motives for the rape of females: power, control, anger, sadism. Rape, regardless of whether the victim is female or male, is more accurately viewed as the sexual expression of violence than as the violent expression of sexuality. If sexual release were the primary motive, a more convenient and ordinary way—less stigmatizing and less fraught with danger for the offender—would be masturbation (Thio, 2010).

A difference exists in how men and women view their experience of being a victim of sexual violence. Men are more likely to report that they think they are less of a *man*, whereas women are more inclined to think that they are less of a *person* (Groth, 1979). A male rape victim may become hypersexual with women after his own sexual victimization, viewing the sexual conquest of them as a way to refurbish his fractured masculinity.

It is possible for a female to rape a male because rape's essential feature is its forcible, nonconsensual nature. Violent women could use physical objects to sodomize male victims anally, or males could be forced in one way or another (e.g., at gunpoint) to perform oral sex on a female whom they would rather avoid altogether. A woman could threaten, coerce, cajole, plead with, cry for, or beg an unwilling male to engage in sexual acts with her. If the male is overpowered physically or psychologically, being forced to consummate a sexual act he would rather not, it qualifies as a rape sociologically but not legally according to the FBI's traditional or legacy definition of forcible rape. (As noted earlier, the FBI historically defined forcible rape as something that could only happen to females.)

The tendency of *female* victims of rape to suffer in silence, either refusing to tell anyone of their victimization or denying that it was rape at all, is even more likely with men who are raped (Rumney, 2008). This inclination to suffer in silence is especially likely if a man is raped by a woman. He is more likely to report increased levels of shame and decreased levels of self-esteem, questioning his own ability to be strong and assertive enough to protect himself (Terry, Giotakos, Tsiliakou, & Ackerman, 2010).

A male who reports to police that he has been sexually victimized faces a strong possibility of encountering both scorn and suspicion (Davies & Rogers, 2006). This is especially true if he is perceived by police to be a gay man. Police are more inclined to view gay men as untrustworthy in reporting being raped unless so much force and violence have been used during the sexual assault that it is beyond dispute that a forcible rape occurred. Gay men are generally viewed by police as individuals for whom sexual assaults by other men are likely and thus not something about which they should complain. When it comes to blame, gay men and straight women are held more responsible for their own sexual victimizations than are gay women and straight men (Wakelin & Long, 2003). Whatever institutionalized sexism still exists in the criminal justice system, which extends some sympathy to male *defendants* who are charged with raping women, does not carry over to sympathetic treatment of male rape *victims* (Rumney, 2008). This insensitivity or indifference of police toward male rape victims is particularly disturbing in light of the fact that victims of male-on-male sexual violence are statistically likely to have faced a stranger, and to have been subject to a great deal of physical injury.

Conclusions

Rape is primarily a way for certain individuals to enhance and reaffirm their sense of power, potency, and control by hurting and overpowering others. However, what qualifies as rape in one place and time may be treated very differently in another place and time, regardless of how injurious the assault may be to its victim. Some of the factors used to define rape are the amount of force used and how much resistance a victim offers.

Patterns of sexual violence and attitudes about it are powerfully influenced by social and cultural factors, gender-based associations, the structure of sexual inequality, and interpersonal dynamics. Structured inequality between males and females often leads to conflicts. Sex may come to be viewed by some men as something that they have a right to receive from women. If it is not freely given, they have no reservations about using force to take what they want. They may then attempt to excuse and justify their actions to others or even to themselves.

A classic rape, which is sexual violence done by a stranger, almost always in a public place, against strong victim resistance, causing the victim serious injury, is the type of coercive sexual act that is easiest for most people to define as rape, victims included. It seems that wherever and whenever sexual conflicts increase, forcible rape becomes more likely. The victim herself may even be blamed for her own victimization. Most social conflicts, such as war, entail some rapes of women by men. Men are also raped, sometimes by women, but mostly by other men. The rape of males is a problem that criminal justice system representatives do not always handle sensitively or effectively.

References

Allison, J., & Wrightsman, L. (1993). *Rape, the misunderstood crime.* Newbury Park, CA: Sage.

Alvarez, A., & Bachman, R. (2008). *Violence: The enduring problem.* Thousand Oaks, CA: Sage.

Amir, M. (1971). *Patterns in forcible rape.* Chicago: University of Chicago Press.

Antioch College Community. (1995). Antioch College: A sexual consent policy. In B. Leone & K. Koster (Eds.), *Rape on campus* (pp. 10–22). San Diego, CA: Greenhaven Press.

Armstrong, E., Hamilton, L., & Sweeney, B. (2009). Sexual assault on campus. In P. Adler & P. Adler (Eds.), *Constructions of deviance: Social power, context, and interaction* (6th ed., pp. 485–501). Belmont, CA: Thomson/Wadsworth.

Bahun-Radunovic', S., & Rajan, V. G. J. (2008). Introduction. In S. Bahun-Radunovic' & V. G. J. Rajan (Eds.), *Violence and gender in the globalized world: The intimate and extimate* (pp. 1–7). Burlington, VT: Ashgate.

Bailey, F. Y. (2010). Rape, race, and the media. In R. L. Bing III (Ed.), *Race, crime, and the media* (pp. 10–27). New York: McGraw-Hill.

Barlow, H. (1996). *Introduction to criminology* (7th ed.). New York: Harper Collins.

Baron, L., & Straus, M. (1987). Four theories of rape: A macrosociological analysis. *Social Problems, 34,* 467–489.

Baron, L., & Straus, M. (1989). *Four theories of rape in American society: A state-level analysis.* New Haven, CT: Yale University Press.

Bart, P., & O'Brien, P. H. (1985). *Stopping rape: Successful survival strategies.* New York: Pergamon.

Beck, A. J., & Johnson, C. (2012, May). *National Former Prisoner Survey, 2008: Sexual victimization reported by former state prisoners, 2008.* NCJ 237363. Washington, DC: Bureau of Justice Statistics, U.S. Department of Justice.

Bedau, H. A. (1982). The death penalty for rape: *Coker v. Georgia* (1977). In H. A. Bedau (Ed.), *The death penalty in America* (3rd ed., pp. 299–304). New York: Oxford University Press.

Bergen, R. K. (1996). *Wife rape: Understanding the response of survivors and service providers.* Thousand Oaks, CA: Sage.

Berkowitz, A., Burkhart, B., & Bourg, S. (1994). Research on college men and rape. In A. Berkowitz (Ed.), *Men and rape: Theory, research, and prevention programs in higher education* (pp. 3–19). San Francisco: Jossey-Bass.

Bohmer, C., & Parrot, A. (1993). *Sexual assault on campus: The problem and the solution.* New York: Lexington.

Bonnycastle, K. D. (2012). *Stranger rape: Rapists, masculinity, and penal governance.* Toronto, ON, Canada: University of Toronto Press.

Bourque, L. B. (1989). *Defining rape.* Durham, NC: Duke University Press.

Brownmiller, S. (1975). *Against our will: Men, women, and rape.* New York: Simon & Schuster.

Buchwald, E., Fletcher, P., & Roth, M. (1993). *Transforming a rape culture.* Minneapolis, MN: Milkweed.

Buddie, A. M., & Miller, A. G. (2000). Beyond rape myths: A more complex view of perceptions of rape victims. *Sex Roles, 45,* 139–160.

Bureau of Justice Statistics. (2008). *Criminal victimization in the United States— statistical tables index, May 12, 2011, Table 102.* NCJ 231173. Retrieved March 11, 2015, from http://bjs.ojp.usdoj.gov/content/pub/pdf/cvus08.pdf

Capraro, R. (1994). Disconnected lives: Men, masculinity, and rape prevention. In A. Berkowitz (Ed.), *Men and rape* (pp. 21–33). San Francisco: Jossey-Bass.

Card, C. (2008). The paradox of genocidal rape aimed at enforced pregnancy. *Southern Journal of Philosophy, 46,* 176–189.

Carlson, E. (2006). The hidden prevalence of male sexual assault during war: Observations on blunt trauma to the male genitals. *British Journal of Criminology, 46,* 16–25.

Carosella, C. (1995). Introduction. In C. Carosella (Ed.), *Who's afraid of the dark? A forum of truth, support, and assurance for those affected by rape* (pp. xiii–xxiv). New York: HarperPerennial.

Celes, W. (1991, January 2). Students trying to draw line between sex and assault. *New York Times,* p. Al.

Clover, C. (1992). *Men, women, and chainsaws: Gender in the modern horror film.* Princeton, NJ: Princeton University Press.

Coker v. Georgia, 433 U.S. 485 (1977).

Collins, P. H. (2010). Assume the position: The changing contours of sexual violence. In L. J. Moore & M. Kosut (Eds.), *The body reader: Essential social and cultural readings* (pp. 80–107). New York: New York University Press.

Coronel, S., Coll, S., & Kravitz, D. (2015, April 5). *Rolling Stone's* investigation: A failure that was avoidable. Columbia Graduate School of Journalism. Retrieved June 26, 2015, from http://www.cjr.org/investigation/rolling_stone_investigation.php

Davies, M., & Rogers, P. (2006). Perceptions of male victims in depicted sexual assaults: A review of the literature. *Aggression and Violent Behavior, 11,* 367–377.

Dunn, J. L. (2010). *Judging victims: Why we stigmatize survivors and how they reclaim respect.* Boulder, CO: Lynn Rienner.

Dworkin, A. (1987). *Intercourse.* New York: Free Press/Simon & Schuster.

Dworkin, A. (1995). Preface. In A. Dworkin, *Intercourse* (pp. vii–xi). New York: Free Press/Simon & Schuster.

Eller, J. (2006). *Violence and culture: A cross-cultural and interdisciplinary approach.* Belmont, CA: Thomson/Wadsworth.

Emerson, R., Ferris, K., & Brooks, C. (1998). On being stalked. *Social Problems, 43,* 289–314.

Erdely, S. R. (2014, November 19). A rape on campus: A brutal assault and struggle for justice at UVA. *Rolling Stone.* Retrieved October 5, 2015, from http://web.archive .org/web/20141219172210/http://www.rollingstone.com/culture/features/a-rape-on-campus-20141119

Estrich, S. (1987). *Real rape.* Cambridge, MA: Harvard University Press.

Farhi, P. (2014, December 9). *Rolling Stone* never asked U-Va. about specific gang rape allegations, according to newly released e-mails and audio recording. *Washington Post.* Retrieved March 15, 2015, from https://t5m.co/fi6y

Farr, K. (2009). Extreme war rape in today's civil-war-torn states: A contextual and comparative analysis. *Gender Issues, 26,* 1–41.

Federal Bureau of Investigation. (2012). *Attorney General Eric Holder announces revisions to the Uniform Crime Report's definition of rape.* National press release. Retrieved May 1, 2012, from https://t5m.co/fi60

Federal Bureau of Investigation. (2014). Rape addendum. *Crime in the United States, 2013.* Washington, DC: Government Printing Office. Retrieved March 14, 2015, from http://www.FBI.gov

Felson, R. (2003). Motives for sexual coercion. In M. Silberman (Ed.), *Violence and society: A reader* (pp. 194–206). Upper Saddle River, NJ: Prentice Hall.

Ferraro, K. (1996). Women's fear of victimization: Shadow of sexual assault? *Social Forces, 75,* 667–690.

Fitzgerald, L. (1993). Sexual harassment: Violence against women in the workplace. *American Psychologist, 48,* 1070–1076.

Freeh Sporkin & Sullivan, LLP. (2012, July 12). *Report of the Special Investigative Counsel Regarding the Actions of The Pennsylvania State University related to the child sexual abuse committed by Gerald A. Sandusky.* Retrieved October 31, 2015, from https://www.documentcloud.org/documents/396512-report-final-071212.html

Frohmann, L. (2005). Sexual assault. In E. Rubington & M. Weinberg (Eds.), *Deviance: The interactionist perspective* (9th ed., pp. 188–200). Boston: Pearson/Allyn & Bacon.

Funk, R. (1993). *Stopping rape: A challenge for men.* Philadelphia: New Society.

Gámez-Guadix, M., Straus, M. A., & Hershberger, S. L. (2011). Childhood and adolescent victimization and perpetuation of sexual coercion by male and female university students. *Deviant Behavior, 32,* 712–714.

Garrett-Gooding, J., & Senter, R., Jr. (1987). Attitudes and acts of sexual aggression on a university campus. *Sociological Inquiry, 57,* 348–371.

Gebhard, P., Gagnon, J., Pomeroy, P., & Christiansen, C. (1965). *Sex offenders: An analysis of types.* New York: Harper & Row.

Geis, G. (1977). Forcible rape: An introduction. In D. Chappell, R. Geis, & G. Geis (Eds.), *Forcible rape: the crime, the victim, and the offender* (pp. 1–44). New York: Columbia University Press.

Gilligan, J. (1996). *Violence: Reflections on a national epidemic.* New York: Vintage/Random House.

Gilmartin, P. (1994). *Rape, incest, and child sexual abuse.* New York: Garland.

Gilmartin-Zena, P. (1988). Gender differences in students' attitudes toward rape. *Sociological Focus, 21,* 279–292.

Goode, E. (1996). Rape. In E. Goode (Ed.), *Social deviance* (pp. 284–287). Boston: Allyn & Bacon.

Goodman, L., Koss, M., Fitzgerald, L., Russo, N., & Keita, G. (1993). Male violence against women: Current research and future directions. *American Psychologist, 48,* 1054–1058.

Gordon, M., & Riger, S. (1989). *The female fear.* New York: Free Press.

Gray, E. (2014, May 26). Rape: The crisis in higher education. *Time, 183,* 20–27.

Greenfeld, L. (1997). *Sex offenses and offenders.* Washington, DC: Government Printing Office.

Gregersen, E. (1983). *Sexual practices: The story of human sexuality.* New York: Watts.

Gregor, T. (1982). No girls allowed. *Science Magazine, 3,* 26–31.

Groth, N. (1979). *Men who rape.* New York: Plenum.

Hall, R. (1995). *Rape in America.* Santa Barbara, CA: ABC-CLIO.

Hartmann, M. (2015, January 13). Everything we know about the UVA rape case [updated]. *New York News & Politics.* Retrieved March 15, 2015, from http://nymag.com/daily/intelligence/2014/12/everything-we-know-uva-rape-case.html

Haskett, M., Portwood, S., & Lewis, K. (2010). Physical child abuse. In C. Ferguson (Ed.), *Violent crime: Clinical and social implications* (pp. 207–228). Thousand Oaks, CA: Sage.

Higgins, L., & Silver, B. (1991). Introduction: Rereading rape. In L. Higgins & B. Silver (Eds.), *Rape and representation* (pp. 1–11). New York: Columbia University Press.

Holmes, R., & Holmes, S. (2009). *Profiling violent crimes: An investigative tool* (4th ed.). Thousand Oaks, CA: Sage.

Hudson, V. M., Ballif-Spanvill, B., Caprioli, M., & Emmett, C. F. (2012). *Sex and world peace.* New York: Columbia University Press.

Iversen, T., & Rosenbluth, F. (2010). *Women, work, and politics: The political economy of gender inequality.* New Haven, CT: Yale University Press.

Jackson, S. (1995). The social context of rape: Sexual scripts and motivation. In P. Searles & R. Berger (Eds.), *Rape and society* (pp. 16–27). Boulder, CO: Westview.

Janeway, E. (1975). The weak are the second sex. In U. West (Ed.), *Women in a changing world* (pp. 5–24). New York: McGraw-Hill.

Jayaraman, T. V. (2008). Rape as a war crime. *UN Chronicle, 45,* 76–77.

Kaiser, M. (2014, May 26). What about our sons? The debate: How should college campuses handle sexual assault? *Time, 183,* 28–29.

Kanin, E. (1967a). An examination of sexual aggression as a response to sexual frustration. *Journal of Marriage and the Family, 29,* 428–433.

Kanin, E. (1967b). Reference groups and sex conduct norm violations. *Sociology Quarterly, 8,* 495–504.

Kanin, E. (1984). Date rape: Unofficial criminals and victims. *Victimology: An International Journal, 9,* 95–108.

Kanin, E. (2003). Date rapists: Differential sexual socialization and relative deprivation. In M. Silberman (Ed.), *Violence and society: A reader* (pp. 207–214). Upper Saddle River, NJ: Prentice Hall.

Kanin, E., & Parcell, S. (1981). Sexual aggression: A second look at the offended female. In L. H. Bowker (Ed.), *Women and crime in America* (pp. 223–233). New York: Macmillan.

Katz, J. (1988). *Seductions of crime: Moral and sensual attractions of doing evil.* New York: Basic Books.

Kirkpatrick, C., & Kanin, E. (1957). Male sex aggression on a university campus. *American Sociological Review, 22,* 52–58.

Koss, M. (1993). Rape: Scope, impact, interventions, and public policy responses. *American Psychologist, 48,* 1062–1069.

Koss, M., Goodman, L., Browne, A., Fitzgerald, L., Keita, G. P., & Russo, N. P. (1994). *No safe haven: Male violence against women at home, at work, and in the community.* Washington, DC: American Psychological Association.

Krakauer, J. (2015). *Missoula: Rape and the justice system in a college town.* New York: Doubleday.

Krebs, C. P., Lindquist, C. H., Warner, T. D., Fisher, B. S., & Martin, S. L. (2007). *The campus sexual assault (CSA) study.* Washington, DC: National Institute of Justice.

Lally, W., & DeMaris, A. (2012). Gender and relational-distance effects in arrests for domestic violence. *Crime & Delinquency, 58,* 103–123.

Larragoite, V. (1994). Rape. In T. Hirschi & M. Gottfredson (Eds.), *The generality of deviance* (pp. 159–172). New Brunswick, NJ: Transaction Publishers.

Leatherman, J. L. (2011). *Sexual violence and armed conflict.* Cambridge, UK: Polity Press.

LeVine, R. (1959). Gusii sex offenses: A study in social control. *American Anthropologist, 61,* 965–990.

Lewin, T. (1991, April 28). In short: Nonfiction. *New York Times.* Retrieved October 4, 2015, from http://www.nytimes.com/1991/04/28/books/in-short-nonfiction-871291.html

Lisak, D., & Miller, P. M. (2002). Repeat rape and multiple offending among undetected rapists. *Violence and Victims, 17,* 73–84.

Llewellyn, K. N., & Hoebel, E. A. (1941). *The Cheyenne way: Conflict and case law in primitive jurisprudence.* Norman: University of Oklahoma Press.

Lowney, J., Winslow, R., & Winslow, V. (1981). *Deviant reality* (2nd ed.). Boston: Allyn & Bacon.

MacKellar, J. (1975). *Rape: The bait and the trap.* New York: Crown.

MacKinnon, C. (1982). Feminism, Marxism, method, and the state: An agenda for theory. *Signs, 7,* 515–544.

MacKinnon, C. (2003). The legal regulation of sexual harassment: From tort to sex discrimination. In M. Silberman (Ed.), *Violence and society: A reader* (pp. 259–270). Upper Saddle River, NJ: Prentice Hall.

Madison, L. (2012, October 23). Richard Mourdock: Even pregnancy from rape something "God intended." *CBS News.* Retrieved October 5, 2015, from http://www.cbsnews.com/news/richard-mourdock-even-pregnancy-from-rape-something-god-intended/

Mandery, E. (2012). *Capital punishment in America: A balanced examination* (2nd ed.). Sudbury, MA: Jones & Bartlett.

Martin, P., & Hummer, R. (2003). Fraternities and rape on campus. In M. Silberman (Ed.), *Violence and society: A reader* (pp. 215–225). Upper Saddle River, NJ: Prentice Hall.

McKinney, K. (1994). Sexual harassment and college faculty members. *Deviant Behavior, 15,* 171–191.

Meadows, R. (2004). *Understanding violence and victimization* (3rd ed.). Upper Saddle River, NJ: Pearson/Prentice Hall.

Meadows, R., & Kuehnel, J. (2005). *Evil minds: Understanding and responding to violent predators.* Upper Saddle River, NJ: Pearson/Prentice Hall.

Medea, A., & Thompson, K. (1974). *Against rape.* New York: Farrar, Straus & Giroux.

Meloy, M. L., & Miller, S. L. (2011). *The victimization of women: Law, policies, and politics.* New York: Oxford University Press.

Miller, J., & Schwartz, M. (1995). Rape myths and violence against street prostitutes. *Deviant Behavior, 16,* 1–23.

Monckton-Smith, J. (2010). *Relating rape and murder: Narratives of sex, death and gender.* Hampshire, UK: Palgrave Macmillan.

Palmer, C. (1989). Is rape a cultural universal? A re-examination of the ethnographic data. *Ethnology, 28,* 1–16.

Pelka, F. (1995). Raped: A male survivor breaks his silence. In P. Searles & R. Berger (Eds.), *Rape and society* (pp. 250–256). Boulder, CO: Westview.

Pleck, E. (1979). Wife beating in nineteenth-century America. *Victimology, 4,* 60–74.

PLoS Medicine Editors. (2009). Rape in war is common, devastating, and too often ignored. *PLoS Medicine, 6,* 1–3.

Pound, R. (1910). Law in books and law in action. *American Law Review, 44,* 12–36.

Quinn, B. (2003). Sexual harassment—adult workplace. In M. Silberman (Ed.), *Violence and society: A reader* (pp. 271–277). Upper Saddle River, NJ: Prentice Hall.

Reiss, I. L. (1986). *Journey into sexuality.* Englewood Cliffs, NJ: Prentice Hall.

Reyns, B. W., Henson, B., & Fisher, B. S. (2012). Stalking in the twilight zone: Extent of cyberstalking victimization and offending among college students. *Deviant Behavior, 33,* 1–25.

Roiphe, K. (1995). A critique of "rape-crisis" feminists. In B. Leone & K. Koster (Eds.), *Rape on campus* (pp. 74–83). San Diego, CA: Greenhaven Press.

Rumney, P. (2008). Policing male rape and sexual assault. *Journal of Criminal Law, 72,* 67–86.

Sanday, P. R. (1981). The socio-cultural context of rape. A cross-cultural study. *Journal of Social Issues, 37,* 5–27.

Sanday, P. R. (1990). *Fraternity gang rape: Sex, brotherhood, and privilege on campus.* New York: New York University Press.

Sanday, P. R. (1996a). Rape-prone versus rape-free campus cultures. *Violence Against Women, 2,* 191–208.

Sanday, P. R. (1996b). *A woman scorned: Acquaintance rape on trial.* New York: Doubleday.

Sanday, P. R. (2007). *Fraternity gang rape: Sex, brotherhood, and privilege on campus* (2nd ed.). New York: New York University Press.

Schultz, J. (1978). Appendix 1: The Ingham case. In P. Wilson (Ed.), *The other side of rape* (pp. 112–125). Brisbane, Queensland, Australia: University of Queensland Press.

Schwartz, P. (1995). A negative view of the Antioch Plan. In B. Leone & K. Koster (Eds.), *Rape on campus* (pp. 33–38). San Diego, CA: Greenhaven Press.

Schwendinger, H., & Schwendinger, J. (1983). *Rape and inequality.* Beverly Hills, CA: Sage.

Scott, J., Crompton, R., & Lyonette, C. (Eds.). (2010). *Gender inequalities in the 21st century: New barriers and continuing constraints.* Cheltenham, UK: Edward Elgar Publishing.

Scully, D. (1990). *Understanding sexual violence: A study of convicted rapists.* Boston: Unwin Hyman.

Scully, D., & Marolla, J. (1984). Convicted rapists' vocabulary of motive: Excuses and justifications. *Social Problems, 31,* 530–544.

Siddiqui, S. (2012, August 22). *Paul Ryan responds to Todd Akin, clarifies abortion position: "Rape is rape."* Retrieved October 31, 2015, from http://www .huffingtonpost.com/2012/08/22/paul-ryan-todd-akin-abortion_n_1821284.html

Sinozich, S., & Langton, L. (2014, December). Rape and sexual assault victimization among college-age females, 1995–2013. *Special Report.* Washington, DC: U.S. Department of Justice, Bureau of Justice Statistics. Retrieved May 25, 2015, from http://www.bjs.gov/content/pub/pdf/rsavcaf9513.pdf

Smith, M. D., & Bennett, N. (1985). Poverty, inequality, and theories of forcible rape. *Crime & Delinquency, 31,* 295–305.

Sommers, C. H. (2014, May 15). Campus hysteria. The debate: How should college campuses handle sexual assault? *Time, 183,* 28–29.

Stemple, L. (2009). Male rape and human rights. *Hastings Law Journal, 60,* 605–647.

Svalastoga, K. (1962). Rape and social structure. *Pacific Sociological Review, 5,* 48–53.

Tellis, K. (2010). *Rape as a part of domestic violence: A qualitative analysis of case narratives and official reports.* El Paso, TX: LFB Scholarly Publishing.

Terry, K., Giotakos, O., Tsiliakou, M., & Ackerman, A. (2010). Sex offenders: Rape and child sexual abuse. In C. Ferguson (Ed.), *Violent crime: Clinical and social implications* (pp. 229–256). Thousand Oaks, CA: Sage.

Thio, A. (2010). *Deviant behavior* (10th ed.). Boston: Allyn & Bacon.

Tieger, T. (1981). Self-rated likelihood of raping and the social perception of rape. *Journal of Research in Personality, 15,* 147–158.

True, J. (2012). *The political economy of violence against women.* New York: Oxford University Press.

Wakelin, K., & Long, K. M. (2003). Effects of victim gender and sexuality on attributions of blame to rape victims. *Sex Roles, 49,* 477–487.

Ward, S., Dziuba-Leatherman, J., Stapleton, J. G., & Yodanis, C. (1994). *Acquaintance and date rape: An annotated bibliography.* Westport, CT: Greenwood.

Weis, K., & Borges, S. (1973). Victimology and rape: The case of the legitimate victim. *Issues in Criminology, 8,* 71–115.

Weiss, K. G. (2013). *Party school: Crime, campus, and community.* Boston: Northeastern University Press.

Wemple, E. (2014, December 11). The full demise of *Rolling Stone*'s rape story. *Washington Post.* Retrieved March 15, 2015, from http://www.washingtonpost .com/blogs/erik-wemple/wp/2014/12/11/the-full-demise-of-rolling-stones-rape-story

Williams, L. (1984). The classic rape: When do victims report? *Social Problems, 31,* 459–467.

Winslow, R., & Zhang, S. (2008). *Criminology: A global perspective.* Upper Saddle River, NJ: Pearson/Prentice Hall.

Wolff, A. (2012, July 30). Is this the end for Penn State? *Sports Illustrated, 117,* 38–41.

Wolfgang, M. (1958). *Patterns in criminal homicide.* Philadelphia: University of Pennsylvania Press.

Yancey, P., & Hummer, R. (1989). Fraternities and rape on campus. *Gender and Society, 3,* 457–473.

Young, C. (1992, May 31). Women, sex and rape: Have some feminists exaggerated the problem? *Washington Post,* p. C1.

7

Suicide

Social Frames and Definitions of the Situation

Understanding Suicide

Suicide refers to an intentional killing of oneself, by oneself, for the sole purpose of ending one's life and existence. The term is based on the Latin pronoun *sui,* meaning "self," and the Latin verb *cide,* "to kill" (Farberow, 1975, p. 1). According to the *Oxford English Dictionary,* the term was first used in English in 1651, but it actually appeared a bit earlier in a work by Sir Thomas Browne, published in 1642 (Alvarez, 1972). Before the mid-1600s, self-killings were treated as murder rather than placed in a category all their own.

Why did the term *suicide* appear when it did? Throughout the Middle Ages (approximately AD 476 to 1450), nearly everyone believed, completely and without question, in the influence and power of supernatural forces and spiritual beings. Heaven and hell were real places, and their existence exerted a shadow over practically everything that people did. With this worldview, it was impossible for anyone—certainly for anyone with even a hint of religious belief—to conclude that a self-inflicted killing would end all existence and send one into a state of nothingness. A self-inflicted death, it was believed, would simply move one to a different realm of existence—perhaps better, perhaps worse, but an existence nonetheless. The secularization of human experience that occurred in the years following the Middle Ages promoted a worldview that had less room for spiritual matters. Perhaps heaven and hell did not exist; maybe humans were physical beings without souls; and, just possibly, death might usher in a permanent state of nothingness, devoid of any sensation or cognition. For the first time, suicide—choosing to end it all—became a real possibility (Shneidman, 1985).

Discourses about suicide have been overly influenced by reductionist models coming from medicine or psychology, making it more difficult to recognize just how much suicide is a collective experience (Gaines, 1990). It is characterized by a diversity of motives, methods, forms, rationalizations, and circumstances. The principal factor that suicidal deaths have in common is that they have all been called suicides by somebody, who is usually in a position of authority. The classification of a death as a suicide is a social process—as is the process of dying itself—and it must be understood in its own right. Suicide is not an automatic classification that naturally flows from a death scene.

People can die in many ways (e.g., naturally, accidentally, or through murder or suicide), and the determination that a death is a suicide hinges on conjectures or presumptions about the inner experience and state of the deceased. The problem is that the deceased is unable to tell us anything directly about his or her reasons for dying. Even when a suicide note is present—and it usually is not—it is not irrefutable proof that a suicide has occurred. A clever murderer could certainly leave a suicide note if he or she wanted to muddy the waters and make it more difficult to know what really happened. Even when they are present at the death scene, suicide notes are usually too sketchy to give the kind of information that would be necessary in order to really know why an individual committed suicide. It is also very possible that the suicide was done by an individual unsure of his or her own motives or for reasons only dimly understood.

Framing Deaths

The sociologist Erving Goffman (1974) explored the value of a "frame analysis" for understanding human behavior. For him, *frames* were definitions of social situations that individuals develop in order to give some meaning and organization to their collective experiences. Framing is a process of constructing images that help people to interpret, understand, describe, and deal with social events. Framing always involves selection, presentation, and accentuation, and frames always package social experiences for both producers and users of them (Papke, 1987). Frames help people who are confronting a hard-to-understand or ambiguous event to make some sense of it (Goffman, 1974).

Framing a death as a suicide is not a straightforward process. Reluctance may be found among the living to call a death a suicide if another option exists. Alvarez (1972) offers an instructive example of how this can work. A West of Ireland coroner decided that a man who shot himself in the head by placing the barrel of his gun in his own mouth and then pulling the trigger had actually died accidentally. How could this clear example of a suicide be framed as an accident? The coroner concluded that the gun had discharged inadvertently as the man cleaned the barrel with his tongue.

Sometimes, disagreement exists over how a death should be framed, and the final decision is the result of a convoluted and contentious history. On November 14, 1997, Moshe Pergament, due to his sideswiping of several cars on the Long Island Expressway, was pulled over by a police officer. Pergament exited his automobile and advanced toward the officer's patrol car with a gun drawn. The officer ordered the man to drop the weapon, but he refused. The officer drew his own revolver and killed Pergament. Although this is a clear case of self-defense by an officer in the line of duty, it is also something more. Subsequent investigation found that the gun Pergament carried was actually made of plastic (which, of course, was unknown to the officer at the time). On the front seat of Pergament's automobile was a note that was addressed "To the officer who shot me." In it, Pergament exonerated the officer in the death, apologized to the officer, and assumed full responsibility for what happened.

The medical examiner classified this death as "homicide caused by gunshots," and the police report classified it as "justifiable homicide." Lindsay and Lester (2004) claim that it was really "suicide-by-cop" (p. 3). Other writers (e.g., Hutson et al., 1998) think that deaths like these are best classified as "law enforcement–forced assisted suicides" because an officer is left little choice in the matter. Little uniformity exists in how deaths like these are classified, with some medical examiners and coroners calling them homicides and others calling them suicides. It is unknown (and unknowable) how many times individuals who want to die provoke police officers to shoot them but fail to leave a suicide note.

Individuals who kill themselves may do it for many reasons—both personal and social—and the presence of a self-inflicted death is not a perfect indicator of suicidal intent. Some people who do not wish to die still do very dangerous and risky things, and not all suicidal deaths can reasonably be viewed as intended (Canetto & Lester, 1995). The spark that leads to a suicide is usually transient, and a large number of people who commit suicide are actually ambivalent about it (Hendin, 1995b). They do something in an agitated and perturbed state that commits them to a plan of action that is irreversible and deadly.

We need a term to describe those acts that are self-inflicted, self-destructive, and suicide-like, but that do not result in the deaths of individuals who commit them. Instead of using the more common term of *attempted suicide,* a more fitting one is *parasuicide* (Shneidman, 1985, p. 19). Parasuicide covers the use of excessive dosages of drugs or dangerous mutilations of self. The term can also be used to cover situations in which an individual does something life-threatening but in a way that death is an unlikely occurrence. It can also cover situations in which the methods were deliberate and deadly enough to do the job, but death just did not occur.

According to Brown (1996), a 28-year-old male was once brought to an emergency room (ER) at a hospital in Ashland, Virginia. He was badly bruised on the upper part of his body. What caused his injuries? Hours earlier, he had tried to kill himself (or that's how paramedics framed it) by drinking a bottle of vodka and swallowing several nitroglycerin tablets. The bruises resulted from the man forcibly ramming himself into a wall many times in order to make the nitroglycerin explode and end his life in a flash (p. 8). The parasuicide of a young man who walked into an emergency room in Akron, Ohio, seems different from the one just described. Days before his arrival at the ER, he had decided to take his own life. He downed a bottle of Valium tablets and drank a bottle of vodka, intending never to regain consciousness. He did awake, however, 36 hours later and with a huge hangover. He subsequently made another attempt to kill himself. He filled his bathtub with water and got in. He used a razor blade to slit both wrists, expecting to die. However, he had cut only veins, not arteries, so the blood clotted quickly and the flow stopped. He was left sitting in a lukewarm bath of pinkish water and still alive. He then made another attempt. He got his belt and used it to hang himself from his dining room light fixture. The light fixture was not up to the task, however, and it tore from the ceiling, sending the man crashing to the floor with such force that the floor broke. He fell through and ended up in the basement. The fall did not kill him either. He searched around to find something that might finish the job where the drugs, the razor, the belt, and the fall had not. He found a bullet (.22 caliber) but no gun. He also found a pair of pliers and a ball-peen hammer. Holding the single bullet as best he could against his sternum with the pliers, he hit the compression end of the bullet several times with the hammer. On the third try, the bullet fired, knocking him to the ground. However, pliers apparently are not as good as pistols when it comes to suicide, because the bullet pierced the left side of his chest where it harmlessly bounced off a rib to lodge in subcutaneous tissue. He drove himself to the hospital (pp. 82–83).

The two incidents show us something of value about the social process of framing deaths as suicides. Both men tried to kill themselves and failed (making each one an example of a parasuicide). Sometimes, people live through an attempt because their methods are really not deadly enough to kill them (e.g., running into a wall, hoping to explode); sometimes, they live because the methods they have chosen are lethal enough to kill them, but they just do not die (e.g., the shooter from Ohio). The concept of *inchoate suicide* can be used to cover those parasuicidal incidents where methods, motives, and intents are lethal enough to do the job, but death still does not result. We will find that inchoate suicides have more in common with completed suicides than they do with other kinds of parasuicide. Muddying the waters even more is the fact that a parasuicide can evolve into a completed suicide, as when an overdose of drugs, taken only to get high, leads to the accidental death of the user. It may be impossible for an outside observer to know enough details of an individual's death to be able to place it in the "right" category. Inherent difficulties exist in any naming process, however, and the determination of cause of death is no exception (Douglas, 1967).

It is true that most people who eventually commit suicide have spoken to others about it, just as it is true that suicidal individuals usually give some warnings about their plan to die (e.g., verbal statements, putting finances in order, withdrawing from social relationships) (Granello & Granello, 2007). However, a distinction must be drawn between those who successfully commit suicide (completed suicide) and those who commit parasuicide, because they are separate events in many important ways. Completed suicides are done by suicidal individuals, and parasuicides are done by parasuicidal individuals. Maris (1981) reports that about 75% of the people who successfully kill themselves only made one attempt, the one that killed them. Furthermore, only a small percentage of those people who commit parasuicides will successfully kill themselves (p. 267). All deaths should be identified as *intentional*, *subintentional* (where the deceased played an unconscious or latent role in producing his or her death), or *unintentional* (Shneidman, 1985).

Suicide is a violent act, so it should not be surprising to learn that it and homicide are related (Henry & Short, 1954). A study of how levels of violence affect suicide in a sample of adolescents in Chicago neighborhoods (from 1994 to 2002) shows that a complex relationship exists between other kinds of violence and suicide (Zimmerman, 2013). A desensitization effect was found: An aggressive individual is more likely than a peaceful individual to commit suicide. The principal reason is that a history of using violence numbs an individual to subjective pain and suffering, removing one of the significant impediments to the commission of suicide. A relationship was found among depression, violence, and suicide. High levels of neighborhood violence lead to an increase in residents' reported levels of depression, which increases their likelihood of committing suicide. The correlation between depression and suicide is lowest for violent individuals living in nonviolent neighborhoods and highest for nonviolent individuals living in violent neighborhoods (p. 375).

The Meanings of Suicide

A definition of suicide—one that has stood the test of time—was offered over 115 years ago by Émile Durkheim (1897/1951) in his book *Suicide:* "Suicide is applied to all cases of death resulting directly or indirectly from a positive or negative act of the victim himself, which he knows will produce this result" (p. 44). Durkheim was confident that his definition of suicide would allow all objective observers to recognize the suicides they saw and to differentiate them from other forms of death. He rejected motive and intent as a way to explain and classify suicides, because he believed these two inner states were not objective enough to be measured. The defining feature of suicide for Durkheim was the renunciation of existence and the purposeful sacrifice of life.

Durkheim's aim to construct a purely objective definition of suicide was laudable but unrealistic (Pope, 1976). It is impossible to accurately and reliably separate a suicidal death from all other kinds of death, and suicide does not exist independently from human thoughts about it. A great deal of subjectivity enters into the classification of a death as a suicide (S. Taylor, 1990). For example, the difference in suicide rates of Catholics and Protestants in the Netherlands during the years 1905 to 1910 was directly related to a classification bias. A large proportion of the deaths of Catholics that had been recorded as "death from ill-defined or unspecified cause" or "sudden death" would have been recorded as suicides if the deceased had been Protestants (Poppel & Day, 1996, pp. 505–506).

As noted previously, Durkheim rejected the variables of motivation (the reasons people kill themselves) and intent (a knowledge or awareness of possible outcomes or consequences), but motive and intent worked their way into his analysis of suicide nonetheless. He apparently never considered that the instances of suicide that he was objectively studying were determined by coroners, medical examiners, police officers, judges, and other authorities, who based their decisions on what constituted a suicide on all those subjective variables that Durkheim did not want to use (Pope, 1976). The *intrinsic ambiguity* of suicide recognized by Douglas (1967, p. 251) exists because human actions are contextual, and the meaning of any social event requires observers to infer a great many details about what happened.

Suicide holds distinctive meanings for an individual contemplating it (Douglas, 1967). It offers the prospect of starting over again as a new being, in a different realm of existence. It offers the hope that changes will occur in how one is viewed by others. It offers the possibility of changes in human relationships. (If the suicide is successful, it produces an immediate reinterpretation of the deceased's life and relationships by surviving family members, friends, and acquaintances.) Suicide also offers an opportunity to avenge some actual or imagined injustice. ("This will serve them right for treating me so badly.") These social meanings exert a powerful influence over why suicide occurs and any interpretation of self-destructive acts.

Suicide attempts (i.e., parasuicides) can be rational, a way for an individual in desperate straits to do something that will significantly improve, or at least change, his or her life (Duhigg, 2007). On the island of Tikopia, in the western Pacific, individuals take *suicide swims* out into the ocean. These swims are one legitimate way for them to handle life's problems. The swimmers have time alone in a watery world to think, and these swims actually enhance their standing in the community. Community ties are reaffirmed because the swimmers allow themselves to be rescued and returned to shore (Littlewood & Lipsedge, 1987, p. 292). The swims are a cry for help, and everyone knows it.

People can change their views of suicide in light of events, such as the suicides of others or perhaps even their own suicide attempts. Consider Alvarez's (1972) own effort to kill himself. He took 45 barbiturates and waited for death, but his wife discovered him and called an ambulance. He was in a deep coma, and he had a rapid pulse, vomit in his mouth, and blue skin. Medical technicians pumped his stomach and got him breathing normally. He was unconscious for 3 days but finally recovered. Alvarez had the following to say about his experience:

> I thought death would be like that: a synoptic vision of life, crisis by crisis, all suddenly explained, justified, redeemed, a Last Judgment in the coils and circuits of the brain. Instead, all I got was a hole in the head, a round zero, nothing. I'd been swindled. (p. 282)

As a result of his experience with suicide, he concluded that when his death finally came, it would be nastier than suicide and a lot less convenient.

The Curious Case of Autoerotic Asphyxiation

The ambiguity that exists in framing a death as a suicide can be seen with a curious—and arguably risky—form of human activity called *autoerotic asphyxiation,* which can lead to autoerotic fatalities. *Autoerotic fatalities* are deaths that occur from oxygen deprivation (asphyxiation) during solitary sexual activity. (The technical name for restriction of airflow for the purpose of sexual arousal is *hypoxyphilia.*) Typically, when death occurs in this case, the deceased is found alone; wearing physical restraints, such as handcuffs, gags, or blindfolds; and behind a locked door, with a rope or other ligature around his or her neck. Oxygen deprivation can also have been achieved through the use of plastic bags, chemicals, chest compression, or a tub of water in which the face was immersed (R. Holmes & Holmes, 2009, pp. 190–195). Evidence of masturbatory activities usually can be found, and one goal in autoerotic asphyxiation is to heighten the pleasure of orgasm (Evans & Farberow, 1988). An escape mechanism is usually found in the individual's hand or within reaching distance (e.g., a knife to cut the rope once the "game" is over). The decedent is usually completely or partially naked, and erotic materials may be present at the death scene, although many documented cases of autoerotic fatalities are not characterized by nudity (Turvey, 2009). Hypoxyphilia is most often practiced by young, white, middle- or upper-middle-class males (Lowery & Wetli, 1982). Data collected from England, the United States, Canada, and Australia show that 1 to 2 erotic asphyxiations per million population are detected and reported each year (APA, 2000, p. 573). (The word *hypoxyphilia* does not appear in *DSM-5,* but a synonym—*asphyxiophilia*—does. *Asphyxiophilia* is listed as one consideration in diagnosing sexual masochism disorder [APA, 2013, pp. 694–695].)

The reason that some people engage in erotic asphyxiation is that it is supposed to be sexually stimulating. The carotid arteries (on either side of the neck) carry oxygen-rich blood from the heart to the brain. When these are compressed, as in strangulation or hanging, the sudden loss of oxygen to the brain and the accumulation of carbon dioxide can increase feelings of giddiness, lightheadedness, and pleasure, all of which will heighten masturbatory sensations. Autoerotic asphyxia was described in writing as far back as the 1600s, where it was proclaimed to be a cure for male impotence. The basis of this belief may well have been the observation that men who were executed by hanging attained an erection. Men in Victorian England could visit "Hanged Men's Clubs," where prostitutes would administer enough asphyxiation for these men to be sexually satisfied but not so much that they would be in any danger (Uva, 1995, p. 575).

Turvey (2009) insists that autoerotic fatalities are accidental deaths, not suicides, because autoerotic asphyxiates restrict airflow to the brain to heighten their sexual pleasures, not to intentionally die. It is hard to believe, however, that erotic asphyxiates are unaware of the riskiness of their chosen sexual practice. The carotid arteries are sensitive, and even a minor miscalculation can lead to unconsciousness and death (R. Holmes & Holmes, 2009). Even if death does not occur, brain damage still can take place if the oxygen supply stops for too long. Though the precise details of what can happen may be unknown to practitioners of erotic asphyxia, they must at least know something about the risks involved. Autoerotic asphyxia is called "terminal sex" in the adult bondage subculture (Uva, 1995, p. 578), but it could just as easily be called sexual termination. The distinction between "intends to die" and "knows death could easily occur" is a fine line.

A suicide note, if present, is usually taken by authorities as proof that the death is a suicide. However, a suicide note itself may be part of an autoerotic game—a prop to aid the decedent's fantasy that it is possible to "die" and then be "reborn" (Hazelwood, Dietz, & Burgess, 1982, pp. 766–767). Another possibility is that a murder will be disguised as an autoerotic fatality. In fact, Wright and Davis (1976) reported just such an occurrence. A 31-year-old single male was found hanging by his neck from a necktie tied to a shower curtain rod in his apartment. His feet touched the floor. He was blindfolded with another necktie, a belt was around his neck, and his hands had been tied behind his back. He was fully clothed except that he wore no shoes. Some of his personal possessions were missing, and two females had been seen leaving his apartment. The death scene and subsequent autopsy provided enough evidence to indicate that the death was an autoerotic asphyxiation. It was ultimately decided, however, that the two females had actually robbed and murdered the man. An important clue was the fact that the victim's hands were tied behind his back, a seeming impossibility if the autoerotic activities had been completely solitary. However, even here we must be cautious. Because some people practice hypoxyphilia with others around, the man's hands could have been tied by a sexual partner.

In 2009, the actor David Carradine (best known for his role as the wandering spiritual advisor and martial arts expert in the *Kung Fu* television series, as well as for his role in the *Kill Bill* films), age 72, was found dead in his hotel room in Thailand. He was hanging by a rope in the closet, and a shoelace was wrapped around his neck and another around his genitals. His hands were also tightly bound and reported initially to be behind his back. (It was subsequently reported that the hands were actually tied over his head.) The death appeared to be a clear case of suicide, but this is not what was eventually decided.

The official classification was accidental death during solitary sexual activity. This would be unlikely if his hands were tied behind his back—making it either a murder or a suicide—but possible if his hands were over his head in a position that would allow them to be freed when he tired of the sexual game. (Because he was believed to have been alone at the time of his death, murder was ruled out.) Carradine's two ex-wives both reported to authorities that the actor did have unusual sexual interests, including self-bondage. On *Larry King Live,* however, the family lawyer disputed the official interpretation, suggesting that the death could have been a murder, because Carradine was in Thailand to unmask groups that were operating in the martial arts underworld. The assessment of one of the investigating officers may be closest to the mark: death by masturbation.

Sociocultural Variations in Suicide: Motive, Intent, and Interpretation

Historical Meanings

Purposeful self-killings are not unusual, and they have occurred throughout human history and in most places (R. Holmes & Holmes, 2005). Some of these self-inflicted lethal acts reflect an individual's isolation from social groups, and they are a response to loneliness and the absence of meaningful relationships. This type is called *egoistic suicide,* and it occurs when social integration becomes too low and the feelings of separation and despair become too high for an individual to manage (Durkheim, 1897/1951). If an individual who is isolated and separate from others (i.e., experiences too-low levels of social integration) is exposed to deeply frustrating experiences, suicide becomes more likely because the only available target of the individual's aggression is himself or herself (Henry & Short, 1954; Unnithan, Huff-Corzine, Corzine, & Whitt, 1994). Egoistic suicides may be characterized by *encore anxiety,* in which individuals believe that they cannot repeat their past accomplishments, and a *fraud complex,* in which individuals believe that even if they were to be successful, it would be undeserved (or fraudulent). Urbanization and modernity are positively correlated with higher rates of suicide, because they lead to increases in individualism and autonomy, which means that instances of aggression will more frequently be directed toward the self (Whitt, 2010).

Attitudes toward suicide can range from strong opposition to spirited support if it were to be done in the proper way and for all the right reasons. In some places and times, suicide, successful or not, was viewed as an abomination. Individuals were threatened with harsh penalties if they took their own lives. The corpse of anyone who committed suicide was abused, and the family name of the decedent was dishonored. In other places and times, the decedent was highly admired for committing suicide, and it was a death that he or she freely chose because of the benefits that it offered. In still other places and times, a suicide was viewed as a tragedy. It diminished the entire social fabric, and it was a time of sadness; survivors may have felt responsible for the death. In still other places and times, a suicide was viewed as a trivial matter because death itself was unimportant. What mattered was how one lived—how completely and how productively—not how one died (Fedden, 1938/1980). The many forms of suicide, the many reasons it occurs, the many methods people use to self-destruct, the wide array in social meanings of suicide, and the great variety in social reactions to suicide all make for a great deal of relativity in regard to it.

Death in ancient Egypt was considered to be a passage from one type of existence to another. The living and the dead were viewed as not too different from one another, and they were believed to have some of the same needs and interests. Because death was seen as no big deal, it really did not matter to anyone exactly what caused it. However, if an Egyptian who committed suicide were somehow magically transported to another culture just as the last breath left the body, attitudes of indifference would not be found there.

> If [an] ancient Egyptian had killed himself in pre-Christian Scandinavia, for example, he would have been guaranteed a place in Viking paradise. If he had taken his life during the Roman Empire, his death would have been honored as a glorious demonstration of his wisdom. If he had cut open his stomach in feudal Japan, he would have been praised as a man of principle. If he had killed himself in fifteenth-century Metz [now a French republic], however, his corpse would have been crammed into a barrel and floated down the Moselle, sending the tainted body beyond city limits. In seventeenth-century France his corpse would have been dragged through the streets, hanged upside down, then thrown on the public garbage heap. In seventeenth-century England his estate would have been forfeited to the crown and his body buried at a cross-roads with a stake through the heart. (Colt, 1991, p. 131)

Some groups fervently believe that suicide is a good and noble way to die, whereas other groups, with equal enthusiasm, view it as a sign of biological dysfunction, immorality, or psychological abnormality. These meanings are not without consequence for the cause, course, and outcome of self-inflicted deaths and how deaths are categorized and interpreted.

The Vikings of pre-Christian Scandinavia viewed suicide as a good way to die because it was a ticket into Valhalla, the eternal home of all heroes who had died violently. The surest way to get into Viking heaven was to die heroically in battle, but a self-inflicted violent death came in a close second. The Vikings believed that people who entered Valhalla would fight mock battles and then feast for all time, drinking from the skulls of their dead enemies. The founder of the feast was none other than Odin, the Scandinavian god of war, who was supposed to have committed suicide himself. Self-respecting Vikings who saw no prospect of dying in battle often killed themselves with their swords or jumped to their deaths. This sanctification of a violent death helped to encourage and justify a violent life. Being encouraged to die by the sword usually means that you will live by the sword, an important requirement in a warrior society like that of the Vikings, which required a proper fighting spirit for its survival (Colt, 1991).

The best term to describe the attitudes of inhabitants of the Greco-Roman world toward suicide would be ambivalence or even confusion. Greek culture condemned suicide, but Greeks were not particularly intolerant of it. Homer himself regarded suicide, if it were done voluntarily and for good reasons, as heroic (Droge & Tabor, 1992). Whatever disapproval of suicide existed in the ancient world was almost entirely dependent on the motives for it. Self-killings done out of honor, devotion, or duty; to avoid dishonor; or as a response to unbearable grief were likely to be viewed as good and noble deaths. Only when self-killings evidenced signs of weakness, cowardice, or irresponsibility were they viewed as disgraceful. To the Romans, the reasons that one died were of fundamental importance in how the death was judged (Plass, 1995). Suicides to avoid dishonor or as a response to the unbearable pain of the death of a loved one or of a love affair gone sour were not considered at all unreasonable (Farberow, 1988).

Christians were ultimately responsible for changing the ambivalence of the Greco-Roman world into condemnation, but initially they were not particularly intolerant of suicide. The Apostles did not moralize against it, and neither the Old nor the New Testaments directly forbade it. In fact, in the early days of Christianity, suicide was viewed as a way to achieve martyrdom and to enter the kingdom of heaven. Everybody who wanted to get to heaven (and who didn't?) could get there in a direct and expeditious way by committing suicide. The icing on the cake was that church members took care of the surviving family members of someone who committed suicide, which significantly eased the conscience of anyone who was planning to self-destruct (Farberow, 1988). However, suicide became a too-attractive option for Christians, so around the sixth century, the Church began working to harden attitudes toward it and to redefine it as an offense against God.

The moral justification for the Christian condemnation of suicide was found in the sixth commandment, "Thou shalt not kill." Life was declared to be a gift from God, and it was asserted that only God could determine when life was to end. People who were considering taking their own lives were assured by Church doctrine that they would be harshly dealt with in the hereafter. The threat of eternal damnation gave the ban on suicide a supreme moral authority and increased its ability to deter the act (Barry, 1994). Though most Christians still wanted to get into heaven and viewed life on earth as transitory and unimportant, the surest route to paradise had been taken away. However, even here, the prohibitions against suicide were not absolute. When done for the right reasons—as a response to a loss of faith, personally disgraceful behavior, being captured by an enemy, or unbearable torture—suicide was still viewed as an honorable death (Farberow, 1977). A study of suicide acceptability in Korea reports that Protestants were less likely than Catholics or Buddhists to be accepting of it. The principal reason is that Protestants went to church more regularly than did Catholics and Buddhists and were more likely to claim that religion was an important part of their lives (Jung & Olson, 2014).

The Victorians sensationalized murder and dreaded and feared suicide (Gates, 1988). A suicide was culturally defined as despicable, so surviving family members did all they could to hide one. The Crown could take all the property of a suicide, and the only way to avert this catastrophe was to convince authorities that the deceased was actually insane and thus unaware of the consequences of his or her action. Clerics were enlisted to aid in the deception, because people who had intentionally killed themselves were not allowed to be buried on church property. It was customary for the corpse of a suicide to be buried at a crossroads with a stake through the heart and a heavy stone over the face so that it could not return to harm the living. The last official record of a degradation of the corpse of a suicide in England was made in 1823, but the degradation did not stop then. Bodies of suicides who had been poor during their lives or that were unclaimed were sent to medical schools for dissection and study for 50 years after that (Alvarez, 1972).

During the twentieth century, attitudes toward suicide continued to fluctuate. Some tolerance could be found among the educated, but the Christian Church remained steadfast in its opposition. Industrialization made it possible for some people to attain great prosperity, while others became dismal failures. Poverty was equated with badness, and prosperity was equated with goodness. The normlessness produced by a drastic and dramatic change in one's economic standing—especially from prosperity to poverty—was conducive to suicide (Durkheim, 1897/1951; Lehmann, 1995). This type, called *anomic suicide* by Durkheim, was caused by too-low levels of social regulation.

The rapid change in one's social situation and living conditions produced an absence of direction and focus that spilled over into a suicidal act by a desperate individual. The growth of a middle class meant that more and more families had a stake in conformity and in maintaining their status and prominence in their communities. When they could do this no longer, suicide seemed to be the only option. The stigma of suicide was only partly lessened by the predilection of authorities to define suicide as an irrational act of an individual who was suffering from severe psychological problems. The medical and the sociological emerged as the two principal paradigms for making sense of suicide.

Suicide in Different Places

People in non-Western, nonindustrialized societies tend to have a generalized horror of the wandering spirits of dead people anyway, but the fear is all that much greater if the deceased died violently (Colt, 1991). Whereas the spirit of a murdered individual is believed to have it in for only his or her killer, the spirit of a suicide is more likely—or so it is believed—to blame the entire group and to be bent on revenge of the worst kind toward the living (Fedden, 1938/1980). A person who commits suicide is generally seen as having shown an alarming indifference to others. He or she probably has put surviving family members, friends, and acquaintances in the position of shouldering the additional and difficult responsibilities that the decedent was unwilling or unable to manage when alive. It is not hard to understand how some of the anger, regret, and sorrow that the living experience in response to the suicide of one of their own could get translated into a generalized fear of the deceased.

Some groups go to great efforts to keep the wandering spirit of a suicide from causing any mischief among the living. It was customary among a Central African tribe called the Baganda to take the corpse of a suicide to a crossroads and burn it. When females passed the spot of cremation, they would hurl grass or sticks at it as a way to keep the spirit from entering their living bodies to be reborn. The Bannaus of Cambodia took the corpses of suicides far away to a corner of the forest to be buried, and the corpses of suicides in Dahomey were abandoned in the fields so that they would be eaten by wild animals. The Alabama Indians unceremoniously pitched the corpses of suicides into a river, and the Wajagga of East Africa would hang a goat in the same noose that the human had used to commit suicide, hoping that it would placate the deceased's wandering spirit. In cultures all across the world, a suicide's spirit is blamed for a host of catastrophes, such as diseases, plagues, storms, famines, droughts, and bad harvests (Colt, 1991, p. 132).

According to Balikci (1970/1989), one non-Western group with a high rate of suicide was the Netsilik Eskimo (Inuit). Like the Vikings, the Netsilik believed that the souls of individuals who died violently (and suicide qualifies) went to a paradise, one of the three afterworlds they recognized.

However, this is not the entire story because, if it were, practically everybody would have committed suicide to get to paradise. A more important factor in causing the high suicide rate was the deterioration of interpersonal relationships and the disappearance of traditional sources of mutual help and support, beginning in the 1920s. Families had left the region or been torn apart by the departure of family members, and kinship bonds had become tenuous. The availability of rifles in the 1920s made it easier for a lone hunter to kill a caribou or seal without the help of others, but the new technology produced further isolation from traditional sources of support and assistance. Men were also very jealous over their wives, and considerable tension and insecurity characterized the marital relationship.

When a Netsilik suffered a personal misfortune—sickness, injury, loss of a loved or valuable friend, depression, despair, marital discord, divorce—too few people were available to offer relief. Suicide was culturally defined as a quick road to a better existence, and people in the community rarely had the interest or inclination to stop a suicide or to help a suicidal individual find reasons to live. In the usual case, a desperate individual faced an uncertain future without the effective support of family and friends (Bergman & Dunn, 1990). Most suicidal individuals hanged themselves using animal skins; about one-third used guns, usually fired into the head; and a small number drowned or suffocated themselves. The primary reason for a suicide was an injury to, or a loss of, a loved one, followed by personal problems, such as injury, illness, or marital discord. Males killed themselves more often than did females (Balikci, 1970/1989).

A breakdown in cohesion, intimacy, and traditional sources of group support seems to be conducive to an increase in suicide, and these disrupting forces can occur anywhere. The rate of suicide can also increase significantly as a response to stresses and strains caused by outside intervention or by migration to a new territory (e.g., the slave trade in Africa or the confinement of Native Americans on reservations). Different ethnic and racial groups adjust to new cultures and to new groups of people in different ways. The accommodation to patterns of prejudice and discrimination in a host culture can cause an increase in suicide among members of an oppressed or exploited minority group (Group for the Advancement of Psychiatry, 1989). It is also true, however, that claims about high rates of suicide by members of some out-group may reflect ethnocentrism and faulty reasoning among members of the defining group (Webb & Willard, 1975).

An exploration of the attitudes in the African American community toward self-destruction shows how subcultural meanings and suicide are related (Early, 1992; Early & Akers, 1993). Other-directed violence, alcohol abuse, and drug use are understandable responses, albeit unfortunate, to the racism of U.S. society. However, these same experiences have promoted the development of a culture of resilience to factors that would otherwise result in an increase in suicide. "Suicide is the ultimate, unforgivable, and unredeemable offense. Abuse of alcohol and drugs, participation in the drug trade, and even violence, although strongly condemned, are not viewed as inexplicable, unforgivable, or unredeemable" (Early & Akers, 1993, p. 291). These social meanings of suicide make it not only unacceptable but practically unthinkable for most members of the African American community.

A study in *JAMA Pediatrics Online* (Bridge et al., 2015) reports that a change occurred in the rates of suicide for black children (ages 5 to 11) in the United States from 1993 to 2012. The rate almost doubled, going from 1.36 to 2.54 per million children, while it declined for white children (falling from 1.14 to 0.77 per million children). This was the first national investigation to find higher rates of suicide for blacks than for whites in any age group. Though suicide is rare for children, this study suggests that something happened among U.S. children that affected their suicide rates. One possibility is that changes occurred in African Americans' degree of social capital, weakening their social networks and family supports and, ultimately, black children's sense of well-being and optimism. Variations in African American suicide rates may result from the existence of weak social bonds between African Americans who go on to kill themselves, and others in their social environment (Clinard & Meier, 2016, pp. 331–332).

Obligatory Suicide

One of Durkheim's (1897/1951) more provocative observations is that suicide can occur *wherever* social integration is too high and the group becomes more important than any individual in it. An example of this type—Durkheim called it *altruistic suicide*—is the death of a soldier who jumps voluntarily on a live grenade to protect other members of the platoon. In certain times and places, altruistic suicide ceases to be optional, and some individuals are under great pressure to kill themselves or be scorned by other members of the group. These obligatory suicides are interesting in their own right, but they also show the importance of definitions and social constructions. One might ask, is not an obligatory suicide actually a murder?

A good example of obligatory suicide is the East Indian custom of *suttee* or *sati,* in which a widowed woman threw herself upon the flames of her deceased husband's funeral pyre, forfeiting her own life. It was named in honor of a heroine from Hindu mythology who committed suicide to prove her wifely devotion. The options confronting a widowed woman in some parts of Asia were very few, and none of them was particularly attractive from her standpoint. She could choose not to commit suicide and lead a miserable and unrewarding life for her remaining days, or she could leap onto the flames and receive the honor and respect of all who knew her (Roy, 1987). A widowed woman in Hindu society had no identity apart from her husband (Sharma, 1988). Marriage to a second husband was rare, and it usually meant that the woman was rejected by her own family. She might even have been blamed for her husband's death in the first place (Saxena, 1975). (The British outlawed *suttee* in all its territories in 1829, but the custom has never been entirely eliminated.)

The rewards of committing suicide, coupled with the punishments for refusing, were sufficient to propel most widowed women in those places that followed the custom of suttee to self-immolate (Rao, 1983). Even those women who were reluctant to follow their husbands into death were easy enough to manipulate. The average widow was young—in some cases no older than 10—grief stricken, and suggestible. To guarantee that she joined her husband, the bereaved widow might have been given opium, marijuana, or some other drug that would make it even more likely that she would do what she was told without complaint (Datta, 1988). By taking her own life upon the death of her husband, it proved both her devotion to him and her respect for tradition. It kept her from having to live the rest of her days as an outcast, scorned for her unmarried status, though it was no fault of her own (Eller, 2006). If the deceased was well-to-do, he would be followed in death by *several* wives, slaves, and servants. Others who felt the pinch of bereavement might also have committed suicide to be with the decedent: mother, sisters, sisters-in-law, minister, and even nurses (Thakur, 1963).

Death before dishonor was the rule to live by in "the Orient," at least among samurai warriors. The Japanese institutionalized suicide in what was called *hara-kiri* (belly slitting) or the more elegant term of *seppuku*. For centuries, it was a privilege reserved by law for the samurai (though it was outlawed in 1868). A ritualized suicide such as hara-kiri was the only way for a dishonored warrior to reclaim his honor. Sometimes, it was done to display allegiance to a fallen leader or to avoid the dishonor of a public execution (Evans & Farberow, 1988, pp. 175–176). Hara-kiri was usually done according to a precise ritual, in special surroundings, in front of a group of invited guests.

> The samurai knelt on a white hassock on a white-edged *tatami* (reed mat), facing a small white table on which lay a short sword with its blade wrapped in white paper. Taking the blade by its middle in his right hand, the samurai made an incision in the left side of his abdomen, drew the blade to the right,

and then made an upward cut. It was meritorious then to make another incision in the chest and a downward cut, allowing the entrails to spill out. (O'Neill, 1981, pp. 12–13)

Because dying could take several hours, a friend was usually close at hand to end the warrior's suffering by beheading him with a sword. The samurai's wife might choose to die with her husband by stabbing herself in the throat with a short dagger known as a *jigai*, a wedding present given to her explicitly for this purpose.

The *kamikaze* pilots of World War II were the heirs apparent to the samurai warriors. In a last-ditch effort to win the war, Japanese pilots flew their planes into ships of their enemy, killing themselves in the process (O'Neill, 1981). The young men who volunteered for the suicide missions were motivated by strong feelings of loyalty and patriotism. Doggedly pursuing victory, regardless of the chances of winning, was a Japanese tradition. The greater the prospect of defeat, the more committed the Japanese became to continuing the fight. The emperor was divine, and so was his word. Any war that he authorized automatically became a holy war, and losing it was not only unacceptable; it was unimaginable. Japanese soldiers believed that if they died heroically, they would become gods themselves and join the guardian spirits of the country at Yasukuni Shrine on Kudan Hill. The kamikazes were willing to die for the sake of their families and their emperor in the fervent belief that by sacrificing their lives, they would make a difference in the world (Naito, 1989). Put simply, a suicide mission was viewed as "a glorious way to die" (Spurr, 1981).

Revenge Suicide

Why would individuals kill themselves to get revenge on someone else? Here, Durkheim (1897/1951) helps us again. He thought that *fatalism*—a condition of overregulation and excessive discipline—produced feelings of unhappiness and hopelessness in the regulated individuals to such an extent that death was the only way out for them. For example, the rate of suicide for married women in rural China is higher than it is for single women. Though many things account for this difference (e.g., mental problems, poor relationships with parents and low levels of social support from them, increases in role conflicts and social strains), one important factor is that marriages are excessively regulated by the government, generating a fatalism that is experienced most acutely by wives (Zhang, 2010).

Durkheim did not seem to imagine that suicide could be carried out to hurt or get even with the source of one's misery or pain. Fedden (1938/1980) offers a bizarre example of a *revenge suicide*. A nineteenth-century Frenchman had been betrayed by his mistress. He was so upset over her unfaithfulness that he killed himself. He had instructed his servant to get his corpse and fashion a candle from its fat, light it, and carry it to his ex-lover. The servant did so, and it was accompanied by a letter in the Frenchman's own hand that stated that as he had burned for her in life, he now burned for her in death. She read these words by the light given off by his burning flesh (p. 45)! Douglas (1967) claimed that committing suicide as a way to get revenge on someone and to blame him or her (or them) for the death is one of the distinctive meanings of suicide in the Western world. However, Douglas was too restrictive; revenge suicide is found all across the planet.

In many non-Western societies, suicide is viewed as a good way for people to get back at others who have wronged them. Malinowski (1926) described revenge suicides among the Trobriand Islanders of the New Guinea coast. They would shinny up a palm tree, loudly name their tormenters, and then jump to their deaths. The rule was a suicide for a suicide, so the marked individual had to respond in kind (or take some effort to placate the spirit of the decedent or to compensate the decedent's family). The Tshi-speaking people of Africa believe that one person can drive another person to suicide. If a person commits suicide and blames the death on another, the named party is required by native custom to commit suicide, too (Counts, 1990, p. 95).

Revenge suicide is socially patterned (Counts, 1990). It occurs in cultures that recognize the possibility that a living individual can be held responsible for the suicidal death. This requires some ethic of shared or collective responsibility, where, for example, a husband can be blamed for his wife's misery and subsequent suicide. The culture must also provide definite mechanisms whereby the individual who kills himself or herself can clearly show who is responsible for the suicide and make the living willing to punish the responsible party. In some cases, the living come to believe that if they fail to avenge the death, they themselves will be haunted by the angry spirit of the deceased.

A revenge suicide is most likely to be successful, and the living are most likely to administer some punishment to the guilty party, if the individual commits the suicide in a public place, forewarns others of the upcoming suicide, and clearly identifies whomever is being held responsible for the death. Revenge suicides are usually done by powerless individuals, often females, who have been used and abused by people in their lives. The only way for these individuals to retaliate against those people who have hurt them, they conclude, is to kill themselves in a public way. Their hope is that they will shame their tormentors enough that these people will also want to kill themselves for all the injury that they have caused.

Sometimes, the desire to hurt others is so direct and immediate that an individual murders family members, friends, or strangers prior to taking his or her own life. Though we can't know for sure, it seems that the suicide is done so that the decedent will not have to suffer all the legal and social consequences (e.g., guilt over having killed someone) of the murderous rampage. Wolfgang's (1958) study of homicide in Philadelphia in the middle of the last century uncovered that approximately 4% of those who committed homicide ended up committing suicide. A study of murder-suicide in the United States (Langley, 2012) reported that the murderer/suicide was almost always a male who killed one or many others, usually members of his family, before taking his own life. The weapon of choice was a firearm and the murder victims were almost always females. Most murder-suicides were between two intimate partners, with a man killing his wife or female dating partner, usually because the relationship had soured, and then killing himself. Most of them were done in a home. When older people were involved in a murder-suicide, the principal factor was the declining health of the killer, the victim, or both.

Suicide Bombers

The fact that some humans are *suicide bombers*—individuals who kill themselves violently so as to kill others and destroy property to strike a blow at an enemy—would probably come as a surprise to Durkheim. The complexity of suicide in today's world is far greater than it was in nineteenth-century France, transcending any straightforward placement in Durkheim's typology based on variations in the level of social integration and social regulation. The typical suicide bomber is male, young, single, and middle class. He considers himself to be a freedom fighter or a martyr, not a terrorist, and he has decided that a suicide bombing is the only way for him to fight an enemy that possesses superior military power. The most important element of suicide bombings is to be found in their militaristic function (Kelsay, 2008, p. 228).

Suicide bombing is not a singular phenomenon (Abufarha, 2009). One type involves waging a campaign against military targets in which no possibility exists of surviving the battle. Death is a certainty, and the combatant knows it. You embark on a mission knowing *for certain* you will be killed by your enemy. An example would be the desperate, last-ditch *banzai* attacks by Japanese soldiers in World War II, human waves of charging men. Another type of suicide bombing involves an individual using suicide to attack military targets, but death is at his or her own hand (e.g., Japanese kamikazes). One other type of suicide bombing involves death by the suicide's own hand, but the targets are civilians and not military installations (e.g., the September 11, 2001, attack on the U.S. World Trade Center).

Suicide bombers embody the *Sampson complex,* in which individuals kill themselves in such a way that ensures they will be able to bring everyone else down with them. Suicide bombing reflects "the power of the powerless" to wage war against even the most fearsome adversary (Reuter, 2008, p. 78). If it is possible for 19 terrorists, armed with little more than box cutters and a seething hatred, to produce the death and destruction that they did on September 11, 2001, on U.S. soil, it is easy to see why suicide bombing is attractive to any powerless group involved in an asymmetrical war. Suicide bombers have strong ties to groups, and they are influenced by what relatives, friends, and religious leaders think about both suicide bombers and bombings in general (Atran, 2007; Reuter, 2008). Human bombs engage in voluntary acts of self-sacrifice that have (or at least *can* have) dramatic consequences (Abufarha, 2009).

It is a suicide bomber's sense of righteousness, coupled with the power that a total absence of fear of death gives to an individual, that allows us to understand why suicide bombing is being used in struggles in Chechnya, Kashmir, Kurdistan, Iran, Iraq, Pakistan, Israel, Afghanistan, Turkey, Sri Lanka, Lebanon, Indonesia, Morocco, Tunisia, Mombasa, and the United States. Parents of suicide bombers tend to share the sentiments of their suicidal children. They are proud of them and the sacrifice they have made, and they view their children as martyrs for a just and noble cause. They would be just as proud if all their children did the same thing, and their main regret may be that they have no more offspring to sacrifice to the struggle (Reuter, 2008, p. 82). Simply, the attraction of suicide bombings is that they work, are inexpensive, and are generally less complicated than other types of terrorism. They get media attention at the same time that their brutal efficiency tears at the social fabric and undermines public trust and confidence in the power of government to protect its citizens (Hoffman, 2014).

Suicide bombers consider themselves to be warriors or soldiers, a belief that both motivates and justifies their suicide missions. It is the willingness to die for a cause greater than oneself that shows in a very clear and public way that no personal interest or stake is involved (S. Holmes, 2005). Suicide bombers consider their acts to be both altruistic and moral. Female suicide bombers, though rarer than their male counterparts, interpret their suicides as a way to strike a blow against a despised enemy while empowering themselves in the face of the humiliation and disgrace that they and their families have had to endure (Bloom, 2007, 2009; Patkin, 2007). Female suicide bombers' other motives are to avenge some personal loss, to redeem the family name, or to escape a dreary life.

Not only must individuals be socially supported in their willingness to die for a cause, but an enemy must also exist that is defined as the embodiment of evil (Patkin, 2007). What this does is to make the suicide bomber into someone to model and copy. He or she is a warrior, someone whose sacrifice is even more heroic and enviable because it is against such great odds and targets such a powerful and diabolical enemy. The *Werther effect* describes the case where one person's suicide triggers other people's suicides; it is suicide by imitation. This term is based on a 1774 novel by Goethe about a spurned lover named Werther. One fateful evening, Werther sits down, writes a letter to his beloved, and then shoots himself in the head. After publication of the novel, men copied the character in the book by dressing like him (blue waistcoat and yellow vest), opening books in front of them, and shooting themselves. The novel was banned in Denmark, Germany, and Italy.

Durkheim (1897/1951) gave little attention to the influence of imitation on suicide, primarily because he viewed imitation as a psychological process that was incapable of explaining the social fact of suicide. However, suicide is at times a fad in which some individuals take their own lives because it seems like the thing to do; those who die in clusters probably would not have killed themselves if they had been isolated from others (Grigoriadis, 2007). It does seem true that a suicide by a friend—more so for females than for males—increases the likelihood of an imitative suicide because it shows that suicides are one way to handle emotional distress (Abrutyn & Mueller, 2014). Some suicide bombings seem to have a suicide-by-imitation quality. Very few suicide bombings are done by lone, marginal, desperate individuals. More often than not, terrorist organizations recruit bombers, prepare the bombs, select the targets, and may even do the initial scouting work to ensure the success of the terrorist operation (Hoffman, 2014).

The ability to define and then attach labels to disliked groups is a form of political power, making it possible for powerful groups to manufacture new realities out of old rubble. On April 12, 2002, Ari Fleischer, then–White House press secretary, offered a new term to the Washington Press Corps. It was designed to further the political agenda of the George W. Bush administration and to reconstruct the prevailing view of Palestinian suicide bombers, demonizing them even more. The new term was *homicide bombers*. Fleischer's contribution to the propaganda war was just one more piece of ammunition in the ongoing battles between Israel and Palestine. The Palestinians, wanting to glamorize suicide bombings, prefer to call suicide *bombers* by the name of "martyrs" and suicide *bombings* by the name "martyrdom operations." Arabs prefer to use the phrase "human bomb" to describe suicide bombers. Israelis, however, prefer to call them "homicide bombers" because it emphasizes their criminal, antisocial nature. The term *homicide bomber* never caught on with the U.S. public or the pundits. First of all, it is redundant (of course a bomber kills people). Second, it was not really inflammatory enough to show the disdain with which terrorist bombings are held in the West. (A term such as *exploding excrement* or *scatological suicide* would have been better in this regard but too offensive to too many people to become popular.)

Suicide, Stigma, and Responsibility

Blame and Loss

Suicidal deaths offer fertile ground for feelings of social discomfort and embarrassment among relatives and friends of the deceased. Individuals who must cope with the suicidal death of a family member or friend may find that outsiders make the healing process more difficult. Many people continue to hold negative views of suicide, and they may blame relatives or even friends of the decedent for what happened. The general social context is far less supportive when the death is a suicide than when it results from a murder, accident, or natural causes; even those people who wish to offer aid and comfort to surviving family members may find themselves paralyzed by a lack of clarity over just what should be done or said (Calhoun & Selby, 1990).

Compared to other kinds of death, suicides precipitate more guilt, a greater search for what caused the death, and lower levels of social support (Sudak, Maxim, & Carpenter, 2008). Although public attitudes have become more accepting of suicide with the passage of time, attitudes have not changed so much that suicide is generally or widely viewed as a good and noble way to die (Clinard & Meier, 2016). Suicide continues to be viewed as either unnecessary or unacceptable, and attitudes toward suicide tend to be generally negative (though the strength of the condemnation is conditioned by characteristics of the suicide itself).

People who attempt but do not complete suicide (i.e., who commit parasuicide) may be condemned because they are considered to be responsible for self-centered attempts at attention getting. People who successfully complete suicide may be dishonored and stigmatized because what they did seems cowardly and selfish. The decedent may be viewed as an individual who expected others to bear the burden that he or she could not or would not bear, while being indifferent to the survivors' pain of losing a loved one. Even though suicide may be painless for the one who does it, this is rarely true for surviving family and friends, whose pain may be acute.

Sadness over the loss of a loved one may be the principal emotion experienced by surviving family and friends, even while many additional emotions can be present, such as anger, shock, denial, disbelief, grief, guilt, depression, anxiety, self-blame, and confusion. Survivors might automatically assume that people who attempt or complete a suicide are mentally ill or insane. Some suicidal individuals do have a history of mental illness or substance abuse, but this is not the primary reason for most suicidal deaths (Granello & Granello, 2007; Sudak et al., 2008). Suicide is an act, not a disease, so what might work to cure a physical illness (e.g., drugs) is woefully inadequate when it comes to a complex happening like suicide (Szasz, 2007). Making it harder for individuals to take their own lives seems to be an effective way to reduce rates of suicide. Where guns are both available and accessible, suicide rates are higher. (Men are more likely to kill themselves with guns than are women.) This is one of the reasons that suicide rates are higher in Montana and Wyoming than they are in New York and New Jersey ("An Awful Hole: Suicide in America," 2015). Likewise, when it is easier to down many pills all at once because they are stored in the same bottle, rather than individually wrapped in blister packs, overdoses and suicides increase (pp. 21–22).

Understandings about what happened so that the death can be fit into some comprehensible whole or pattern of meaning are particularly difficult to ascertain with suicide. The problem is that it is not easy to convince oneself that the suicide of a family member or friend was inevitable or that the individual was unaware of what he or she was doing. Surviving family and friends may be inclined to believe that the death could have been prevented and that the suicidal person could have been helped by some kind of counseling. If the death had been from an accident or natural causes, it could more easily have been defined by surviving individuals as unavoidable or inevitable (Henslin, 1970). When it is viewed as an intentional, deliberate act, surviving family and friends may be more inclined to feel some guilt and responsibility for the death.

Excusing and Justifying Suicide

Jacobs's (1967) analysis of suicide notes shows that some of the same processes that survivors go through in trying to understand and deal with a suicide of one of their own are also found among those individuals who are on a pathway to the commission of suicide. Suicidal individuals, too, must come to attach some positive meaning to the suicidal act and neutralize conventional forces of social control that strongly forbid suicide. They must reconcile their views of themselves as good and decent persons—trustworthy—with the fact that they are planning with full intent to violate the sacred trust of life that suicide represents.

Individuals who are contemplating suicide typically first convince themselves that their problems in living are not of their own making, attaching blame to others or to external situations over which they have no control. They then conclude that their problems are unsolvable but not from any lack of effort on their part. Finally, they convince themselves that death is the only option for them, a view that is more likely if these individuals have character structures marked by rigidity and inflexibility. They transform a *choice* to die into a *commandment* to die, removing all voluntariness and deliberation from it. Non-suicidal alternatives come to be viewed increasingly as impossibilities. After convincing themselves that no reason exists to feel guilty or embarrassed about a self-inflicted death, they are prepared to kill themselves (Rodgers, 1995).

A discussion of adolescent suicide reaffirms Jacobs's suggestion that rigid cognitive structures and poor coping skills make suicide a more likely event. Adolescents who are unable to come up with practical solutions for their problems are more likely to fixate on suicide as an option (Granello & Granello, 2007). Changing technologies and access to cell phones, which may bring users in contact with websites that convey personal attacks that are cruel and often untrue (e.g., Ask.fm, an anonymous website often used to make abusive comments about people). This can lead to increases in depression and despair. A fragile and insecure individual may conclude that suicide is the only way out of an intolerable situation. A social world interpenetrated by electronic networking characterized by backstabbing, meanness, cruelty, and duplicity may not seem to be the kind of world worth living in for many adolescents (Dickey, 2014).

The shame and stigma attached to suicide can sometimes deter it, and their absence can make suicide more likely. Gladwell (2000) observes that suicide among young males in Micronesia has become ordinary and commonplace, a ritual of adolescence to which no stigma or shame attaches. One teenager killed himself because his father yelled at him, and another took his own life because his parents refused to buy him a graduation gown. Another hanged himself because his brother criticized him for making too much noise. Some adolescent males committed suicide because they saw their girlfriends chatting with other males or because their parents would not give them enough money to buy beer. Stigma, however, is a double-edged sword. While it can deter some suicides, its existence can be an additional burden for surviving family members and friends to carry.

Whatever religious proscriptions exist in regard to suicide are easily neutralized by an individual who is serious about it. The individual simply convinces himself or herself that no sin will have occurred because no choice exists, the suicide being an act of necessity or even sacrifice (Jacobs, 1970). If this belief is coupled with the individual's certainty that he or she will finally be rid of life's problems, it is easy enough to understand how religion and suicide can go together. The prospect of a hell complicates the picture, but not too much. The suicidal individual can simply conclude that hell promises fewer problems than continuing a wretched life on Earth. In one fell swoop, religion makes it possible for an individual contemplating suicide to be able to convince himself or herself that the present troubles will be gone and that things will be better for all eternity in an afterlife.

Assisted Suicide

The issues of blame and stigma are the bedrock of the controversy in the United States over assisted suicide. An important event in the battle over it was the involvement of Dr. Jack Kevorkian in the death of Janet Adkins. Ms. Adkins was a happily married, 54-year-old mother of three grown sons, who was afflicted with Alzheimer's disease. She wanted to end her own life before the degenerative disease made it impossible for her to take care of herself. She had tried to get help from physicians in Portland, Oregon, the city where she lived, but everyone she asked refused to help her die.

Adkins learned of Kevorkian in 1989, and she even saw him explain his procedures for assisted suicide on a national television show. Her objective was to die with dignity and without pain, and Kevorkian seemed to be the only professional who could help her. She sent him records of her medical history, and he wanted to know more. She and her husband flew from Portland to Royal Oak, Michigan, where Kevorkian lived. After talking to Ms. Adkins, Kevorkian was convinced that she was rational and that she was suffering from an irreversible physical condition. He decided to help her die. Her final exit came on June 4, 1990, in a rather unceremonious setting: the back of Kevorkian's Volkswagen van, parked in a Michigan campsite. When she was ready, Adkins pushed a button, and Kevorkian's suicide machine did the rest: One drug put her to sleep, and another drug killed her. Ms. Adkins's husband awaited news of her death at a nearby hotel because his wife would not allow him to be present at the actual death scene (Humphry, 1991).

How assisted suicide is framed is critical in determining the levels of support for it. Successful presentation of an assisted suicide as self-deliverance from an irreversible terminal illness, as a dignified death, or as a simple medical procedure makes it much more likely that it will be viewed favorably than if it is called suicide, lethal injection, or euthanasia (Worsnop, 1995). Support rises if safeguards exist—clear and consistent ones that make assisted suicides fully voluntary and fully informed on the part of those choosing to die—and if the people are truly suffering from an incurable, irreversible, painful disease (Cosculluela, 1995). The Roman Catholic Church remains steadfast in its opposition to physician-assisted death. The U.S. Supreme Court has taken the position that an individual has no constitutional right to end his or her own life and that it is up to the states to make this decision for their citizens (Ball, 2012). (As of this writing, physician-assisted suicide is legal in the states of Washington, Oregon, California, New Mexico, Vermont, and Montana through their right-to-die laws.)

Because of the secrecy and mystery that surround physician-assisted suicide, a great fear exists that this type of suicide could be carried out for an individual who was merely tired of living or depressed, rather than a person who was terminally ill. Adkins had played tennis with one of her sons a few days before her death (although she was too mentally incapacitated to keep the score). Some critics of assisted suicide are fearful that a *right* to die could easily evolve into an *obligation* to die (Hendin, 1995a). How do we know or recognize an incurable disease when we see one? Once active euthanasia is firmly in place in a society, it could become more likely that it will be called into service to get rid of people who are not terminally ill and who have not given their full and informed consent. It might be used to get rid of the friendless or despised, for example.

Most patients who seek physician assistance in the termination of life typically do not do it to avoid unbearable pain. (The U.S. medical profession is skilled at pain control.) The principal reasons are constant nausea, discomfort, difficulty breathing, incontinence, or increasing dependence on others. Those who seek a self-assisted death are individuals who do not want to be a burden to their family and friends, desiring to remain independent and self-reliant up until the end of life. They want to control how they die as much as possible, just as they control how they live (M. Taylor, 2007).

On December 3, 1990, Kevorkian was charged with the murder of Janet Adkins. A few weeks later, all charges were dismissed because of lack of evidence that Kevorkian had planned her death and intentionally caused it. An additional factor was that Michigan had no law directly forbidding an individual from helping another to commit suicide. In 1992, the Michigan legislature passed a bill that banned assisted suicide, and the Michigan Supreme Court decided that assisted suicides could be prosecuted as felonies. However, Michigan prosecutors still found it difficult to get Kevorkian convicted of a crime. Five times they tried, and five times they failed. The trials ended either in acquittals or, in one instance, a mistrial.

On April 13, 1999, however, Kevorkian was sentenced to 10 to 25 years in prison for the murder (second degree) of 52-year-old Thomas Wouk, who had suffered from Lou Gehrig's disease (amyotrophic lateral sclerosis). Kevorkian had not only supplied the drugs used to kill Wouk, but he had also injected the drugs himself into the man. What's more, he had recorded the whole thing on film. With all this evidence, prosecutors were able to charge Kevorkian with murder and make it stick. He was released from prison on June 1, 2007, after serving about 8 years of his sentence, vowing never to assist or advise on any more suicides. Battles over assisted suicide show that the core of the controversy is not really over how or when an individual should die, but about who should decide. (Kevorkian passed away on June 3, 2011, at the age of 83, in a hospital in Royal Oak, Michigan. His death was painless, and no artificial attempts were made to prolong his life.)

A new or at least newer face on the "death with dignity" position was Brittany Maynard. On November 1, 2014, at the age of 29, the woman ingested legally prescribed barbiturates—she was living in Oregon at the time, having moved from California to take advantage of Oregon's Death With Dignity Act—to end her suffering from a terminal brain cancer that she had been diagnosed with in January. She emerged as a strong and effective spokesperson for rational suicide. Maynard appeared in several videos where she described her debilitating illness and her deteriorating health. As the day of her final exit neared, she celebrated her life and the joys of living, not her impending death. She had the opportunity and resources to be able to enjoy time with her loved ones and to be able to visit some of the places she always wanted to visit (e.g., the Grand Canyon). Her joy in living was a testimony to her and serves as an enduring inspiration to others.

Conclusions

At some times, in some places, suicide has been admired and has received widespread social support. At other times, in other places, suicide has been condemned and treated as evidence of immorality, disease, or antisocial tendencies. Suicides are one possible outcome of interpersonal relationships and social situations, and they reflect different patterns of social organization, ethnic and racial concentrations, and cultural beliefs. These social factors can have direct and important influences on suicide that are separate from an individual's levels of hopelessness, helplessness, or depression.

Death is symbolized in many different ways, and death of the physical body does not always denote death of the soul or spirit. Historical and cross-cultural variations in the symbolization of suicide show that contradictions exist regarding death and what it means. Before people frame a death as a suicide, they must put together what can be ambiguous bits of information into some consistent whole that will satisfactorily explain what happened, why, and who is responsible.

Suicide may be a response to normlessness, social isolation, and low levels of integration, or it may be a cultural prescription (e.g., *suttee* or *hara-kiri*). Durkheim identified four types of suicide that were correlated with changes in the two social factors of social integration and social regulation. When integration gets too low, egoistic suicide becomes more likely, and when it gets too high, altruistic suicide becomes more likely. When social regulation gets too low, anomic suicide is more likely, and when it gets too high, fatalistic suicide is more likely.

Suicide may be a way for a powerless individual to get revenge on some disliked individual or group. It may also be used as a military strategy in an asymmetrical war, the function it provides for suicide bombers. Because of the stigma that still attaches to suicide in U.S. society, an individual contemplating it may try to convince himself or herself it is both necessary and unavoidable so as to diminish, or remove entirely, whatever stigma is attached to it. Controversies over assisted suicide are founded on determinations about how necessary it is and who should have the power to decide when and how an individual should die.

References

Abrutyn, S., & Mueller, A. S. (2014). Are suicidal behaviors contagious in adolescence? Using longitudinal data to examine suicide suggestion. *American Sociological Review, 79,* 211–227.

Abufarha, N. (2009). *The making of a human bomb: Ethnography of Palestinian resistance.* Durham, NC: Duke University Press.

Alvarez, A. (1972). *The savage god: A study of suicide.* New York: Random House.

American Psychiatric Association. (2000). *Diagnostic and statistical manual of mental disorders* (4th ed., text rev.). Washington, DC: Author.

American Psychiatric Association. (2013). *Diagnostic and statistical manual of mental disorders* (5th ed.). Washington, DC: Author.

An awful hole: Suicide in America. (2015, January 31). *The Economist, 414,* 21–22.

Atran, S. (2007). The moral logic and growth of suicide terrorism. In T. Badey (Ed.), *Violence and terrorism 07/08* (10th ed., pp. 26–35). Dubuque, IA: McGraw-Hill.

Balikci, A. (1989). *The Netsilik Eskimo.* Prospect Heights, IL: Waveland. (Original work published 1970)

Ball, H. (2012). *At liberty to die: The battle for death with dignity in America.* New York: New York University Press.

Barry, R. (1994). *Breaking the thread of life: On rational suicide.* New Brunswick, NJ: Transaction Publishers.

Bergman, B., & Dunn, J. (1990, June 4). Northern agony. *Maclean's,* p. 14.

Bloom, M. (2007). Many women suicide bombers are sexual abuse victims. In P. Connors (Ed.), *Suicide* (pp. 102–111). Detroit, MI: Greenhaven Press.

Bloom, M. (2009). Female suicide bombers: A global trend. In T. Badey (Ed.), *Violence and terrorism 08–09* (11th ed., pp. 144–149). New York: McGraw-Hill.

Bridge, J. A., Asti, L., Horowitz, L. M., Greenhouse, J. B., Fontanella, C. A., Sheftall, A. H., et al. (2015, May 18). Suicide trends among elementary school-aged children in the United States from 1993 to 2012. *JAMA Pediatrics Online First.* Retrieved June 27, 2015, from http://www.archpedi.jamanetwork.com/article.aspx?articleid=2293169

Brown, M. (1996). *Emergency! True stories from the nation's ERs.* New York: Villard.

Calhoun, L., & Selby, J. W. (1990). The social aftermath of a suicide in the family: Some empirical findings. In D. Lester (Ed.), *Current concepts of suicide* (pp. 214–224). Philadelphia: Charles Press.

Canetto, S. S., & Lester, D. (1995). Women and suicidal behavior: Issues and dilemmas. In S. S. Canetto & D. Lester (Eds.), *Women and suicidal behavior* (pp. 3–8). New York: Springer-Verlag.

Clinard, M., & Meier, R. (2016). *Sociology of deviant behavior* (15th ed.). Boston: Cengage Learning.

Colt, G. H. (1991). *The enigma of suicide.* New York: Summit.

Cosculluela, V. (1995). *The ethics of suicide.* New York: Garland.

Counts, D. A. (1990). Abused women and revenge suicide: Anthropological contributions to understanding suicide. In D. Lester (Ed.), *Current concepts of suicide* (pp. 95–106). Philadelphia: Charles Press.

Datta, V. N. (1988). *Sati: A historical, social and philosophical enquiry into the Hindu rite of widow burning.* Riverdale, MD: Riverdale.

Dickey, J. (2014, July 7). The antisocial network: Inside the dangerous online world kids can't quit. *Time, 184,* 40–45.

Douglas, J. (1967). *The social meanings of suicide.* Princeton, NJ: Princeton University Press.

Droge, A. J., & Tabor, J. D. (1992). *A noble death: Suicide and martyrdom among Christians and Jews in antiquity.* San Francisco: HarperSanFrancisco.

Duhigg, C. (2007). Attempted suicide can be a lucrative economic decision. In P. Connors (Ed.), *Suicide* (pp. 68–71). Detroit, MI: Greenhaven Press.

Durkheim, É. (1951). *Suicide: A study in sociology* (J. Spaulding & G. Simpson, Trans.). New York: Free Press. (Original work published 1897)

Early, K. (1992). *Religion and suicide in the African-American community.* Westport, CT: Greenwood.

Early, K., & Akers, R. (1993). "It's a white thing": An exploration of beliefs about suicide in the African-American community. *Deviant Behavior, 14,* 277–296.

Eller, J. (2006). *Violence and culture: A cross-cultural and interdisciplinary approach.* Belmont, CA: Thomson/Wadsworth.

Evans, G., & Farberow, N. (Eds.). (1988). *The encyclopedia of suicide*. New York: Facts on File.

Farberow, N. (1975). Cultural history of suicide. In N. Farberow (Ed.), *Suicide in different cultures* (pp. 1–15). Baltimore: University Park Press.

Farberow, N. (1977). Suicide. In E. Sagarin & F. Montenino (Eds.), *Deviants: Voluntary actors in a hostile world* (pp. 503–570). Morristown, NJ: General Learning Press.

Farberow, N. (1988). Introduction: The history of suicide. In G. Evans & N. Farberow (Eds.), *The encyclopedia of suicide* (pp. vii–xxvii). New York: Facts on File.

Fedden, H. R. (1980). *Suicide: A social and historical study*. New York: Arno. (Original work published 1938)

Gaines, D. (1990). *Teenage wasteland*. New York: Random House.

Gates, B. T. (1988). *Victorian suicide: Mad crimes and sad histories*. Princeton, NJ: Princeton University Press.

Gladwell, M. (2000). *The tipping point: How little things can make a big difference*. Boston: Little, Brown.

Goffman, E. (1974). *Frame analysis: An essay on the organization of experience*. New York: Harper & Row.

Granello, D., & Granello, P. (2007). *Suicide: An essential guide for helping professionals and educators*. Boston: Pearson/Allyn & Bacon.

Grigoriadis, V. (2007). Suicide can be a fad among teenagers. In P. Connors (Ed.), *Suicide* (pp. 87–91). Detroit, MI: Greenhaven Press.

Group for the Advancement of Psychiatry. (1989). *Suicide and ethnicity in the United States*. New York: Brunner/Mazel.

Hazelwood, R., Dietz, P. E., & Burgess, A. W. (1982). Sexual fatalities: Behavioral reconstruction in equivocal cases. *Journal of Forensic Science, 27,* 763–773.

Hendin, H. (1995a). Assisted suicide, euthanasia, and suicide prevention: The implications of the Dutch experience. In M. Silverman & R. Maris (Eds.), *Suicide prevention: Toward the year 2000* (pp. 193–204). New York: Guilford.

Hendin, H. (1995b). *Suicide in America* (Expanded ed.). New York: Norton.

Henry, J., & Short, A. (1954). *Suicide and homicide*. New York: Free Press.

Henslin, J. (1970). Guilt and guilt neutralization: Response and adjustment to suicide. In J. Douglas (Ed.), *Deviance and respectability: The social construction of moral meanings* (pp. 192–228). New York: Basic Books.

Hoffman, B. (2014). The logic of suicide terrorism. In J. L. Feldkamp (Ed.), *Theory and politics of terrorism* (pp. 377–386). San Diego, CA: Cognella.

Holmes, R., & Holmes, S. (2005). *Suicide: Theory, practice, and investigation*. Thousand Oaks, CA: Sage.

Holmes, R., & Holmes, S. (2009). *Profiling violent crimes: An investigative tool* (4th ed.). Thousand Oaks, CA: Sage.

Holmes, S. (2005). Al-Qaeda, September 11, 2001. In D. Gambetta (Ed.), *Making sense of suicide missions* (pp. 131–172). New York: Oxford University Press.

Humphry, D. (1991). *Final exit: The practicalities of self-deliverance and assisted suicide for the dying*. Eugene, OR: Hemlock Society.

Hutson, H., Anglin, D., Yarbrough, J., Hardaway, K., Russell, M., Strote, J., et al. (1998). Suicide by cop. *Annals of Emergency Medicine, 32,* 665–669.

Jacobs, J. (1967). A phenomenological study of suicide notes. *Social Problems, 15,* 60–72.

Jacobs, J. (1970). The use of religion in constructing the moral justification of suicide. In J. D. Douglas (Ed.), *Deviance and respectability: The social construction of moral meanings* (pp. 229–251). New York: Basic Books.

Jung, J. H., & Olson, D. V. A. (2014). Religion, stress, and suicide acceptability in South Korea. *Social Forces, 92,* 1039–1059.

Kelsay, J. (2008). The "just war" debate, Islamic style. In R. Heiner (Ed.), *Deviance across cultures* (pp. 227–231). New York: Oxford University Press.

Langley, M. (2012). *American roulette: Murder-suicide in the United States* (4th ed.). Washington, DC: Violence Policy Center. Retrieved April 6, 2015, from http://www.vpc.org/studies/amroul2012.pdf

Lehmann, J. (1995). Durkheim's theories of deviance and suicide: A feminist reconsideration. *American Journal of Sociology, 100,* 904–930.

Lindsay, M., & Lester, D. (2004). *Suicide-by-cop: Committing suicide by provoking police to shoot you.* New York: Baywood.

Littlewood, R., & Lipsedge, M. (1987). The butterfly and the serpent: Culture, psychopathology and biomedicine. *Culture, Medicine, and Psychiatry, 11,* 289–335.

Lowery, S., & Wetli, G. (1982). Sexual asphyxia: A neglected area of study. *Deviant Behavior, 4,* 19–39.

Malinowski, B. (1926). *Crime and custom in savage society.* London: Routledge/Kegan Paul.

Maris, R. (1981). *Pathways to suicide: A survey of self-destructive behavior.* Baltimore: Johns Hopkins University Press.

Naito, H. (1989). *Thunder gods: The kamikaze pilots tell their story.* Tokyo: Kodansha.

O'Neill, R. (1981). *Suicide squads.* London: Salamander.

Papke, D. R. (1987). *Framing the criminal.* Hamden, CT: Archon.

Patkin, T. (2007). Explosive baggage: Female Palestinian suicide bombers and the rhetoric of emotion. In T. Badey (Ed.), *Violence and terrorism 07/08* (10th ed., pp. 170–179). Dubuque, IA: McGraw-Hill.

Plass, P. (1995). *The game of death in ancient Rome: Arena sport and political suicide.* Madison: University of Wisconsin Press.

Pope, W. (1976). *Durkheim's Suicide: A classic analyzed.* Chicago: University of Chicago Press.

Poppel, F. van, & Day, L. H. (1996). A test of Durkheim's theory of suicide—without committing the ecological fallacy. *American Sociological Review, 61,* 500–507.

Rao, A. V. (1983). India. In L. Headley (Ed.), *Suicide in Asia and the Near East* (pp. 210–237). Berkeley: University of California Press.

Reuter, C. (2008). Suicide bombing: The power of the powerless. In A. Thio, T. Calhoun, & A. Conyers (Eds.), *Readings in deviant behavior* (5th ed., pp. 77–86). Boston: Pearson/Allyn & Bacon.

Rodgers, L. (1995). Prison suicide: Suggestions from phenomenology. *Deviant Behavior, 16,* 113–126.

Roy, B. B. (1987). *Socioeconomic impact of sati in Bengal and the role of Raja Rammohun Roy.* Calcutta, India: Naya Prokash.

Saxena, R. K. (1975). *Social reforms: Infanticide and sati.* New Delhi, India: Trimurti.

Sharma, A. (1988). *Sati: Historical and phenomenological essays.* New Delhi, India: Motilal Banarsidass.

Shneidman, E. (1985). *Definition of suicide.* New York: Wiley.

Spurr, R. (1981). *A glorious way to die.* New York: Newmarket.

Sudak, H., Maxim, K., & Carpenter, M. (2008). Suicide and stigma: A review of the literature and personal reflections. *Academic Psychiatry, 32,* 136–142.

Szasz, T. (2007). Collegiate suicide prevention programs may increase the number of suicides. In P. Connors (Ed.), *Suicide* (pp. 207–211). Detroit, MI: Greenhaven Press.

Taylor, M. (2007). The legality of Oregon's physician-assisted suicide law is a victory for patients and doctors. In P. Connors (Ed.), *Suicide* (pp. 133–138). Detroit, MI: Greenhaven Press.

Taylor, S. (1990). Suicide, Durkheim, and sociology. In D. Lester (Ed.), *Current concepts of suicide* (pp. 225–236). Philadelphia: Charles Press.

Thakur, U. (1963). *The history of suicide in India: An introduction.* New Delhi, India: Munshi Ram Manohar Lal Oriental Publishers.

Turvey, B. (2009). Autoerotic sexual asphyxia. In P. Adler & P. Adler (Eds.), *Constructions of deviance: Social power, context, and interaction* (6th ed., pp. 451–462). Belmont, CA: Thomson/Wadsworth.

Unnithan, N. P., Huff-Corzine, L., Corzine, J., & Whitt, H. P. (1994). *The currents of lethal violence: An integrated model of suicide and homicide.* New York: State University of New York Press.

Uva, J. (1995). Review: Autoerotic asphyxiation in the United States. *Journal of Forensic Sciences, 40,* 574–581.

Webb, J., & Willard, W. (1975). Six American Indian patterns of suicide. In N. Farberow (Ed.), *Suicide in different cultures* (pp. 17–33). Baltimore: University Park Press.

Whitt, H. P. (2010). The civilizing process and its discontents: Suicide and crimes against persons in France, 1825–1830. *American Journal of Sociology, 116,* 130–186.

Wolfgang, M. (1958). *Patterns in criminal homicide.* Philadelphia: University of Pennsylvania Press.

Worsnop, R. (1995, May 5). Assisted suicide controversy. *CQ Researcher, 5,* 393–416.

Wright, R. K., & Davis, J. (1976). Homicidal hanging masquerading as sexual asphyxia. *Journal of Forensic Sciences, 21,* 387–389.

Zhang, J. (2010). Marriage and suicide among Chinese rural young women. *Social Forces, 89,* 311–326.

Zimmerman, G. M. (2013). Does violence toward others affect violence toward oneself? Examining the direct and moderating effects of violence on suicidal behavior. *Social Problems, 60,* 357–382.

8

Sexual Diversity

Sex, Gender, and Sexuality

Because so little is known about what people around the world actually do (or have done) in bed (or in a hut, tent, igloo, cave, or the great outdoors), most statements about human sexual diversity and deviance are speculative and contentious. Studies that purport to tell us what really happens in our sexual lives really do not. They offer little more than biased information, coupled with a few anecdotes, about some of the sexual experiences that some people were willing to share with researchers (Carter & Sokol, 1989). These pictures or portraits of human sexuality are ripped from the social context that defines them and gives them meaning, so they are stripped of much of what makes them sexual in the first place. For example, a special report was issued by the Gallup organization on the number of U.S. adults who define themselves as lesbian, gay, bisexual, or transgender (Gates & Newport, 2012). To date, it is the largest single study of its kind (with a sample of 121,290 individuals). Sexual identity, however, was tapped with but a single question: "Do you, personally, identify as lesbian, gay, bisexual, or transgender?" (asked in a phone interview between June 1 and September 30, 2012). The researchers reported that 3.4% of adults said that they are lesbian, gay, bisexual, or transgender, with more females (3.6%) than males (3.3%) so identifying.

Even if all the respondents were being honest on the survey, which seems unlikely given the way the data were collected and the personal nature of the question, the data are still not representative enough to give anything close to a satisfactory picture of human sexual identities. As the authors of the report honestly confess, their results can only be understood as responses by adult Americans who were willing to publicly identify themselves as part of the LGBT community when asked about it on a survey. A 2013 survey of 33,557 individuals, between the ages of 18 and 64, by the Centers for Disease Control and Prevention in the first-ever large-scale government study of sexual orientation reported that 1.6% of the respondents identified as gay or lesbian, and an additional 0.7% claimed they were bisexual. Most of the respondents (96.6%) defined themselves as straight (Somashekhar, 2014).

While the term *sex* is principally about biological placement as male or female, *gender* is about attitudes and feelings in regard to masculine and feminine (Moon, 1995; Tewksbury, 1994). Sex reflects the operation of chromosomes and body chemicals (testosterone or estrogen) on the development of anatomical structures (e.g., ovaries, testes, uterus, scrotum, vagina, clitoris), along with the development of secondary sex characteristics (e.g., body hair, breasts, voice pitch, menstruation). Gender, however, refers to the psychological aspects of being masculine or feminine, as well as the social statuses, roles, and cultural prescriptions and proscriptions for acting, thinking, and feeling in sex-appropriate ways. Alcohol consumption, smoking, wage differences, and wearing panty hose are more about gender than sex.

Sex and gender, of course, are not separate from one another, and interactions exist between them. An infusion of testosterone may produce increased levels of masculinity, and exercise can change the degree of muscularity and hormone levels. Sexuality, though related to both sex and gender, is separable from them both. *Sexuality* refers to those experiences that lead to erotic arousal and a genital response. Erotic arousal is a state of feeling "turned on," which produces a wish to continue with the relationship and its central activity; genital response is a physiological response to some stimulus that is defined as sexual (e.g., erection, ejaculation, or vaginal lubrication) (Reiss, 1986, p. 21).

Gender is continually constructed and reconstructed, made and transformed, in the context of our relationships to others (West & Zimmerman, 2000; Wijngaard, 1997). It is not a "thing" a human has as much as it is a constellation of actions and presentations that one *does* in anticipation of the actual or imagined reactions of others. Sexual identities are interactional social accomplishments more than they are inborn traits (Pfeffer, 2014). We all become gendered in a gendered society, and as societies and cultures change, gender does, too (Chou, 2012; Martin, 1998; Ridgeway, 2011).

When parents teach gender to their children, they not only express their own beliefs about how their children ought to "do" gender, but they also must take account of prevailing gendered social structures and what other people think. Most parents do not want their children to be viewed as odd or strange for gender bending, even if the parents themselves find it appropriate. Parents who have an enlightened view of sexual equality and want gender equality between their sons and daughters may still find that they cannot ignore broader sociocultural pressures or currents that discourage gender bending of one form or another (Kane, 2012). Some countries (e.g., Sweden) have moved much closer to full gender equality in child-rearing practices and other aspects of family life, as well as in the worlds of work and politics, than have other countries (Abend, 2013).

Sexuality: A Sociocultural Understanding

Body, Brain, and Sexuality

One view of the relationships among sex, gender, and sexuality gives genes the preeminent position. According to this approach—going by names such as *evolutionary biology, evolutionary psychology,* or *sociobiology*—practically all sexuality, human and nonhuman, is designed to increase the reproductive success of an individual creature or a species. Anything that makes reproductive success more likely will prosper over anything that does not (Ridley, 1993). This approach generates a rather dismal appraisal of human sexual experiences. Men, the story goes, try to acquire power and resources and then use them to attract women who will bear them offspring to ensure that their male genes are passed on to future generations. Simply put, wealth and power are the means to attaining women, and women are the road to genetic immortality. The story continues that women search for men with abundant resources who will be able to support and protect them and their children. Women are portrayed as genetically determined to be more selective and choosy in picking mates, as well as more faithful to them, and men are portrayed as preferring to spread their genes around (Buss, 1994).

Human sexual customs are related to human biological characteristics, but exactly how is a matter of dispute. It is customary to assert that biological factors are the cause and that social and sexual relationships are the effect, but this interpretation of the direction of causality is too one-sided (Fine, 2010; Jordan-Young, 2010). Sexual relationships and other human experiences change the human body and brain in all kinds of ways. When men are actively involved in sexual relationships, their testosterone levels increase dramatically, much more than if they achieve sexual release through solitary acts of masturbation (Kemper, 1990). Men may actually have higher sperm counts in response to the possibility that their female mates are being unfaithful (Small, 1995). The human brain is not only an organ that causes things to happen. Its structure and function are also dependent on what happens in an individual's social and sexual relationships.

Theories that suggest differences in gender are caused by differences in the brain are almost always based on the idea that the left and right hemispheres develop differently in males and females. It is usually hypothesized that a male brain is more *lateralized* (the hemispheres are specialized in their abilities), whereas a female brain is more *symmetrical*, because her corpus callosum (the part of the brain that joins its two sides) is larger and contains more fibers. So, the story goes, because women have more and better interconnections between brain hemispheres than men do, women excel in talk, feelings, intuition, and quick judgments. Wolf (2012) even goes so far as to insist that the neurology of the vagina and the biochemical processes in the brain are "virtually inseparable," forming one integrated network (p. 5). It may be true that males and females have different brains and that these account for male–female differences. However, the research on brain differences between males and females is often of limited value, because it reaches questionable conclusions based on small samples. Sometimes it does little more than reaffirm preexisting sex and gender stereotypes.

Jordan-Young's (2010) analysis of more than 300 studies, published between 1967 and 2008, led her to conclude that the evidence for masculine and feminine brains—known collectively as *brain organization theory*—is mostly smoke and mirrors.

> [E]vidence that human brains are hormonally organized to be either masculine or feminine turns out to be surprisingly disjointed, and even contradictory— and the stakes involved in prematurely promoting the theory to a "fact" of human development are high. (p. 3)

Our sexual behaviors and our personal outlooks are far more complex than the distinction between right brain and left brain would allow (Tavris, 1992). The range of differences *within* a sexual category (i.e., male or female) is always greater than the differences *between* the "average" male and the "average" female (Kimmel, 2000). More similarities than differences exist between boys and girls, and males and females are more like close neighbors than they are residents of different planets (Friedman, 2013; Kimmel, 2000). The expedition to find brain differences as the root cause of every sex and gender difference misses (or refuses to consider) the interactive effects, overlaps, and blurred or nonexistent boundaries that exist between males and females.

The interest in possible brain differences between males and females has spilled over into the study of brain differences between heterosexuals and homosexuals. Is there a homosexual brain? LeVay (1993) conducted some research that suggests there is. He autopsied hypothalamuses from 19 homosexual men who had died from AIDS and 16 heterosexual men, 6 of whom had died from AIDS. Brains from six women were also autopsied, but their sexual orientation was unknown. LeVay reported that his male specimens had a thickening in brain cells not found in females, and that heterosexual men had thicker brain cells than homosexual men. LeVay concluded that sexual orientation is directly related to brain structure. However, the differences in brain structure that he found, *if* valid and reliable, may simply have been caused by the impact of the AIDS virus on brain chemistry and not the impact of brain structure on sexual orientation (Byne, 1994).

Researchers at the Karolinska Institute in Sweden conducted brain scans of 90 gay and straight males and females. They started with the familiar premise that heterosexual males have brain hemispheres that are lateralized and heterosexual females have brain hemispheres that are symmetrical. They reported from their research that the two hemispheres of the brains of gay *men* resembled the brains of straight *women* more than they did the brains of straight men; the brains of gay *women* looked more like the brains of straight *men* than those of straight women (Park, 2008). Much like LeVay, the researchers concluded that it is the anatomy of the brain that determines sexual orientation. This is the twenty-first–century version of the view—it has lasted long beyond its shelf life—that gays are trapped in the body of the wrong sex, which explains why they are sexually aroused by same-sex individuals.

Problems galore may be found in the claim that gays and straights have different brain structures that account for their sexual orientation, beyond its oversimplification of a complex human experience. The most fundamental problem, however, is that it doesn't fit enough of the facts of human sexuality to be of much value. Some humans do conclude that they are trapped in the body of the wrong sex, and some may even wish to change their anatomy (i.e., their sex) to be consistent with their gender. However, these individuals—called *transsexuals* or *transgenderists*—strongly resist any suggestion that they are homosexual. Homosexuals are individuals who are attracted to members of the same sex; they are not (in the case of males) feminine beings trapped in masculine bodies or (in the case of females) masculine beings trapped in feminine bodies.

The most charitable—and scientifically defensible—view of research on brains and sexual orientation is that the role of the brain in sexual orientation is a complex one, far more than is implied by the male brain–female brain distinction. We really don't know much about why *heterosexuals* are aroused by members of the *opposite* sex, and, likewise, despite the voluminous writings and research, the issue of gay sexuality is also a mystery. Children who eventually come to define themselves as gay, regardless of gender, do report being aware of their sexual attraction to same-sex individuals early in life, and they also exhibit a greater number of gender-bending behaviors and traits during childhood than do their soon-to-become heterosexual peers (Jenkins, 2012). However, nobody has yet provided a convincing explanation for how something as complex and dynamic as sexual orientation could be determined by brain structure or any other innate characteristic (Fine, 2010; Jenkins, 2012; Jordan-Young, 2010; Lewontin, 2000; Lewontin, Rose, & Kamin, 1984). Though certain biological markers must be present for an individual to be sexual—some brain characteristics and some features of sexual orientation are related—social factors are also implicated in the making of sexual orientation and gender. Sexual orientation has prenatal and postnatal causes that work together to produce an orientation that gets more stable over time (Money, 1988).

Sexual Variance and Sexual Scripts

Regardless of the biological or psychological roots of sexual impulses—and these certainly do exist—the additional dimension of society and culture cannot be ignored. Even if we did have a comprehensive and thoroughly satisfying explanation of why some humans are heterosexual and some are not, this would still not tell us why human sexuality is so relative. Homosexuality at one time and place is condemned and homosexuals are persecuted; at another time and place, it is deviant for *only* the "passive" partner; at still another time and place, it is a *required* act for both partners (i.e., males), ensuring that they will both develop appropriate levels of masculinity (Carrier, 2007).

The terms *homosexual* and *homosexuality*, like *heterosexual* and *heterosexuality*, are culture-bound and historically specific, and they can mean different things to different groups and at different points in time. Most certainly they are not homogeneous categories of human experience, and it is unlikely that they include humans who are all alike in attitudes, behaviors, and conditions (Jordan-Young, 2010). Whatever makes heterosexuality more "normal" than homosexuality—if it is—is not intrinsic to any particular kind of sex act between partners. It has to do with who does it, when, where, why, and how; it also matters a great deal who knows about it and what they think and do about it.

Because most societies are so strongly committed to encouraging heterosexuality, exclusive homosexuality is usually strongly discouraged for both males and females. However, a wide range of alternative forms of sexuality do exist at most times and places. When we consider the wide range of persons, experiences, and objects that humans have found sexually arousing, it should come as no surprise that some people in every society have found members of the *same* sex more attractive and sexually arousing than they have members of the opposite sex (Shneer & Aviv, 2006). Gays are continually in a process of constructing and reconstructing their collective identity, both in terms of what it is (or should be) and its relationship to the dominant or majority group(s) (Taylor, Kimport, Van Dyke, & Andersen, 2009). Scheitle and Hahn (2011) report that U.S. states with the highest levels of religious fundamentalism (e.g., evangelical Protestantism) are the most antagonistic to homosexuals and their interests.

No important and enduring human act (e.g., eating or sleeping) or social relationship (e.g., dating, marriage, or child rearing) is going to be ignored by human beings and left entirely either to biology or chance. It will be scripted by human groups, and these scripts will be incorporated into human culture, passing from generation to generation. This is true with human sexuality. *Sexual scripts* have been constructed to tell individuals the appropriate and inappropriate ways of acting, thinking, and feeling in regard to things sexual. Each social group will usually have a main sexual script that is known to most of its members (Gagnon & Simon, 1973), along with additional sexual scripts that are known to only a relative few (Laumann, Gagnon, Michael, & Michaels, 1994). With sexual deviance, as with perhaps no other type of activity, we see that people go beyond the prevailing cultural and subcultural scripts and invent their own (Tewksbury, 1996). Human sexuality always involves interplay, the expectation and experience of compromise, as well as competition and cooperation (Laumann et al., 1994). Increases in sexual freedom can mean that a great deal of confusion exists over just what sexual behaviors should be enjoyed and to what degree (Kelly, 2011).

Some of the dominant themes in U.S. culture and society—practicality, competitiveness, individualism, consumerism—can interpenetrate the American way of sex and set the foundation for too great a degree of emotional emptiness in our most intimate relationships. According to Schur (1988), the American way of sex has become too impersonal, coercive, and self-centered. Casual sex is defined as a problem by its critics because it seems to be too irresponsible and too self-indulgent. It is also defined as a problem because it is correlated with other things that are viewed as troubling: illegitimate births, teenage pregnancy, AIDS, sexually transmitted diseases, marital instability, divorce, and drug use. A letter sent to Dear Abby from a 23-year-old woman makes the point. She tells the advice columnist that she has been on birth control pills for 2 years. The expense of the drug has gone up, and she thinks her boyfriend should share in the cost. However, she tells the columnist what the real problem is: "I don't know him well enough to discuss money with him" (Van Buren, 1981, p. 242).

Adolescents who have sexual intercourse in the context of relationships that are casual and superficial fare much worse than do abstainers on several educational outcomes. They are found to have lower grade point averages and weaker attachments to school, while having more truancies, problems in school, and negative school sanctions (B. McCarthy & Grodsky, 2011). A study drawn from surveys of U.S. undergraduates at 21 four-year colleges and universities, suggests that "hooking up" (meeting for casual sexual encounters) among these students was both normal and normative (though hooking up could have involved only kissing it usually involved more) (Bearak, 2014). By their senior year, only about a fifth of the women (23%) and about a third of the men (30%) reported they had abstained from sexual intercourse. For students who reported that they had engaged in sexual intercourse during their college years, 57% of the freshmen and 66% of the seniors claimed it had occurred outside of an exclusive relationship (p. 490). This means that most of the students who have had sexual intercourse during their college years claim that they experienced it in the context of casual relationships.

Narrow-mindedness or lack of empathy is what usually dooms efforts by adults to regulate adolescent sexuality (Barcelos & Gubrium, 2014). Sex education classes usually accomplish little because they use a single-minded (and often simpleminded) framework in which the principal component is an "abstinence only" message. A study of teen pregnancy across 75 U.S. high schools uncovered that pregnancy rates were lowest in those schools that had formalized a norm against adolescent pregnancy that was defined by most of the students as reasonable and legitimate (Mollborn, Domingue, & Boardman, 2014). It is possible to be *both* sexually responsible and sexually active, or at least that is one of the conclusions from a study of Latina adolescents in Chicago (Garcia, 2012). For this sample of women, what was central to their definition of themselves as both respectable and responsible sexual beings is that they practice safe sex.

Fields's (2008) study of sex education classes in three North Carolina schools (one private and two public) indicates that these classes—and others by implication—are irrelevant to students' sexual lives. They are too long on discussions of human anatomy and sexual activities and too short on examinations of the sociocultural factors that so powerfully impact and influence humans' sexual lives and experiences. Classrooms, Fields insists, should be organized in such a way that an atmosphere exists in which teachers and students can and do listen to one another so that students better understand personal sexual desire, cultural sex-role expectations, interpersonal power, and sexual inequalities. In the absence of a more comprehensive understanding of social and cultural dimensions of human sexuality, knowledge of how to put on a condom or check for sexually transmitted diseases will be of little value.

A study of close to 50 parents, mostly mothers, from a city in Texas indicates that their views of their own teenagers' sexual experimentations and sexual experiences were not entirely correct (Elliott, 2012). They believed their own kids were more innocent and less sexually experienced than the teenagers actually were. Even parents who had evidence that their teenagers were sexually active (e.g., pregnancy scares) still did what they could to exonerate their offspring for their sexual trespasses. They figured that their kids must have been seduced by a culture soaked in sexual images or by scurrilous predators who had not been taught correct behavior by their own parents or who were under the sway of unruly sex drives.

The Curious Case of the Berdache

Some Native American groups have a sex/gender status in addition to male or female called *berdache*. Almost always, a berdache is an anatomical male who combines parts of the masculine and feminine gender into a unique role (Williams, 1986). Berdaches move freely between men's and women's groups because of their unique status, and berdachism is not always permanent. Some men are berdaches for a while but eventually change and act like regular men. Transgender statuses, like that of the berdache, show us quite clearly that the division of the human race into two mutually exclusive categories of male and female or masculine and feminine fails to convey adequately the full range of possibilities with regard to sex, gender, and sexuality. (Societies in many parts of the globe—Oceania, Africa, India, Siberia, Asia, and Australia—have a gender category comparable to the berdache.)

Early Native American groups were some of the most egalitarian on Earth. This sexual equality meant that females were of great importance to the life of the community, and their contributions—social, economic, and political—were valued as highly as those of males.

> Because women had high status, there was no shame in a male taking on feminine characteristics. He was not giving up male privilege or "debasing" himself to become like a woman, simply because the position of women was not inferior. (Williams, 1986, p. 66)

Where women have high status, no loss of esteem accrues to a male who moves in a feminine direction. If anything, he may be viewed as the possessor of exceptional qualities. Berdaches are able to transcend the confines of a two-gender worldview, and they are respected for it. Their secure position in the social life of the community practically ensures that they will enjoy both personal and social success.

It would be incorrect to conclude that the berdache status is universally respected or that berdaches are uniformly honored. However, some of the hostility directed at berdaches by their fellows reflects the impact of early Europeans and their Christian ideals on Native Americans. These early Europeans tended to be intolerant and inflexible when confronted with any sexual practices or gender roles that were different from their own. The persecution of homosexuals and "sodomites" made a great deal of sense to these visitors to the New World. It gave them one way to establish—in their own minds, at any rate—their superiority over other people, while convincing themselves that theirs was the only natural and proper way. By the thirteenth century in Europe, the suppression of homosexuality was well underway, and by the fourteenth century, male sodomy was viewed throughout Europe as a capital crime. Sodomites, homosexuals, and pederasts were lumped together with heretics, Jews, and lepers, all of whom were branded as extreme threats to Christianity and Christians. The "abominable sin" of sodomy was suppressed wherever it was found (Moore, 1987, pp. 93–94).

A clear—and fascinating—illustration of the challenges that gender benders must deal with when their society has no institutionalized third gender role for them to occupy is found in the life of a jazz musician named Billy Tipton. This musician was born a female, in Oklahoma City, December 29, 1914. Her birth name was Dorothy Lucille Tipton, but in 1933, she changed her name to Billy and began dressing as a man, portraying herself as a *male* jazz musician (Middlebrook, 1998). Although a few close family members knew about Billy Tipton's gender bending, most of the people he met did not.

In January 1989, Billy Tipton's health had deteriorated so much that he was too weak to do much of anything for himself, but he refused to go to a hospital. One of his adopted sons (William), who had been caring for his father, phoned his mother (Kitty) to ask for assistance when Billy collapsed. (She and Billy had been divorced for almost 10 years, and she had remarried.) Kitty instructed William to call 9-1-1 and have Billy taken to a hospital. When the paramedics arrived, they placed the unconscious Billy on the floor of his trailer so that they could search him for a heartbeat. It was then that they—and a very shocked son—learned that Billy Tipton was, indeed, a biological woman. Billy Tipton died in the emergency room of Valley

General Hospital, in Spokane, Washington, on the day of his collapse without regaining consciousness. Tipton had lived as a man from the age of 19 until his death at the age of 74, having been a successful cross-dresser, gender bender, and jazz musician for over 50 years.

The brutal economic conditions of the 1930s and the sexism of the U.S. music industry worked together to demand a dramatic response from Dorothy Tipton. Playing music required much more from her than the ability to play notes on an instrument. It required that she wear trousers and play music as a man. Billy eventually developed all the social and personal fronts—the accoutrements—that were needed to present a façade of heterosexual masculinity, and he was considered to be a sharp-dressing, warm-hearted, good-humored individual. He was good enough as a musician to form his own trio (the Billy Tipton Trio) and good enough as a gender bender to be married to several different women, as well as being a father to three adopted sons.

Dorothy Tipton passed as Billy for most of her life in order to do something that she loved to do in an unequal, sexist society. Sometimes, however, things happen to humans that make it problematic for them to be placed into either one of the two dominant sex categories. One possibility is that they lack the "normal" anatomy that is used as a primary cue for classifying individuals as male or female. The usual term for individuals such as this is *hermaphrodite* or *intersexed,* an individual who possesses identifiable characteristics of *both* male and female. In the United States, the usual way this sexual ambiguity is resolved is that representatives of the medical profession determine which sex category fits the child best (i.e., male or female) based on what kind of genitals the newborn is deemed to possess.

Usually, things are routine. A newborn is inspected shortly after birth and easily and confidently placed into one of the two available sex/gender categories. A phallus that is long enough to be called a penis, along with the presence of a scrotum, signifies that a boy has entered the world, and a phallus that is small enough to be called a clitoris, along with a vagina, signifies that a girl has been born. (The penis and the clitoris develop from the same body tissues, as do the scrotum and vagina.) However, in a relatively small number of births, inspection of the newborn's genitals leads to the conclusion that the phallus is indeterminate (i.e., too large for a girl but too small for a boy). The child then exists in a limbo world and is defined as a hermaphrodite or an intersexed individual. A newborn could also have external genitals of one sex (e.g., penis/scrotum) but the internal sexual structures of the opposite sex (e.g., ovaries). These individuals, more difficult to classify from a quick physical examination, are also deemed to be hermaphrodites. If a newborn's sex/gender is impossible to determine from an external examination, more extensive tests can be done if the society has the technology (e.g., chromosomal analysis or hormonal evaluation).

Most of the medical personnel who regularly deal with intersexuality are inclined to define it as a liability that can and should be corrected to make the child "normal" and to make the child's development less difficult. This usually requires them to determine which sex best fits the child and then to reconstruct the child's body and indeterminate genitals through surgery and/ or drugs. Sometimes this medical strategy has the desired effect, but sometimes it does not. Some hermaphrodites have been irreparably damaged by being assigned to a sex category to which they never adjust. The possibility of mistakes like this occurring justifies a different strategy in dealing with the intersexed. This alternate approach *absolutely* rejects the claim that hermaphroditism is a disorder that should be "fixed" through medical intervention, and it also rejects the idea that the two-sex, binary model of sex describes a natural and necessary division of the human race (Weinberg, Williams, & Laurent, 2005). Advocates of this approach are inclined to view any effort to surgically reconstruct the genitals of an intersexed child as a form of genital mutilation and a human rights abuse.

Humans are wired but not programmed for gender in the same way that they are wired but not programmed for language (Money & Tucker, 1975). Gender development reflects the joint influence of both innate factors and environmental learning. Money and Tucker hold that a *gender identity gate* is open during the early days of life and stays that way for a time. As long as the "gate" is open, gender is flexible and open to change, even though gender identity will become more rigid as the days pass (p. 90). They relate the case of twin boys in the 1960s, one of whom experienced a bizarre and ultimately tragic event, to demonstrate the nature of gender.

> A young farm couple took their sturdy, normal, identical twin boys to a physician in a nearby hospital to be circumcised when the boys were seven months old. The physician elected to use an electric cauterizing needle instead of a scalpel to remove the foreskin of the twin who chanced to be brought into the operating room first. When this baby's foreskin didn't give on the first try, or on the second, the doctor stepped up the current. On the third try, the surge of heat from the electricity literally cooked the baby's penis. (pp. 91–92)

After the botched circumcision of the boy, whose name was Bruce Reimer, he was taken to the burn ward. His parents, Ron and Janet Reimer, were summoned to the hospital. When they arrived, Dr. Huot, the physician who had injured their son, told them about the "accident," a rather charitable and self-serving way to describe what he had done to their child. When Ron and Janet were allowed to see their son, what they saw was unforgettable.

The child's penis was blackened like a piece of charcoal. Over the next couple of days, the penis dried up and then broke away in pieces. It was not long before nothing remained of the organ (Colapinto, 2000).

The Reimers found a glimmer of hope after seeing a television interview with the sexologist Dr. John Money at Johns Hopkins. They arranged to meet with Dr. Money early in 1967, and he quickly developed an interest in the case. He was interested in part because he cared about the Reimers and what had happened to their son, but he also saw the case as a test of his theories of the gender identity gate. Here was a child with an identical twin brother (to serve as a comparison), who was normal at birth but who had been irreparably damaged through physician error. Money's career could benefit enormously from his involvement with a case like that of the Reimers. He laid out the options for the parents, nudging them toward the conclusion that it would be best to change their "son-without-a-penis" into their "daughter-with-a-vagina." Money assured the parents that Bruce's young age meant that he would accept the new gender and pattern his erotic interests and activities accordingly. Money emphasized that gender reassignment for their son would work best if it were started immediately.

Ron and Janet Reimer decided to follow Money's advice. Shortly after their return to their home in Winnipeg, Canada, they came up with a new name for the child—Brenda Lee Reimer—and they started treating Brenda like a girl and as if she had always been one. Her hair was allowed to grow long, and she was dressed in feminine clothing. Brenda was given toys appropriate for girls, and in all ways possible she was encouraged to be feminine. At 22 months, she was taken back to Johns Hopkins where she was surgically castrated. Both testicles were removed (bilateral orchiectomy), the ducts that would have carried sperm to the urethra were tied off, and the scrotal tissue was used to make external genital structures. More extensive surgery would be needed to construct a vaginal opening and canal. Hormone treatments would promote breast development, create a widening of the pelvis, and suppress both hair growth and a masculine voice. Intensive therapy sessions by trained professionals would add to the efforts of her family to erase any memories of the child's life as a boy and to get her to live as a female. At the appropriate time, additional surgery would be done to enhance Brenda's feminine appearance. No one could know, of course, how things would turn out for this family. Any predictions would have to be guarded because the case was so unique.

Brenda, according to photographs, looked the part of a pretty, brown-eyed, brown-haired girl. However, according to those who knew her, that's as far as her femininity went. When participating in the activities of childhood, she acted like a typical boy. The toys she preferred were those of her brother, and she used her girl toys to play boys' games. She used her jump rope to tie up people or to whip them; the sewing machine that she was given as a present was totally ignored. Brenda even insisted on standing to urinate, a position that meant the urine would shoot directly out and get all over the toilet seat. She went as far as to sneak out into an alley so she could urinate in a standing position without making a mess. Despite the family's intensive efforts, Brenda never felt she was a girl. Even her regular visits with John Money at Johns Hopkins, her surgeries, and the drugs she was given to feminize her anatomy did little to change her mind. She was not a girl and never would be, no matter what anyone said. She found the physical changes produced by the feminizing drugs to be very embarrassing (i.e., her developing breasts and the accumulation of fat on her hips).

On the afternoon of March 14, 1980, when Brenda was 14 years old, her father picked her up from school and drove her home. In the family's driveway, he broke down in tears as he told her the details of the botched circumcision. Brenda's primary feeling was one of relief. She finally understood why she felt the way she did. Brenda decided that she would no longer live as a female. The first thing she did was select a new name. Thinking her birth name, Bruce, a name for "geeks and nerds," she came up with two possibilities, Joe or David, and let her parents make the final decision. "Brenda" became "David." Second on the agenda was to go public with the news. In August, a week after he turned 15, David told his extended family that he was no longer Brenda (and never had been). Next, he had to get his female form changed. After receiving injections of testosterone, he sported peach fuzz on his face and a few hairs over an inch in length. He later had a painful double mastectomy. A month before his sixteenth birthday (July 2, 1981), David had surgery to construct male genitals. A penis was crafted from tissue and muscles on the inside of his thighs, and an artificial urethra and testicles were fashioned out of plastic and placed in his reconstructed scrotum. David was very pleased with the results.

In 1988, David's brother introduced him to Jane Fontane, a divorced woman and mother of three. The two hit it off, and they started to date regularly. On September 22, 1990, approximately 2 years after they were introduced, David and Jane were married at Regents Park United Church in Winnipeg. David continued to struggle, unsuccessfully, with what had happened to him. He eventually lost his job and separated from his wife. He lost most of his life savings in a questionable golf shop investment. After three unsuccessful attempts at suicide, David Reimer finally put an end to his suffering. On May 4, 2004, at the age of 38, David Reimer sat alone in a car and shot himself in the head. (His twin brother had also killed himself, in 2002.)

Despite the way that life turned out (and ended) for David Reimer, the case should not be taken as indisputable proof that sexuoerotic identity is formed in the womb. As Brenda, David's sexual interests and views were continually explored and relentlessly examined by adults who were bent on uncovering any hint or trace of lingering masculinity and eliminating it. Brenda was repeatedly given physical exams and questioned incessantly about her sexual interests and views. She was even forced to simulate sexual intercourse ("dry humping") with her brother, supposedly to help her develop a female role and overcome her sexual inhibitions (Jordan-Young, 2010). Though Brenda was fully clothed during the simulated sexual intercourse, it might very well have been traumatic enough that it failed to achieve its intended objective of making Brenda embrace femininity. The trauma for the child of this unrelenting effort to feminize her as "all girl" might be what best explains Brenda's distaste for femininity.

One routine complaint by the intersexed themselves is that they believe too much significance is given to the "power of the penis" to determine how decisions are made about sex assignment and surgical reconstruction (Kessler, 1998). Most sexologists and medical personnel believe that a lack of male genitals means that an individual will be better off being raised as a female (Weinberg & Williams, 1994). Yet, the situation of the intersexed is not understood adequately by focusing on what anatomical structures they have or lack. It is their feeling of not fitting in, of not being like everyone else, that leads them to seek medical assistance to change their anatomy. The way that intersexed children are treated is a matter of time and place. The ancient Greeks tolerated them; Romans found them disgusting and destroyed them; the Navajo respected them; and a tribe from eastern Africa (the Pokot) defined them as mistakes, either to be kept or thrown away in the same fashion that one might treat a chipped coffee cup (Geertz, 1975).

Intersexed individuals are critical of the separation of the world into two mutually exclusive, non-overlapping categories of male–female or masculine–feminine (M. Holmes, 2009). They both resent and challenge the medicalization of their condition, and they refuse to look at intersexuality as a disease to be "cured" or "corrected" through surgery and gender reassignment (Greenberg, 2012). Kessler's (1998) intersexed respondents defined *their* happiness in terms of increased societal acceptance of them and of their genital anomalies. Trans activists (such as actress Laverne Cox or Caitlyn Jenner, the latter an Olympic gold medalist and reality-TV star whose birth name was Bruce Jenner) have been able to present themselves in such a way that public attitudes have become more accepting, and transgenderism has become more mainstream (Steinmetz, 2014).

The position of the Intersexed Society of North America (ISNA) is that intersexed children should be allowed to wait until they are both old enough and mature enough to make an informed decision about gender reassignment that will be best for them. This may mean that these intersexed persons will live their entire lives completely free from *any* surgical alteration. A central objective of ISNA is to make it possible for the intersexed to live physically unaltered in a society that is understanding and accepting of them (Weinberg et al., 2005).

Sexual Differentiation and Sexual Asymmetry

Double Standards

Sexologists and physicians in the United States in the early twentieth century took it for granted that the world was naturally divided into two, mutually exclusive categories of masculine and feminine or of male and female, and that heterosexuality was more normal than homosexuality. They did what they could to convince everyone that what they believed was true (Birken, 1988). This rigid view of sexual differentiation offered sexologists and physicians abundant riches. It allowed them to seize control of the sex–gender–sexuality complex, deciding what was normal and what was not. They could then devise and promote "fixes" or "cures" for the sex-related problems that they had had a pivotal role in defining and interpreting. This approach to sex, gender, and sexuality, anchored heavily on notions of innateness and naturalness, offered advantages to these early sexologists and physicians that a more dynamic, relativistic view never could (Irvine, 1990).

Any system of sexual differentiation that divides the world into two categories that are construed as mutually exclusive is almost always coupled with the tendency to prize some characteristics and condemn others. This socially constructed asymmetry is then used by the dominant group to maintain its dominance by continuing to suppress and subdue members of the opposite group and what they are and do (Kimmel, 1996; Spain, 1992). One of the more enduring double standards or asymmetries is between males and females, with things "female" almost always being considered not as valuable as things "male" (Boryczka, 2012; Marsden, 2012). Gender is a frame through which people are defined; differentiated; and then partitioned into statuses in the family, the world of work, and other institutions in the social world (Ridgeway, 2011; Roychowdhury, 2014).

In some places on Earth, every female child undergoes an extreme and traumatizing mutilation of her genitals. It is known as circumcision, genital alteration, genital cutting, or—the most accurate term—*female genital mutilation* (Mackie, 1996). This procedure is done most often on a girl between ages 2 and 9, but in some places (e.g., Ethiopia or the Sudan), it has been done to females no more than a few days old (Dorkenoo & Elworthy, 2007). The young girl is grabbed and held down by several adults until the cutting is complete. Sometimes, the only body part that is amputated is the clitoris in a procedure called *clitoridectomy,* usually done by untrained and perhaps unskilled individuals (Saadawi, 1982). At other times, the procedure is a more radical one, called *infibulation.* All the genital organs—clitoris and portions of the labia—are cut away with a knife, a razor, a pair of scissors, or even a sharp rock. The remaining flesh is then sewn together with a sharp needle, and the female's legs are bound together for many weeks to allow the skin to heal. A small hole for the passage of urine and menstrual blood is all that remains (Burstyn, 1997). Beyond the violence and betrayal this mutilation evidences to the child is the possibility of infection, infertility, and even death (Dorkenoo & Elworthy, 2007). Africa is the region where the custom is most frequent, but it is also found in parts of South America, Southeast Asia, and the Middle East (Ziv, 1997).

The custom of female genital mutilation is kept alive principally by cultural beliefs that terrible consequences will befall a female who does not undergo the procedure. One belief is that an uncircumcised clitoris will grow so large that it will drag on the ground. Another is that uncircumcised females will be unruly, oversexed, unclean, childless, and unmarriageable (Burstyn, 1997). The Bambara of Mali believe that a man will die if his penis comes in contact with the clitoris during sexual intercourse, and in Nigeria, some groups believe that a child will die if his or her head brushes against the mother's clitoris during the birthing process. All of these beliefs are, of course, not based on reality, but the people who practice genital mutilation are caught in a *belief trap:* No one is brave enough to risk the costs of what might happen if the procedure is not performed (Mackie, 1996, p. 1009).

In some societies, male genitals may be mutilated, too, through piercing, cutting, or inserting foreign objects into them. The most frequently occurring male genital alteration is *circumcision,* a practice that may have started during the Stone Age (Gregersen, 1983). In circumcision, the foreskin of the penis is removed, a practice that is almost always justified by claims that it will improve a man's personal hygiene. *Castration,* another form of male genital alteration, is a procedure in which one or both testicles are removed. The Khoi, a native people of southwestern Africa, used to remove one testicle from all males (called *hemicastration* or *semicastration*) with the goal of preventing the birth of twins, which was considered a very bad omen (Gregersen, 1983, p. 104). Male genital alteration and female genital alteration, however, are different social events, principally because of differences in the cultural justifications for them. Rarely (or never) will a male be circumcised or castrated in order to make him more attractive to a woman or in order to make him more marriageable.

Sexual Identities and Social Inequalities

Sexual asymmetry is not confined to male and female categories. It is found almost anytime and anywhere that mutually exclusive categories are created. A study of the imaging of prostitution in nineteenth-century Canada shows the relational and asymmetric nature of the social construction of deviance (Ball, 2012). The images of the prostitute varied from time period to time period, but each new image of Prostitute was a reflection of her opposite, Ideal Woman. Each time the image of Ideal Woman changed, an accompanying change in the image of Prostitute was not far behind.

In nineteenth-century Canada, man was economic and woman was domestic, a situation paralleled in the United States (Gregersen, 1983). While woman was not considered the equal of man, one type of woman *was* elevated above all other *women*: the Angel or Saint of the Household. Her feminine opposite was the Fallen Woman, embodied in the image of the Prostitute, who symbolized all the imperfections that had been avoided by the Angel or Saintly Woman. Prostitution was constructed as sin and, like all sin, was seen as a result of moral imperfection and personal weakness.

Female activists at this time in Canada worked to spread their view that the problem of women was men. If true, this meant that prostitutes were more sinned against than sinning. Prostitution came to be understood less in moral terms and more in political ones. Women were viewed as having been forced into prostitution by ruthless men, so prostitution was reconstructed as "white slavery." Demands for governmental intervention and control of it increased.

The final dichotomization came when the Ideal Woman was constructed as the Nurturing Mother, and the Prostitute was constructed as intrinsically pathological. The Prostitute was defined as embodying the traits of hypersexuality, immorality, and impulsivity; she was defined as lacking any maternal instincts. The reconstruction went so far as to declare that the Prostitute was not a woman at all. Her incessant and inexorable sex drive meant that she was genetically closer to man than woman.

In the United States, Nevada is the only state that permits legalized prostitution (and not in every county). The lynchpin of this world of impersonal sex is the *illusion* of intimacy, one more commodity to be peddled. Postmodern flesh peddlers have learned how to package physical intimacy and what seems to be authentic emotional engagement. The women use a warm smile and engaging eye contact to seduce clients who really need little coaxing (Brents, Jackson, & Hausbeck, 2010). Men who frequently use prostitutes may be searching for intimacy, but it is actually an intimacy demarcated by its casualness and superficiality. (It is possible, Kipnis [2010, p. 2] concludes, that what men are actually paying prostitutes for is their willingness to leave after the sex is over.)

When men purchase sex from women, the relationship reflects broader concerns of consumption, financial gain, status, self-affirmation, hypermasculinity, and femininity (Hoang, 2014). Social structural conditions play a powerful role in shaping and directing the experiences of prostitutes and their customers (Weitzer, 2012). The legal sex industry in Nevada is inextricably entwined with U.S. capitalist development, and its organization and structure change all the time (Brents & Hausbeck, 2012). Brothels are part of Nevada's tourist economy and a central feature of the state's prosperity. The brothels reaffirm the state's image as a sexual playground, where freedom and pleasure coexist in a climate of discretion and privacy. ("What happens in Vegas stays in Vegas.") Social acceptance of prostitution is most likely when it is conceptualized as "sex work" rather than "human exploitation" or "trafficking" (Cao & Maguire, 2013, p. 201; Chin & Finckenauer, 2012).

A study of exotic dancers shows how nudity and seminudity, along with seductive sex talk, can be used to earn income, but these women lose both power and self-respect in the process (Deshotels, Tinney, & Forsyth, 2012). Although exotic dancers do have some control over what they do and how much they work, thereby increasing personal wealth, they are still tightly boxed in by rigid expectations regarding how they should look and how they should express their sexuality (Hardy, Kingston, & Sanders, 2010). Their provocative dancing and overall sexiness does give them a measure of interpersonal power over their customers, but it is a hollow victory. The money tap only flows if they are willing to do whatever their patrons will financially reward. Exotic dancers must embrace a thoroughly other-directed view of their bodies and their sexual expressions and be willing to do and be whatever the market demands (Pasko, 2009; Stone, 2014).

Logan (2010) found that when it comes to gay male sex in the escort service, customers place a premium on masculinity, a penetrative sexual position ("topping"), aggressive sexual behavior, and muscular physiques. Generally, the closer a gay male sex worker is to embodying an image of hegemonic masculinity, the more coveted he is and the more handsomely he is paid. This spells substantial disadvantage for anything that hints of femininity, such as receptive sexual positions ("bottoming"); submissiveness; or a body build that is viewed as too fat, too thin, or too soft. Black men in the gay escort service do particularly well, because gay men are willing to pay the most for escorts whom they deem to fit the image of a large, muscular, aggressive, dominant, penetrating, insatiable sex brute. Walby's (2012) study of 30 men in the male-to-male escort service in England (London), Canada, and the United States reports that it is possible for customers and their escorts to form deeper and more meaningful intimate relationships, even though they start out as simple exchanges of sex for money.

The term *effeminate* and its derivatives (e.g., "sissy," "faggot," "fag," "girly-man") symbolize what is unattractive and unacceptable for men to do or be. Men, regardless of sexual orientation, are expected to eschew any traces of femininity in their own personal style of acting and being. This may be easier for straight men than for gay men because of the influence of the effeminacy effect. The *effeminacy effect* is the belief, both stigmatizing and insulting, that gay men are in fact more feminine than straight men and that homosexuality is what men turn to who have failed at masculinity. This belief has played a role in how gays have forged their own sexual identities (Hennen, 2008).

Gray (2009) studied gay identity construction (i.e., queer identity) in parts of rural Kentucky. Unlike their counterparts in urban metropolises, these rural gays and lesbians were more inclined to utilize a program of *circulation* rather than *separation* to show their opposition to conventional heterosexuality. Gray's research shows that the "we're here and we're queer" approach, based on gay congregation, visibility, and open confrontation with straights, is not the only way to establish a gay identity (Ghaziani, 2011). A mobile, fluid process was used by Gray's sample to express their queer identity while remaining sensitive to local community standards in regard to propriety, decency, and respect of others. Bible Belt gays (those in the socially conservative southeastern and south-central United States)—some of them—experience prejudice and discrimination, being forced by the actual or imagined hostility of others to maintain secrecy and seclusion about their sexual lives and orientations (Barton, 2012). Staying in the closet is not a uniform, homogenous, invariant state of being for individuals who work to hide their sexual orientations, and coming out is also a dynamic, relational, relativistic process (Guittar, 2014).

The Myth of the Universal Turn-On

Human Variability and Sexual Arousal

Though humans can separate everyday reality from erotic reality, experiencing them as two distinct realms, components of one realm can easily intrude on the other. We may alternate between the two without intending to do so, and the sexual can impact the everyday and vice versa (Davis, 1983). It is also true that human sexual deviance overlaps with human sexuality so much that what is true about sexuality in general also tends to be true about deviant sexuality. There need be no intrinsic differences between sexual deviance and sexual conformity. All that is required for sexual deviance to exist is for some group to forbid certain kinds of sexuality and condemn those individuals who participate in them.

For some people, the principal fascination with sexuality that is exotic, bizarre, or maybe even perverted is that it upsets or alarms representatives of conventional society. According to Davis (1983), it is the fact that this sexuality is impure that makes it worth doing in the first place. Woody Allen's character in the film *Everything You Wanted to Know About Sex* expresses just this sentiment when he states that the only time sex is dirty is when it's done right. Although most types of sexual deviance have no specific procreative function—though they may be a prologue to reproductive acts—this fact alone is insufficient to account for their deviancy. Sex for pleasure is an integral part of human sexual experiences, and even some nonhuman primates seem to participate in sexuality for purposes other than reproduction (de Waal, 2005).

Biology influences sexual expression in many ways. For example, no amount of cultural conditioning or socialization is going to make it possible for a human to orgasm indefinitely. Physical limits exist regarding how many sexual episodes one can have in a day, a year, or a lifetime. We can predict that some things are more likely than other things to turn people on, and we will be right more often than not. This is true, but it's not the whole truth. Humans can gain access to an intricate world of sexual experiences, sexual objects, and sexual activities that is unique because it offers so much diversity and variation (Chodorow, 1994). Expanding sexual freedom and a culture of eroticism can lead to new forms of sexual pleasure and self-expression, along with new sexual identities and the formation of new sexual communities (Seidman, 1991).

Biological sexual urges and drives are harnessed by social and cultural factors (Gagnon & Simon, 1970). Goode and Troiden (1974) made an observation over 40 years ago that is still relevant today:

> Sexual behavior is not dictated by the body, not by our animal chemistry, but by the mind, by our human relationships, by civilization, by what has historically come to be accepted as good or bad—in short, by convention. We do what we do in bed because we have learned to do so. And what we do *could* have been otherwise; by growing up surrounded by different customs, we would have been completely different sexual beings. (p. 14)

The degree of variability and flexibility in human sexual experiences surpasses what is found in *all* nonhuman animal species, even the more sexually playful ones. Human sexuality is *distinctly* human.

Bullough's (1976) comprehensive exploration of sexual variance throughout history makes it quite clear that wherever human sexuality is found, so is human sexual deviance. In addition, what qualifies as sexual deviance varies considerably from place to place and time to time:

> Some [societies] emphasized chastity and tolerated intercourse only in a marriage relationship with procreation specifically in mind, others had a double standard in which almost everything was tolerated for the male but not for the female, and still others tolerated, if not encouraged, almost any sexual activity, there being all kinds of variation in between. (p. 19)

Even kissing, defined as an enjoyable and necessary part of lovemaking in some cultures, is seen as aberrant and unnatural in other societies (Tiefer, 1978). What one group defines as the epitome of sensuality, sophistication, and normalcy, another group brands as obscene, dangerous, and in need of immediate eradication (Beisel, 1993).

Humans may not yet have imagined the boundaries of their sexual potential, let alone exhausted all of its possibilities (Sanger, 2010). They are continually finding new sexual turn-ons, using the same old body parts but in new ways, finding new sexual paraphernalia to increase their sensual pleasures, establishing new relationships that provide new pleasures in the old ways, or enjoying solitary sex. Alfred Kinsey, a biologist who eventually directed his attention to surveying and describing human sexuality, was more aware of the diversity of human sexuality than were many of his successors. He knew that practically *any* stimuli could be sexualized by someone (Kinsey, Pomeroy, & Martin, 1948; Kinsey, Pomeroy, Martin, & Gebhard, 1953). How else can we explain the fact that for some people, riding horses is sexually arousing, while others are aroused by the smell of automobile exhaust fumes?

Some individuals may become part of what Gregersen (1983) called the *chastity underground*. These are individuals who have no interest in sexual activities or in forming sexual relationships. The scanty information available suggests that these people do not have any noticeable sexual dysfunction. They simply have a marked disinterest in sexual activities. The authors of *Sex in America* (Michael, Gagnon, Laumann, & Kolata, 1994) stated that approximately 1 out of 3 women and 1 out of 6 men report a lack of interest in sex (for at least 1 of the 12 months before data collection); in addition, 1 woman in 5 and 1 man in 10 report that sex gives them no pleasure (p. 126).

Moreover, 37% of single U.S. males and 36% of single U.S. females, ages 18 to 19, report that they have never had sexual intercourse (Bearak, 2014, p. 490). (Of course, at this young age, the study subjects could simply have decided to wait to have sex, or lacked the opportunity, rather than lacked interest.) Some of the individuals in the chastity underground do worry about their lack of sexual interest, thinking it shows that something is wrong with them. It may simply be that asexual individuals do not get sexually aroused as quickly as do other individuals (Kelly, 2011).

The speed, anonymity, and reach of the Internet give sexual deviants of all stripes unprecedented opportunities for sexual thrills and vicarious titillation (S. T. Holmes & Holmes, 2009). The Internet offers access to websites, chat rooms, discussion groups, newsletters, contacts, parties, names of potential participants/partners, and photos/videos, covering an incredible array of sexual interests and unusual turn-ons (Durkin, Forsyth, & Quinn, 2006). The Internet has an openness and accessibility that is lacking in most other parts of culture and society, with an almost unlimited capacity to expand its coverage of things sexual (Streeter, 2011). It is one of the most unregulated social domains ever created, and it offers quick access to the dark side of human sexuality to practically anyone who wants it (Sandywell, 2006). In fact, the more extreme or bizarre the sexual deviance, the more useful the Internet becomes (Adler & Adler, 2006).

Maratea (2011) collected data from an Internet message board oriented toward a discussion of *zoophilia* (sexual desire for, and emotional attachment to, nonhuman animals) and *bestiality* (sex with nonhuman animals devoid of any emotional attachments to them). The nonrandom sample (with unknown characteristics) consisted of 4,983 individual posts, made mostly between September and November 2008. Sex with nonhuman animals was justified in many ways, but most of these accounts claimed that no harm was done to the animals. In fact, some of the posts declared that the acts of *bestiosexuality* had been caused by the nonhumans themselves, making them, at least in the humans' minds, both consensual *and* positive for the nonhuman creatures. The human participants portrayed their sexual interests and activities as more normal and ordinary than they might appear to nonparticipants. They endeavored to convince others that they were doing nothing harmful to their nonhuman consorts. Participants on this message board condemned their critics for doing cruel things to animals.

The Internet plays another role in the construction of sexual deviance. It gives moral entrepreneurs abundant opportunities to find something new, disturbing, and seemingly out of control to worry about and condemn. The Internet—and what it makes possible—is fertile ground for the origination of new moral crusades and moral panics. The "threat" of *cyberporn,* for example, can be presented as yet one more example of the many risks that youngsters face. This claim can then be used to substantiate the further claim that youngsters are growing up too fast, in a climate of self-indulgence and irresponsibility that can only be interrupted by strong parental monitoring of youngsters' leisure time and government oversight (Potter & Potter, 2009). Cyberporn is now added to the list of threats to the purity and innocence of childhood and adolescence.

Patterning Paraphilias

Some sexual turn-ons—such as *formicophilia* (sexual arousal from insects), *emetophilia* (sexual arousal from vomiting), *klismaphilia* (sexual arousal from enemas), *eproctophilia* (sexual arousal from flatulence), *urophilia* (sexual arousal from urine), *coprophilia* (sexual arousal from feces), or *necrophilia* (sexual arousal from corpses)—are found among a relatively small number of individuals (who may be suffering from psychological disorders of one type or another). Few, if any, group and cultural supports exist for these far-side sexual thrills. Once called perversions, things like this are now classified as paraphilias in much of the psychiatric literature.

The term *paraphilia,* which literally means "a love beside," is used to refer to sexual arousal in response to objects or situations that are considered to *not* be a part of the *usual* arousal-activity patterns. The term is best thought of as describing sexual arousal in response to "inappropriate" objects or acts, or acts that occur in "inappropriate" settings. The American Psychiatric Association's (2013) manual of mental disorders (see Chapter 4) instructs that the term paraphilia "denotes any intense and persistent sexual interest other than sexual interest in genital stimulation or preparatory fondling with phenotypically normal, physically mature, consenting human partners" (p. 685). This definition really doesn't tell us what it is as much as what it is not. Anything even slightly deviant if it is "intense and persistent" seems to qualify (i.e., could be classified) as a paraphilia, though very few paraphilias are actually discussed in the manual. The APA has made it even easier to find a paraphilia, however. It reasons that the criteria of "intense and persistent" may not fit all people because some of them do not have intense sexual interests of any kind (e.g., the very old or medically ill are singled out for attention). In these cases, the definition of paraphilia changes to "any sexual interest greater than or equal to normophilic sexual interests" (p. 685). If these definitions were not squishy (or incomprehensible) enough, the APA concludes that there are some paraphilias that are best described as *preferential* rather than as *intense* sexual interests (p. 685).

Paraphilia is a term that covers a wide range of far-side sexual turn-ons that involve nonconsenting partners, nonhuman animals, inanimate objects, or acts that can cause pain or humiliation for the individuals involved. Although some individuals who have paraphilias may be found to be "sick" or "mentally ill" in the clinical sense of the term, this finding is of limited value for a relativist approach. What the existence of paraphilias and people who engage in them *does* show is that there is incredible variety in what humans find sexually arousing and that new turn-ons are found (or made) all the time (Rosewarne, 2011; Stoller, 1979, 1985).

Paraphilias are predominantly a Western, culture-specific happening, and it is their medicalization as a form of disease or disorder that requires as much analysis as does the question of why people have them in the first place (Bhugra, 2008). Though some paraphilias are rigid and incomprehensible to most people most of the time, many are concordant with conventional sexuality and overlap with it quite a bit. At times, paraphilias are best viewed as inclinations that are followed, altered, modified, and amended, rather than as concrete, invariant, abnormal conditions.

Some individuals who dabble in paraphilic sex—Rosewarne (2011) calls them part-time perverts—are neither physically sick nor psychologically maladjusted. They simply manage their expressions of their sexual fantasies through far-side sexuality. For example, *fetish* (sexual arousal from inanimate objects, such as clothing) is common among men (and found less often among women), and it is widely viewed as both normative and normal (Steele, 1996). Yet fetish is defined as a paraphilia (APA, 2013, pp. 700–702). *Voyeurism* (sexual arousal from viewing forbidden things), another paraphilia, has a variant in which a number of voyeurs will get together to spy on people. Sometimes they use telescopes, and they may even be viewing people who know that they are being watched (Forsyth, 1996).

Even this brief discussion of paraphilias shows that the term is value-laden and judgmental. It transforms something that is inherently ambiguous and relative (not part of the *usual* arousal-activity patterns; *inappropriate* acts, objects, or settings) into something that is more likely to be viewed as sick or degenerate—as a disorder. Paraphilic sexual acts are (or can be) done by people who make contributions to a society, are well-integrated in it, and have full consent of their sexual partners (i.e., no involvement with children or nonhuman animals). In addition, paraphilias can be acted upon in ways that are neither dangerous nor hurtful for the participants.

Beckmann's (2009) study of individuals involved in the subculture of BDSM (bondage/discipline/sadism/masochism) in London, England, concludes that these individuals are involved in sexual activities that are better understood as sexual variations than as inherent individual pathologies.

Members of her sample used bondage, discipline, dominance, and submission, along with the physical and psychological pain that can accompany them, as ways to achieve altered mental states and emotional transcendence. It is true that BDSM sex is rarer than mainstream sex, but it is still found throughout the world and all through human history. It can be done in safe and responsible ways, Beckmann's study indicates, that are neither coercive nor exploitative.

The existence of sadomasochistic sex (SM) between willing partners shows that the same sexual act, no matter how bizarre or dysfunctional it might seem to some individuals, is evaluated in positive or even glowing terms by other individuals. When SM is consensual and done by fully informed adults—as it almost always is—it is wrong to dismiss it out of hand as evidence of mental illness or social pathology. For the bulk of SM practitioners, an interest in the sex practice developed well after childhood (i.e., in their twenties or later) and was not a response to some childhood trauma or abuse. The principal way that most SM practitioners get introduced to sadomasochism is by someone they know rather than from private discovery and experimentation (Powls & Davies, 2012).

A study of 66 professional dominatrices (or *pro-dommes*) and 10 of their male clients in BDSM clubs and public meetings in New York City and San Francisco shows that the relationship between dominatrix and client is more a commercial transaction than a perverted, dysfunctional relationship (Lindemann, 2012). The dominatrix must take her client's tastes, interests, and well-being into consideration while getting him to submit to her. The client's main reason for submission is the quest for personal pleasure; the pro-domme's main reason for participating in the sexual activity is that it gives her the opportunity to demonstrate her skill and ingenuity. Although the pro-domme does get paid, she does not want to be understood in a pay-for-services-rendered way. It would make her feel like a whore, something she does not want to be. Pro-dommes believe that indiscriminate sex with strangers for money is a more tainted terrain than what they do with their customers (Levey & Pinsky, 2015).

Newmahr (2011) did a participant observation study of sadomasochism being acted out at parties, clubs, and dungeons in various locales in a northeastern U.S. metropolis she calls Caeden. Her findings offer a counterpoint to an approach that paints SM as a sexual deviance that is inherently abnormal and essentially dysfunctional. She reports that sadomasochism is a way for participants to purposefully and voluntarily take extreme risks (physical, psychological, emotional) in the quest for novel experiences. Newmahr reaches the arguable conclusion that sadomasochism, as the administration of extreme though controlled violence (e.g., whipping, spanking, beating, caning), expertly delivered, is a form of intimacy that allows females who experience it to develop a sense of empowerment by successfully surviving male sadistic acts (p. 183). The Eulenspiegel Society, founded in New York City in 1971, and the Pansexual Society of Janus, founded in San Francisco in 1974, are the oldest and most populated sadomasochistic organizations in the United States (p. 4).

In 2010, the APA's Sexual and Gender Disorder work group was petitioned by the National Coalition for Sexual Freedom (NCSF) (2010) to remove all paraphilias from the *DSM-5*. The request by NCSF was founded on its belief that keeping them in the manual is based more on morality than on science. The NCSF has concluded that BDSM practitioners, fetishists, and cross-dressers are the targets of discrimination, bias, and negative social sanctions because of APA diagnostic decisions. The APA refused to comply with the request, but it did draw a distinction between *paraphilia* and *paraphilic disorder* in *DSM-5*. Unlike a *paraphilia*, which "by itself does not necessarily justify or require clinical intervention" (APA, 2013, p. 686), a *paraphilic disorder* refers to the situation in which a paraphilia is causing significant long-term distress or impairment for an individual (of at least 6 months' duration) or when that individual is causing harm to others because he or she has a paraphilia. Just because an individual is diagnosed as having a paraphilia, the APA reasons, does not necessarily mean that he or she has a disorder that requires clinical intervention or medical treatment (pp. 685–686).

The social and legal definitions of specific forms of sexuality as "unnatural" or "crimes against nature" (legally known as *sodomy*) developed in colonial America to protect women and children—even livestock—from sexual assault, not to regulate the sexual acts of consenting adults, especially when they were done in private. However, sodomy statutes were eventually used in more expansive ways. The prospect of greater political freedoms and economic prosperity attracted waves of immigrants to the United States. Sodomy laws were used against ethnic and racial minorities to maintain a generally conservative social order and the conventional morality on which it was based. The principal function of sodomy laws, however, was to suppress the sexuality of homosexuals, particularly gay men (Eskridge, 2008). Gays experienced so much persecution at the hands of heterosexuals that they learned they would have to hide their sexual orientation, establishing an identity-based community that was separate from heterosexual society (Adam, 1987).

A worldwide shift is discernible away from the view that sex is only for reproduction and toward the view that sex is an expressive and enjoyable activity (Frank, Camp, & Boutcher, 2010). A principal decision rule in deciding whether to criminalize and punish a given sexual act has been whether it is voluntary for its participants. Consensual sex is treated more leniently, while sexuality that is coercive and nonconsensual—or is viewed that way—is treated more severely. (For example, adult-to-adult incest is more often defined as consensual and treated more leniently than is adult-to-child incest, which is more often viewed as coercive and sanctioned more severely.) The global trend toward making the independent person the foundation of social order meant that characteristics of families, communities, societies, and nations became less important reasons for changing global sex laws.

Rigid rules of sexual conduct, coupled with punitive sanctions, have the primary effect of causing individuals to talk less and less about their sexuality and to conduct their sexual activities with greater caution and secrecy (Foucault, 1978; Gay, 1986). It is less likely that a valued and enjoyable sexual practice, done in private, will be given up, no matter how harsh the possible penalties are. The restrictions on sexual expression in nineteenth-century U.S. culture were rigid and uncompromising. Chastity before marriage and fidelity after it were cultural imperatives. Sexual moderation was expected, and sexual intercourse was allowed only if it was intended to lead to the birth of a child. However, cultural rules against forbidden sex (e.g., masturbation, oral sex, anal sex) were not as absolute as they appeared. Nineteenth-century Americans enjoyed a wide range of sexual pleasures, and they privately rejected the ideal culture that called for a monotonous and unemotional sex life (Lystra, 1989).

Kinsey's studies of sexuality (Kinsey et al., 1948, 1953) indicated that the sexual activities of Americans were far more flexible and diverse than ideal culture permitted and more than most people suspected. By the middle of the twentieth century, ideal culture itself started to change. More was learned about sexual pleasure and the multitude of ways that humans could achieve it. Conception could be separated from sexual enjoyment as more and better methods of birth control became available. The double standard began to erode as women experienced some movement away from their traditional position as caretakers of home and children to seek their fortunes in jobs and attain advanced degrees in colleges and universities. Homosexuals and prostitutes became better organized and more insistent that they be left alone because their sexuality was their business and nobody else's (Bullough, 1976).

People felt freer than they ever had to embark on their own journey into sexuality and to use their imaginations to discover new sources of sexual pleasure with less concern for what prevailing sexual standards dictated. People became confident (or brazen) enough to divulge publicly that they violated traditional sexual standards, at least some of the time. The acclamation of sexuality as a pleasurable and important human experience for both males and females went a long way toward legitimating the kinds of sexual experimentation—collective and individual—that would have been shocking in earlier times (Peiss & Simmons, 1989).

Sexual Politics and the Transformation of Intimacy

Culture Wars and Sexual Politics

As the twentieth century churned on, the whiff of revolution was in the air. Sexuality became more open and pleasure-oriented than it ever had been before. People discussed and reflected on sexual matters incessantly and publicly while they reassured one another that sexuality was a private and largely insignificant pastime (Foucault, 1978). Women's pursuit of sexual pleasure, more effective contraceptive techniques, and changing feminine identities were correlated with increasing tensions between males and females, as well as between the young and the not-so-young (Giddens, 1992). Problems surrounding teenage pregnancy, both probable and improbable, were used as a way to justify the regulation of the sexuality of adolescent females because moral and medical controls were becoming less effective (Nathanson, 1991).

With the arrival of what Janus and Janus (1993) called the *second sexual revolution* in the early 1980s, the casual sex of previous years was replaced by something close to sexual anarchy. The cornerstones were increased sexual activity among the mature and post-mature generations and participation by more and more people in more and more far-side sexual deviances. In a process of defining deviancy down, people were prepared to accept sexual activities among others—or even to try some themselves—that would have been extremely shocking to the moral sensibilities of earlier times. The specter of AIDS and other sexually transmitted diseases was one restraint (Burroway, 2010), but the prospect of contracting a communicable disease—even one that could be fatal—was not enough for some people to substantially alter their sexual activities. Sexual pleasure was just too important to individuals for them to allow too much to interfere with their pursuit of it. People used sexuality as a way to achieve self-liberation and find rewarding personal experiences (Quadagno & Fobes, 1995).

The civil rights movement and the Black Freedom movement provided the opportunity for both white and black females to liberate themselves from traditional sex roles and a stifling femininity by challenging male chauvinism, patriarchy, and the double standard through organizing demonstrations, giving speeches, and writing essays for public outlets (Giardina, 2010). Prominent African American women (e.g., Beyoncé Knowles, Janet Jackson, Jill Scott, Serena Williams, Tyra Banks) became erotic revolutionaries by embodying a "new feminist chic." They are smart, edgy, ambitious, socially conscious, and independent women who embody virtue while they inspire others to work toward greater empowerment, liberation, and sexual agency (Lee, 2010, p. xiv).

Battles over the legality and morality of same-sex marriage will be a constant feature on the social landscape in the years ahead (Moscowitz, 2013; Negro, Carroll, & Perretti, 2013; Taylor et al., 2009). Intolerance of same-sex marriage is highest in areas characterized by traditional gender roles, high rates of residential instability, high crime rates, and low levels of home ownership. These are sites of weak or nonexistent social capital. Residents are inclined to define same-sex marriage as yet one more threat to their values at a time and place where they already feel vulnerable. Though they may not know what to do about high crime rates or neighborhood instability, they do know what to do about same-sex marriage when given the opportunity to vote on the issue: reject it (McVeigh & Diaz, 2009).

A variety of motives and objectives are reported by gays and lesbians who marry, beyond a wish to challenge heterosexual marriage and its traditional family norms. Some do marry to show that marriage is not only for heterosexuals, but others marry for love, to get legal rights that they lacked as single individuals, or to be faithful to the movement (Kimport, 2014). The disagreements and conflicts over same-sex marriage are not only between social conservatives and everybody else. Members of the LGBT community *themselves* disagree over the function, purpose, and importance of marriage for advancing their collective interests (Bernstein & Taylor, 2013). Marriage and family life reflect the intersections of sexual orientation, parental status, race, gender, class, nationality, and geography (Acosta, 2013).

The Gallup Organization interviewed about 1,000 persons (age 15 or older) in each of 123 countries to ask if they lived in a gay-friendly community. Just about 3 in 10 of the respondents (in 2013) agreed that they did live in a place that was hospitable to gays (J. McCarthy, 2014). A great deal of variation existed from country to country, from a high of 83% of respondents in the Netherlands expressing the view that their region was gay-friendly to a low of 1% in Senegal and Pakistan saying it. Seventy percent of U.S. respondents claimed that their country was a good place for gays and lesbians to live. (The country rankings exclude information from over a dozen countries in which the question about gays and lesbians was too sensitive to ask, such as Egypt, Saudi Arabia, Kuwait, Uzbekistan, and Yemen.) Most of the countries that are gay-friendly have marriage equality laws.

In fact, the most gay-friendly country, the Netherlands, was the first country to legalize same-sex marriage (in 2001).

Marriage equality is a rapidly changing social terrain with court decisions, legislative actions, and electoral mandates impacting it on a regular basis (Doan, Loehr, & Miller, 2014). As president, Bill Clinton signed the Defense of Marriage Act (DOMA) into law in September of 1996, reaffirming the view that marriage was a union between one male and one female. His support seemed to be a contradiction because he was a strong advocate of gay rights and a supporter of gay interests. It is likely that Clinton, the consummate politician, was convinced that his support of DOMA was something that most voters wanted and would lead to his reelection. (He was reelected, but it's not clear that DOMA was the reason.) A majority of the states (38) went on to pass their own versions of DOMA. (The U.S. Supreme Court struck down the Defense of Marriage Act in 2013 in *United States v. Windsor*, which meant that same-sex marriage partners were legally permitted to receive the same federal benefits as opposite-sex marriage partners.)

The 2012 U.S. election was a historic one for gay equality, at least as far as marriage was concerned. The electorate in three states (Maryland, Maine, and Washington) voted to legalize same-sex marriage. The electorate in a fourth state (Minnesota), while not voting for marriage equality, did vote against a measure that would have amended the state constitution to read that marriage is only between a man and a woman. Although a minority of states already recognized civil unions between same-sex couples, and an even smaller minority already had legalized same-sex marriage, this was the first time that same-sex marriage was approved of by a popular vote in U.S. states. A 2015 joint poll by the *Washington Post* and ABC News showed that support of marriage equality was at record highs (Clement & Barnes, 2015). A total of 64% of the respondents supported same-sex marriages, 61% opposed state prohibitions on same-sex marriages, and 62% supported recognition of same-sex marriages across state lines. In that same year, Ireland became the first country to approve same-sex marriage by popular vote (with 62% support). By early 2015, a total of 37 states and the District of Columbia had legalized same-sex marriage, while the remaining (13) still had constitutional or statutory bans on it (Karimi & Pearson, 2015).

On Friday, June 26, 2015, by a vote of 5 to 4, the U.S. Supreme Court in *Obergefell v. Hodges* put some of the controversy and confusion to rest, temporarily. It made same-sex marriage legal in all 50 states. While supporters of the decision heralded it as a human rights equality victory or as proof that love conquers all, it was mostly about consistency and coherence. Imagine, for example, a situation in which a same-sex couple and an opposite-sex couple are both legally married in California but then both couples move to Kentucky. Would it be fair or consistent with the equal protection clause of the Fourteenth Amendment of the Constitution for Kentucky to recognize the male/female union but not the same-sex one? The highest court in the land decided that it would not. Opponents of same-sex marriages are certain that legalizing them will lead to increasing homosexuality in schools, as well as endanger the entire fabric of the nation. Only further research and the passage of time will allow us to know how legalization of same-sex marriage will affect the country. However, it is clear that it will become increasingly difficult for any state legislature, state court, or public official to maintain with any legitimacy or credibility that heterosexual marriage is the only correct and proper form of it.

Little doubt exists that the legalization of same-sex marriage was a historic ruling, reflecting changing views of sexuality, intimate relationships, marriage, and legal rights. Obergefell brought suit because he was disallowed from putting his name on his deceased husband's death certificate. The Supreme Court's ruling means that each state now must license same-sex marriages (and can dissolve them legally), as well as legally recognize same-sex marriages from other states. Opponents of the Court's decision believe that this is an example of the federal government usurping powers that are better left up to the individual states. Despite the clarity of the decision, challenges will continue, as will the fight. In some places after the Supreme Court decision (e.g., Kentucky, Texas, and Oregon), public officials (e.g., county clerks or judges) simply refused to grant marriage licenses to gay couples, and in some cases, to *anyone*, gay or straight, citing religious beliefs as the principal justification. Supporters of marriage equality, despite the existence of pockets of resistance, can celebrate the Supreme Court ruling as an important victory, but they should not take off the gloves just yet.

Masculinity, Femininity, and Family Life

Ideas about the ideal way to parent, as if there were only one perfect way, fluctuate over time and from place to place. In the United States, the idea of co-nurturing has been challenged by a view that the mother must once again become the pivotal player in the parenting trip. *The Battle Hymn of the Tiger Mother* was originally supposed to be Chua's (2011) glorification of the skill of Chinese parents as compared to Western parents to raise their children. Instead, it was seen as a book that glorified highly authoritarian and rigid, demanding and unyielding, *mother-centered* child-rearing techniques as the road to raising perfect kids. The only two instruments that Chua permitted her two daughters to play were the violin or piano, and she never allowed them to attend a sleepover or have a playdate. The book could easily have been titled *A Message to My Daughters: My Way or the Highway*. *Tiger mothering* is based on the principle that the child must do the bidding of the mother no matter what she says, because it is she who knows what is in the best interests of the child.

A counterpoint to tiger mothering is *attachment parenting*. Mothers still play the pivotal role, but a very different relationship exists between mother and child than is found between tiger moms and their cubs. Attachment parenting is fundamentally and totally *child-centered* (Sears & Sears, 2003). The trifecta of attachment parenting is a lengthy period of breast-feeding (sometimes for years, even into toddlerhood), co-sleeping (in the mother's bed or in a bed next to hers), and "baby-wearing" (use of baby slings to keep infants in constant contact with their mothers and their mothers' body rhythms). Children are in charge, and every cry is considered to be a cry for help. These cries can only be ignored at the peril of the child's well-being.

Attachment mothering, due to its intensity, puts mothers in a position where they are pressured to select either motherhood or careers. The response to this role conflict has *not* entailed a simple reversion back to the double standard of the 1950s where dads bring home the bacon and moms fry it up in a pan while raising children. What *has* happened is the rise of a cultural frame of *egalitarian essentialism*. This allows mothers to stay at home to follow the principles of attachment parenting while still believing that they embody the feminist ideals of choice and equality.

> We believe this cultural explanation [egalitarian essentialism] is . . . consistent with the broader changes that . . . shifted in the mid-1990s. Married mothers' labor force participation began to decline at about the same time. Women's entry into previously male occupations slowed in the 1990s. Even women's state-level political office holding seems to have peaked in that decade. The gender gap in earnings that had been narrowing since the late 1970s stopped changing in the 1990s. The convergence in husbands' and wives' housework time stopped well short of equality. (Cotter, Hermsen, & Vanneman, 2011, pp. 261–262)

One outcome of these sociocultural changes has been a "mommy war," in which a central conflict has been between working mothers and stay-at-home mothers.

Attachment mothers have insisted that what seemed to be traditional gender roles and a sexual double standard really were not. Even though women giving up their career aspirations (at least for a while) made the family look traditional and the relationships between spouses seem unequal, this was an incorrect view. They were not betraying the sisterhood. Because women's decision to stay at home to raise children was voluntary and done in the best interests of their children, not specifically to further their husbands' career goals, it was both reasonable and constructive. The division of labor between husband and wife was simply a better way to raise children. (Research does indicate that women may be disadvantaged in career mobility if they stay home to raise children and support their husbands [Petersen, Penner, & Høgsnes, 2014]. If they can only work part-time, or not at all for a while, this keeps them from taking the kinds of risks and accepting the kinds of assignments that promote job success [Cha & Weeden, 2014; Sandberg, 2013].)

Regardless of whether the parenting style is co-nurturing, tiger mothering, or attachment parenting, one problem for U.S. children may be that they are now overprotected, monitored so closely by parents that they fail to develop sufficient levels of independence, self-reliance, and ingenuity to be able to take risks (Rosin, 2014). Some responsible risk seems to be a good thing for children as they mature into adults, making it possible for them to develop abilities they will need to be able to succeed in a constantly changing world filled with both opportunities and dangers. Compared to earlier generations of children, Rosin concludes, the current generation has far less free time away from adult supervision and far less free space in which to do things with other children. This "erosion of child culture" and "overprotection," ostensibly to keep kids safe, means that children fail to develop their own understandings and strategies for making their way in the world as they mature.

Marriage does not have the same function or fascination that it once did—at least for some individuals—and family life is becoming increasingly diverse (Bello, 2015; Bergstrand & Sinski, 2010; Fox, 2009; Illouz, 2012; Van Hooff, 2013). In this setting, it becomes ever more difficult to define alternate lifestyles as inherently pathological and dysfunctional. Fewer people are getting married now than in the last century, more children are being born out of wedlock, and college graduates are now more likely to marry than are those individuals who never went to college (Luscombe, 2010). Many individuals, even as adults, continue to live with their parents, an arrangement that Newman (2013) calls the *accordion family*. Some never left or have not yet left ("failed to launch"); others left and returned ("boomerangs").

Women who are inclined to marry no longer simply want to find a mate. They want to have a *good* marriage, or the trade-off of giving up their independence is not worth it. Women want careers, good marriages, and children, but they realize it will be difficult to have all three successfully. Though

U.S. women do have expanding opportunities for personal fulfillment and professional success, especially when compared to earlier generations, these unprecedented opportunities generate new anxieties and dilemmas about how to manage their sexual and nonsexual relationships (Bell, 2013; Regnerus & Uecker, 2011).

Men have changed, too (Aboim, 2010). Part of this was in response to economic and political changes, and part of it was in response to criticisms of men and traditional masculinity.

> Buffeted by changes not of their making, increasingly anxious in an economic and political arena that erodes their ability to be breadwinners and confused by new demands about emotional responsiveness and involved fatherhood, men seem uncomfortable in that new spotlight, shifting uncomfortably, shielding their eyes, even railing against the glare. (Kimmel, 2010, p. 2)

As masculinity became ever more difficult for men to figure out, let alone embody, the declaration that full equality between the sexes offered the only real possibility for personal growth and social progress seemed promising. A strong argument was made that gender equality would enrich *both* males and females (Kimmel, p. 11).

When men become fathers, they have to deal with the stresses and strains, as well as with the rewards and opportunities, that come from balancing private family roles and public work roles. A study based on over 300 lengthy interviews with all kinds of U.S. fathers (i.e., biological dads, adoptive dads, gay dads, dads in prison, dads who share child custody with ex-wives) shows the dilemmas that fathers face (Marsiglio & Roy, 2012). Differences exist from one man to another in what it means to be a good father and how fatherhood is defined. One point of agreement is that a good father must be a man who provides economically for his kids. The sample also was inclined to agree that good fathers do *not* have to be skillful in taking care of their children's emotional and physical needs. The overstatement of the father's breadwinning role and the understatement of his emotional-support-and-caretaking role are what can make parenting difficult and generate some of the conflicts and disagreements between mothers and fathers over how to raise their kids.

Kaufman (2013) identified from her study of 70 fathers (in North Carolina and California) three fathering types: old dads, new dads, and super-dads. *Old dads* have a traditional view of fathering and fathers' rights and duties. They define themselves principally as breadwinners, and they accept other parts of the parental role reluctantly and only when work demands don't interfere. It is not that they dislike being fathers. Fathering is simply not their principal identity peg. *New dads*, by contrast, define themselves as parents, and they work to balance family life and public life. For example, if a new dad were to miss his child's ball game because of a work obligation, he would feel a need to apologize and somehow make it up to the child. (Old dads would feel neither a need to apologize nor any guilt over having missed the game.) New dads are the ones who experience the greatest stress and difficulty in being parents because they are committed to *both* work and family. *Superdads* put family first and spend all the time they can with their youngsters, making substantial changes to their work routines in order to do so. Any decisions about work—what kind to do, where to do it, how much of it do, or whether to work outside the home at all—are made with their children's interests and well-being in mind.

Many gay men are dads, too. Some have biological offspring from previous heterosexual relationships, and others decide that they want to adopt children so that they and their same-sex partners can take the parenting trip together. Much like heteronormative parenting, gay parenting is a mirror of society, impacted by other institutions (politics, economics, law); demographic shifts; and cultural changes regarding homosexuality, gender, and marriage equality (Goldberg, 2012). Gay dads, like dads most everywhere, must be creative and resolved if they are successfully to juggle work, child care, child-rearing, community involvement, and sexuality. Transitioning from being partners in a same-sex relationship to being parents is filled with some of the same problems and possibilities that any shift in status would bring, made even more challenging by the fact that no moms are present. (Some biological mothers who put their children up for adoption actually want them to be placed with gay dads so that these women will be the only female figures in their children's lives.)

Deviantizing Sexual Matters

Moral enterprises have existed, do exist, and will continue to exist in regard to sexual matters. Whether it is gay marriage, teenage pregnancy, pornography, extramarital sex, prostitution, or something else, sexual patterns of one group can generate a great deal of distress and anxiety for other groups, whose members set about to make things right. Social reactions can reach the point of being moral panics, where worry evolves into something widespread and mightily upsetting (Lancaster, 2011). Some of the concern of moral entrepreneurs (people who work to impose their views and values on others) over sexuality, of course, may be both reasonable and justified, but history shows us that some of it is silly and irrelevant, nothing more than dust in the wind. At times, the reaction is so disproportionate to the actual threat, it is the *reaction* that is the real problem.

Genital Hysteria

Penis size seems to be a near-universal concern of men (and sometimes of their mates), which generally boils down to "the bigger the better" (at least up to a point). It is no surprise, then, that if males think that their penises are shriveling up and disappearing, it would cause enough concern, anxiety, and fear to qualify as a moral panic. Women, too, share a similar fear, but with different organs (i.e., vulvas, breasts, and nipples).

> In parts of Asia entire regions are occasionally overwhelmed by terror-stricken men who believe that their penises are shriveling up or retracting into their bodies. Those affected often take extreme measures and place clamps or string onto the precious organ or have family members hold the penis in relays until an appropriate treatment is obtained, often from native healers. Occasionally women are affected, believing their breasts or vaginas [i.e., vulvas] are being sucked into their bodies. Episodes can endure for weeks or months and affect thousands. (Bartholomew, 2014, p. 389)

The shrinking of the penis to the point of being absorbed back into the body—or the belief that this is happening—is known as koro. *Koro* is a word of Malayan-Indonesian origin that means "tortoise," and it is used because of the similarity between the head and wrinkled neck of a tortoise and the tip and shaft of the human penis.

The belief that penis absorption is possible is widespread in Chinese culture, where medical texts as far back as the 1800s described the reality of penis shrinkage and its deadliness if left untreated. (The origin of females' anxieties over the absorption of their sex organs is unclear.) A number of "penis panics" occurred in regions of China, Singapore, Thailand, and India in the twentieth century (Bartholomew, 2014). The first well-documented one occurred in the fall of 1967 in Singapore. Hospitals in the area were treating increasingly higher numbers of anxious males, who were convinced that they had koro, portending their immediate death. The sufferers had tried various remedies themselves—rubber bands and even clothespins—in a futile attempt to stop the shrinkage. The penis panic ended (amid a number of sore and injured penises) when the populace was assured by medical specialists that nothing out of the ordinary was happening. Another penis panic occurred in the Guangdong province of China, starting in 1984 and ending a year later (in August 1985). Approximately 5,000 inhabitants of the region believed they were experiencing genital-shrinking episodes. Between November and December of 1976, approximately 2,000 people in northeastern Thailand thought they had koro, and in 1982, a koro epidemic occurred in northeastern India, where thousands of individuals were afflicted. A popular local remedy in the Indian epidemic was to have the sufferer hold the affected body part tightly while he or she drank lime juice and was thoroughly soaked with cold water (Bartholomew, 2014).

Koro has tended to afflict individuals in rural regions of a country who were poorly educated and without much sophistication or an abundance of intellectual skills. However, in the examples given above, sociocultural factors were also at work. Rumors about the rapid spread of koro, coupled with the belief that humans could actually experience the absorption of a body part, set the stage for the panic. It helped that of all the body parts, the penis, scrotum, breasts, and nipples are the most physiologically capable of changing size in response to changes in climate, sexual arousal, stress, depression, anxiety, fear, illness, or the ingestion of certain drugs. Idiosyncratic events (e.g., anxiety) and a cultural system that authenticates koro as a real possibility made it possible for some humans to perceive and then believe that their sexual anatomy was undergoing an unwanted and dangerous transformation. When local remedies failed to work, medical intervention was required. In these cases, the individuals themselves, with the support of group and cultural factors, defined an ordinary and temporary change in sexual anatomy as more ominous than it actually was.

Attacking Autostimulation

Masturbation (also known as *autostimulation* or *automanipulation*) is a regular sexual practice. In one study, 40% of females and approximately 60% of males (ages 18 to 59) reported that they had masturbated at least once during the previous year; about 25% of the male and 10% of the female respondents reported that they masturbated at least once a week (Michael et al., 1994, p. 158). The Janus report on human sexuality indicated that 5% of the 1,338 males in their sample and 8% of the 1,398 females stated that masturbation was their *preferred* way to achieve orgasm (Janus & Janus, 1993, p. 98). A survey of 223 college undergraduates about their masturbatory activities during the 3 months prior to data collection provides evidence that masturbation is a common way for individuals to achieve sexual pleasure or sexual release (Pinkerton, Bogart, Cecil, & Abramson, 2002). These researchers found that only 2% of the males ($n = 1$) and 36% of females ($n = 40$) reported that they had *never* masturbated, meaning that 98% of males and 64% of females reported that they *had* masturbated. Men averaged 12 times per month, and women averaged 5 times per month (p. 111). The National Survey of Sexual Health and Behavior (NSSHB) reported that 86% of males and 69% of females ages 14 to 94 reported they had masturbated at some point in their lives (Herbenick et al., 2012). People who are most likely to masturbate are individuals who have partners with whom they are sexually active, suggesting that the practice is found most frequently among individuals with the *fullest* sex life (Michael et al., 1994, p. 165).

Both Judaism and Christianity condemn masturbation. (The literal meaning of the word *masturbation* is "self-abuse.") The biblical inspiration for this denunciation is the sin of Onan. Rather than consummate a sexual relationship with his sister-in-law after the death of his brother, Onan spilled his semen on the ground, and the Lord struck him dead for his deed. It is not entirely clear if his sin was masturbation or his failure to honor the custom of *levirate* and impregnate his sister-in-law, but over the years the religious interpretation came to dominate, and the cardinal sin of Onan came to be his masturbation. Good Christians quickly learned that all righteous sexuality had to be oriented toward reproduction, and even then it must be done with a minimum of excitement and pleasure. Spending the seed without a good reproductive reason led to tragic results.

The condemnation of masturbation gained a stronger foothold as it went from being branded as badness to sickness. The prevailing and authoritative medical view of human afflictions during the eighteenth century was that good health came from a perfect balance among bodily substances of blood, bile, and sexual fluids. Any practice that upset this balance, the story went, would cause harmful results. Masturbation especially was suspect. Not only did it lack any apparent reproductive purpose, but it also depleted the body of essential fluids and generated far too much excitement in the masturbator. Physicians in the eighteenth century blamed every physical, nervous, and mental illness that they could on masturbation. It is what explained pathological singularity (Foucault, 2003, p. 60).

Richard von Krafft-Ebing (1947), a neurologist and psychiatrist born in Germany in the nineteenth century, concluded from his case studies that four categories of sexual deviation existed—masochism, sadism, fetishism, and homosexuality—all of which were caused by masturbation. Male gynecologists were inclined to view women's sexual urges as quite unnecessary or even as dangerous distractions. The most troublesome of the lot was female masturbation. Once a female fell under its spell, all was lost, and her obsession with the "solitary vice" would know no bounds (Barker-Benfield, 1976). Even at the beginning of the twentieth century, female masturbation was seen as a major cause of women's lack of sexual responsiveness in marriage (Jacquart & Thomasset, 1988).

The social reformers of the nineteenth century believed that the only way to halt the creeping social decay that they believed was plaguing U.S. society was for every individual to develop a strong personal moral code, especially with regard to food, drink, and sexuality. A moral man or woman was an individual who was safe from all temptations because of his or her ability to control the ever-present dangers posed by the unholy trinity of sexual desire, stimulating food, and unhealthy practices. No challenge or temptation was so great that it could not be bested by a well-managed body. Sylvester Graham (1794–1851) was confident that total individual control was the one virtue that could truly make people free (cited in Sokolow, 1983, p. 122). Graham's views were supported by others, such as John Harvey Kellogg (1852–1943). Kellogg identified 39 warning signs of masturbation in a book published in 1888 (cited in Money, 1985). Some of these were weakness, untrustworthiness, bashfulness, unnatural boldness, emaciation, paleness, underdeveloped breasts (females), gluttony, pain in the limbs or joints, tobacco use (by boys), acne, fingernail-biting, obscene talk, and bed-wetting. Kellogg believed that masturbation was the principal cause of most of the paleness, feebleness, nervousness, and general good-for-nothingness that he saw all around him.

Both Graham and Kellogg had great faith in the power of correct food and proper eating habits to keep humans morally upright. Both believed that masturbators were attracted to excessive amounts of spicy or upsetting foods, such as pepper, salt, cloves, mustard, horseradish, or vinegar. They also believed that chronic masturbators were inclined to consume non-nutritious substances, such as clay or plaster. If chronic masturbators avoided both nutritious and bland foods, Graham and Kellogg reasoned, the path to salvation was clear. Masturbation was much less likely if individuals learned proper nutrition at an early age. Graham developed a mild foodstuff called the Graham cracker, and Kellogg developed the cornflake, to help keep individuals from touching themselves in sexual ways (Money, 1985).

If the dietary restrictions were unsuccessful, other things still might work. Parents were instructed to wrap up their children's genitals, cover the genitals with some protective device, or bind their children's hands to make self-touching impossible. Devices were invented and peddled that supposedly would prevent male masturbation. Most of these contraptions combated masturbation by making it difficult, if not impossible, for a male to have an erection. One of these, a large ring with sharp spikes on its inside, was positioned to encircle a male's penis while he slept. If the penis were to become erect (*tumescence*), the spikes would come in contact with the organ, and pain, along with a rapid *detumescence*, would result. Another device was more elaborate and far less painful. It sounded an alarm when an erection occurred, alerting the vigilant, who would take the necessary steps to stop whatever was happening (Gregersen, 1983, p. 30). One treatment that was guaranteed to cure female masturbation was for the masturbator's parents to apply pure carbolic acid to her clitoris (Michael et al., 1994).

The rationale for maligning masturbation reflected how it was practiced and how it was understood. It was a sexual practice that was accessible to the young of *both* sexes. The democratic nature of masturbation—its status as equal-opportunity sex, accessible to practically anyone at practically any time—was compounded by the fact that it was defined as uniquely capable of excess (the "crack cocaine of sexuality," according to Laqueur [2003, p. 21]). The last straw in the demonization of masturbation was that it cut its practitioners off from the world of work and responsibility, moving them into the world of fantasy and self-indulgence. Sex panics are less about protecting children, Lancaster (2011) instructs, than they are about preserving adults' recollections about childhood—that it is *supposed* to be a time of innocence and purity.

Most people now define masturbation as relatively harmless, even though about half of the women and men who masturbate still report some guilt over it (Michael et al., 1994, p. 166). (Foucault [2003] declares masturbation to be the "universal secret shared by everyone but disclosed to no one" [p. 59].) The comic David Steinberg once divulged on *The Tonight Show* that he felt guilty about his own masturbation. The reason was because he did it so badly (or so he said). Masturbation exists in a changing moral terrain. It is no longer viewed as the road to disease and moral decay. It is not even widely viewed as deviant unless it is excessive and comes to supplant other forms of sexuality that are defined as better and healthier. In general, masturbation is now viewed as a form of personal pleasure instead of self-pollution. However, could another Graham or Kellogg happen along and successfully attach new meanings to old practices?

Maligning Menstruation

A biological event such as *menstruation,* found only among women of a particular age and physical status, is one that can hardly be ignored, certainly not by a woman herself and likely not by her peers, either. The variable meanings attached to this natural event remind us once again that social groups and social relationships must be at the center of our understandings of what is proper and improper. At some places and times, menstruation was taken as a sign of woman's high status, and menstruating women were treated with respect. Menstrual blood was believed to have the power to cure leprosy, warts, hemorrhoids, epilepsy, and headaches. It was used as a love charm, a sacrifice to the gods, and a protection against evil spirits. A virgin's first menstrual pad was saved and used as a curative for disease. At other places and times, this periodic bleeding was viewed as a sign of contamination and pollution. Pliny, the Roman naturalist, thought that menstrual blood could ruin crops, dull steel knives, make ivory tarnish, cause iron to rust, and make new wine turn sour. Dogs were supposed to be driven mad from the taste of menstrual blood, and bees supposedly died from it. Women were disallowed from working in the Saigon opium industry in the 1800s because opium was supposed to acquire a bitter taste if menstruating women were near it (Delaney, Lupton, & Toth, 1988, p. 9). At still other places and times, menstruation was viewed as an ordinary part of everyday life, and people did not worry very much about it one way or the other.

Women's ability to produce blood that neither appreciably weakened nor killed them, and that was associated with life and living rather than with death and dying, spurred a measure of envy among those men who were willing to think about it at all. Male initiation rites among native populations in Melanesia, Africa, the Americas, and Australia contain rites of passage in which men actually mimic female menstruation by slitting the underside of their penises to facilitate bleeding. Sometimes the incision is short, but at other times it extends the entire length of the shaft (Tannahill, 1992, p. 44). Why would men attempt to simulate female menstruation unless they viewed it as the source of a power that they wanted for themselves (Knight, 1991)?

The way menstruation came to be symbolized—its social construction—reflected, at least in part, the conflicts and struggles between men and women for power and control of *women's* bodies. Men tried to increase their influence over women by constructing an ideology that defined women as naturally inferior. A cultural establishment of what menstruation meant and how it should be handled by women and responded to by men was a central part of this ideology (Laws, 1990). Times and places can be found where women most certainly did suffer a loss of status. They were secluded and isolated in special dwellings where they had little to do other than to handle their menstrual cramps as best they could and follow the rules that regulated only them (Mead, 1949).

Even when the seclusion was forced, however, women may have turned it to their own advantage (Buckley & Gottlieb, 1988). It was usually a group event, and it provided opportunities for fellowship, relaxation, and growth. It was a time for women to get in touch with other women while they got in touch with themselves and the rhythms of their own bodies (Hathaway, 1998). The segregation of menstruating women was an important event in the life of the entire community, and men's activities were strongly influenced by the menstrual cycles of women. Some men even had illicit love affairs—or tried to—with menstruating women during their period of isolation (Buckley, 1988).

To those women and men who consider menstruation to be impure and debilitating, here is an alternative view of this very natural process. The biologist Margie Profet (1993) argues that it is most unlikely that women would lose as much blood and tissue as they do, and potentially be incapacitated for so long, simply to slough off unnecessary uterine lining. It is more likely that menstruation also evolved as a way for a female to purge herself of infectious microorganisms (p. 338). Bacteria can be carried from the woman's vagina into her uterus by getting on the heads or tails of swimming sperm, and seminal fluid can transport viruses from the male to the female reproductive organs. Menstrual blood offers some protection to a female. It helps remove uterine tissue that might be infected, and it also contains chemicals that kill a wide range of pathogens in the uterus, cervix, vagina, and oviducts (pp. 345–346). This take on menstruation is part of an emerging image of female sexuality. It views females' sexual responses as having evolved to allow them to be sexually active with whomever they like, in rapid succession, without getting sick in the process from any intimate contact that they might have had with unclean or infected males. The so-called "curse" comes to an end by being defined as more of a blessing.

Menstrual activists are highly critical of the social construction of menstruation as a debilitating disorder because they believe this interpretation subjugates and controls women. The bedrock of menstrual activism is the belief that menstruation is neither shameful nor unclean, a claim that leads to a critique of the political economy of capitalism and the environmental impact of the feminine hygiene industry. Some menstrual activists believe that menstruation is an event that is integrative, binding women to one another. They want it to be understood as something to be celebrated as a form of female empowerment rather than dreaded. Others condemn the feminine hygiene industry for relentless profiteering, manipulation of women, and environmental destruction, all perpetrated under the façade of care and concern for women. Menstrual activists want to make women aware of the harm that comes from defining menstruation as nothing more than an individual matter of discomfort and pain management (Bobel, 2010).

Conclusions

Various possibilities arise from the interplay of biology, personality, culture, and society in regard to sexual attitudes, behaviors, and conditions. When pigeonholes are created, and people and what they do are forced into them, our ability to recognize the full range of human sexual diversity is restricted. When this sexual differentiation is coupled with differences in power between categories, one category of individuals is usually devalued more than the other. Human sexuality—deviant and otherwise—and how it is defined and understood are powerfully influenced by social and cultural factors. Because of this, sexual customs are relative, and the evaluations of sexual experiences and responses are variable.

The distinctive aspect of human sexuality is its relativity, as well as the importance it is given in practically every society. A wide range of things are sexually stimulating to humans, from sexual intercourse to far-side paraphilias (e.g., necrophilia or coprophilia). Though many varied sexual acts are available to humans, the sex/gender roles that are available in U.S. culture are limited and limiting. Gender benders (like Dorothy/Billy Tipton) do not have easy access to a legitimate institutionalized status.

A crucial part of a relative understanding of sexual deviance is to know about moral enterprises in regard to sexual matters. Groups of people develop views of the propriety or impropriety of sexual experiences, and they force these views on other groups. Fluctuations in the social meanings of both masturbation and menstruation are particularly instructive. They show us that any human experience, trait, or practice can be the source of differentiation and evaluation. Depending on place, time, and situation, people's sexual experiences and sex/gender attributes are the objects of reverence, scorn, or anything in between.

The experiences of people who are stigmatized and persecuted for their sexual outlooks and sexual interests are not appreciably different from the experiences of people who are scorned for other reasons. Sometimes, humans even become mightily concerned over their own sexuality and do what they can to control what they view as unwanted sexual changes in themselves. This is clear with the genital hysteria and penis panics of the twentieth century. It is also clear in the way menstruation is defined and understood.

References

Abend, L. (2013, December 16). Boys won't be boys. *Time, 182,* 40–44.

Aboim, S. (2010). *Plural masculinities: The remaking of the self in private life.* Burlington, VT: Ashgate.

Acosta, K. L. (2013). *Amigas y amantes: Sexually nonconforming Latinas negotiate family.* New Brunswick, NY: Rutgers University Press.

Adam, B. (1987). *The rise of a gay and lesbian movement.* Boston: Twayne.

Adler, P. A., & Adler, P. (2006). The deviance society. *Deviant Behavior, 27,* 129–148.

American Psychiatric Association. (2013). *Diagnostic and statistical manual of mental disorders* (5th ed.). Washington, DC: Author.

Ball, R. A. (2012). Changing images of deviance: Nineteenth-century Canadian anti-prostitution movements. *Deviant Behavior, 33,* 26–39.

Barcelos, C. A., & Gubrium, A. C. (2014). Reproducing stories: Strategic narratives of teen pregnancy and motherhood. *Social Problems, 61,* 466–481.

Barker-Benfield, G. J. (1976). *The horrors of the half-known life: Male attitudes toward women and sexuality in nineteenth-century America.* New York: Harper & Row.

Bartholomew, R. (2008). Penis panics. In R. Heiner (Ed.), *Deviance across cultures* (pp. 79–85). New York: Oxford University Press.

Bartholomew, R. (2014). Penis panics. In R. Heiner (Ed.), *Deviance across cultures: Constructions of difference* (pp. 389–394). New York: Oxford University Press.

Barton, B. (2012). *Pray the gay away: The extraordinary lives of Bible Belt gays.* New York: New York University Press.

Bearak, J. M. (2014). Casual contraception in casual sex: Life-cycle change in undergraduates' sexual behavior in hookups. *Social Forces, 93,* 483–513.

Beckmann, A. (2009). *The social construction of sexuality and perversion: Deconstructing sadomasochism.* New York: Palgrave Macmillan.

Beisel, N. (1993). Morals versus art: Censorship, the politics of interpretation, and the Victorian nude. *American Sociological Review, 58,* 145–162.

Bell, L. C. (2013). *Hard to get: 20-Something women and the paradox of sexual freedom.* Berkeley: University of California Press.

Bello, M. (2015). *Whatever . . . love is love: Questioning the labels we give ourselves.* New York: HarperCollins.

Bergstrand, C. R., & Sinski, J. B. (2010). *Swinging in America: Love, sex, and marriage in the 21st century.* Santa Barbara, CA: Praeger.

Bernstein, M., & Taylor, V. (Eds.). (2013). *The marrying kind? Debating same-sex marriage within the lesbian and gay movement.* Minneapolis: University of Minnesota Press.

Bhugra, D. (2008). Paraphilias across cultures. In R. Heiner (Ed.), *Deviance across cultures: Constructions of difference* (pp. 106–116). New York: Oxford University Press.

Birken, L. (1988). *Consuming desire: Sexual science and the emergence of a culture of abundance, 1871–1914.* Ithaca, NY: Cornell University Press.

Bobel, C. (2010). *New blood: Third-wave feminism and the politics of menstruation.* New Brunswick, NJ: Rutgers University Press.

Boryczka, J. M. (2012). *Suspect citizens: Women, virtue, and vice in backlash politics.* Philadelphia: Temple University Press.

Brents, B. G., & Hausbeck, K. (2012). Marketing sex: U.S. legal brothels and late capitalist consumption. In L. Salinger (Ed.), *Social deviance* (pp. 249–259). San Diego, CA: Cognella.

Brents, B. G., Jackson, C. A., & Hausbeck, K. (2010). *The state of sex: Tourism, sex, and sin in the new American heartland.* New York: Routledge.

Buckley, T. (1988). Menstruation and the power of Yurok women. In T. Buckley & A. Gottlieb (Eds.), *Blood magic: The anthropology of menstruation* (pp. 187–209). Berkeley: University of California Press.

Buckley, T., & Gottlieb, A. (1988). A critical appraisal of theories of menstrual symbolism. In T. Buckley & A. Gottlieb (Eds.), *Blood magic: The anthropology of menstruation* (pp. 3–50). Berkeley: University of California Press.

Bullough, V. (1976). *Sexual variance in society and history.* New York: Wiley.

Burroway, R. (2010). Schools against AIDS: Secondary school enrollment and cross-national disparities in AIDS death rates. *Social Problems, 57,* 398–420.

Burstyn, L. (1997). Female circumcision comes to America. In L. Salinger (Ed.), *Deviant behavior 97/98* (2nd ed., pp. 19–23). Guilford, CT: Dushkin.

Buss, D. (1994). *The evolution of desire: Strategies of human mating.* New York: Basic Books.

Byne, W. (1994, May). The biological evidence challenged. *Scientific American, 270,* 50–55.

Cao, L., & Maguire, E. R. (2013). A test of the temperance hypothesis: Class, religiosity, and tolerance of prostitution. *Social Problems, 60,* 188–205.

Carrier, J. (2007). Homosexual behavior in cross-cultural perspective. In J. Macionis & N. Benokraitis (Eds.), *Seeing ourselves: Classic, contemporary, and cross-cultural readings in sociology* (7th ed., pp. 204–214). Upper Saddle River, NJ: Pearson/ Prentice Hall.

Carter, S., & Sokol, J. (1989). *What really happens in bed: A demystification of sex.* New York: M. Evans.

Cha, Y., & Weeden, K. A. (2014). Overwork and the slow convergence in the gender gap in wages. *American Sociological Review, 79,* 457–484.

Chou, R. S. (2012). *Asian American sexual politics: The construction of race, gender, and sexuality.* Lanham, MD: Rowman & Littlefield.

Chin, Ko-Lin, & Finckenauer, J. O. (2012). *Selling sex overseas: Chinese women and the realities of prostitution and global sex trafficking.* New York: New York University Press.

Chodorow, N. (1994). *Femininities, masculinities, sexualities: Freud and beyond.* Lexington: University Press of Kentucky.

Chua, A. (2011). *Battle hymn of the tiger mother.* New York: Penguin.

Clement, S., & Barnes, R. (2015, April 23). Poll: Gay-marriage support at record high. *Washington Post.* Retrieved April 25, 2015, from http://www.washingtonpost .com/politics/courts_law/poll-gay-marriage-support-at-record-high/2015/04/22/ f6548332-e92a-11e4-aae1-d642717d8afa_story.html

Colapinto, J. (2000). *As nature made him: The boy who was raised as a girl.* New York: HarperCollins.

Cotter, D., Hermsen, J. M., & Vanneman, R. (2011). The end of the gender revolution? Gender role attitudes from 1977 to 2008. *American Journal of Sociology, 117,* 259–289.

Davis, M. (1983). *Smut: Erotic reality/obscene ideology.* Chicago: University of Chicago Press.

Delaney, J., Lupton, M. J., & Toth, E. (1988). *The curse: A cultural history of menstruation* (Rev. ed.). Urbana: University of Illinois Press.

Deshotels, T. H., Tinney, M., & Forsyth, C. J. (2012). McSexy: Exotic dancing and institutional power. *Deviant Behavior, 33,* 140–148.

De Waal, F. (2005). *Our inner ape: A leading primatologist explains why we are who we are.* New York: Riverhead Books/Penguin.

Doan, L., Loehr, A., & Miller, L. R. (2014). Formal rights and informal privileges for same-sex couples: Evidence from a national survey experiment. *American Sociological Review, 79,* 1172–1195.

Dorkenoo, E., & Elworthy, S. (2007). Female genital mutilation. In J. Macionis & N. Benokraitis (Eds.), *Seeing ourselves: Classic, contemporary, and cross-cultural readings in sociology* (7th ed., pp. 425–432). Upper Saddle River, NJ: Pearson/Prentice Hall.

Durkin, K., Forsyth, C., & Quinn, J. (2006). Pathological Internet communities: A new direction for sexual deviance research in a post-modern era. *Sociological Spectrum, 26,* 595–606.

Elliott, S. (2012). *Not my kid: What parents believe about the sex lives of their teenagers.* New York: New York University Press.

Eskridge, W. (2008). *Dishonorable passions: Sodomy laws in America, 1861–2003.* New York: Viking.

Fields, J. (2008). *Risky lessons: Sex education and social inequality.* New Brunswick, NJ: Rutgers University Press.

Fine, C. (2010). *Delusions of gender: How our minds, society, and neurosexism create difference.* New York: Norton.

Forsyth, C. (1996). The structuring of vicarious sex. *Deviant Behavior, 17,* 279–295.

Foucault, M. (1978). *The history of sexuality* (Vol. 1). New York: Pantheon.

Foucault, M. (2003). *Abnormal: Lectures at the Collège de France. 1974–1975* (V. Marchetti & A. Salomoni, Eds.; G. Burchell, Trans.). New York: Picador.

Fox, B. (2009). *When couples become parents: The creation of gender in the transition to parenthood.* Toronto, Ont., Canada: University of Toronto Press.

Frank, D. J., Camp, B. J., & Boutcher, S. A. (2010). Worldwide trends in the criminal regulation of sex, 1945–2005. *American Sociological Review, 75,* 867–893.

Friedman, A. (2013). *Blind to sameness: Sexpectations and the social construction of male and female bodies.* Chicago: University of Chicago Press.

Gagnon, J., & Simon, W. (1970). Perspectives on the social scene. In J. Gagnon & W. Simon (Eds.), *The sexual scene* (pp. 1–21). New Brunswick, NJ: Transaction Publishers.

Gagnon, J., & Simon, W. (1973). *Sexual conduct.* Chicago: Aldine.

Garcia, L. (2012). *Respect yourself, protect yourself: Latina girls and sexual identity.* New York: New York University Press.

Gates, G. J., & Newport, R. (2012, October 18). *Special report: 3.4% of U.S. adults identify as LGBT.* Retrieved October 29, 2012, from http://www.gallup.com/poll/158066/special-report-adults-identify-lgbt.aspx

Gay, P. (1986). *The tender passion: The bourgeois experience, Victoria to Freud* (Vol. 2). New York: Oxford University Press.

Geertz, C. (1975). Common sense as a cultural system. *The Antioch Review, 33,* 5–26.

Ghaziani, A. (2011). Post-gay collective identity construction. *Social Problems, 58,* 99–125.

Giardina, C. (2010). *Freedom for women: Forging the women's liberation movement, 1953–1970.* Gainesville: University Press of Florida.

Giddens, A. (1992). *The transformation of intimacy: Sexuality, love and eroticism in modern societies.* Stanford, CA: Stanford University Press.

Goldberg, A. E. (2012). *Gay dads: Transitions to adoptive fatherhood.* New York: New York University Press.

Goode, E., & Troiden, R. (Eds.). (1974). *Sexual deviance and sexual deviants.* New York: William Morrow.

Gray, M. L. (2009). *Out in the country: Youth, media, and queer visibility in rural America.* New York: New York University Press.

Greenberg, J. A. (2012). *Intersexuality and the law: Why sex matters.* New York: New York University Press.

Gregersen, E. (1983). *Sexual practices: The story of human sexuality.* New York: Franklin Watts.

Guittar, N. A. (2014). *Coming out: The new dynamics.* Boulder, CO: FirstForumPress.

Hardy, K., Kingston, S., & Sanders, T. (Eds.). (2010). *New sociologies of sex work.* Burlington, VT: Ashgate.

Hathaway, N. (1998). Blood rites: Myths, taboos, and the eternal rhythm of the female body. In L. Salinger (Ed.), *Deviant behavior 98/99* (3rd ed., pp. 22–25). Guilford, CT: Dushkin.

Hennen, P. (2008). *Fairies, bears, and leathermen: Men in community queering the masculine.* Chicago: University of Chicago Press.

Herbenick, D., Reece, M., Schick, V., Sanders, S. A., Dodge, B., & Fortenberry, J. D. (2012). Sexual behavior in the United States: Results from a national probability sample of men and women ages 14–94. In L. Salinger (Ed.), *Social deviance* (pp. 235–247). San Diego, CA: Cognella.

Hoang, K. K. (2014). Flirting with capital: Negotiating perceptions of Pan-Asian ascendency and Western decline in global sex work. *Social Problems, 61,* 507–529.

Holmes, M. (Ed.). (2009). *Critical intersex.* Burlington, VT: Ashgate.

Holmes, S. T., & Holmes, R. M. (2009). *Sex crimes: Patterns and behaviors* (3rd ed.). Thousand Oaks, CA: Sage.

Hooff, J. van (2013). *Modern couples? Continuity and change in heterosexual relationships.* Burlington, VT: Ashgate.

Illouz, E. (2012). *Why love hurts: A sociological explanation.* Malden, MA: Polity Press.

Irvine, J. (1990). *Disorders of desire: Sex and gender in modern American sexology.* Philadelphia: Temple University Press.

Jacquart, D., & Thomasset, C. (1988). *Sexuality and medicine in the Middle Ages.* Cambridge, UK: Polity.

Janus, S., & Janus, C. (1993). *The Janus report on sexual behavior.* New York: Wiley.

Jenkins, W. (2012). Can anyone tell me why I'm gay? What research suggests regarding the origins of sexual orientation. In L. Salinger (Ed.), *Social deviance* (pp. 311–322). San Diego, CA: Cognella.

Jordan-Young, R. M. (2010). *Brain storm: The flaws in the science of sex differences.* Cambridge, MA: Harvard University Press.

Kane, E. W. (2012). *The gender trap: Parents and the pitfalls of raising boys and girls.* New York: New York University Press.

Karimi, F., & Pearson, M. (2015, February 13). The 13 states that still ban same-sex marriage. *CNN.com.* Retrieved October 31, 2015, from http://www.cnn.com/2015/02/13/us/states-same-sex-marriage-ban/

Kaufman, G. (2013). *Superdads: How fathers balance work and family in the 21st century.* New York: New York University Press.

Kelly, G. F. (2011). *Sexuality today* (10th ed.). New York: McGraw-Hill.

Kemper, T. (1990). *Social structure and testosterone.* New Brunswick, NJ: Rutgers University Press.

Kessler, S. (1998). *Lessons from the intersexed.* New Brunswick, NJ: Rutgers University Press.

Kimmel, M. (1996). *Manhood in America: A cultural history.* New York: Free Press.

Kimmel, M. (2000). *The gendered society.* New York: Oxford University Press.

Kimmel, M. (2010). *Misframing men: The politics of contemporary masculinities.* New Brunswick, NJ: Rutgers University Press.

Kimport, K. (2014). *Queering marriage: Challenging family formation in the United States.* New Brunswick, NJ: Rutgers University Press.

Kinsey, A. C., Pomeroy, W. B., & Martin, C. E. (1948). *Sexual behavior in the human male.* Philadelphia: W. B. Saunders.

Kinsey, A. C., Pomeroy, W. B., Martin, C. E., & Gebhard, P. H. (1953). *Sexual behavior in the human female.* Philadelphia: W. B. Saunders.

Kipnis, L. (2010). *How to become a scandal: Adventures in bad behavior.* New York: Metropolitan Books.

Knight, C. (1991). *Blood relations: Menstruation and the origins of culture.* New Haven, CT: Yale University Press.

Krafft-Ebing, R. von. (1947). *Psychopathia sexualis* (12th ed.). New York: Pioneer.

Lancaster, R. N. (2011). *Sex panic and the punitive state.* Berkeley: University of California Press.

Laqueur, T. W. (2003). *Solitary sex: A cultural history of masturbation.* Brooklyn, NY: Zone Books.

Laumann, E. O., Gagnon, J. H., Michael, R. T., & Michaels, S. (1994). *The social organization of sexuality: Sexual practices in the United States.* Chicago: University of Chicago Press.

Laws, S. (1990). *Issues of blood: The politics of menstruation.* New York: Macmillan.

Lee, S. (2010). *Erotic revolutionaries: Black women, sexuality, and popular culture.* Lanham, MD: Hamilton Books.

LeVay, S. (1993). *The sexual brain.* Cambridge: MIT Press.

Levey, T. G., & Pinsky, D. (2015). A constellation of stigmas: Intersectional stigma management and the professional dominatrix. *Deviant Behavior, 36,* 347–367.

Lewontin, R. (2000). *It ain't necessarily so: The dream of the human genome and other illusions.* New York: New York Review of Books.

Lewontin, R., Rose, S., & Kamin, L. (1984). *Not in our genes: Biology, ideology, and human nature*. New York: Pantheon.

Lindemann, D. J. (2012). *Dominatrix: Gender, eroticism, and control in the dungeon*. Chicago: University of Chicago Press.

Logan, T. D. (2010). Personal characteristics, sexual behaviors, and male sex work: A quantitative approach. *American Sociological Review, 75*, 679–704.

Luscombe, B. (2010). Marriage: What's it good for? *Time, 176*, 48–56.

Lystra, K. (1989). *Searching the heart: Women, men, and romantic love in nineteenth-century America*. New York: Oxford University Press.

Mackie, G. (1996). Ending footbinding and infibulation: A convention account. *American Sociological Review, 61*, 999–1017.

Maratea, R. J. (2011). Screwing the pooch: Legitimizing accounts in a zoophilia on-line community. *Deviant Behavior, 32*, 918–943.

Marsden, L. R. (2012). *Canadian women and the struggle for equality*. New York: Oxford University Press.

Marsiglio, W., & Roy, K. (2012). *Nurturing dads: Social initiatives for contemporary fatherhood*. New York: Russell Sage Foundation.

Martin, K. (1998). Becoming a gendered body: Practices of preschools. *American Sociological Review, 63*, 494–511.

McCarthy, B., & Grodsky, E. (2011). Sex and school: Adolescent sexual intercourse and education. *Social Problems, 58*, 213–234.

McCarthy, J. (2014, August 27). Nearly 3 in 10 worldwide see their areas as good for gays. *Gallup*. Retrieved June 30, 2015, from http://www.gallup.com/poll/175520/nearly-worldwide-areas-good-gays.aspx

McVeigh, R., & Diaz, M. E. D. (2009). Voting to ban same-sex marriage: Interests, values, and communities. *American Sociological Review, 74*, 891–915.

Mead, M. (1949). *Male and female: A study of the sexes in a changing world*. New York: William Morrow.

Michael, R. T., Gagnon, J. H., Laumann, E. O., & Kolata, G. (1994). *Sex in America: A definitive study*. Boston: Little, Brown.

Middlebrook, D. (1998). *Suits me: The double life of Billy Tipton*. Boston: Houghton Mifflin.

Mollborn, S., Domingue, B. W., & Boardman, J. D. (2014). Norms as group-level constructs: Investigating school-level teen pregnancy norms and behaviors. *Social Forces, 93*, 241–267.

Money, J. (1985). *The destroying angel*. Buffalo, NY: Prometheus.

Money, J. (1988, February). The development of sexual orientation. *Harvard Medical School Mental Health Letter, 4*, 1–4.

Money, J., & Tucker, P. (1975). *Sexual signatures: On being a man or a woman*. Boston: Little, Brown.

Moon, D. (1995). Insult and inclusion: The term fag hag and gay male "community." *Social Forces, 74*, 487–510.

Moore, R. I. (1987). *The formation of a persecuting society: Power and deviance in Western Europe, 950–1250*. New York: Basil Blackwell.

Moscowitz, L. (2013). *The battle over marriage: Gay rights activism through the media.* Urbana: University of Illinois Press.

Nathanson, C. (1991). *Dangerous passage: The social control of sexuality in women's adolescence.* Philadelphia: Temple University Press.

National Coalition for Sexual Freedom (NCSF). (2010). *DSM-V Revision Project.* Retrieved October 15, 2015, from https://ncsfreedom.org/key-programs/dsm-v-revision-project/dsm-v-program-page.html

Negro, G., Carroll, G. R., & Perretti, F. (2013). Challenger groups, commercial organizations, and policy enactment: Local lesbian/gay rights ordinances in the United States from 1972 to 2008. *American Journal of Sociology, 119,* 790–832.

Newmahr, S. (2011). *Playing on the edge: Sadomasochism, risk, and intimacy.* Bloomington: Indiana University Press.

Newman, K. S. (2013). *The accordion family: Boomerang kids, anxious parents, and the private toll of global competition.* Boston: Beacon Press.

Park, A. (2008, June 17). What the gay brain looks like. *Time.* Retrieved October 15, 2015, from http://www.time.com/time/printout/0,8816,1815538,00.html

Pasko, L. (2009). Naked power: Stripping as a confidence game. In P. Adler & P. Adler (Eds.), *Constructions of deviance: Social power, context, and interaction* (6th ed., pp. 476–484). Belmont, CA: Thomson Wadsworth.

Peiss, K., & Simmons, C. (1989). Passion and power: An introduction. In K. Peiss & C. Simmons (Eds.), *Passion and power: Sexuality in history* (pp. 3–13). Philadelphia: Temple University Press.

Petersen, T., Penner, A. M., & Høgsnes, G. (2014). From motherhood penalties to husband premia: The new challenge for gender equality and family policy, lessons from Norway. *American Journal of Sociology, 119,* 1434–1472.

Pfeffer, C. A. (2014). "I don't like passing as a straight woman": Queer negotiations of identity and social group membership. *American Journal of Sociology, 120,* 1–44.

Pinkerton, S. D., Bogart, L. M., Cecil, H., & Abramson, P. R. (2002). Factors associated with masturbation in a collegiate sample. *Journal of Psychology and Human Sexuality, 14,* 103–121.

Potter, R. H., & Potter, L. A. (2009). The cyberporn and child sexual predator moral panic. In P. Adler & P. Adler (Eds.), *Constructions of deviance: Social power, context, and interaction* (6th ed., pp. 176–183). Belmont, CA: Thomson Wadsworth.

Powls, J., & Davies, J. (2012). A descriptive review of research relating to sadomasochism: Considerations for clinical practice. *Deviant Behavior, 33,* 223–234.

Profet, M. (1993, September). Menstruation as a defense against pathogens transported by sperm. *Quarterly Review of Biology, 68,* 335–386.

Quadagno, J., & Fobes, C. (1995). The welfare state and the cultural reproduction of gender: Making good girls and boys in the Job Corps. *Social Problems, 42,* 171–190.

Regnerus, M., & Uecker, J. (2011). *Premarital sex in America: How young Americans meet, mate, and think about marrying.* New York: Oxford University Press.

Reiss, I. (1986). *Journey into sexuality.* Englewood Cliffs, NJ: Prentice Hall.

Ridgeway, C. L. (2011). *Framed by gender: How gender inequality persists in the modern world.* New York: Oxford University Press.

Ridley, M. (1993). *The Red Queen: Sex and the evolution of human nature.* New York: Penguin.

Rosewarne, L. (2011). *Part-time perverts: Sex, pop culture, and kink management.* Santa Barbara, CA: Praeger.

Rosin, H. (2014, April). The overprotected kid. *The Atlantic.* Retrieved June 29, 2015 from http://www.theatlantic.com/features/archive/2014/03/hey-parents-leave-those-kids-alone/358631/

Roychowdhury, P. (2014). Brothers and others: Organizing masculinity, disorganizing workers. *Social Problems, 61,* 22–41.

Saadawi, N. (1982). *The hidden face of Eve: Women in the Arab world.* Boston: Beacon.

Sandberg, S., with Scovell, N. (2013). *Lean in: Women, work, and the will to lead.* New York: Knopf.

Sandywell, B. (2006). Monsters in cyberspace: Cyberphobia and cultural panic in the information age. *Information, Communication & Society, 9,* 39–61.

Sanger, T. (2010). *Trans people's partnerships: Towards an ethics of intimacy.* New York: Palgrave Macmillan.

Scheitle, C. P., & Hahn, B. B. (2011). From the pews to policy: Specifying Evangelical Protestantism's influence on states' sexual orientation policies. *Social Forces, 89,* 913–934.

Schur, E. (1988). *The Americanization of sex.* Philadelphia: Temple University Press.

Sears, W., & Sears, M. (2003). *The baby book: Everything you need to know about your baby—from birth to age two* (2nd ed., Rev. ed.). Boston: Little, Brown.

Seidman, S. (1991). *Romantic longings: Love in America, 1830–1980.* New York: Routledge.

Shneer, D., & Aviv, C. (Eds.). (2006). *American queer, now and then.* Boulder, CO: Paradigm.

Small, M. (1995). *What's love got to do with it? The evolution of human mating.* New York: Anchor.

Sokolow, J. (1983). *Eros and modernization: Sylvester Graham, health reform, and the origins of Victorian sexuality in America.* Rutherford, NJ: Fairleigh Dickinson University Press.

Somashekhar, S. (2014, July 15). Health survey gives government its first large-scale data on gay, bisexual population. *Washington Post.* Retrieved June 30, 2015, from https://www.washingtonpost.com/national/health-science/health-survey-gives-government-its-first-large-scale-data-on-gay-bisexual-population/2014/07/14/2db9f4b0-092f-11e4-bbf1-cc51275e7f8f_story.html

Spain, D. (1992). *Gendered spaces.* Chapel Hill: University of North Carolina Press.

Steele, V. (1996). *Fetish: Fashion, sex & power.* New York: Oxford University Press.

Steinmetz, K. (2014). America's transition. *Time, 183,* 38–46.

Stoller, R. (1979). *Sexual excitement: Dynamics of erotic life.* New York: Pantheon.

Stoller, R. (1985). *Observing the erotic imagination*. New Haven, CT: Yale University Press.

Stone, M. M. (2014). "This could be a good avenue for you": Influential strategies in the hiring of exotic dancers. *Deviant Behavior, 35,* 727–741.

Streeter, T. (2011). *The net effect: Romanticism, capitalism, and the Internet*. New York: New York University Press.

Tannahill, R. (1992). *Sex in history* (Rev. ed.). Chelsea, MI: Scarborough House.

Tavris, C. (1992). *The mismeasure of woman*. New York: Simon & Schuster.

Taylor, V., Kimport, K., Van Dyke, N., & Andersen, E. A. (2009). Culture and mobilization: Tactical repertoires, same-sex weddings, and the impact on gay activism. *American Sociological Review, 74,* 865–890.

Tewksbury, R. (1994). Gender construction and the female impersonator: The process of transforming "he" to "she." *Deviant Behavior, 15,* 27–43.

Tewksbury, R. (1996). Cruising for sex in public places: The structure and language of men's hidden, erotic worlds. *Deviant Behavior, 17,* 1–19.

Tiefer, L. (1978, July). The kiss. *Human Nature, 1,* 29–37.

Van Buren, A. (1981). *The best of Dear Abby*. Kansas City, MO: Andrews McMeel.

Walby, K. (2012). *Touching encounters: Sex, work, and male-for-male Internet escorting*. Chicago: University of Chicago Press.

Weinberg, M., & Williams, C. (1994). *Dual attraction: Understanding bisexuality*. New York: Oxford University Press.

Weinberg, M., Williams, C., & Laurent, B. (2005). Medicalizing and demedicalizing hermaphroditism. In E. Rubington & M. Weinberg (Eds.), *Deviance: The interactionist perspective* (9th ed., pp. 472–486). Boston: Allyn & Bacon.

Weitzer, R. J. (2012). *Legalizing prostitution: From illicit vice to lawful business*. New York: New York University Press.

West, C., & Zimmerman, D. (2000). Doing gender. In M. Kimmel (Ed.) (with A. Aronson), *The gendered society reader* (pp. 131–149). New York: Oxford University Press.

Wijngaard, M. van den. (1997). *Reinventing the sexes: The biomedical construction of femininity and masculinity*. Bloomington: Indiana University Press.

Williams, W. (1986). *The spirit and the flesh: Sexual diversity in American Indian culture*. Boston: Beacon.

Wolf, N. (2012). *Vagina: A new biography*. New York: HarperCollins.

Ziv, L. (1997). The tragedy of female circumcision: One woman's story. In L. Salinger (Ed.), *Deviant behavior 97/98* (2nd ed., pp. 9–12). Guilford, CT: Dushkin.

9

Drugs and Drug Taking

The Social Reality of Drug Use

Get any textbook on drugs, and you will find that a *drug* is defined as a chemical substance that, when ingested, alters or changes the functioning of the mind and/or body. A textbook definition gives the impression—incorrectly, as it turns out—that drugs have uniform and universal characteristics that make it possible for them to be classified as drugs. The truth is that no uniform feature is found in all substances called drugs that differentiate them from all substances called nondrugs, except that all drugs have been classified as drugs by somebody.

> Some drugs, such as heroin, alcohol, valium, nicotine, and caffeine, may lead to withdrawal symptoms upon discontinuance of use; but drugs such as peyote, LSD, and marijuana do not. Some drugs, such as cocaine and amphetamines, stimulate the central nervous system while others, such as barbiturates and alcohol, depress it. Some drugs have medicinal value, others have none at all. In fact, efforts to argue that drugs are defined by their action on our bodies or mind[s] lead only into absurdity since everything we eat and drink is a chemical that affects our bodies and minds. (Matveychuk, 1986, p. 9)

The naming of some substance as a drug or a drug of abuse is a highly relative, value-laden, culture-specific, often personal judgment, and it cannot be separated either from the sociocultural context or from who is doing the defining. Practically any claim about drugs is contentious, and discussions about drugs are almost always highly charged.

The Greek word for drug, *pharmakon,* contained three images: The substance was a poison (bad), a remedy (good), or a magical amulet (wonderful). Drugs and drug use have been viewed in many different and often contradictory ways: as demonic, deadly, enslaving, monstrous, curative, spiritual, liberating, fun, or interesting (Montagne, 1988, pp. 418–419). It seems to be true that one group's medicine can be another group's poison. A former Mississippi lawmaker and judge named Noah Sweat Jr. (a.k.a. "Old Soggy") gave a short speech on the floor of the Mississippi state legislature in 1952. It was prompted by the issue of legalizing alcohol. The speech was masterful in the way it reconciled contradictory views of alcohol by allowing Sweat to declare that he was *both* emphatically against whisky and emphatically for it. He shows how to straddle a fence with style and a satiric flair (Safire, 1997), while showing that drugs can have multiple meanings. (His nickname "Old Soggy" came not from his love of liquor but from the phrase, "sorghum top," because his appearance resembled a sugar cane plant.)

> If when you say "whisky" you mean the devil's brew, the poison scourge, the bloody monster that defiles innocence, dethrones reason, destroys the home, creates misery and poverty, yea, literally takes the bread from the mouths of little children; if you mean the evil drink that topples the Christian man and woman from the pinnacle of righteous, gracious living into the bottomless pit of degradation, and despair, and shame, and helplessness, and hopelessness— then certainly I am against it.
>
> But, if when you say "whisky" you mean the oil of conversation, the philosophic wine, the ale that is consumed when good fellows get together, that puts a song in their hearts and laughter on their lips, and the warm glow of contentment in their eyes; if you mean Christmas cheer; if you mean the stimulating drink that puts the spring into the old gentleman's step on a frosty, crispy morning; if you mean the drink that enables a man to magnify his joy, and his happiness, and to forget, if only for a little while, life's great tragedies, and heartaches, and sorrows; if you mean that drink the sale of which pours into our treasuries untold millions of dollars, which are used to provide tender care for our little crippled children, our blind, our deaf, our dumb, our pitiful aged and inform [*sic*]; to build highways and hospitals and schools—then certainly I am for it.
>
> This is my stand. I will not retreat from it. I will not compromise. (Address to the legislature by a Mississippi state senator, 1958, "Whiskey Speech")

It practically goes without saying that with a little effort and some fine-tuning, Old Soggy's speech could be extended to cover practically *any* chemical substance, not just whisky.

If the term *drug* is slippery, then the term *drug abuse* is even slipperier. Even if it is true that the use of a particular drug can be harmful to users— what chemical substance *couldn't* be abused if the user were to try hard enough?—the potential for harm is not the only or even the principal reason that one drug is branded as a substance of abuse and another is not. Scientific evidence about the harmfulness of a particular drug almost always comes *after* the declaration by authorities that it is being abused (Szasz, 1985). "People in positions of social responsibility have greater credibility and authority to prove, create and maintain their reality, while some have no credibility and must suffer the consequences of the reality created by others" (Matveychuk, 1986, p. 11).

Cultural meanings and personal experiences work together to help drug users perceive, interpret, respond to, and remember the pharmacological effects of drugs (Montagne, 1988). This symbolic universe of discourse also makes it possible for drug users to describe and discuss their private experiences with drugs with other people. Those societies that have an extensive drug-user culture are the ones most likely to provide users with positive images of their drug experience. Where this user culture is absent or poorly developed, an antidrug message is more common, and drug effects are more likely to be portrayed as dangerous and debilitating. Even users themselves may hold negative views of their own drug experiences (Becker, 1967). Individuals who stop using drugs interpret and describe their former drug-using experiences differently from those who continue to use them (Woodward, Misis, & Griffin, 2014).

Some college students who use stimulating drugs construct narratives to excuse or justify their drug use as both functional and responsible. They claim (and probably believe) that their drug use is controlled, making it possible for them to be successful at school by being able to work harder and longer on their assignments. By contrasting their controlled and functional use with what they see as the irresponsible and dysfunctional drug use of others not like themselves, it allows them to maintain a conventional, ordinary prosocial personal identity. They believe that they are worthy of respect for being able to maintain their drug usage and some measure of academic success (Kerley, Copes, & Griffin, 2015).

A yearlong study (March 2010 to March 2011) of marijuana use by participants in New York City's hip-hop and jam band scenes shows the significant role played by subcultural values and social norms in the social organization of drug-taking experiences (Pawson & Kelly, 2014). Even though members of both the hip-hop and jam band subcultures used marijuana recreationally, the ways they used it and their reasons differed. The jam band subculture was more interactive and friendly, with members who searched for people with whom to establish new friendships. In contrast, hip-hop subculture was interpenetrated by themes of masculinity and toughness, wherein members remained aloof and separate from most others. They were inclined to interact only within an immediate circle of close friends. In the jam band subculture, marijuana was social glue that brought people together and was a way to make new friends. Marijuana use and sharing it with others, regardless of who they were, reflected the central values of kindness, trust, generosity, and congeniality. Things were different in the hip-hop scene. The values of hypermasculinity, toughness, and dominance of public space glided into a disinclination to share marijuana with anyone other than close and trusted friends. Patterns of marijuana use reflected subcultural dynamics, while it also served to reaffirm its central values.

Every drug experience reflects a user's expectations and background with regard to a chemical substance—called the *set*—as well as the *setting,* the history of where a chemical substance has been used, with whom, when, and why (Weil, 1972). The sociocultural environment and its repository of meanings and understandings, as well as a user's accumulated experiences with a particular drug, introduce a great deal of variability and relativity into *every* drug experience (Ford, 2014; Hoffman, 2014). Molecular structure of a drug is one factor that will help to determine its effects, but pharmacological effects of any drug are always mediated by social meanings, social contexts, past experiences with the drug, and social relationships. For instance, when you think or know that your peers are using drugs, it increases your likelihood of using them, too (Schaefer, Vito, Marcum, Higgins, & Ricketts, 2015). The reality of drugs, drug use, and drug abuse is a socially constructed one (Miller & Stogner, 2015).

Getting Stoned in the Animal Kingdom

Our human ancestors may have learned much of what they knew about intoxication from observing the kinds of effects that nonhuman animals derived from the plants they consumed. Getting "stoned" in the animal kingdom does seem to be influenced by something chemical and physiological, because certain substances produce similar effects among dissimilar creatures.

After sampling the numbing nectar of certain orchids, bees drop to the ground in a temporary stupor, then weave back for more. Birds gorge themselves on inebriating berries, then fly with reckless abandon. Cats eagerly sniff aromatic "pleasure" plants, then play with imaginary objects. Cows that browse special range weeds will twitch, shake, and stumble back to the plants for more. Elephants purposely get drunk on fermented fruits. Snacks on "magic mushrooms" cause monkeys to sit with their heads on their hands in a posture reminiscent of Rodin's *Thinker.* (Siegel, 1989, p. 11)

Siegel labeled intoxication the *fourth drive,* little different from the other basic drives of hunger, thirst, or sex (p. 10). He stated that the fourth drive does not simply motivate organisms to consume external substances to feel good. It also motivates them to attain some altered state, and the direction of that change—up or down or good or bad—is of secondary importance. Sometimes nonhuman animals will stop their regular activities—eating, drinking, mating—and take psychoactive chemicals if they have the chance.

Studies of the drug use of nonhuman animals in the wild are interesting. They suggest that a part of the variation in drug-taking experiences is accounted for by the relationship between biological structures and chemical substances. However, naturalistic studies are flawed. They credit nonhuman animals with far too many human qualities, and they suffer from insurmountable problems of interpretation and measurement. It is impossible to know for sure exactly what is going on when a nonhuman animal gets intoxicated. Because little is known (or knowable) about the creature's needs, its unique biological characteristics, the quality of its group life, how much of a psychoactive drug is in its body, its stresses and strains, its specific body weight, its fat composition, or its psychological characteristics, the demonstration that some nonhuman animal is intoxicated tells us little of value about drugs, drug use, or drug abuse.

Laboratory studies of drug-taking behaviors of nonhumans, though more artificial than studies in the wild, allow more precision in determining how drugs work. Test animals in laboratories do engage in drug-taking behaviors when given the opportunity. Monkeys allowed to press a bar to get an injection of morphine (a central nervous system depressant) will press it hundreds of times for one injection even if they only receive a small amount of the drug (Ray & Ksir, 1996). Rats, dogs, and several species of monkey will go through a series of complicated physical maneuvers and forgo practically all other pleasures if cocaine is the reward. A laboratory animal might have to press a bar 100 times for its first injection. On subsequent trials, the number of presses is then doubled to 200, 400, 800, and so on. At some point, an animal will either stop responding or be too exhausted to continue, and this is called the *breaking point.* Cocaine's breaking point is 2 to 16 times higher than that for other drugs, and some monkeys have been found to be willing to press a bar 12,800 times for one cocaine injection (Siegel, 1989, pp. 183–185). By contrast, laboratory animals do not seem to like alcohol or tobacco, and they will not use either of them to the point of either addiction or dependency. However, humans in their natural settings like these two chemicals very much (Goode, 2008a).

Lab studies clearly show that certain drugs are powerfully reinforcing to laboratory animals with free access to them. They may indulge themselves to the point where other pursuits become irrelevant. What the lab studies *mean*, however, is not as clear. These studies do *not* prove that some inevitable, inexorable, physical addiction process exists to account for compulsive drug use among members of the animal kingdom (Peele, 1985). The lab animals might self-administer drugs simply because they are attached to implanted catheters that make it easy for them to get drugs and are frightened; under stress; in pain; and living in overcrowded, uninteresting, and unfamiliar environments. Because these studies maximize the chance that a hapless creature will self-inject drugs, they really do not prove that drug-taking behavior is determined by the molecular properties of drugs. If animal research has any relevance for understanding *human* drug experiences, it is in its demonstration that one important source of a drug habit is a life filled with wretchedness. Humans may develop a drug habit when they do not have the kinds of rewarding experiences or quality relationships that make a drug-free life worth living.

Addiction: Imprecise Definitions and Arbitrary Meanings

How we define or label a human activity affects greatly the way we will react to it. If drug use is classified as an addiction and the user as an addict, this designation alone makes it much less likely that the drug use will be viewed as anything other than a sickness or disease. If it were to be defined in some other way—as sin, psychological malfunction, an outgrowth of social disorganization, a problem in living, a central activity, a form of self-help, or ordinary behavior—it would generate entirely different understandings and evoke entirely different responses. Representing drug use as an addiction makes it appear inexorably and inherently compulsive, self-destructive, and in need of cure. The disease model of drug addiction, Schaler (2000) instructs, was created and actively promoted by individuals who had a lot to gain from widespread acceptance of it. Its prominence and influence can be traced to its familiarity rather than to its empirical credibility as a theory of why people do things they shouldn't.

Before the twentieth century, the word *addiction* was used to refer to a habit that could be *either* good or bad but was most often good. Back then, addiction meant no more than a preference, interest, or inclination that people had (Alexander & Schweighofer, 1988). They might be addicted to religion, hard work, reading, sobriety, their families, or even the devil (Szasz, 1985). If addiction were to be viewed as something that could be positive or negative, drug-related or not, then it could be claimed that Beethoven was addicted to music, and da Vinci was addicted to painting; Mickey Mantle was addicted to baseball, and Buddy Holly was addicted to rock and roll; Proust was addicted to writing, and Goethe was addicted to reading. Schaler (2000) describes what he considers one of the most difficult and uncomfortable of all addictions, associated with upsetting physical reactions, which can be negative or positive depending on situational elements. The addiction is what we humans call "love" (p. 6). Goffman (1952) would agree with Schaler. He used the word "hooked" to refer both to persons who fall in love and those who take drugs (p. 453). The word *addiction* ultimately attained its current meaning as a relentless and self-defeating pursuit. The words *addiction* and *addict* were expanded to cover a large number of things that really had little in common with one another.

Changes in the meanings of addiction and addict always produce changes in the kinds of substances that are defined as addicting, the kinds of drug-taking patterns that are viewed as problematic, and the kinds of people who are classified as troublesome (Murphy, 2011). Some drugs that were once considered inconsequential and recreational are now considered dangerous and addicting, and some drugs that were once considered addicting and dangerous no longer are. The terms *addiction* and *addict* are now used, often indiscriminately, by individuals to condemn whatever they think is bad, compulsive, and in need of correction, regardless of whether they are discussing sex, drugs, or some other activity that they do not like. When the brush sweeps this wide, it is probably time to rethink seriously our understanding and use of the terms (Staley, 1992).

The word *addiction* reached a point where it meant not only something generally bad but also something invariant, uniform, and universal. In order to make the process of addiction seem uniform and invariantly debilitating, physical changes supposedly associated with drug use and abuse were identified. Drugs that were associated with: (1) *withdrawal* (physical changes in heavy users if the drug were discontinued) and (2) *tolerance* (the physical capacity to withstand higher and higher doses of a drug; diminishing effects upon subsequent use at the same dose) were branded as addicting. Other drugs were defined as nonaddicting (i.e., only habituating) because users experienced neither tolerance nor withdrawal.

Drug-use patterns continued to change throughout the twentieth century, and the meaning of addiction changed right along with them. Drug patterns were becoming more diverse, and more and more people were using more and more drugs. The traditional meanings of addict and addiction were considered too restrictive by authorities to encompass all the new drug users and patterns of drug use that they believed needed to be included. Addiction was transformed into more of a psychological process than it had been, but a psychological process that still had universal and uniform biological underpinnings.

An individual was defined as addicted if he or she craved a drug, used it uncontrollably, and remained indifferent to the actual or potential adverse consequences of its use. It became the prevailing scientific view that psychological dependence, based on reinforcement, was the driving force behind all drug addiction; physical changes could still occur, but these were no longer considered necessary to identify an addiction or an addict. By the 1980s, drugs like cocaine and marijuana were included in the category of addictive substances, whereas at one time they had been defined as only habituating.

The reinforcement that addicts receive, the story now goes, comes from a jolt of pleasure and exhilaration associated with the flow of brain chemicals (Volkow, Wang, Fischman, et al., 1997; Volkow, Wang, Fowler, et al., 1997). Experiences of the addict, such as craving, compulsion, and loss of control, may also be due to these same brain chemicals. The prevailing view is that practically anyone can become addicted to practically anything under the right circumstances because of something going on in his or her brain (Goode, 2015; Hanson, Venturelli, & Fleckenstein, 2015).

We can appreciate some of the difficulties with the terms *addiction* and *addict* by looking at their application to an aspect of behavior that at one time would never have been called an addiction: human sexuality. Are some people addicted to sex, or is the concept of sex addiction nothing more than a silly fad? Opinions vary, and different groups give different answers to these questions. Some people believe that no such thing as a sex addiction exists. Sexual behavior is not a substance, they claim, and it is not associated with tolerance and withdrawal symptoms at too-low doses. To call certain erotic feelings and behaviors "addictions" is to brand them as abnormal and as both uncontrolled and uncontrollable (Henkin, 1996). Does this contribute anything to our understanding of either addiction or sexuality, or does it merely stigmatize those people who are unhappy with their sex lives but feel powerless to change them?

Other people believe wholeheartedly in the existence of sex addictions. According to them, a sex addiction is a life-threatening condition where people's lives are dominated by a pattern of compulsive, destructive sex that they would like to change but cannot. Sex makes them "high" because it releases chemicals in the brain (Rice, 1998, p. 218). It is claimed that sex addictions lead to suicide, unwanted pregnancies, family disintegration, violence, major health care costs, and child abuse. People who refuse to believe that sexuality can be an addiction are themselves branded as suffering from an illness: the denial of an illness (Carnes, 1991).

A messy term like *sex addiction* gets even messier when it is applied to concrete cases. Who is a sex addict? This category seems to include a diverse group of people whose only qualification is that they have had their lives made difficult—tragically so, in some cases—by sex. Carnes (1991) offers the following as actual examples of sex addicts and their addictions: a woman who had burned herself using a vibrator and had to go to an emergency room for treatment; a priest who stole money from his parish to pay for visits to prostitutes; a dentist who drugged his unresponsive wife in order to have sex with her; a corporate technician who sexually harassed people; and a male youth leader who had sex with boys (pp. 9–10). What is true is that these individuals seem to be out of control in regard to features of their sexuality. It is *not* true, however, that our understanding of complex human activities and relationships is improved by calling them "addictions," applying the term to sexual activities that seem indecipherable in other ways.

Our most damaging addiction may be our addiction to the addiction terminology (Henkin, 1996). The addiction terminology can come to serve as a vocabulary of motive in which individuals become convinced that they have no capacity for self-control and no responsibility for the consequences of their actions (Raikhel & Garriott, 2013; Schaler, 2000). How on Earth can people control something that they truly believe is relentless and uncontrollable? Why would they even try? Regardless of how it is defined, addiction does not automatically denote danger: A substance that is nonaddictive can still be used destructively and harmfully, and an addictive substance can still be used safely and responsibly.

Carr's (2011) study of an outpatient drug treatment program for homeless women in the Midwest (which she refers to as "Fresh Beginnings") shows how important it is to the lifeblood of a therapeutic agency that its members (therapists, clients, administrators, case managers) use the language of addiction and in similar ways. Agency personnel had an unshakable belief that addiction was real and that all of the clients' problems in living erupted from their enslavement to drugs. A major objective of the agency's personnel was for them to get their clients to fall into line and start using the addiction terminology to interpret their own personal experiences and habits. Central to this project was the expectation that clients would reach a point where they would be willing to disclose a personal history of suffering and misery that was caused by their drug use. Clients were expected to be able and willing to articulate the official view at Fresh Beginnings and come to speak like the addicts they were defined to be.

Unsurprisingly, clients learned on their own, as well as from more experienced and knowledgeable clients, how to use the vocabulary of addiction, helplessness, and recovery to please their caretakers. In Carr's (2011) words, they "flipped the script" (p. 191). *Flipping the script* involved a presentation of self in which clients were willing to use the narratives and vocabularies that agency personnel both wanted and expected to hear without clients making any personal investment in the content or correctness of their statements. It is recovery through impression management. These interpersonal strategies allowed clients to be better able to get things they wanted and were of value to them (e.g., housing, transportation vouchers, medical care, job training, legal aid, and therapeutic assistance). The therapy at Fresh Beginnings focused more on getting clients to use the words that agency personnel wanted to hear than it did on changing clients' actual relationship to drugs.

The relatively benign treatment that clients at Fresh Beginnings received is not found everywhere, however. McCorkel's (2013) study reveals a darker side of drug-addiction programs, at least when they take place in a state prison for women and where outside contractors are in charge of them. The prison was overcrowded, underfunded, understaffed, and receiving rougher and tougher inmates to control. The U.S. war on drugs was increasing the number of African American women in the prison drug program. Either due to racism or to practical decision making—it is unclear which was operating—staff's view of incarcerated addicts changed from looking at them as good people who had temporarily lost their way to viewing them as ruthless predators. A treatment-oriented, compassionate, and caring approach to addicts and addiction was supplanted by a coercive, punitive, mean-spirited, tough-on-crime approach.

According to McCorkel (2013), the orienting theme of this drug program was that inmates were both untrustworthy and unworthy, damaged individuals who deserved heavy doses of abuse and incivility from the staff. Name-calling and status degradation were regular features of how the women were treated, and much of what happened to them was an outcome of staff's belief that the inmates were fruits of the tainted tree. They were defined as incompetent mothers, irresponsible sexual partners, and leeches on the welfare system. In order to have any hope of getting through the program, the inmates had to redefine themselves in ways that coincided exactly with what the staff expected to hear. They were forced to present themselves and their lives in highly negative and stereotypical ways, much of which bore little relationship to what they actually were or to how they actually viewed themselves. Though a minority of the women could insulate themselves from staff's assaults on their self-concepts and personal identities, most of them could not remain unscathed by the barrage of criticism, contempt, and condemnation they received.

The Social Dynamics of Human Drug-Taking Experiences

Organizing Drug Use

The addiction model fails to account for the diversity, uniqueness, and ineradicably social nature of human drug-taking experiences. Humans may use drugs because they expect them to bring pleasure, to eliminate psychic discomfort, or to interrupt the onset of physical pain (Grilly, 1994; Lindesmith, 1968). Humans may even have what Inciardi (1992) calls a *psychogenic addiction,* in which they believe they are addicted and so must continue their drug use when no physical basis for their addiction exists; it is only in their minds.

One thing that seems clear from studies of drug abusers and addicts is that they use drugs in order to get high and to stay in an altered state for as long as possible, not simply to maintain a habit or to avoid the onset of unpleasant withdrawal symptoms (Goode, 2008a). Drug use, especially of stimulating drugs, is a form of *edgework:* risky behaviors that overwhelm the body with a sense of exhilaration and excitement, along with a measure of nervousness and fear (Pine, 2010). The risk *is* the reward, and the excitement and exhilaration are ways to achieve increasing levels of freedom and self-determination. Users may experience a sense of supreme, self-realized sovereignty. A study of 55 users of amphetamines or methamphetamines in Norway indicated that they were used for ordinary reasons rather than for subversive or marginal ones. This sample used them so that they could party longer than would ordinarily have been the case, work longer and harder at their jobs, or self-medicate their self-diagnosed disorders (e.g., attention disorders) (Pedersen, Sandberg, & Copes, 2015, p. 152).

Of all living things, only humans use drugs because of peer pressure or because they want to be part of a drug subculture or drug-using scene (Whaley, Smith, & Hayes-Smith, 2011). A drug-using group gives its members the opportunity to develop new identities, relationships, lifestyles, and ideologies, all centered on drug use (Anderson, 1995). Users will be able to find others who are like them, and they may find that this connectedness is the most "intoxicating" part of their drug-taking experiences. Moreover, only humans can self-consciously and willfully discontinue their drug use because it becomes unattractive to them or inconsistent with other self-images or values that they have developed.

With drugs that are illegal, difficult to get or use, or expensive, a *hassle factor* is present. As the burden of continuing some particular activity increases, it becomes less likely that it will continue for very long (Goode, 2008a, pp. 437–438). This is what increases in criminal penalties for illegal drug use are supposed to do: make drug use so risky or inconvenient that it is no longer worth the trouble to do it. If drugs do become less of a hassle to get and use, it *is* likely that drug use will increase. This increase will be found, however, principally among the heaviest users (Goode, 2008b).

On July 1, 2001, Portugal embarked upon a program of nationwide decriminalization of all drugs, and no distinction was drawn between "hard" and "soft" drugs. Possession for personal consumption incurred no criminal penalties at all. It didn't matter if the drugs were used in private or in public, to maintain a habit or simply to get "high." Technically, use of controlled drugs continued to be prohibited under Portuguese law, but use was treated as an administrative matter, not a criminal offense. Decriminalization was adopted as public policy, because it was clear that criminalization was making a serious problem much worse. One major obstacle to Portugal's efforts to deal with drug abuse in an effective way had been that criminalization drained resources that could have been used for prevention and treatment. Another obstacle was that users were scared to enter treatment facilities because of their fear that they would be arrested and imprisoned for their illegal drug use.

A review and analysis of the success of the Portuguese program by Greenwald (2009) reports impressive results, leading to the conclusion that the decriminalization framework has been a success. Drug use did not increase. In fact, it decreased in absolute terms in some categories of drugs and increased only slightly in other categories (e.g., for older groups). The capital city of Lisbon did not become a haven for drug tourists. Newly reported cases of AIDS and HIV among drug addicts declined substantially. Drug-related mortality rates went down. One *increase* is notable: More individuals sought treatment in the decriminalized setting than they ever did in the criminalized one, substantially *reducing* drug-related harms for the country. According to Greenwald,

> By freeing its citizens from the fear of prosecution and imprisonment for drug usage, Portugal has dramatically improved its ability to encourage drug addicts to avail themselves of treatment. The resources that were previously

devoted to prosecuting and imprisoning drug addicts are now available to provide treatment programs to addicts. Those developments, along with Portugal's shift to a harm-reduction approach, have dramatically improved drug-related social ills, including drug-caused mortalities and drug-related disease transmission. (p. 28)

Another, more recent evaluation of the Portuguese program (Hollersen, 2013) reports that 12 years after its adoption, it can be considered a success, having done more good than harm.

One lesson from the Portuguese experience is that stringent laws and harsh criminal penalties do little, if anything, to reduce the number of addictions or the number of addicts. They also do not eradicate the harms that drugs do. In fact, the opposite may be the case. (However, it would be a mistake to give sole credit to decriminalization for whatever successes the Portuguese program has achieved. Expanded treatment services and an aging population's dwindling interest in using drugs [e.g., heroin] can also be counted as part of the reason for the program's success [Hughes & Stevens, 2010].)

The Limits of Criminal Penalties

The continuing and serious drug-related problems in the United States, existing in tandem with a highly criminalized approach to drug abuse, offer compelling evidence that criminalization does not work well enough to justify its continued use in its current form. The problem is not simply that it hasn't worked. The problem is that it *can't* work, and the Portuguese decriminalization program shows some of the reasons why. Criminalization increases the profits from drug trafficking for those individuals who do not mind breaking the law to benefit themselves; it increases drug-related violence; it corrupts law enforcement; and it keeps drug users away from seeking medical help, exposing them to intense pressures to break the law to support their habits. Arguably, in the end, criminalization does little to affect the demand for drugs and not much more to affect the supply. Disrespect for the law may go up, and the quality and safety of street drugs may drop even more (Walker, 2011).

In 1996, California voters passed Proposition 215, which legalized use of marijuana for medical purposes, though it violated federal law ("California Proposition 215," 2015). Marijuana continues to be classified (as of this writing) by the federal government as a drug that has high potential for abuse and no medical benefits (Schedule I in the federal Controlled Substances Act). Since California's legal approval of medical marijuana, 22 other states, the

District of Columbia, and Guam all enacted similar laws. Eleven other states passed laws that allowed use of medical marijuana but that were more restrictive than California's (e.g., the pot had to be low in THC, the psychoactive substance in marijuana with the greatest effects). In recent years, Colorado, Washington, and Oregon legalized marijuana for recreational use for individuals 21 and over, as did Alaska. On June 18, 2015, Delaware became the nineteenth state to ease the restrictions on marijuana, decriminalizing possession of small amounts of it. The National Organization for the Reform of Marijuana Laws (NORML) applauded all of the above changes as a significant victory. No doubt efforts to legalize pot use, both for medical and recreational purposes, will continue in the years ahead (Black & Joseph, 2014).

The Food and Drug Administration is reviewing evidence on the addictive potential and medical value of marijuana, which could lead to marijuana being classified as a less habituating, medically beneficial substance. It does seem true that the earlier a human starts using marijuana, the more often he or she uses it, and the higher the percentage of psychoactive ingredients the drug contains (i.e., THC), the greater will be the likelihood of long-term damage to the user (Goode, 2015, p. 179). The U.S. government's approach to marijuana has meant that research has been difficult to do—the only federal pot farm in the United States is at the University of Mississippi—and much ignorance exists about both the risks and benefits of the drug for people with different health problems and of different ages (Barcott, 2015). In June 2015, the White House announced that research on marijuana would no longer have to be cleared by the U.S. Public Health Service, a policy change that removed a major bureaucratic obstacle to uncovering valid and reliable information about the drug.

U.S. prohibition of alcohol from 1920 to 1933—the Volstead Act (also known as the National Prohibition Act), which made the sale, production, and distribution of alcoholic drinks (beer, wine, and liquor) illegal—provides lessons about *all* drug-taking experiences and the limited use of criminal sanction (Goode, 2008b). One lesson is that criminal penalties can work with some people, some of the time, to discourage their use of drugs. The demand for heroin is little affected by variations in criminal penalties associated with its use, but the demand for marijuana does drop when penalties for use increase (Goode, 2008b, p. 387). Another lesson is that criminalization of a drug *always* produces unanticipated consequences, some of which are counterproductive for achievement of the initial objective. A prohibition on drugs can, for example, produce a *crime tariff* in which criminalization of a drug sets up barriers (i.e., tariffs) that actually protect criminal activities, financially rewarding anyone who is willing to break the law to supply drugs to people who want them (Packer, 1968). Prices go up because little or no competition exists, and quality goes down. When this happens, criminalization has made a bad situation even worse, and the efforts to stop drug use actually produce more problems, not fewer. Walker (2011) concludes that convictions for drug crimes are the principal reason for the "spectacular" increase in the U.S. prison population during the last 35 to 40 years (p. 311).

The Volstead Act, almost immediately upon its passage, provided both the incentive and the opportunity for some groups to figure out how to evade the new law so that they could keep on drinking alcohol, and other groups to figure out how to benefit financially from alcohol's illegal status. "Speakeasies" (establishments that sold illegal alcohol) replaced saloons. Hardware stores started stocking and selling stills that could be used to make booze at home. If an individual didn't know how to use a still, it was no problem. Libraries had books that contained detailed information about how to use stills to distill liquor at home. Vintners in California *expanded* the total acreage they devoted to grape production, because they had developed a grape juice (called Vine-Glo) that would ferment into wine with little work. The juice was delivered to a customer's home, accompanied by explicit directions for how to turn it into wine. If it were allowed to sit on a shelf in a warm room, in about 2 months, it would have an alcoholic content of about 12%. The whole process of buying the grape juice, fermenting it, and then drinking it was entirely legal if the wine were not sold or taken outside of the home (Mendelson, 2009, p. 4). Brewers developed a half-brewed beverage for distribution and sale (called *wort*) that was also entirely legal if kept in the home. It could be transformed into beer by adding yeast to the concoction. If someone who really wanted a drink had neither a warm room nor a yeast packet, it was still no problem. The Volstead Act did not forbid medicinal use of ethyl alcohol, so physicians were writing prescriptions for alcohol, and pharmacists were filling them in record numbers (Ruane & Cerulo, 2015, p. 182).

A 2011 global commission on drugs and drug policy issued a report that concluded that the global war on drugs has been a failure in reducing both consumption of illegal drugs and their supply (Global Commission on Drug Policy, 2012). It reported that tougher policies had not made the global environment safer, and they had done nothing to promote healthier patterns of drug use. The commission's main recommendation was for nations to regulate drugs in such a way that organized crime's power would be decreased, while the health and security of citizens would be increased. The commission concluded that drug policies based on a war mentality and zero tolerance are counterproductive if sensible drug policies and harm reduction are our objective. Legalization of cannabis, it reasoned, would be a positive and beneficial change. Drum (2009) would agree. He concluded that too many lives have been ruined and too many scarce societal resources have been squandered in a vain effort to stop people from smoking pot.

In a newer report, a different global commission (Global Commission on Drug Policy, 2014) gives its informed views about worldwide drug use. Much like its predecessor, this commission asserts that drug policies across the planet err significantly by being too punitive and too ineffective. Enforcement of these policies has led to increasing violence, corruption, community deterioration, and expanding prison populations, while draining social, economic, and human resources that could have been better used elsewhere. The thrust of the commission's suggestions is to target organized crime and leave the low-level users and suppliers alone whenever possible. The gist is that criminal law should be used sparingly because it is both costly and ineffective. The report of this global, well-respected commission should serve as a warning to anyone who continues to think that a war on drugs is the best way to deal with drug abuse. Jablecki (2012) sees some light at the end of the tunnel. He thinks a harsh, retributive approach, making drug abusers into enemies of the state, is slowly being replaced by a more compassionate, reasoned approach to drug abuse and its control.

Central Activities and Role Engulfment

In a book titled *Heavy Drinking,* Fingarette (1988) explored the human dimension of drug use as he critiqued the claim that alcoholism is a disease. Though Fingarette concentrated on alcohol, his discussion has great value for understanding *any* human drug-taking experience. Heavy drinking and alcoholism are not really physical disorders, he explains. They are labels that cover a wide array of social and individual problems that are the result of a complex and poorly understood interrelationship among biological, psychological, social, and cultural factors. The cardinal feature of alcoholism is its seeming uncontrollability and dysfunctionality. Reaching for that next drink without considering the complications seems to make no sense. Why would anyone sacrifice health, wealth, and happiness for what seems to be a transitory pleasure? A common explanation is that drug use can become a disease. Just as an individual with a cold cannot stop sneezing, an individual with an addiction supposedly cannot stop drinking, smoking, snorting, or injecting.

Some people start using a drug and reach a point where they throw all caution to the wind, doing things that are self-defeating. In these cases, it seems that a powerful momentum—a craving—is at work, and that no amount of persuasion or coercion will be sufficient to create the self-restraint necessary to interrupt the bout of drug taking (Costello, Anderson, & Stein,

2014). The evidence strongly suggests, however, that even individuals who claim that they have uncontrollable cravings for drugs—and it doesn't seem to matter what kind of drug it is—do moderate their use of them as the drugs become unavailable (Schaler, 2000).

Fingarette (1988) insists that heavy drinkers are neither sick nor addicted. They are those individuals for whom drinking alcohol has become a *central activity*, not all that different from other central activities around which people organize their lives, such as jobs, hobbies, family pursuits, or community service. When drinking alcohol evolves into a central activity, an individual's life is defined by drinking, and his or her major preoccupation becomes the pursuit of drink, drinking situations, and drinking companions. Central activities exert a great deal of power over us because they involve significant relationships, activities, values, and views of the self and others. Research has shown that some college students view drinking alcohol as a central and valued activity (Peralta, 2005). Drinking and intoxication are one way for them to show their independence while bonding with peers (Vander Ven, 2011).

A longitudinal study of 449 young couples shows that romantic partners during adolescence have an influence on an individual's drinking patterns (Kreager & Haynie, 2011). Romantic partners can be conduits to a new world of relationships, possibilities, and understandings about the self and others. These new things can lead to risky behaviors of illegal or excessive alcohol use. Even friends of an individual's romantic partner can influence the person's own drinking patterns. This influence may continue even if the romantic relationship ends. Peers play an important role in how much and how often an individual consumes alcohol, and so do the parents of peers (Ragan, Osgood, Wayne, & Feinberg, 2014). (This influence is also found with other types of drugs, such as ecstasy/MDMA or marijuana [Gilliard-Matthews, Stevens, Nilsen, & Dunaev, 2015; Norman & Ford, 2015].)

People cannot always (or easily) change what they are and what they do entirely by themselves. A great deal more than good intentions and personal resolve may be required to reconstruct one's life and to change one's central activities. However, it would be a mistake to discount the power and importance of willpower in the transformation of central activities. Determination and dedication are important parts of any change—personal or social—and they are important in moving from one central activity to another or in shifting the priorities of one's central activities. We must not allow the tenets of the addiction model to blind us to the important role played by will, determination, and true grit in human behavior.

It is unlikely that the future holds some remarkable scientific break-through that will prove indisputably that ongoing drug use either is or is not an addiction. People who believe human addictions exist have no trouble finding the elements of an addiction in drug-taking behavior, just as they do in certain sexual behavior, violence, gambling, nail-biting, and overeating. Likewise, people who believe that the term *addiction* fails to fit human drug-taking experiences have no trouble in finding inconsistencies and contradictions in the addiction model. One thing is true: The word *addiction,* if it is designed to describe drug use as a uniform, universal, debilitating, biologically determined experience, is woefully inadequate to account for the relativity and variability that exist in human drug-taking experiences.

The best thing might be simply to admit that the words *addiction* and *addict* are so mired in controversy and confusion that they have no value and no purpose other than to criticize and condemn. They contribute little to a better understanding of human drug use. In fact, these terms increase the likelihood that we will miss the huge impact of social, cultural, and personality factors on drug taking. They also make it more likely that we will see more uniformity and consistency in human drug-taking experiences than actually exist. It may be best to "just say no" to the terms *addiction* and *addict,* avoiding them whenever possible (Alexander & Wijngaart, 1992).

Moral Entrepreneurs and Drug Crusades

Demonizing Drugs

Drugs are nothing more than inert substances until they are ingested by people who experience effects from them. What determines their moral status—good or bad—is how they are viewed and described by human groups.

> The use of antihistamines to avoid cold symptoms seems unlikely to be defined as deviant, that is, unless the user is a Christian Scientist or a member of any one of several other religions that advocate treating disease by spiritual means only. Drinking alcohol is permitted in our society, but its manufacture and sale were once illegal nationwide, and in some areas it is still illegal to sell alcoholic beverages. . . . Amphetamines are widely available through medical prescription, but taking them without a prescription makes one liable to imprisonment for using a dangerous drug. (McCaghy & Capron, 1997, pp. 283–284)

A drug of abuse at one time and place is not so at another, and groups that are despised and harassed for their drug use in one situation may be ignored or even praised in some other situation. Because images of drugs and drug users change over time, and because so many groups have vested interests in what the images are, we must understand what we can about crusades against drugs and drug users.

A crusade against drugs and drug users will be unsuccessful without broad public support (Ryan, 1994). To achieve this, drug crusaders must have sufficient time, influence, and resources to be able to define a chemical substance and its use as problematic; convince others that what the crusaders say is true; invent or find a way to cure or correct the problem that is affordable, effective, and acceptable to others; and overcome any resistance to the crusade that might exist (Tuggle & Holmes, 1997, p. 80). Moral crusaders may subtly—and not so subtly—create new kinds of deviance and new profiles of deviants by hunting, catching, and sanctioning people who had never been punished before (Victor, 1994). They are helped mightily if they can garner the support of scientific, medical, religious, or legal authorities. Politicians and other representatives of government, along with media spokespersons, play a central role in creating and legitimating wars on drugs (Goode, 2008a; Wysong, Aniskiewicz, & Wright, 1994). Media images of the "addict" and "addiction" usually exaggerate or overstate the damage drugs do to the body, both in regard to how the "addicted" body looks and how it functions. The addict is usually portrayed as a marginal "other," both geographically (i.e., a threat from abroad) and socially (Huggins, 2010). Anything positive or beneficial about street drugs either goes unrecognized or unacknowledged.

Wars on drugs are usually legitimated on the grounds that they, like their military counterparts, can be won only if the cause is just and the soldiers are strong and noble (Kraska, 2003). The major outcome of drug wars, however, is not a victorious conquest. It is usually little more than increased social control over subordinate groups and greater surveillance of them (Fagan, 1994). Drug crusades are almost always launched against groups of people who are already defined as a problem by some dominant group, and their patterns of drug use are used to justify the attack on them (Reinarman, 1996). These ceremonies of exclusion have less to do with the molecular structure or pharmacological effects of drugs than they do with what dominant groups want to encourage or discourage and with whom they want to interact. A war on drugs is a convenient smokescreen for waging a war on certain kinds of *people* (Helmer, 1975; Schaler, 2000; Szasz, 1985). A strange irony is that the war on drugs may do greater damage to the social fabric and ruin more lives than the drugs themselves ever could (Trebach & Inciardi, 1993).

U.S. history is filled with examples of drug crusades that boiled over into public hysteria (Musto, 1987). Alcohol, cocaine, cigarettes, opium, morphine, methamphetamines, marijuana, and heroin have all been the targets of moral reformers in the past, and these chemical substances and those who use them continue to be the object of periodic concern and attack (Tiger, 2013). Any usable chemical substance can be viewed as *abusable* by some group, somewhere, and its members can then set about to punish or correct these drug abusers (Acker, 1991; Brandt, 1991). People with long enough memories can usually recall when today's "most dangerous substance on earth" was at one time proclaimed to be a safe and effective corrective for some human affliction (Inciardi, 1992).

Prior to their criminalization and designation as dangerous substances, the major psychoactive drugs—opium, heroin, morphine, cocaine, marijuana—were administered freely to get people to work harder and longer at dangerous and exhausting jobs. These drugs increased productivity because they were a reward for hard work, and they took some of the edge off the pain of backbreaking labor (Szasz, 1985). In colonial times in the United States, alcohol was widely viewed as a cure-all for a range of psychological and physical ailments, and physicians and ministers encouraged its use (Levine, 1984). In the closing years of his life, Benjamin Franklin used laudanum on a daily basis (opium dissolved in an alcoholic liquid), principally to manage the pain he suffered from kidney stones. Narcotics were available through mail-order catalogs (e.g., Sears, Roebuck & Co.), and the soda pop known as Coca-Cola started life (in 1886) as an alcohol-free beverage that contained cocaine as a key ingredient (which was removed in 1900). Marijuana is a widely used, albeit generally illegal, chemical substance. In fact, no other illegal drug comes even close (Goode, 2008a; Substance Abuse and Mental Health Services Administration [SAMHSA], 2014, p. 15).

An excellent example of how a chemical substance can be demonized and its negative effects exaggerated, thereby producing a drug scare, is the portrayal of *phencyclidine* (PCP) in the U.S. media. At one time, phencyclidine was used as an anesthetic-analgesic in surgery (which dulled pain while the patient remained conscious), but it was eventually abandoned because of its side effects. It can produce hallucinations, disorientation, and a range of unpleasant or upsetting physical symptoms (vomiting, rashes, numbness, lack of coordination, and excitement). When mixed with other drugs, usually LSD, phencyclidine is known on the street as *angel dust*. PCP eventually earned a reputation as a "devil drug," and it came to be viewed as a substance capable of precipitating ghastly acts of violence and self-inflicted injury.

Descriptions of the drug in the print media and portrayals of it on television relied heavily on horror stories, especially ones that reported PCP users as being unusually prone to gouge out their own eyes. If a stronger image than this one exists, it is hard to know what it could possibly be. It shocks, scares, repels, and creates a sense of urgency, while conveying an image of a drug user who is insane, crazy, and totally out of control. Were the negative images of PCP and its users totally false? Probably not—drug crusades may contain a kernel of truth—but facts about drugs are not usually the driving force behind drug scares (Schaler, 2000, p. 39). A gruesome tale such as the gouged-eye story is told and retold so often that it comes to offer instant proof of the correctness of the fears of drug crusaders. Eye gouging is an image that is so meaningful *and* so horrendous that facts alone cannot constrain it (Morgan & Kagan, 1995).

One thing worse than horrific examples of the self-inflicted injury that eye-gouging represents is when horrific injuries are inflicted on *others*. The bar was raised again over Memorial Day, 2012 (May 26), in Miami, Florida. Rudy Eugene, naked and growling, ate about 75% of a homeless man's face before he was killed by police when he refused to stop eating his victim. The homeless man was permanently disfigured from the mauling, but he survived it (Szalavitz, 2012). The attack was blamed on "bath salts," a synthetic stimulant, described in the media as a cocaine substitute or synthetic LSD. The drug is poorly understood, but like all designer drugs, it can contain a variety of different chemical compounds that affect the human organism in multiple ways. (Usually, bath salts contain mephedrine, methylenedioxypyrovalerone, or other amphetamine-like substances.)

Another unusual feature of this admittedly bizarre happening is that the toxicology report on Rudy Eugene found no evidence of bath salts, synthetic marijuana, or LSD in the man's system. The only substance detected was marijuana, a substance that is currently believed to be incapable of provoking what happened during the Memorial Day attack. This fact will probably mean little to those individuals who are prepared to conclude that bath salts are the newest "most dangerous substance on earth." The truth of this incident may be far less complicated and far less sensational. Rudy Eugene may simply have been a seriously disturbed individual who did not receive the kind of care he needed during his life, which led to his attack on the homeless man (Szalavitz, 2012).

A horror story about drugs can sensationalize or even demonize certain events and make new chemical substances and new patterns of drug use the object of heightened public concern. What it cannot do, however, is ensure that a demonized drug is actually the one thing responsible for all the bad effects blamed on it. Some of the problems associated with drugs and their use exist because of how a drug is taken, how much is taken, why it is taken, where it is taken, who is taking it, and what impurities get into the body along with the psychoactive substance. Drugs purchased on the street, where a user can never be sure what psychoactive substance or how much of it is being taken, can be dangerous. Some people can do destructive things to themselves (or others) when they are under the influence. People use these substances at their own risk.

The demonization of drugs and the persecution of drug users, curiously enough, are not necessarily intended to create a drug-free world. The war *against* certain drugs is almost always coupled with a war *for* other drugs.

> The abuse of tobacco, alcohol, and prescription drugs leads to far more serious consequences in terms of public health, violent behavior, spiritual deterioration, family disruption, death and disease—consequences that are all but ignored in the quest for a so-called drug-free culture. The drug-free culture being pursued is in fact a culture which allows citizens to consume culturally integrated drugs but excludes the drugs of other cultures. (Johns & Borrero, 1991, p. 79)

Representatives of the pharmaceutical industry do more than push drugs legally. They push a faith in the power of drugs to cure the afflictions of human existence by constantly reinforcing the message that the solution to personal problems can be found in a tablet, capsule, or dose of syrup.

The drug pushing by drug companies has serious consequences: death and injury to consumers from their use of inappropriate or dangerous legal drugs and a colossal waste of patients' money and national health resources (Chetley & Mintzes, 1992). No doubt exists that drug companies' pushing of both prescription and over-the-counter drugs has an enormous impact on the kinds of drugs that consumers demand and that physicians prescribe (Hanson et al., 2015). Drug companies do all they can to suppress reports of the dangers of drugs or of test results that are unfavorable to their economic interests.

Drug companies spend far more money on pushing (a.k.a. advertising) than on researching and developing drugs (Frances, 2013). When research is done, it is most often poorly constructed and poorly executed, designed more to generate company profits than to learn something of value about drugs and their effects. Having drugs tested by the people who make and profit from them is much like putting Dracula in charge of the blood bank. The human subjects on which drugs are tested are usually parts of samples that are so unrepresentative that they fail to give valid information about what drugs will really do to consumers in the real world. The clinical trials for a drug almost always end up exaggerating its benefits and whitewashing its dangers and risks (Goldacre, 2012). If concealment fails and whitewashing is ineffective, every effort is made to direct attention to the dangers of illegal drugs rather than to the dangers of those drugs that are an important source of company profits (Clinard & Yeager, 1980; Coleman, 2006; Simon, 2008).

Overdoses of prescription pain remedies and deaths from legal chemical substances (i.e., nicotine and alcohol) kill far more people than cocaine and heroin (Reiman & Leighton, 2010).

Drug pricing has no relationship to the costs of research and little relationship to a drug's medicinal value. Profit is a product of the popularity of a drug, which is determined largely by how much advertising monies are spent on it, market position of the drug (which is a reflection of monopoly position of the drug company), and a drug company's lobbying expertise (Frances, 2013). The billions and billions of dollars the pharmaceutical industry spends to push its drugs and to influence the decisions of politicians go a long way toward increasing the profitability of its products. The heavy promotion of drugs can easily nudge some individuals in the direction of believing that they are sick, at least sicker than they once thought they were, and in need of a drug to make themselves feel better.

Drug Bans and Social Bedevilment

Helmer (1975) insists that deception is the core of U.S. drug policy. Past crusades against opium, marijuana, and cocaine were not only about the dangers, real or imagined, of psychoactive substances, but they were also perfect covers for relentless attacks on U.S. minorities, such as the Chinese, Mexicans, and African Americans, supposedly because these people were addicted to drugs and dangerous to themselves and to others. The primary objective of these drug crusades was actually the exclusion of minorities from social life and the eradication of any threats that they might have posed to moral crusaders' interests (Helmer, 1975; Latimer & Goldberg, 1981; Musto, 1987; Szasz, 1985). A drug crusade generates new images of drug use and drug users, and these images become part of the weaponry that some groups use to battle other groups.

The 1960s, 1970s, and 1980s were a perplexing time in the United States. Social diversity and cultural heterogeneity were upsetting to those individuals who viewed them as disorganizing forces. A constellation of problems was particularly alarming: family breakdown, economic decline, disorder in schools, premarital sexuality, illegitimacy, pornography, adultery, community deterioration, crime, delinquency, violence, and America's loss of influence abroad. If the problems were many, so went the official view, the causes were few. Too many people had lost their moral rudders, turning on with drugs and thereby neglecting their social responsibilities and failing to honor the social contract.

Sensitization to the dangers of drugs, especially crack cocaine, provided a scapegoat on which people could lay the blame for some of the social and personal problems that seemed to have increased dramatically as the years had passed. The transformation of the image of cocaine use from a harmless, recreational activity to a dangerous, if not deadly, addiction was accompanied by shifts in the symbolization of both cocaine and its users (Scheibe, 1994). Stricter drug laws and harsher punishments for drug offenders became a central part of the overall plan to rebuild the United States.

In September 1986, the U.S. House of Representatives passed a sweeping drug abuse law. It allocated more monies for enforcement than treatment, increased sentences for drug-related crimes, and increased sanctions against foreign nations that refused to cooperate with efforts to eradicate foreign sources of illicit drugs coming into the United States. This act authorized the *100-to-1 rule,* which established a glaring (and illogical) discrepancy between the penalties for crack cocaine and powdered cocaine use by penalizing users of the former more severely. The criminal penalty was the same for someone possessing 5 grams of crack as it was for someone possessing 500 grams of powdered cocaine. Although the way a drug is taken (e.g., swallowed, inhaled, or injected) does influence the speed and duration of its effects, this is insufficient justification for penalizing users of crack cocaine so much more harshly than users of powdered cocaine. The Fair Sentencing Act of 2010, passed by the 111th Congress and signed into law by President Obama that same year, reduced the disparity between mandatory minimums for users of crack cocaine and powdered cocaine from 100 to 1 to 18 to 1. Under this new law, the threshold to be charged with a felony for possession of crack is 28 grams, but it remains at 500 grams for powdered cocaine. (In June 2012, the U.S. Supreme Court ruled that the new law applied retroactively, covering people who had been convicted before the act was passed, which resulted in the release of many of those incarcerated for cocaine-related offenses.)

George H. W. Bush, forty-first president of the United States, delivered his first major prime-time speech to the nation from the Oval Office of the White House on September 5, 1989. The core of his address was his pledge that he and his administration would achieve a victory over drugs. To show the nation just how accessible drugs were, he held up a clear plastic bag of crack cocaine marked "EVIDENCE." He reported to the nation that the bag had been seized by drug enforcement agents in Lafayette Park, directly across from the White House. The implication was clear: No place was safe from drugs. Bush insisted that "crack" was destroying our cities, turning them into battle zones and killing our children. A picture of the president, cocaine bag held defiantly aloft, appeared on the front pages of newspapers all across the country (Reinarman & Levine, 1997).

The president, however, was not telling the truth. His handlers and speech writers thought he needed a prop to show his viewing audience to enhance his message. The president had agreed. He even wanted the drug to be seized from someone (anyone) in Lafayette Park so that he could claim that "crack" was everywhere, even right in front of the White House. Reinarman and Levine (1997) tell us what happened next.

> White House Communications Director David Demarest asked Cabinet Affairs Secretary David Bates to instruct the Justice Department "to find some crack that fit the description in the speech." Bates called Richard Weatherbee, special assistant to Attorney General Dick Thornburgh, who then called James Millford [sic], executive assistant to the DEA chief. Finally, Milford phoned William McMullen, special agent in charge of the DEA's Washington office, and told him to arrange an undercover crack buy near the White House. (pp. 22–23)

The president's plan may have been good politics, but it was based on bad sociology and even worse economics. Drug agents could find nobody selling crack or any other drug anywhere near the White House, because nobody would be there to buy it. The sale of crack cocaine was concentrated in the poorer neighborhoods of Washington, D.C.

All was not lost, however. Drug enforcement agents were able to find someone who was willing to journey to the White House to make the sale. They enticed Keith Jackson, an 18-year-old African American high school student, to make the trip. He had to be coached, however, because the man did not even know where the White House was, let alone how to get there. The agents did not actually seize the cocaine, either. They bought it from Jackson for $2,400 and then sent him on his way. When reality did not conform to the script, the speech, or the wishes of the president and his advisors, things were done to create a reality that would fit the scripted image.

One claim that received strong support in scientific writings and the popular press was that cocaine poses exceptional threats to a user's health and well-being. Leading authorities asserted with confidence and usually much fanfare that cocaine was too dangerous to be tried even once and posed extraordinary threats to any user. These claims, especially because they seemed beyond dispute, were used as one more bit of ammunition in the war on drugs in general and the war on cocaine in particular. Fewer and fewer people were willing to speak on behalf of cocaine, as they had in the past (Erickson, Adlaf, Murray, & Smart, 1987; Trebach, 1987). The indisputable fact that certain drugs at high doses are deadly was transformed into a more general and bogus indictment of *all* illicit drugs at *any* dose as unusually dangerous.

Cocaine is a heart stimulant, so any imprudent or recreational use is cause for concern. However, *moderate* use of cocaine seems to be no more cardiotoxic than other stimulating activities, and the claim that no safe dose of cocaine exists is false. A link does seem to exist between *prolonged* and *heavy* use of cocaine and cardiotoxicity, but even here we must be cautious if truth is our objective. If a heavy user were to die from a heart attack while using cocaine—a rare event—it still would not prove that cocaine was the cause. The death might have been an atypical reaction to the drug, comparable to the deaths some people experience from using aspirin. It might also have been due to an already existing health problem, such as high blood pressure or arteriosclerosis. If this person had tried to jog, to have sex, or gotten too excited over a sporting event, the outcome likely would have been the same. Another possibility is that it was not the cocaine itself but some adulterant in the street variety of the drug, or some other drug used along with it, that caused the death (Alexander & Wong, 1990, p. 260).

A prominent scare story associated with cocaine use is the claim that large numbers of children are born addicted because of their mothers' use of the drug. The initial studies of babies who were born to mothers who used cocaine during pregnancy were not at all encouraging. They reported that these infants were more likely to be born prematurely; have a significantly lower birth weight; have smaller heads; suffer seizures; have genital and urinary tract abnormalities; have poor motor abilities; have brain lesions; and exhibit behavioral aberrations, such as impulsivity, moodiness, and lower sensitivity to environmental stimuli (Goode & Ben-Yehuda, 1994, p. 216). Findings such as these were picked up quickly by the media and just as quickly transmitted to the general public. However, according to Goode and Ben-Yehuda, enough evidence had accumulated by the 1990s to suggest strongly that the *crack-baby syndrome* is a medical fiction. Mothers who smoke crack are more likely to engage in a variety of practices that strongly correlate with poor infant health, such as smoking tobacco, drinking alcohol, using other psychoactive drugs, refusing to exercise, following poor eating habits, failing to visit physicians regularly, and maintaining a generally reckless lifestyle.

> With crack babies, what we saw was [sic] pathological conditions *associated with* the use of cocaine that was [sic] automatically *assumed to have been caused* by the drug which later, careful research indicated, were in fact caused by very conventional conditions *about which there was very little subjective concern.* (p. 216)

Many things work together to determine the health of a newborn, and a mother's use of crack cocaine is just one of them.

Not only were helpless infants defined as an at-risk population, but so were the hale and hearty. In the 1980s, increasing attention was directed toward the illicit drug use of professional athletes (Leiber, Jamieson, & Krohn, 1993). Once again, the reason has less to do with drugs than it does with social relationships and group interests. Drug use among professional athletes, real or imagined, was used by owners as a trump card in the difficult and contentious contract negotiations that were underway. Players were mainly concerned with their freedom to determine with which team(s) they would play and other features of their professional careers, as well as their pension plans, but management artfully focused most of the attention on illicit drug use among players.

The players' wish to be free from the intrusion of drug testing was branded by the owners as an example of their selfishness and irresponsibility. Their thinking was, why not go along with the plan unless something was being hidden? Media representatives tended to side with owners and portrayed players as the deviant ones for being generally ignorant of, or indifferent to, how damaging their drug use was to themselves and to the game. This alignment of the media with owners increased the owners' power and effectively undercut players' demands for higher salaries, more control over the game, and more control over their own personal careers.

Professional and nonprofessional athletes alike are increasingly being singled out for their illegal use of steroids. Any objective analysis of athletes' use of steroids must conclude that legitimate health risks exist, but that the risks have been exaggerated (Perry, 2008). Physicians have used steroids to treat patients since the 1930s with a reasonable measure of safety. The current claims of horrible side effects from steroid use correctly describe the experiences of only long-term, heavy users who use steroids without medical advice and supervision (Hanson et al., 2015). Making steroids more difficult to get by making their use a crime had a predictable effect: It produced a black market for steroids in which prices and risk went up and quality went down. Drug testing in professional athletics, ostensibly to get rid of illegal steroid use, was done principally for public relations purposes by a business that is highly interested in protecting its image and its profits.

The sense of panic and urgency that the war on drugs generates may be one of its biggest liabilities. The use of *club drugs* or *designer drugs*, specifically by adolescents and young adults at nightclubs, raves, or concerts, has generated a disproportionate amount of public attention and concern. The use of designer drugs such as Ecstasy (MDMA), GHB, Rohypnol (the "date rape drug"), and ketamine has involved a relatively small number of individuals, even among the drug-using population, and the frequency of use of most designer drugs has declined with the passage of time (Goode, 2008a, p. 268;

Hanson et al., 2015). Although the club drugs are a heterogeneous collection of psychoactive chemicals, each one having distinctive effects, they are still (mistakenly) lumped together into the same category. This mistake, however, pales in comparison to a more serious one, namely, treating these drugs as uniformly the same in terms of their potential to hurt or kill users.

A study in the state of Florida reported that from 1994 to 2000, exactly 254 individuals had died from their use of rave or club drugs (discussed in Goode, 2008a, p. 267). However, it turns out that the study was flawed, and the panel that prepared the report had based their conclusions on dogma and political interest. Too many types of drugs were included in the category of club drugs, some of which did not even fit the panel's *own* working definition of what qualified as one (e.g., nitrous oxide or laughing gas was included, and though it is sometimes abused, it does not qualify as a club drug). In addition, some of the 254 deaths the panel blamed on club drugs stretched things a bit too far. One woman died after being hit by an automobile, and she was included in the deaths. Another man committed suicide after losing his job. His blood tested positive for amphetamine, so he was included in the tally, too. Although some of the club drugs can be dangerous, condemnation of a chemical substance for the purpose of public relations or political advancement may do more harm than good if it breeds distrust. Even a well-meaning lie is still a lie.

Portrayals or conceptualizations of drug use that pathologize or demonize adolescent drug use give pictures of it that are too distorted to do us much good if we wish to understand users' motivations and methods. The typical participant in the rave scene is neither an enslaved victim of a drug epidemic nor a self-centered risk-taker who needs to be locked up for the protection of others. Adolescents' drug-use patterns are flexible and almost always voluntary, and adolescent nightlife behaviors change all the time (Hunt, Moloney, & Evans, 2010).

Any evidence of an increase in drug use, no matter how slight and no matter what drug it is, or any evidence of a shift in drug-use patterns, is dramatized by the U.S. press. The print media created a cocaine drug scare in the summer of 1986 by using "shocking numbers and graphic accounts" (Orcutt & Turner, 1993) to make cocaine use, especially crack cocaine, appear widespread and dangerous. These media representatives took raw data from surveys of drug use among high school seniors and young adults and fiddled with the numbers until they could be used to prove the existence of a drug epidemic.

> We found ample evidence of media workers snatching at shocking numbers
> from ISR [Institute for Social Research at the University of Michigan] press

releases, smothering reports of stable or decreasing use under more ominous headlines, and distorting the cocaine problem to epidemic proportions as high as 40 percent of high school seniors. (p. 203)

When cocaine use could no longer be portrayed as an epidemic—stories about it had disappeared from all the major news magazines by the end of 1986—media magicians simply produced a new plague from the ashes of the old. *Newsweek* reported in its February 3, 1992, issue that LSD use was "rising alarmingly" among U.S. teens (quoted in Orcutt & Turner, p. 201). Like previous media claims, this one was based on omissions, exaggerations, and distortions. According to Orcutt and Turner, the "alarming rise" in LSD use from 1989 to 1990 was countered by a much larger *drop* in cocaine use, but little was made of this decrease (p. 201). It seems that decreases in drug use are not nearly as newsworthy as increases.

Practically any claim or declaration about patterns of drug use or the social or personal consequences of using drugs must be tentative. Users of most drugs are inclined to be deceptive or evasive about their drug use, so estimates of drug-use patterns are very likely to be unreliable and invalid (Andreas & Greenhill, 2010; Page & Singer, 2010). A substantial number of people understate on surveys the extent of their drug use, and some people are more likely to lie on surveys than others.

Drug Fears

A growing concern in the twenty-first century combines societal distress over drugs with societal distress over international terrorism. The term *narcoterrorism* covers a multitude of activities in which terrorist groups manufacture and distribute illegal drugs in order to accumulate capital to further their terrorist activities. With the end of the Cold War and the relative decline in the influence of communism on world events, state-sponsored terrorism started to fade in importance. U.S. retaliation against Islamic radicals for the terrorist attacks of September 11, 2001, has crippled their ability to raise funds from mosques and charities. Today, surviving as a terrorist requires the ability to raise funds in independent ways, and trafficking in drugs is one of the most profitable activities around. Al-Qaeda's leadership has avoided involvement in drug smuggling, but practically nobody else has. Terrorist organizations and organized crime syndicates show increasing levels of cooperation all across the planet (Treverton, Matthies, Cunningham, Gouka, & Ridgeway, 2014, p. 116). The United States now officially views drug trafficking and terrorism as sharing the same ground of geography, money, and violence (Madsen, 2014; Winslow & Zhang, 2008). The war on terror now goes hand in hand with the war on drugs. (The two countries that are currently principal sites of narcoterrorism are Afghanistan and Pakistan.)

Drugs, even without their tie to terrorism, are still associated with global crime and violence. Mexican drug lords and the cartels they command are engaged in an ongoing, bloody turf war, fueled both by guns and money (Madsen, 2014). The weapons can be assault rifles or even grenade launchers, and the targets are rival gang members, police officers, soldiers, or even civilians. Anybody in the way of their relentless profiteering is fair game (Gibler, 2011). The death and destruction from these power struggles seem never-ending, a threat to the entire fabric of a society. The tremendous profits to be made from drug trafficking have led to widespread corruption in Mexico of the police, judiciary, and military. The local police can be working for one cartel, the state police for another, and the federal police for still another (Vulliamy, 2010).

Ordinary citizens—even journalists—may be reluctant to travel in Mexico for fear that they will be stopped at a checkpoint, robbed of what they have, and then murdered and left to rot on the side of the road. Even if the criminal justice system is free from corruption, convictions are difficult to get because evidence is lacking and witnesses are either afraid to testify or are simply murdered prior to trial. This unchecked violence and cartel competition has spawned an arms race that can only lead to further violence and bloodshed. It may be tempting to conclude that Mexico's drug problems are its own, better dealt with at a local level. This kind of thinking, however, would be a mistake. The huge U.S. demand for drugs is what fuels much of the profit engine in Mexico—giving cartels economic incentives to put money first—and arms imported from the United States are what help to make the violence as deadly as it is (Vulliamy, 2010; Young, 2011).

Two Mexicos exist. One is a place where Mexican authorities fight drug cartels by waging a war on drugs, where U.S. financial aid plays a role, and where the Mexican Army is a central part of the fight. This Mexico has both drug laws and a criminal justice system that is enlisted in the war on drugs. The U.S. government views this society as its ally in the international effort to stop drug abuse. This is the Mexico reported on by U.S. media. The other Mexico, however, is the real deal. It is a place where the war is fought to *get* drugs, and the police and military actively go after as much money as they can get from drugs and the U.S. demand for them. In this latter Mexico, the coin of the realm is fear, intimidation, bribery, and corruption. Murder of the innocent is a common occurrence, and survival is either a matter of luck or of brute force. It is a lawless place, pervaded by violence and greed (Bowden, 2009). The drug cartels have expanded their influence into the

United States, bringing not only drugs but also murder, kidnapping, and corruption of U.S. law enforcement. In July 2015, drug lord Joaquín "El Chapo" (Shorty) Guzmán escaped from a Mexican prison (by using a motorcycle on rails in an underground tunnel). He is the head of the Sinaloa Cartel, one of the most powerful and ruthless cartels that has ever existed. It is estimated to be the supplier for at least 80% of Chicago's illegal drugs (Vick, 2015). (Guzmán was recaptured by Mexican authorities in January 2016.)

The ties between Mexico and the United States are real, and the border between the two countries is porous. In 2008, over 50 victims of drug violence in Ciudad Juárez were treated at Thomason Hospital in El Paso, Texas, and U.S. and Mexican firefighters helped out one another (Vulliamy, 2010). Narcotics running across the border and along the borderland between the United States and Mexico—which is 2,100 miles long and 50 miles wide, stretching from the Pacific Ocean to the Gulf of Mexico—has made this vast area even more forbidding and dangerous than it once was. It is a world unto itself (which Vulliamy calls *Amexica*). The drug war in Mexico, according to Vulliamy, is unique because it is about nothing that matters. It lacks both a propelling cause and any convincing ideology. "Mexicans are mutilating, decapitating, torturing, and killing each other ostensibly over money and the drug-smuggling routes that provide it" (p. 11). It is a war only to show who is the coolest by making it possible for drug pushers and drug traffickers to own and display symbols of conspicuous consumption.

Conclusions

Though animals, regardless of species, are sensitive to certain chemical substances, for humans it is their cognitive and symbolic abilities, as well as their complex and intricate social lives, that are most responsible for their drug-taking experiences. Ongoing disputes over fundamental questions are real and important: What is a drug? What is addiction? What is abuse? Who is an addict? These questions are at the foundation of the interpretation of drug experiences.

Some groups advocate using an addiction terminology to interpret the use of drugs; other groups advocate staying clear of the words *addiction* and *addict* because they believe these terms are used more to condemn than to clarify. Human drug experiences are unique and show a great deal of relativity. Understandings about drugs and drug use are forged in the context of struggles between different groups, some of which take charge of interpreting social reality for everybody else.

What is most valuable is to develop an understanding of the cause, course, and consequence of the many crusades that have been initiated against drugs and drug users. Opiates, alcohol, marijuana, cocaine, PCP, steroids, designer drugs, and stimulants have all been the target of moral entrepreneurs at some point in U.S. history. These crusaders have done what they could to have their drug of concern identified as the most dangerous substance on Earth. A "new" menace is narcoterrorism, which merges two of our fears together: the fear of terrorist attack and the fear of drug addicts. Mexico-based drug cartels are having an influence on the relationship between the United States and Mexico. The war on drugs, whatever it is designed to do, is not going to usher in a drug-free world. The war is simply filled with too many contradictions and ironies for it ever to be able to accomplish its intended objectives.

References

Acker, C. (1991). Social meanings of disease: Changing concepts of addiction in the twentieth century. *Magazine of History, 6,* 28–29.

Alexander, B. K., & Schweighofer, A. (1988). Defining "addiction." *Canadian Psychology, 29,* 151–162.

Alexander, B. K., & Wijngaart, G. F. van de. (1992). The disease of addiction: It's sick and tired. In A. Trebach & K. Zeese (Eds.), *Strategies for change* (pp. 275–279). Washington, DC: Drug Policy Foundation.

Alexander, B. K., & Wong, L. S. (1990). Adverse effects of cocaine on the heart: A critical review. In A. Trebach & K. Zeese (Eds.), *The great issues of drug policy* (pp. 257–267). Washington, DC: Drug Policy Foundation.

Anderson, T. (1995). Toward a preliminary macro theory of drug addiction. *Deviant Behavior, 16,* 353–372.

Andreas, P., & Greenhill, K. M. (Eds.). (2010). *Sex, drugs, and body counts: The politics of numbers in global crime and conflict.* Ithaca, NY: Cornell University Press.

Barcott, B. (2015). *Weed the people: The future of legal marijuana in America.* New York: Time Books.

Becker, H. (1967). History, culture and subjective experience: An exploration of the social bases of drug-induced experiences. *Journal of Health and Social Behavior, 7,* 163–176.

Black, P., & Joseph, L. J. (2014). Still dazed and confused: Midlife marijuana use by the baby boom generation. *Deviant Behavior, 35,* 822–841.

Bowden, C. (2009). We bring fear. *Mother Jones, 34,* 28–43.

Brandt, A. (1991). Up in smoke: How cigarettes came to be a controlled substance. *Magazine of History, 6,* 22–24.

California Proposition 215, the Medical Marijuana Initiative (1996). (2015). *Ballotpedia.* Retrieved April 3, 2015, from http://ballotpedia.org/California-Proposition-215-the-Medical-Marijuana-Initiative-(1996)

Carnes, P. (1991). *Don't call it love: Recovery from sexual addiction*. New York: Bantam.

Carr, E. S. (2011). *Scripting addiction: The politics of therapeutic talk and American society*. Princeton, NJ: Princeton University Press.

Chetley, A., & Mintzes, B. (Eds.). (1992). *Promoting health or pushing drugs? A critical examination of marketing of pharmaceuticals*. Amsterdam, The Netherlands: Health Action International.

Clinard, M. B., & Yeager, P. (1980). *Corporate crime*. New York: Free Press.

Coleman, J. W. (2006). *The criminal elite: Understanding white-collar crime* (6th ed.). New York: Worth.

Costello, B. J., Anderson, B. J., & Stein, M. D. (2014). Self-control and adverse "drinking" consequences. *Deviant Behavior, 35,* 973–992.

Drum, K. (2009). The patriot's guide to legalization: Have you ever looked at our marijuana policy? I mean really looked at it? *Mother Jones, 34,* 49–52.

Erickson, P., Adlaf, E., Murray, G., & Smart, R. (1987). *The steel drug*. Lexington, MA: Lexington.

Fagan, J. (1994). Do criminal sanctions deter drug crimes? In D. L. MacKenzie & C. Uchida (Eds.), *Drugs and crime: Evaluating public policy initiatives* (pp. 188–214). Thousand Oaks, CA: Sage.

Fingarette, H. (1988). *Heavy drinking: The myth of alcoholism as a disease*. Berkeley: University of California Press.

Ford, J. A. (2014). Poor health, strain, and substance use. *Deviant Behavior, 35,* 654–667.

Frances, A. (2013). *Saving normal*. New York: William Morrow/HarperCollins.

Gibler, J. (2011). *To die in Mexico: Dispatches from inside the drug war*. San Francisco: City Lights Books.

Gilliard-Matthews, S., Stevens, R., Nilsen, M., & Dunaev, J. (2015). "You see it everywhere. It's just natural": Contextualizing the role of peers, family, and neighborhood in initial substance use. *Deviant Behavior, 36,* 492–509.

Global Commission on Drug Policy. (2012, June). *The war on drugs and HIV/AIDS: How the criminalization of drug use fuels the global pandemic*. Retrieved September 4, 2012, from http://global commissionondrugs.org/wp-content/themes/gcdp_v1/pdf/GCDP_HIV-AIDS_ 2012_REFERENCE.pdf

Global Commission on Drug Policy. (2014, September). *Taking control: Pathways to drug policies that work*. Retrieved April 3, 2015, from http://www.globalcommissionondrugs.org/reports/

Goffman, E. (1952). On cooling the mark out. *Psychiatry, 15,* 451–463.

Goldacre, B. (2012). *Big pharma: How drug companies mislead doctors and harm patients*. New York: Faber & Faber/Farrar, Straus & Giroux.

Goode, E. (2008a). *Drugs in American society* (7th ed.). Boston: McGraw-Hill.

Goode, E. (2008b). Legalize it? A bulletin from the war on drugs. In J. Goodwin & J. Jasper (Eds.), *The contexts reader* (pp. 384–391). New York: Norton.

Goode, E. (2015). *Deviant behavior* (10th ed.). Boston: Pearson.

Goode, E., & Ben-Yehuda, N. (1994). *Moral panics: The social construction of deviance*. Cambridge, MA: Blackwell.

Greenwald, G. (2009). *Drug decriminalization in Portugal: Lessons for creating fair and successful drug policies.* Washington, DC: Cato Institute.

Grilly, D. (1994). *Drugs and human behavior* (2nd ed.). Boston: Allyn & Bacon.

Hanson, G. R., Venturelli, P. J., & Fleckenstein, A. E. (2015). *Drugs and society* (12th ed.). Burlington, VT: Jones & Bartlett.

Helmer, J. (1975). *Drugs and minority oppression.* New York: Seabury.

Henkin, W. (1996). The myth of sexual addiction. In R. Francoeur (Ed.), *Taking sides: Clashing views on controversial issues in human sexuality* (5th ed., pp. 58–65). Guilford, CT: Dushkin.

Hoffmann, J. P. (2014). Religiousness, social networks, moral schemas, and marijuana use: A dynamic dual-process model of culture and behavior. *Social Forces, 93,* 181–208.

Hollersen, W. (2013, March 27). "This is working": Portugal, 12 years after decriminalizing drugs. *Speigel Online International.* Retrieved April 2, 2015, from http://www.spiegel.de/international/europe/evaluating-drug-decriminalization-in-portugal-12-years-later-a-891060.html

Huggins, R. (2010). Images of addiction: The representation of illicit drug use in popular media. In L. J. Moore & M. Kosut (Eds.), *The body reader: Essential social and cultural readings* (pp. 384–398). New York: New York University Press.

Hughes, C. E., & Stevens, A. (2010). What can we learn from the Portuguese decriminalization of illicit drugs? *British Journal of Criminology, 50,* 999–1022.

Hunt, G., Moloney, M., & Evans, K. (2010). *Youth, drugs, and nightlife.* New York: Routledge.

Inciardi, J. (1992). *The war on drugs II.* Mountain View, CA: Mayfield.

Jablecki, L. T. (2012). The death of the war on drugs. In J. Naughton (Ed.), *Annual editions: Criminal justice 11/12* (35th ed., pp. 16–18). New York: McGraw-Hill.

Johns, C. J., & Borrero J. M. (1991). The war on drugs: Nothing succeeds like failure. In G. Barak (Ed.), *Crimes by the capitalist state* (pp. 67–100). Albany: State University of New York Press.

Kerley, K. R., Copes, H., & Griffin, O. H., III. (2015). Middle-class motives for non-medical prescription stimulant use among college students. *Deviant Behavior, 36,* 589–603.

Kraska, P. (2003). The military as drug police: Exercising the ideology of war. In L. K. Gaines & P. B. Kraska (Eds.), *Drugs, crime, and justice: Contemporary perspectives* (2nd ed., pp. 288–308). Prospect Heights, IL: Waveland Press.

Kreager, D. A., & Haynie, D. L. (2011). Dangerous liaisons: Dating and drinking diffusion in adolescent peer networks. *American Sociological Review, 76,* 737–763.

Latimer, D., & Goldberg, J. (1981). *Flowers in the blood: The story of opium.* New York: Franklin Watts.

Leiber, M., Jamieson, K., & Krohn, M. (1993). Newspaper reporting and the production of deviance: Drug use among professional athletes. *Deviant Behavior, 14,* 317–339.

Levine, H. (1984). The alcohol problem in America: From temperance to alcoholism. *British Journal of Addiction, 79,* 109–119.

Lindesmith, A. (1968). *Addiction and opiates.* Chicago: Aldine.

Madsen, F. G. (2014). Transnational crime and terrorism. In J. L. Feldkamp (Ed.), *Theory and politics of terrorism* (pp. 99–110). San Diego, CA: Cognella.

Matveychuk, W. (1986). The social construction of drug definitions and drug experience. In P. Park & W. Matveychuk (Eds.), *Culture and politics of drugs* (pp. 7–12). Dubuque, IA: Kendall/Hunt.

McCaghy, C., & Capron, T. (1997). *Deviant behavior* (4th ed.). Boston: Allyn & Bacon.

McCorkel, J. A. (2013). *Breaking women: Gender, race, and the new politics of imprisonment.* New York: New York University Press.

Mendelson, R. (2009). *From demon to darling: A legal history of wine in America.* Berkeley: University of California Press.

Miller, B. L., & Stogner, J. M. (2015). Keeping it between the buoys: Assessing self-reported boating under the influence (BUI) in a young adult population. *Deviant Behavior, 36,* 68–86.

Montagne, M. (1988). The metaphorical nature of drugs and drug taking. *Social Science and Medicine, 26,* 417–424.

Morgan, J., & Kagan, D. (1995). The dusting of America: The image of phencyclidine (PCP) in the popular media. In J. Inciardi & K. McElrath (Eds.), *The American drug scene: An anthology* (pp. 204–213). Los Angeles: Roxbury.

Murphy, J. (2011). Drug court as both a legal and medical authority. *Deviant Behavior, 32,* 257–291.

Musto, D. (1987). *The American disease: Origins of narcotic control* (Expanded ed.). New York: Oxford University Press.

Norman, L. B., & Ford, J. A. (2015). Adolescent Ecstasy use: A test of social bonds and social learning theory. *Deviant Behavior, 36,* 527–538.

Orcutt, J., & Turner, J. B. (1993). Shocking numbers and graphic accounts: Quantified images of drug problems in the print media. *Social Problems, 40,* 190–206.

Packer, H. (1968). *The limits of the criminal sanction.* Stanford, CA: Stanford University Press.

Page, J. B., & Singer, M. (2010). *Comprehending drug use: Ethnographic research at the social margins.* New Brunswick, NJ: Rutgers University Press.

Pawson, M., & Kelly, B. C. (2014). Consumption and community: The subcultural contexts of disparate marijuana practices in jam band and hip-hop scenes. *Deviant Behavior, 35,* 347–363.

Pedersen, W., Sandberg, S., & Copes, H. (2015). High speed. Amphetamine use in the context of conventional culture. *Deviant Behavior, 36,* 146–165.

Peele, S. (1985). *The meaning of addiction: Compulsive experience and its interpretation.* Lexington, MA: D. C. Heath.

Peralta, R. (2005). Race and the culture of college drinking: An analysis of white privilege on campus. In W. Palacios (Ed.), *Cocktails and dreams: Perspectives on drug and alcohol use* (pp. 127–141). Upper Saddle River, NJ: Pearson/Prentice Hall.

Perry, D. (2008). Pumped-up panic. In R. Heiner (Ed.), *Deviance across cultures* (pp. 166–176). New York: Oxford University Press.

Pine, J. (2010). Embodied capitalism and the meth economy. In L. J. Moore & M. Kosut (Eds.), *The body reader: Essential social and cultural readings* (pp. 164–183). New York: New York University Press.

Ragan, D. T., Osgood, D., Wayne, & Feinberg, M. E. (2014). Friends as a bridge to parental influence: Implications for adolescent alcohol use. *Social Forces, 92,* 1061–1085.

Raikhel, E., & Garriott, W. (Eds.). (2013). *Addiction trajectories.* Durham, NC: Duke University Press.

Ray, O., & Ksir, C. (1996). *Drugs, society, and human behavior* (7th ed.). St. Louis, MO: C. V. Mosby.

Reiman, J., & Leighton, P. (2010). *The rich get richer and the poor get prison: Ideology, class, and crime.* Upper Saddle River, NJ: Pearson.

Reinarman, C. (1996). The social construction of drug scares. In E. Goode (Ed.), *Social deviance* (pp. 224–234). Boston: Allyn & Bacon.

Reinarman, C., & Levine, H. (1997). The crack attack: Politics and media in America's latest drug scare. In C. Reinarman & H. Levine (Eds.), *Crack in America: Demon drugs and social justice* (pp. 18–51). Berkeley: University of California Press.

Rice, R. (1998). The startling truth about sexual addiction. In L. Salinger (Ed.), *Deviant behavior 98/99* (3rd ed., pp. 217–219). Guilford, CT: Dushkin.

Ruane, J. M., & Cerulo, K. A. (2015). *Second thoughts: Sociology challenges conventional wisdom* (6th ed.). Thousand Oaks, CA: Sage.

Ryan, K. (1994). Technicians and interpreters in moral crusades: The case of the drug courier profile. *Deviant Behavior, 15,* 217–240.

Safire, W. (1997). *Lend me your ears: Great speeches in history* (Rev. & expanded ed.). New York: Norton.

Schaefer, B. P., Vito, A. G., Marcum, C. D., Higgins, G. E., & Ricketts, M. L. (2015). Heroin use among adolescents: A multi-theoretical examination. *Deviant Behavior, 36,* 101–112.

Schaler, J. (2000). *Addiction is a choice.* Chicago: Open Court.

Scheibe, K. (1994). Cocaine careers: Historical and individual constructions. In T. Sarbin & J. Kitsuse (Eds.), *Constructing the social* (pp. 195–212). Thousand Oaks, CA: Sage.

Siegel, R. (1989). *Intoxication: Life in pursuit of artificial paradise.* New York: Dutton.

Simon, D. (2008). *Elite deviance* (9th ed.). Boston: Allyn & Bacon.

Staley, S. (1992). *Drug policy and the decline of American cities.* New Brunswick, NJ: Transaction Publishers.

Substance Abuse and Mental Health Services Administration (SAMHSA). (2014). *Results from the 2013 National Survey on Drug Use and Health: Summary of National Findings,* NSDUH Series H-48, HHS Publication No. (SMA) 14–4863. Rockville, MD: Author. Retrieved April 3, 2015, from http://www.samhsa.gov/data/sites/default/files/NSDUHresultsPDFWHTML2013/Web/NSDUHresults2013.pdf

Szalavitz, M. (2012, June 27). The cannabis cannibal? Miami face-eater didn't take "bath salts." *Time Health & Family.* Retrieved September 3, 2012, from http://healthland.time.com/2012/06/27/the-cannabis-cannibal-miami-face-eater-didnt-take-bath-salts/

Szasz, T. (1985). *Ceremonial chemistry: The ritual persecution of drugs, addicts, and pushers* (Rev. ed.). Holmes Beach, FL: Learning Publications.

Tiger, R. (2013). *Judging addicts: Drug courts and coercion in the justice system.* New York: New York University Press.

Trebach, A. (1987). *The great drug war.* New York: Macmillan.

Trebach, A., & Inciardi, J. (1993). *Legalize it? Debating American drug policy.* Washington, DC: American University Press.

Treverton, G., Matthies, C., Cunningham, K. J., Gouka, J., & Ridgeway G. (2014). Organized crime and terrorism. In J. L. Feldkamp (Ed.), *Theory and politics of terrorism* (pp. 111–118). San Diego, CA: Cognella.

Tuggle, J., & Holmes, M. (1997). Blowing smoke: Status politics and the Shasta County smoking ban. *Deviant Behavior, 18,* 77–93.

Vander Ven, T. (2011). *Getting wasted: Why college students drink too much and party so hard.* New York: New York University Press.

Vick, K. (2015, July 27). A humiliating jail break puts Mexico back in a place it tried to leave behind. *Time, 186,* pp. 9–10.

Victor, J. (1994). Fundamentalist religion and the moral crusade against Satanism: The social construction of deviant behavior. *Deviant Behavior, 15,* 305–334.

Volkow, N. D., Wang, G.-J., Fischman, M. W., Foltin, R. W., Fowler, J. S., Abumrad, N. N., et al. (1997). Relationship between subjective effects of cocaine and dopamine transporter occupancy. *Nature, 386,* 827–830.

Volkow, N. D., Wang, G.-J., Fowler, J. S., Logan, J., Gatley, S. J., Hitzemann, R., Chen, A. D., et al. (1997). Decreased striatal dopaminergic responsiveness in detoxified cocaine-dependent subjects. *Nature, 386,* 830–833.

Vulliamy, E. (2010). *Amexica: War along the borderline.* New York: Farrar, Straus & Giroux.

Walker, S. (2011). *Sense and nonsense about crime, drugs, and communities* (7th ed.). Belmont, CA: Wadsworth/Cengage.

Weil, A. (1972). *The natural mind.* Boston: Houghton Mifflin.

Whaley, R. B., Smith, J. M., & Hayes-Smith, R. (2011). Teenage drug and alcohol use: Comparing individual and contextual effects. *Deviant Behavior, 32,* 818–845.

Winslow, R., & Zhang, S. (2008). *Criminology: A global perspective.* Upper Saddle River, NJ: Pearson/Prentice Hall.

Woodward, V. H., Misis, M. L., & Griffin, O. H., III. (2014). Examining the effects of social bonds and shame on drug recovery within an on-line support community. *Deviant Behavior, 35,* 938–958.

Wysong, E., Aniskiewicz, R., & Wright, D. (1994). Truth *and* dare: Tracking drug education to graduation as a symbolic politics. *Social Problems, 41,* 448–472.

Young, J. (2011). Moral panics and the transgressive other. *Crime, Media, Culture, 7,* 245–258.

Index

About the Author

John Curra is a professor at Eastern Kentucky University, where he has taught since 1975. He received both his bachelor's and master's degrees from San Diego State College (now San Diego State University) in sociology, and his doctorate from Purdue University, also in sociology. He has taught courses in introductory sociology, social deviance, criminology, sociological analysis, social problems, social psychology, juvenile delinquency, and criminological theory. In 1981, he received the prestigious Excellence in Teaching Award from the College of Social and Behavioral Sciences. In 2005, he was selected to be a Foundation Professor, one of the highest honors a professor can receive at Eastern Kentucky University. In 2012, Curra moved to the Department of Criminal Justice in the School of Justice Studies. That same year, he was awarded the Excellence in Teaching Award by the Department of Criminal Justice in the College of Justice and Safety. In addition to the three previous editions of *The Relativity of Deviance*, Curra has authored or coauthored several books, an instructor's manual, and a reader.